WITHDRAWN

Japan in Transition

Japan in Transition
Thought and Action in the Meiji Era, 1868–1912

Edited by
Hilary Conroy, Sandra T. W. Davis, *and*
Wayne Patterson

Rutherford • Madison • Teaneck
Fairleigh Dickinson University Press
London and Toronto: Associated University Presses

© 1984 by Associated University Presses, Inc.

Associated University Presses
440 Forsgate Drive
Cranbury, NJ 08512

Associated University Presses
25 Sicilian Avenue
London WC1A 2QH, England

Associated University Presses
2133 Royal Windsor Drive
Unit 1
Mississauga, Ontario
Canada L5J 1K5

Library of Congress Cataloging in Publication Data
Main entry under title:

Japan in transition.

   Includes bibliographical references.
   1. Japan—History—Meiji period, 1868–1912.
2. Japan—Intellectual life—1868–1912.   I. Conroy,
Hilary, 1919–   .   II. Davis, Sandra T. W.
III. Patterson, Wayne.
DS882.J38   1984   952'.03   82-48577
ISBN 0-8386-3169-X

Printed in the United States of America

To Delmer and Mary Brown
for their tireless encouragement of students and study of Japan
and
To the memory of Peter Ch'en and John Lin,
whose promising careers were cut short by illness

Contents

Preface	9
Chronology of "Japan in Transition"	11
General Introduction, *Hilary Conroy*	13

Part 1. Establishing Order

Introduction	21
1. The Policing of Society, *James B. Leavell*	22
2. Managing the News: Fukuchi Gen'ichirō Attempts to Balance Two Worlds, *James L. Huffman*	50

Part 2. Ideas in the Air

Introduction	75
3. Herbert Spencer and Meiji Japan, *Yamashita Shigekazu*	77
4. Fukuzawa Yukichi and Women's Rights, *Mikiso Hane*	96
5. The French Connection: Emile Guimet's Mission to Japan, A Cultural Context for *Japonisme*, *Ellen P. Conant*	113

Part 3. International Treaties and National Security

Introduction	149
6. Treaty Revision, National Security, and Regional Cooperation: A *Mintō* Viewpoint, *Sandra T. W. Davis*	151
7. The Question of Unilateral Denunciation and the Meiji Government, 1888–92, *Richard T. Chang*	174
8. Western Parameters of Sino-Japanese Relations, *Hilary Conroy*	193

Part 4. Problems and Solutions in Thought and Action

Introduction	207
9. Varieties of *Bunmei Ron* (Theories of Civilization): *Matsuzawa Hiroaki*, with assistance in translating from the Japanese original by *Nagata Yoichi and Hilary Conroy*	209
10. Inoue Kowashi: The Principles of Reform, *H. Peter Ch'en*	224
11. Mutsu Munemitsu in Europe, 1884–85: The Intellectual in Search of an Ideology, *Hagihara Nobutoshi*	235

Part 5. The Darker Side
  Introduction 259
  12. Workers, Peasants, and Women in Taishō Japan: Legacy of the Meiji Mind, *John Lin with Reginald Rajapakse* 261
  13. Fukuda Hideko and the Woman's World of Meiji Japan, *Sharlie C. Ushioda* 276
  14. Japanese Imperialism in Korea: A Study of Immigration and Foreign Policy, *Wayne Patterson* 294

Notes on the Contributors 316

Preface

This collection grew out of several scholarly meetings on Meiji Japan, conducted under the auspices of the Association for Asian Studies and the American Historical Association. Like the meetings, the papers presented here are primarily for specialists. Indeed, the first reviewer of the collection observed with some alarm: "The reader is presumed to know such terms as the *hanbatsu*, the Satcho monopoly of power and *Jiyū minken undō*." Though this may be true, the editors wish to emphasize that the study of Meiji Japan can be rewarding for nonspecialists, and we have therefore inserted definitions of terms to assist them. As explained in the general introduction, though a special place and time, Meiji Japan may be considered a "crucible" for the world of the twentieth century, and that era of Japanese history needs to be explored in depth if the opportunities and problems of rapid change conducted on a nationwide scale in any country are to be understood.

It is to encourage the nonspecialist reader that the following list of dates and events of the Meiji era and a few years before and after is presented.

The illustrations are from a collection of artifically tinted Meiji era photographs collected by Anna Brinton, a Quaker missionary to Japan, and the Interchange for Pacific Scholarship (IPS) is sponsoring this as one of a series of Asian–Pacific area studies.

Chronology of "Japan in Transition"

1600–1868. The Tokugawa Era.
  1603. Shogunate established.
  1641. Seclusion policy established.
  1853. Perry's first visit to Japan.
  1854. Perry "opens" Japan. (Treaty of Kanagawa.)
  1858. Townsend Harris obtains fuller treaty.
  1860. Ii Naosuke, advocate of treaties, assassinated.
  1862–63. Attacks on Westerners in Japan, retaliation at Shimonoseki and Kagoshima.
  1866. Shogunal forces defeated by Chōshū.
  1867–68. Civil war; Satsuma-Chōshū-Hizen-Tosa "Imperial Restoration" coalition victorious over Tokugawa.
  1868. Meiji Restoration; end of Shogunate; emperor moves to new capital (Tōkyō).

1868–1912. The Meiji Era.
  1868. Edo becomes Tōkyō, new imperial capital.
  1869. Four (Satchō-Hito) daimyō surrender fiefs to emperor.
  1871. All fiefs *(han)* replaced by prefectures *(ken)*;government centralization.
  1871–73. Iwakura mission travels abroad seeking Western knowledge.
  1873. Seikanron (Conquer Korea) argument. Saigō and "war party" leave the Meiji government.
  1873–78. Leadership of Iwakura and Ōkubo; course set toward modernization; 1877 Satsuma rebellion, death of Saigō.
  1878. Ōkubo assassinated.
  1870s. Japanese expansion begins: Liu-ch'ius annexed; Formosa expedition, 1874; Kanghwa Treaty (Korea), 1876.
  1881. Hokkaido scandal; Ōkuma demands Parliament, ousted, but promise of Diet in ten years.
  1883. Iwakura dies. Itō Hirobumi studies constitutional issue, prime minister, 1885.
  1889. Meiji constitution promulgated.
  1890. First Diet convenes; General Yamagata, premier.
  1890–94. Liberal and Progressive parties dominate Diet; oppose

oligarchs (Yamagata, Matsukata, Itō).
1894. Treaty revision with England.
1894–95. Sino-Japanese war.
1895. Treaty of Shimonoseki; Triple Intervention.
1898. Ōkuma-Itagaki party cabinet formed; fails; nonparty cabinets resume.
1900. Itō forms Seiyūkai political party. Military (Yamagata) vs. civilian (Itō) factions alternate in control of government, 1900–1914.
1902. Anglo-Japanese alliance.
1904–5. Russo-Japanese war; treaty of Portsmouth.
1910. Annexation of Korea; execution of Kōtoku and other "traitors."
1912. Death of Emperor Meiji.

Post Meiji (Taishō era), 1912–1926.
1914. Japan enters World War I; takes Shantung.
1915. Twenty-one Demands on China.
1918. Siberian Intervention; Hara, party cabinet; rice riots.
1925. Universal (male) suffrage; peace-preservation law.

General Introduction

Hilary Conroy

Meiji Japan was a special time and place, covering the years 1868–1912 in the temporal sense. Spatially it was limited at first to three of the Japanese islands, Honshu, Kyushu, and Shikoku, where the main action took place, but early on encompassing southern Hokkaido, where important development projects were instituted in the 1870s. Then by the turn of the century it had incorporated the Liu-ch'iu islands, through astute diplomacy, and Taiwan by force, and was deeply involved in Korea, which was to be fully incorporated into a growing Japanese colonial empire by 1910. In addition, following the Russo-Japanese war, 1904–5, southern Manchuria became a fertile field for Japanese military and economic penetration.

By 1912 Japan had changed from the slumbering feudal bureaucracy of the late Tokugawa era, often described in contradictory terminology as "centralized feudalism," into a modern nation state, well organized and functioning with aplomb in the highly competitive international system of the time. And beyond that, Japan already was a burgeoning empire, with huge territorial additions to the original four islands (or more precisely three and one-third) possessed in operative fashion in Tokugawa times, with millions of Koreans, Formosans, and Chinese as subject peoples in her colonial system.

Considered as "progress," it was remarkable indeed. Japan had become the first non-Western nation to "modernize," both internally and in its foreign relations. This was not accomplished without great cost, indeed turmoil in the areas of both ideas and actions. In a very real sense Meiji Japan was a crucible for the world of the twentieth century. In a single generation of historical time the Japanese of the Meiji era had to face the mind-wrenching and emotion-searing realization that their past way of life, seemingly tried and true for centuries, had become hopelessly inadequate. They had to adjust their thinking and actions to a new world that had developed outside of and beyond their own experience. The result was a revolution in thought and action.

Why can Meiji Japan be called a "crucible" for our twentieth-century world? The reason, it may be argued, is that the kind of intense, searing pressure for changes of immense magnitude that beset the Meiji generation in Japan has now become characteristic of every generation everywhere in the world, including the so-called developed countries. Within our own lifetimes, and certainly those of our children, changes so vast are occurring that it staggers the mind, to say nothing of the emotions, to keep up with them. Many people, of course, like large numbers of Japan's samurai and peasant classes, cannot keep up and, in Toynbee's picturesque phraseology, become practitioners of "Zealotism," resisters of change to the death. But, as Toynbee also points out, the end result of Zealotism is indeed the death of one's former cherished way of life, however bitter and desperate the resistance to change. Hence, far better to be a pragmatic "Herodian" who bends with the winds of change.[1]

The leaders of Meiji Japan, at least those who survived, were changelings, in ideas or practice, or in both. Having made up one's mind to change, however, even to lead in it, one's course is by no means smooth and unruffled. Viewed from outside and from historical distance the so-called oligarchs and other leaders of Meiji Japan often seem larger than life, men of such long-range vision and skill in molding their country and people that they seem to emerge as models of modernization, at least in the generation in which they operated.[2] (Of course, if one looks ahead to the errant militarism of the 1930s and the Pacific war that followed, one could claim to discover long-range ineptness beyond their short-range success; but the Japan of 1931–45 was managed by the "third generation" from the Meiji beginning, a generation symbolizing ineptness in Japanese tradition, whose mistakes have since been rectified.)

At any rate our study is focused on Meiji Japan, that amazing time and place wherein was accomplished the first successful transition of a backward non-Western state to modernity. And when one compares it to contemporary Russia or Turkey or China in their attempts to accomplish a similar transition, or even midtwentieth-century "Modernizations" in Latin America, Africa, or Asia, the contrast is enormously favorable to Japan.

Although successful in the end, as indicated in the first pages of James Huffman's essay below, there were strange paradoxes and/or anomalies in the process and, as the details in his and the other essays amply demonstrate, the course of Meiji Japan was far from smooth. In addition to the many tribulations discussed below a few observations from the recently published diary of "an American girl in Meiji Japan" well illustrate this point. For example, the great educator and journalist, Fukuzawa Yukichi, whom many would identify as the epitome of the modernizing man of Meiji Japan, in both thought and action, receives the following evaluation under the heading. "Mr. Fukuzawa's English":

> Mr. Fukuzawa has a comical way of speaking, using English and Japanese in the utmost confusion, so that it is difficult to understand

what he really means. For example, speaking of the Governor: "Mr. Kuriyama is *hontō ni*, kind man, *Keredomo* he is *taisō* busy *kono setsu*, yes?" (Mr. Kuriyama is a very kind man, but he is extremely busy of late).³

Mori Arinori, another "modernizer" of high importance, arranged for William C. Whitney, father of the aforementioned "American girl," to come to Japan with his family to found a commercial college, deemed by Mori and his progressive friends to be highly important for putting Japan on a progressive track. But by the time the Whitneys arrived in 1875, Mori had lost his influence and shortly departed for China, leaving five members of the Whitney family stranded in Tokyo with "only a dollar and a half." They were "rescued" by the former Tokugawa official Katsu Awa (Kaishu), who donated $1,000 to the cause.⁴ Three years later Mori did come through with a house for the Whitneys, the rent on which was paid in piano lessons for Mrs. Mori.⁵ On such slender threads did Meiji progress sometimes depend.

It should be remembered also that Meiji modernizers were often in jeopardy of life and limb. Okubo Toshimichi, first and foremost of the "ministers of modernization," was assassinated in May 1878, an event described by our "American girl" as follows: "Toshimichi Okubo was killed by six men while on his way to the Dajokan [Council of State] and not five chō [about 550 yards] from the palace in Akasaka.... Okubo's head was cut in two, a sword driven to the hilt in his breast, his hand cut off, besides many other wounds."⁶ The aforementioned Mori was asassinated in 1889, the same year in which Ōkuma Shigenobu lost a leg to a would-be assassin, and Itō Hirobumi was assassinated by a Korean in 1909, to mention only four.

This is to say nothing of the psychological cost. Most of the leaders discussed in the following pages went through alternating periods of elation and depression as they strove desperately to become modern and at the same time remain Japanese, or at least make some justification of their Japanese heritage. Fukuzawa Yukichi, perhaps, worked out the best formula for this. He told our "American girl" that "Among civilized nations we do not find civilization," a "pretty hard sentiment" which she did not understand,⁷ but which is carefully analyzed in Professor Matsuzawa's essay. Uchimura Kanzō was most uncomfortable at his Christian wedding and guests thought they heard his bride "giggle" at the crucial moment.⁸ But these give only hints of the mental gymnastics Uchimura had to go through before arriving at some kind of mental equilibrium (again explained by Professor Matsuzawa).

Mutsu Munemitsu went from jail to Europe, where he loved England, but settled for the Germanic teachings of Lorenz von Stein in order to make peace with his government (see Nobutoshi Hagihara's careful tracing of Mutsu's peregrination).

In addition to the above-mentioned tribulations, it should be remembered as a backdrop to Meiji diplomacy of the crucial years 1889–96 that the two key foreign ministers of that era, Ōkuma and Mutsu, were suffering from serious physical ailments, Ōkuma from the amputation of his leg and Mutsu from tuberculosis, from which he died a lingering death in 1897. Constitution drafter Inoue Kowashi also was tubercular.

Adding up the problems of transition, it may be little wondered that what could and should be called the "darker side" of little attention to the problems of peasants, women, and workers, discussed in the final section, blotted the escutcheon of Meiji Japan. Perhaps the wonder is that it held together at all.

Notes

1. For a discussion of Toynbee's concept as applied to Meiji Japan, see Hilary Conroy, *The Japanese Seizure of Korea, 1868–1910* (Philadelphia: University of Pennsylvania Press, 1960, paperback ed., 1974), pp. 30–35.
2. See Bernard S. Silberman, *Ministers of Modernization: Elite Mobility in the Meiji Restoration, 1868–1873* (Tucson, Ariz.: University of Arizona Press, 1964) and a review of this book by Douglas H. Mendel, Jr., *Journal of Asian Studies* 24: 3 (May 1965): 510–12.
3. Clara A. N. Whitney, *Clara's Diary*, ed. M. William Steele and Tamiko Ichimata (Tokyo and New York: Kodansha, 1979), p. 221.
4. Ibid., p. 37.
5. Ibid., pp. 190–91.
6. Ibid., p. 183.
7. Ibid., p. 192.
8. Ibid., p. 328.

Japan in Transition

Part 1
Establishing Order

Silkworm culture. *(Photo permission of Anna Brinton Collection. Reproduction by Masako Imai.)*

Introduction

The first problem faced by the new Meiji government in 1868 was that of establishing order. Tokugawa Japan, as indicated in the initial essay by James Leavell, despite control mechanisms, was a relatively unpoliced society in the technical sense. The governing samurai class, entitled to be armed with two swords and to cut down lower-class persons who might get out of line *(kirisute gomen),* had pretty much ceased to utilize or to need this option by 1800 as the pervasive Neo-Confucian philosophy of respect for superiors had come to be accepted at all levels of society.

But the turmoil unleashed by the coming of Perry and the treaties made with the West during the years 1854–65 reached a crescendo in the civil war of the Restoration during the winter and spring of 1867–68, when all manner of violence and challenge to authority broke loose. Hence the new government immediately faced the problem of restoring order, first in action, then in thought. Finding the law-enforcement arrangements of the Tokugawa period wholly inadequate, they undertook to replace "neighborhood watchmen" with "Emperor's policemen" throughout the land. The story of this, with its many vicissitudes, is told in detail in the first essay, entitled "The Policing of Society."

The second essay in this section, entitled "Managing the News," utilizes the career of the longtime (1874–88) editor of *Tokyo-Nichi Nichi,* the "government mouthpiece" newspaper that articulated the course of progress of Meiji Japan. As the author, James L. Huffman, points out, there was much ambiguity in his career, not only ideologically as between Western style and Japanese loyalty, but even on such a basic question as the worth of a newspaper and a newspaper career, such being by no means established as important or even legitimate in the early Meiji era.

1   The Policing of Society

James B. Leavell

During the early Meiji period, the government of Japan instituted a number of reforms that altered political and social life throughout the country. Vital to any society engaged in such a program of rapid change is the maintenance of social control.[1] Marion J. Levy, Jr., in his study of the problems of modernization, lists control among the "three most strategic problems of transition."[2] In Levy's opinion, Japan's success was due to the fact that "the structures of control in Tokugawa Japanese society were convertible to modernized forms with little loss of effectiveness."[3] Like others in the "social control" tradition, he emphasizes normative and voluntary processes (traditional values) as opposed to organized and legitimate coercion (police).[4] Yet, it has been suggested that such an exclusion is indicative of a general failure among works on social control to deal adequately with the contributions of the police as a structure of control in modern societies.[5] The impressive performance of Japan suggests the presence of powerful structures of social control in early Meiji society. This study seeks to ascertain the extent to which the police were mobilized to ensure a stable transition. Did the government depend upon the residual strength of traditional control devices and structures, or did the central government invest in new techniques?

Answers to these questions are sought through an investigation on two governmental levels. The central-government materials provide information on the intended police reforms of the Meiji leadership, and the prefectural data reveal the nature of the actual implementation. The prefecture chosen for this study was Okayama.[6]

Tokugawa Japan as an Unpoliced Society

During the Tokugawa period, the salient structural feature of law-enforcement organization was its highly decentralized character. Throughout Japan, the various domains outside the shogun's personal holdings were autonomous as far as their internal law-enforcement machinery was concerned. Further, this pattern of self-regulation typified the law-enforcement structures within the domains themselves. Domain administrations followed a deliberate policy of placing the police burden on the private sector.

The rural areas were fragmented into village jurisdictions that, ideally, were natural units drawn together through the pursuit of agricultural production requiring intensive and highly cooperative endeavor. Within the village unit, the fundamental law-enforcement institution, the five-man group *(gonin gumi)*, served as the device by which a community protected and policed itself.[7]

The five-man groups provided samurai governments with primary-level regulatory and control machinery in the rural areas of the Okayama domain as well as in Bitchū and Mimasaka, provinces to the west and north that were incorporated into Okayama Prefecture during the Meiji period. With specific regard to crime prevention and detection, the key feature of the five-man group was the burden of mutual responsibility imposed by higher authorities. Crimes committed by one member that were detected by the authorities before being reported by other group members threatened all members with the possibility of punishment. In theory, it was to the advantage of each member to be aware of the misdeeds of others and to disclose such transgressions to the village headman with all possible haste. If the need arose, the five-man groups furnished a vigilante posse as an extension of their self-policing function.

Because the peasants were responsible for the capture of thieves in their villages, the samurai authorities would blame the village headman and the members of the five-man groups if the fact that burglary was a problem in a particular community came to the attention of the domain's samurai officials.[8] Such an official policy discouraged village leaders from requesting police services from the domain. Indeed, the domain did not have any burglary-control officers assigned to the rural areas.

The web of five-man organizations was arranged so as to retard any successful burglary within the community itself. A more likely occurrence would be an act of theft by an outsider. Thus, nonvillage members were viewed with great suspicion even before the discovery of any crime. Further to enforce this hostility to outsiders, the domain authorities decreed that strangers should be detained and questioned, though village authorities were warned not to mistreat such individuals.[9] When possible, villagers employed outcastes to do the actual arresting.[10] A villager who housed criminals, knowingly or unknowingly, was subject to the same punishment as the outlaw himself,[11] and the host's fellow five-man group members were equally subject to punishment. Such a policy was designed to make travel by unauthorized individuals difficult.

For the purpose of crime prevention, domain authorities promulgated further regulations aimed at retarding geographical mobility at its source as well as encouraging surveillance and harassment of a traveler during a journey. If a village member desired to make a visit to another place, he was required to provide the leader of his five-man group[12] details concerning his expected departure and return. If he planned to stay in another place for a while, he was required to inform his village headman. Permanent moves to other areas necessitated obtaining the permission of samurai officials. Former village members who desired to return for a visit of more than a few days were required to join a five-man group temporarily, while anyone returning to the village permanently had to have a certificate from his former employer vouching for his good conduct as a prerequisite to his readmittance.[13]

Beyond the procedures mentioned above, the local communities were entreated to establish sheltered locations called watch houses *(banya)*, which functioned much as police stations. Their primary purpose was to intimidate thieves by presenting the vigilantes in full view of potential lawbreakers. These shelters served as night-watch stations for which the community was responsible. If thieves were encountered, the night watchmen were expected to sound an alarm for help and then attempt to apprehend the criminals.[14] Samurai officials instructed the rural communities to establish watch houses in areas where there had been frequent trouble.[15]

Confucian concerns for proper human relationships ideologically reinforced the five-man group system. Theoretically, society was regarded as a natural moral order in which the highly integrated character of task performance and group maintenance in peasant villages served as an ideal paradigm. Social control was effected by emphasizing group solidarity, a value of functional and ethical importance. Such a society can be unpoliced. The rural law-enforcement organization in Tokugawa Japan was not a separate entity impinging on the local community; control functions were well integrated into the social structure. There were no enforcers who were professional specialists, a situation that might have created the possibilities for alienation. What coercive control machinery the domain bureaucracy did maintain for use in the rural areas was reactive rather than active.

Urban communities, such as the Okayama castle town, were not so socially integrated as the rural ideal and, thus, required some adjustments in the control machinery. Nevertheless, the basic philosophy of self-regulation remained operative. In the urban areas the domain administration provided some supervisory personnel, but organizationally the five-man group structure continued to be the key law-enforcement organ among the commoners. Again, the private sector was held responsible for policing itself.

Among the various officials on the Okayama municipal magistrate's *(machi bugyō)* staff, two men served as municipal inspectors *(machi metsuke)* whose principal function was to act as investigators and prosecutors for the magistrate.[16] In fulfilling their responsibilities as criminal investigators, the municipal inspectors took on some of the characteristics we associate with modern Japanese and American detectives.

In Edo, the official who corresponded to the municipal inspector of Okayama was the investigator *(yoriki)*.[17] Regulations for city administration in Edo stipulated that twenty-five investigators should be assigned to each municipal magistrate; however, only twenty-three customarily served in each of the two jurisdictions.[18]

In the Okayama domain, the municipal inspectors supervised the work of six detectives *(dōshin)*, who were appointed from among the ranks of the foot soldiers *(ashigaru)*—the lowest level of samurai. Of the six officials, one was assigned full time to the city magistrate's residence.[19] The samurai detectives were responsible for the control of the urban population, the arrest, interrogation, and arraignment of criminals, and the surveillance of transient *daimyō* (feudal lords) who were performing alternate attendance duty (sankin kōtai).[20]

In Edo the number of detectives fluctuated, but at the end of the Tokugawa period there were usually about 140 of them assigned to each of the two municipal magistrates' staffs.[21] After 1713, both investigators and detectives were assigned housing in the Hattchobori district of Edo city.[22] Each investigator was granted 300 *tsubo* (1,185 square yards) for the house and garden, while the detectives occupied 100 *tsubo* (395 square yards). These two types of officers not only resided in the same areas of the city, but they also shared a unique hair style called *hatchō-bori ichō*.[23]

Okayama sources simply state that the duty of detectives was to patrol the castle town in pairs;[24] however, Higuchi's study of the Edo detectives enumerates three types of patrols—regular, temporary, and secret. Regular patrols followed a set course for the purpose of visiting each neighborhood citizen's patrol station *(jishinban)*, at which they would inquire about criminal activity. Temporary patrols were organized to investigate areas outside the regular patrol routes, with experienced detectives drawing this class of duty. Finally, two detectives from each municipal magistrate's roster were selected for secret assignments.[25]

Below the detective level, urban police operatives were enlisted from among the commoners or outcaste groups. The Edo detective recruited part-time auxiliaries called *meakashi* (spies). Since their normal employment and residence were among the people, the auxiliaries had access to rumors, gossip, and community knowledge that would be of use to the detectives whose samurai rank and control function tended to isolate them. Some of Edo's police auxiliaries were selected from the retinue of gambling bosses. This source of personnel suggests that physical prowess and close association with known criminal elements in part constituted recruitment criteria for samurai police auxiliaries. Gambling bosses, who were themselves engaged in illegal activity, functioned as police job brokers. Remuneration for police auxiliary duty was paid from government taxes collected in Yoshiwara, Edo's famous licensed quarter.[26] This is to say that police work below the level of detective did not always exemplify the highest professional standards, since those holding many law-enforcement posts in Edo were not full time and in most cases were not even recognized by the government as officers. In Okayama there were developments that caused police auxiliaries to take on status characteristics different from those in Edo. Auxiliaries were recruited from the hereditary outcastes, the *eta*.[27]

Every seven to ten households in the Okayama castle town were organized like a rural five-man group, and the same term was used even though "five" was clearly a misnomer. Such groups functioned on the same principles of collective responsibility as the rural organizations; however, one difference was that in the castle town there was a much higher probability that the groupings were artificial arrangements unrelated to the work relationships, which tended to reinforce the five-man group as a control mechanism in the countryside.

Beyond the self-policing obligations of the five-man group, urban commoners were responsible for maintaining neighborhood patrol stations, which were located in the sixty-two wards of the castle town.[28] Heads of households took turns staffing these offices, where criminal acts were reported and to which foundlings and accident victims were referred. It was to these neighborhood stations that the samurai detectives brought criminal suspects for interrogation. If the questioning sustained the detective's suspicions, he would order the suspect to be transferred to the central detention house to await further ruling by the municipal magistrate.[29]

The streets of the castle town were intersected at several locations by fences and gates, which were opened in the daytime and closed for certain hours during the night. Such barriers provided the authorities with a ready means of physically containing urban disturbances as well as restricting mobility at night when burglary was most common. Some neighborhood patrol stations were located at such gates, thus enabling the duty officers to fulfill the dual functions of gate guard and watchman *(bannin)*. Though heads of households were supposed to maintain these stations by working in shifts, a number of *hinin* (nonpersons, nonhereditary outcastes) was employed to substitute for those who preferred to pay rather than serve.

The Restoration and Military Police

In the early months of 1868, following the announcement of the restoration of imperial rule, the first Meiji police organization was established in Kyoto, where the new regime exercised direct administrative power. Two departments under the newly established Council of State, the Criminal

Law Department *(keihōkan)* and the Military Department *(gunmukan)*, held responsibilities that would eventually fall under the jurisdiction of police agencies.

The Criminal Law Department was assigned tasks that included the maintenance of a court system and judicial police functions such as investigating criminal offenses and making arrests. Arrest officers *(hobōshi)* were appointed to serve in a supervisory capacity much like that of the samurai investigators and detectives of the Tokugawa period. The effective execution of these duties continued to depend upon the cooperation of neighborhood mutual-protection associations and the five-man groups, as had been the case during the Tokugawa period. Some months later, on the twentieth of September and following one of several shifts in the nomenclature of government departments, the authorities issued formal orders to continue the Tokugawa period self-policing system in Kyoto.[30]

The Military Department was charged with maintaining public peace, a responsibility that included suppression of rebels and control of rioters. During the Bakumatsu period, when it became clear that the investigator-detective arrangement could not control the groups of masterless samurai *(rōnin)* who gathered in Kyoto to express growing antigovernment sentiment, the Tokugawa authorities had employed a special police task force with units noted for strict internal discipline and violent tactics. A group known as the *shinsengumi* was the most famous of these elite units.[31] When the loyalists came to power, they did not duplicate this innovation but returned to the more standard practice of appointing certain domains to be responsible for suppression of large-scale violence in the capital. Six domains were requested to provide personnel for what was called the Kyoto City Pacification Patrol, and three other domains were asked to staff the city's fire patrol.[32]

Though Kyoto served as the first Meiji capital, soon after the capitulation of Edo the imperial government moved to the shogun's former seat of administration. For this reason, the central arena of police organizational development was located in Kyoto for only a few months. Edo serves best as the focal point for studying the early experiments in police administration conducted by the Meiji leadership.

Imperial forces entered Edo castle on May 3, 1868, thereby placing the loyalists in nominal control of the city. A contingent of Tokugawa adherents continued to hold a fortified area in the Ueno district; however, at the outset there was hope that they would follow the example of the Edo castle defenders by surrendering without a struggle so that military action within the city could be avoided. The loyalist army had entered Edo without a well-devised plan of occupation. On May 13, Prince Taruhito, the titular commander of the imperial forces in Kantō, set up his headquarters in Edo castle and on the same day ordered the two former municipal magistrates, Ishikawa Toshimasa and Sakuma Nobuyoshi, to resume their responsibilities, chief of which was the maintenance of public peace and order.[33] No alteration of the city's administrative structure, organization, or personnel was prepared for immediate implementation; however, a survey of the samurai police personnel disclosed the fact that only forty-one former investigators and detectives remained available for duty.[34] Thus, the attempt to continue the Tokugawa system with experienced officers proved unworkable, forcing the new government to devise an alternative arrangement for municipal law enforcement.

The maintenance of a state of public order in Edo during the first year of Meiji required the use of armed military patrols. Even had the samurai detective system remained intact, it is doubtful whether order could have been maintained without troops. Thousands of Tokugawa retainers lost their livelihood overnight when the imperial government confiscated Tokugawa land holdings, thereby forcing many samurai to vacate their Tokyo residences and move to the countryside in hopes of making a living. Taking advantage of this circumstance, robbers settled in deserted samurai residences and went forth in groups at night to commit burglary. They openly carried stolen goods in carts even in broad daylight.

Better to cope with the growing atmosphere of lawlessness, on May 23 Prince Taruhito named Tayasu Chūnagon (Tokugawa Yoshiyori) and two former shogunal Junior Elders, Ōkubo Tadahiro and Katsu Kaishu, to take charge of police activities within Edo as joint heads of the Edo City Pacification and Disciplinary Patrol Office.[35] In that the choice of these men for high office gave evidence of the new regime's willingness to treat cooperative Tokugawa retainers favorably, these appointments had immediate propaganda value for the new regime in encouraging intransigent shogunal supporters to surrender.[36] The Junior Elders had constituted the highest police organ in the shogun's administrative system; hence, the appointments showed elements of propriety and continuity as well as generosity.

Although former officials of the shogunate held the top positions, the actual patrolling of the city was performed by representative military units from twelve domains. Ikeda Akimasa, the new lord of the Okayama domain, consented to take charge of suppressing the rebels in the city as well as to provide patrols to keep the peace.[37] By July 26, the domain troops had completely taken over the police functions, and the former Junior Elders were relieved of their command responsibilities.

On July 8, four days after loyalist troops finally acted decisively against the Ueno-based rebels, the Restoration leaders began a series of organizational changes in Edo's administration that commenced with the establishment of the Edo Garrison Headquarters. Two days later the municipal magistrates' offices were transferred to the jurisdiction of the garrison headquarters and ordered to change their names to Municipal Courts.[38] The new names did not signify internal reorganization within the old municipal magistrates' offices, but they did involve relieving the two former magistrates of their positions. The timing of the dismissal of the two former shogunal officials, following immediately as it did the defeat of the Ueno rebels, suggests that their appointment had indeed been largely propagandistic; however, men from Tokugawa collateral houses as well as shogunal housemen continued to receive imperial administrative appointments. Assigned to the two municipal courts were troops from Satsuma, Chōshū, and two other domains which took responsibility for city patrols from the twelve domains that had served under the City Pacification and Disciplinary Patrol Office.[39] There is no indication that the substructure of neighborhood self-policing associations was altered in any way at this time, but clearly the old law-enforcement arrangement was unable to cope with disorder it was designed to prevent but which it was incapable of containing once a breakdown occurred.

Individuals in the new imperial government, chief among them Ōkubo Toshimichi, had advocated moving the capital from Kyoto to Edo. Negotiations were carried out in August; and on September 3, an imperial pronouncement changed the name of Edo to Tokyo.[40] Simultaneously, the administrative structure of the city was revised to provide a stronger civilian image to the government. The Garrison Headquarters was abolished, and the Headquarters of the Pacification Command was instituted with jurisdiction over all of eastern Japan and with Sanjō Sanetomi as its head. On October 2, the two municipal courts were administratively consolidated under the title Tokyo Municipal Government; and the troops that had been assigned to the courts were absorbed by the new unified structure.

With the creation of the Tokyo Municipal Government, an attempt was made to emulate elements of the Kyoto law-enforcement structure. Officers called "arrest agents" (*hobōkata*) were assigned to work within the government in much the same way as samurai detectives had served the municipal magistrates in the Edo period. In the first year of Meiji there were four Arrest Agent/Under Inspectors (*hobōkata shitametsuke*) and twenty-three arrest agents working for the Tokyo administration. There was also a staff of twenty-four court and jail officials.[41] Such a small group clearly had little power to improve law and order in Tokyo. The Tokugawa pattern of dependence on self-regulation with only a few supervisory personnel continued to be ineffective.

Police operational problems in Tokyo were exacerbated following the end of major hostilities by an increase in the number of discharged soldiers and destitute shogunal retainers in the capital. The Tokyo authorities became so overburdened with the task of keeping order that on December 22, 1868, 200 soldiers were dispatched from the Oshi domain, in what is today Saitama Prefecture, to deal with the deteriorating conditions. This contingent was named the Tokyo Municipal Military Police.[42] Within a short period, thirty domains were asked to contribute troops to help keep public order in Tokyo.[43] On January 17, 1869, the city was divided into forty-seven precincts, with the overall leadership of patrol administration placed in the hands of Hitotsubashi Dainagon and Tayosu Chūnagon.[44] By February 4, the new military patrol personnel had completely replaced the troops representing Satsuma, Chōshū, Tottori, and Satohara. This new military contingent would eventually serve as the foundation of the imperial government's own army.

On July 1, 1869, the central government created a special police agency called the Censorate *(danjōdai)* for the purpose of searching out antigovernment agitators. The agents of the Censorate were expected to range throughout the country using tactics similar to those of the former inspectors of the shogunate. It was through the Censorate that the government arranged police protection for the British crown prince, who visited Japan during 1869.[45] Administratively the Censorate was subject to the Criminal Law Department of the central government. In August of the same year, the name of the Criminal Law Department was changed to Ministry of Corrections *(gyōbushō)*, while the name of the other major central government department with responsibilities for maintaining internal law and order, the Military Department, was changed to Armed Forces Ministry *(heibushō)*. The Censorate retained its original name and function.

As evidence of continuing unrest in the capital, the Council of State issued the following directive to the Armed Forces Ministry soon after the reorganization:

> In recent days, night burglary has been on the increase within the urban areas. There have been acts of pillage, murder, and plunder with the use of military weapons, especially in the imperial capital. We hereby urge you to control vigorously the problem.[46]

On December 17, possibly in response to this exhortation, a further reorganization of patrol units was effected by consolidating the forty-seven districts into six large ones, each under the administrative supervision of a district commander. More significantly, along with this structural change in the law-enforcement organization, the government ordered the cessation of feudal designations for the various patrol units that had been supplied to the central administration by the above-mentioned thirty domains. Thenceforth, police troops were referred to by their patrol-district numbers rather than domain origins.

By changing nomenclature and shifting the chain of command, the reorganization attempted to increase centralization. Under the previous arrangement, it was probable that the thirty domain units were distributed among the forty-seven jurisdictions in such a manner that a domain-appointed unit commander was also chief officer in the jurisdiction patrolled by his own troops. Such a situation tended to maintain group solidarity and regional consciousness. The new arrangement by no means erased regional attachments within the organization, but it did create the opportunity for the Tokyo government to appoint six district commanders who would be clearly identified with the new regime. A possible disadvantage was that there would be district commanders who, through identification with some domain, had no domain ties with a large proportion of the men under their commands. Such an arrangement could either promote friction and jealousy or, it was hoped, further weaken regional loyalty and strengthen organizational commitment. The central government's policy seemed aimed at acquiring broad domain participation while promoting within those feudally defined limits an organization of law enforcement that was increasingly responsive to central authority. By April of 1870, the reorganization was completed and the police force numbered about 2,500 men.[47]

A number of attacks on foreigners during the Bakumatsu period had prompted the shogunate to establish in 1860 a special police force in Yokohama. The Settlement Patrol, as the group was called, was on duty from dusk till dawn. The men worked in groups of three. Two carried lanterns and one held a drum. They were armed with wooden swords. In 1863, the Kanagawa magistrate provided the foreign settlement with patrolmen dressed in deep yellow uniforms, which earned them the appellation "Rape Leaf Brigade."[48] A joint British and French patrol was created in 1867 to keep order within the settlement while the Japanese provided twenty foot soldiers to patrol the perimeter of the community. An Englishman served as commandant of this mixed police force. At the outset of the Restoration, soldiers from a number of domains were stationed in Yokohama. In September 1870, the special police unit that protected the foreign settlement in Yokohama was transferred from the Armed Forces Ministry to the Tokyo Municipal Government. By 1870, Yokohama's Japanese patrolmen were wearing a semi-Western uniform with the English word "Police" painted on their helmets and on their paper lanterns. This unique unit was abolished in 1872.[49]

Continuation of the Tokugawa Pattern in Okayama

At the beginning of the Restoration period, the Okayama domain did not have the great social confusion that might have stimulated a lawless atmosphere as it had in Edo in the early Meiji years. Ikeda Mochimasa, *daimyō* of Okayama, was, like most other lords on the eve of the Restoration, neutralized; he could not actively work for or against the imperial cause. The fact that the Okayama lord was in reality the natural son of Tokugawa Nariaki, until his death one of the strongest voices advocating imperial interests, was balanced by the fact that the reigning shogun at the time of the upheaval was Mochimasa's natural brother.[50]

Following the outbreak of fighting between irreconcilable Tokugawa retainers and the loyalist troops in late January 1868, the pressure on Ikeda Mochimasa evidently became intolerable, for he resigned as *daimyō* in favor of Ikeda Masaaki, lord of the Kamogata branch domain west of Kurashiki. Masaaki changed his name to Akimasa and from that time on pursued a solidly proloyalist policy.[51]

On April 3, 1869, Ikeda Akimasa presented his land and tax registers to the imperial government. This action symbolized the *daimyō*'s return of independent political authority to the central administration in Tokyo. On July 25, Akimasa was appointed imperial governor of his former domain.

Immediately following the appointment of Akimasa as governor, a new criminal code was promulgated in the domain. The Tokugawa period legal structure had been maintained during the first year and a half of the Meiji period; and even the new criminal code, known as the *Gyōhō*, retained aspects of the Tokugawa system. For example, a division was maintained between the samurai and the commoner with regard to punishments.[52] Even after the institution of the *Gyōhō*, the night watch, a part of the old domain law-enforcement arrangement, continued to function within the city of Okayama.

In August 1869, the central government began attempting to implement reforms in the organization of Okayama's police system. In the *Kenkan jinin narabini jobikin kisoku* (Rule Concerning the Number of Prefectural Officials and the Reserve Fund),[53] the central government suggested that Okayama institute a new type of law officer in addition to the personnel already performing police duties. Five such officers was the recommended number for a domain the size of Okayama; these new officials were to be known as "arresters" *(hobō)*.[54].

During the early days of the Restoration government's rule, the arresters had been established by the central government in Kyoto to act in a supervisory capacity similar to that of the samurai investigators and detectives. When the imperial government's control was extended to Edo and Osaka, the arresters had been instituted in those areas as well. The officers were described as performing what were later to be viewed as judicial police functions, i.e., investigation, arrest, and arraignment. Arresters were absorbed into the ranks of the Constabulary *(rasotsu)* when this group was founded in December 1871. The chief significance of the arresters was that they represented the first police officer that the imperial government attempted to establish on a comprehensive basis throughout the entire country. There is no evidence that Okayama complied with these early orders, and, as will be shown below, there is in fact evidence for rather tardy adoption of the arresters.

Creation of a Civil Police

In the capital, 1871 was a year of momentous change in the structure of government generally and in the nature of police particularly. On August 24, the Ministry of Corrections (*gyōbushō*) was dismantled, making way for the creation of the Ministry of Justice (*shihōshō*), which began absorbing various police functions throughout the succeeding months. Five days later, on August 29, the feudal domains were legally abolished, and the prefectures were substituted for them. Symbolic of the advent of a new era, the samurai were permitted to put away their swords, and all Japanese men were allowed to cut their hair in the fashion of the West.

The most significant police reform was the transfer of patrol responsibilities from the Armed Forces Ministry to the Ministry of Justice, since, both in administrative accountability and in personnel, the Tokyo police assume, for the first time, the character of civil rather than military officials. The organizational adjustments commenced on October 27, when the Metropolitan Military Office (*fuhei gakari*), which managed the street patrols, had its title changed to Metropolitan Control Office (*torishimari gakari*). On December 5, the Tokyo patrol personnel were totally replaced in an attempt to establish for the first time a genuine civil police under an organizational arrangement designed to be more responsive to the central leadership. The city guards had been recruited from thirty different feudal domains, and the enlistment procedures had followed the accepted policy of unit rather than individual recruitment. The groups or units had remained intact during their duty assignments in Tokyo, and the domain rather than the central government was held responsible for keeping service personnel numbers up to efficient levels. With the abolition of the domains, the imperial government destroyed the organizational basis for the city guard units. These military detachments, which had been patrolling the city as policemen, were disbanded, and the Tokyo Control Unit was completely restaffed with new men,[55] indicating an attempt on the part of central government leaders to effect fundamental change. The recruitment statistics of these new policemen serve as a reminder of the preponderant influence of the Satsuma domain in the early history of the Japanese police. Of the 3,000 men initially enlisted to form the Tokyo Control Unit, 2,000 of them were selected from among Satsuma ex-samurai. One thousand of the men were recruited by Saigō Takamori, and another thousand were selected by Kawaji Toshiyoshi. The remaining thousand were recruited from among former samurai of other prefectures.[56]

More than any other single individual, Kawaji Toshiyoshi can be credited with designing the early modern Japanese police system. His influence is felt even today through the study of his writings by trainees in police schools.[57] Kawaji was born into a Satsuma samurai household. His father, Shōzō, served as an investigator in the Kagoshima castle town. The son, Toshiyoshi, showed a strong aptitude for fencing as a young man; and in his early thirties he studied under the renowned Bakumatsu fencing master, Chiba Shūsaku.[58] Kawaji's belief that training in the art of fencing developed superior physical and mental performance led him to encourage policemen to study the art—a tradition that continues today as a standard part of police training.

During the Bakumatsu period, Kawaji participated in Satsuma political activities in Kyoto. As a result of his meritorious action during the Chōshū uprising at Hamaguri gate in Kyoto in 1864, Kawaji came to the attention of Saigō Takamori. Such recognition led to his eventual appointment by the domain lord, Shimazu Hisamitsu, as head of a Satsuma unit studying modern Western military techniques utilizing advanced firearms. He studied Western military science books under the supervision of Sekiguchi Tetsunosuke in Edo. Kawaji soon had opportunities to make use of his knowledge, for he served in the Imperial Army during the Restoration War and saw action in a number of engagements.

Kawaji, as the protege of Saigō, was appointed Magistrate of Arms for the Satsuma domain government in 1869. Saigō secured a post in the central government for Kawaji during the spring of 1871, and it was in the fall of that year that Kawaji was sent to Kagoshima to recruit for the Control Unit.

For the purposes of Control Unit patrols in the city of Tokyo, the metropolitan area continued to be divided into six jurisdictions, each being administered by its own police station. The station chiefs maintained a staff of four clerks to manage routine business. Under each station there were sixteen substations commanded by a patrol captain with thirty men under his direction. Each patrol captain was assigned three sergeants, who were included among the thirty men assigned to the substation.[59] The thirty men in a given substation were divided into two shifts; fifteen men would be on duty every other day. According to Kawaji, most of the ninety-six substations were located in temples or houses of citizens.[60]

On April 11, 1872, the Tokyo Metropolitan Government changed the name of the six district Control Unit stations to Major District Offices. In May, another thousand recruits, selected from various prefectures, were added to the Tokyo police force, thereby diluting the high proportion of Satsuma men serving in the capital's law-enforcement machinery. In July, the Control Unit and its officers became known collectively as the Constabulary (rasotsu). Kawaji Toshiyoshi was appointed the first chief constable.

In May of 1872, Etō Shimpei, a Restoration leader from Hizen (Saga Prefecture) was appointed head of the Ministry of Justice; and from that time, the rate of reform quickened. Having become a part of the Ministry of Justice, the Constabulary was ordered on September 25 to assume a greater

The Policing of Society

role in the judicial process. Up until this time, the constables had functioned primarily as patrolmen and arresting officers. To these responsibilities were added functions in the prosecutor's office. When carrying out these added tasks, the constables were referred to as "bailiff-solicitors" *(taibu)*, whose role it was to levy indictments, administer pretrial hearings, and act as prosecutors. Combining the roles of arresting officer and prosecutor marked a return to broad responsibilities for the officers, such as had been the case with samurai investigators and detectives during the Tokugawa period. The prosecutorial responsibilities instituted for the Constabulary in 1872 were more closely delimited by Kawaji in subsequent reforms.

Constables had been instituted in a number of prefectures, though not in Okayama. The broadened constable responsibilities delineated by the central government were intended to apply to these prefectural officers as well as to Tokyo policemen. In order to exercise greater control over police administration in the various prefectures, the Ministry of Justice created the Police Bureau *(keihōryō)* on September 29. This was the first serious attempt to unify the nation's police organizationally.

The Police Bureau created new ranks of policemen that included officers called *junsa* (patrolmen), the term currently used for men in the lowest ranks. The Police Bureau patrolmen differed from the present-day patrolmen in that they ranked between the constables and the soon to be officially constituted watchmen *(bannin)*. Further, the position of patrolman was actually created only in the Tokyo area and was not extended to the prefectures until 1875.[61] Each patrolman was expected to supervise ten watchmen.[62] Kawaji Toshiyoshi, who had been serving as head of the Constabulary, was appointed to the position of Chief of Police *(daikeishi)*, which was the top service rank in the Police Bureau.

Soon after the organizational scheme of the Police Bureau became operative, the government leadership clique selected Etō Shimpei to lead a group to Europe and America for the purpose of investigating Western legal codes and procedures. Etō and his associates were to be part of the major governmental mission abroad known as the Iwakura Mission, 1871–73. Etō was granted the right to select the members of the study group; so upon the urging of Saigō Takamori, he chose Kawaji to head the subsection for investigating police organizations.[63] As it turned out, Etō was unable to make the trip with the group.

In January of 1873, the Police Bureau exerted direct control over the primary level of law-enforcement activities in Tokyo by changing the Tokugawa neighborhood watch *(jishinban)* system into what was simply called the *bannin* (watchman) system. Nominally the watchmen became representatives of the government rather than simply guards hired by neighborhood associations, as had been the case during the Tokugawa period.

As a symbol of their new status, the former neighborhood watch employees were given an official uniform and a ranking system. Despite these new signs of centralization and standardization, the neighborhood organizations continued to pay the salaries of these men; however, the salary schedule was fixed by the government. The ranking system prescribed sergeant, corporal, and three grades of watchmen. The uniforms were semi-Western in style with straight pants and a military jacket of dark blue. Ranks were indicated by the color of the jacket cuffs. Sergeants and corporals had uniforms with red cuffs, and the regular watchmen had white-cuffed jackets. The distinctly Japanese touch was the hat, which was large and bowl-shaped. In time, the name of the district in which a watchman served was inscribed on his belt. These patrolmen were armed with staffs.[64]

In June 1873, having completed the absorption of the watchmen into the Tokyo government's law-enforcement organization, the central government attempted to standardize regional police systems along the same lines. Through Council of State decree number 225, all prefectures were instructed to use the term *watchman* for law-enforcement personnel who fulfilled patrol and guard functions.[65] Various prefectural governments expressed opposition to this name change; in the face of the protests, the central government temporized. The watchman system was maintained by the central government in Tokyo, and the prefectures continued to use their old Tokugawa period arrangements on the neighborhood level. Tokyo's watchman system was abolished in 1875 with the promulgation of the Administrative Police Regulations *(Gyōsei keisatsu kisoku)*.

Kawaji and Police Reform

Kawaji Toshiyoshi returned from his study tour abroad in September 1873 to find his patron, Saigō Takamori, involved in a struggle to gain authorization for a military expedition against Korea to punish her for alleged insults to Japan in refusing to recognize the new Japanese government. Etō Shimpei, Itagaki Taisuke, and other leaders of the Restoration supported Saigō's plan. The venture was opposed by Ōkubo Toshimichi, Kido Kōin, Iwakura Tomomi, and others who favored concentrating Japan's energies on domestic reform. The antiwar faction won the argument; therefore, Saigō and his party resigned their positions in government and returned to their provincial homes. A large number of officials from Satsuma followed Saigō's example. Some expressed surprise that Kawaji was not among this group because of his debt to Saigō; however, he remained at his post and continued to serve the central government in anticipation of influencing the development of Japan's law-enforcement machinery.

While abroad, Kawaji had formulated a group of recommendations for police reform that he presented to the government immediately upon his return in September. Kawaji's key points were as follows:

1. The police are an indispensable element in the maintenance of prosperity in a nation.
2. A national police force should be controlled by a home ministry.
3. Within the capital city there should be established a police department under the supervision of the home ministry.
4. The justice police should be divided from the administrative police. The duties of the justice police should be administered by the Ministry of Justice, while the administrative police should be under the jurisdiction of the Home Ministry.
5. Satisfactory small arms should be prepared to equip the police for emergency situations so that the army will not have to be mobilized unnecessarily.
6. The fire department should be placed under the administration of the police.[66]

Kawaji's proposals serve as a prospectus for the study of police organizational reforms during the succeeding years. The Home Ministry (naimushō) was established on November 10, thus satisfying a basic organizational prerequisite for the implementation of the second of Kawaji's six principal proposals. On November 25, the firefighting organizations were transferred from the Tokyo Municipal Government to the Police Bureau to conform with the sixth proposal. January 9, 1874, is the date on which the second proposal was fully realized. The Police Bureau was transferred from the Ministry of Justice to the Home Ministry. The Police Bureau, as we have seen, was designed to control a nationwide police network. Proposal number three, that a special policy agency be created for law enforcement in Tokyo, was actualized on January 15 with the establishment of the Metropolitan Police Agency (keishichō). The agency's officers were initially housed in the Edo headquarters of the former Tsuyama domain, which became a part of Okayama Prefecture.[67] Organizational directives and the duty regulations of the Metropolitan Police Agency were issued on January 27. On February 2, constables were renamed patrolmen (junsa), within which rank there were four grades. The personnel quota for patrolmen called for 6,000 officers.[68]

On February 20, the Metropolitan Police Agency borrowed 7,000 small arms from the army for the purpose of dealing with riots.[69] Kawaji's fifth proposal was thereby put into action. With the acquisition of firearms by the Metropolitan Police Agency, only one proposal remained to be fully implemented, the separation of the administrative and judicial police. The completion of this process took place in 1875 with the promulgation of the Administrative Police Regulations (Gyōsei keisatsu kisoku).

Before an examination of developments on the prefectural level, mention should be made of the fate of Etō Shimpei, whose efforts as minister of justice strengthened the legal basis of the Meiji police. On January 17, 1874, following his return to Saga Prefecture, Etō joined Itagaki and six other prominent men in presenting a petition to the government demanding the establishment of a popularly elected legislative assembly. In early February, Etō led an armed insurrection in Saga in hopes of forcing the government to adopt the defunct Korean invasion plan. The rebellion was suppressed under the personal leadership of Ōkubo, and Etō was executed following his capture.

It has been argued that the creation of the Police Bureau within the Home Ministry was engineered by Ōkubo who was "anticipating internal disturbances created by dissidents, especially those within the ranks of the recently defeated military party."[70] Though such fears may have prompted rapid action, Kawaji's recommendation to adopt such a structure predates even the political resolution of the Korean question. Thus, the police reforms of early 1874 were not born out of the specific desire to establish machinery to control the men who had favored the Korean venture. Such reforms seem to have emerged from a more general appreciation for the value of police over the military as a flexible instrument for dealing with any internal disturbance, thus leaving the mobilization of troops as a contingency of last resort.

Prefectural Resistance to Standardization

On the prefectural level, the tempo of reform increased following the abolition of the domains on August 29, 1871. On December 10, 1871, the Council of State issued a directive outlining local government organization, the Regional System of Administration Act *(Fuken kansei)*,[71] which specified that prefectural administration should consist of three departments: General Affairs *(shomuka)*, Justice *(chōshōka)*, and Tax *(sozeika)*. Judicial police activities were to be administered under the Justice Department.

About a month later, the Council of State issued the Local Administration Act *(Kenji jorei)*, which sought to revise, clarify, and expand upon the Regional System of Administration Act. The addition of a fourth administrative department, called Receipts and Disbursements, was part of the more greatly articulated plan. A specific aim of the Local Administration Act was to standardize the existing profusion of prefectural police organizations by again, as in 1869, directing the local governments to institute a number of high-ranking law-enforcement officers called arresters *(hobō)*. The arresters were to be placed in the Justice Department of each prefecture.[72] Although there was no attempt to go so far as to appoint its own agents to fill these posts, the Ministry of Finance did follow up the Council of State orders with a directive to the prefectural governments that admonished them to appoint suitable personnel as arresters.[73] Exactly what qualities were considered "suitable" was not explained.

In February 1872, the Ministry of Finance ordered the prefectures to disband the former domain military forces that were on active duty as law-enforcement officers and to replace them with arresters.[74] Given the personnel figures for the arresters who were eventually appointed, it appears that they were not intended to replace the troops on a man for man basis. More specifically, this directive was another attempt to bring to an end the system of investigators and detectives in the old domain administrative arrangement. On September 5, 1872, the Council of State issued the Organizational Regulations for the Administration of Justice *(Shihō shokumu teisei)*, which further attempted to standardize the administration of justice in the prefectures. The document directed that a legal department with a prosecutor's section be established in each prefecture. Prefectural constables and arresters were ordered to be administratively attached to this prosecutor's section.[75] In the prefectures where the Legal Department was actually established, the Justice Department was abolished. Police duties were divided between the Legal Department, which administered judicial police functions, and the General Affairs Department, which supervised patrols.

Okayama Prefecture did not comply with the central government's new organizational plan until many months after the issuance of the orders. One possible explanation for this fact, at least with regard to the Justice Department, was that Okayama had completed a reorganization on November 16, 1871, just a few weeks prior to the issuance of the Regional System of Administration Act. Police functions were carried out under a department called Investigation and Adjudication *(chōdansho)*. On January 29, 1872, the Okayama prefectural government again issued reorganization directives listing four departments but using different nomenclature than had been specified in the Local Administration Act.[76] The lack of any functional description makes it difficult to compare this Okayama plan with the central government's decree; however, it is clear that Okayama did not implement the Local Administration Act organization until more than one year later, on January 10, 1873.[77] By that time, the Organizational Regulation for the Administration of Justice ordering the abolition of the Justice Department had already been in force for four months. The duties of six sections within Okayama's Justice Department are as follows:

1. interrogation and responsibility for written confessions;
2. adjudication;
3. supervision of prison labor;
4. jail supervision with responsibility for searching prisoners for weapons;

5. compilation of records including retention of letters of inquiry to government offices, drafting of letters to other prefectures, maintenance of records regarding court actions, and supervision of departmental finances;

6. investigation and arrest.[78]

The Justice Department managed what were later to be designated as judicial police functions; administrative police duties fell under the jurisdiction of the General Affairs Department and the Tax Department.

The creation of a Justice Department in harmony with the Local Administration Act was not the only reform decreed by the central government that Okayama failed to implement readily. Indications are that arresters were not instituted for more than a year after the Council of State reissued orders for their establishment in the prefectures. Local Okayama documents state that arresters were placed under the Justice Department in January 1873.[79] In other words, the Okayama prefectural government was not using the same organizational scheme as that decreed by the central authorities; there was considerable time lag with regard to implementation of centrally dictated structural innovations such as the appointment of arresters. The following personnel statistics provide added evidence supporting the tardy date of establishing arresters in Okayama. There are no figures available for 1871.

Year	Rank	No. of Officers	Monthly Salary
Meiji 5 (1872)	Arrest Sergeant	1	4 yen
	Arrester	30	3.5 yen
Meiji 6 (1873)	Arrest Sergeant	2	4 yen
	Arrester	30	3.5 yen
Meiji 7 (1874)	Chief Arrester	1	10 yen
	Arrest Supervisor	1	5 yen
	Arrest Sergeant	3	4 yen
	Arrester	34	3.5 yen[80]

Arresters were assigned to work at the prefectural headquarters, but when necessary, they were sent to other places on specific assignments. Each prefecture was responsible for paying these officers, and the local, rather than central, government controlled their appointments and dismissals. This meant that, though the nomenclature had been standardized, the qualifications had not. The acceptance of the arresters, even though belated in the case of Okayama, represented a major first step toward the realization of a standardized prefectural police system. The arresters continued to fulfill the role of arresting offices, primarily emphasizing the apprehension of lawbreakers after the crime. This judicial police role provided functional continuity with the investigator/detective system of the Tokugawa period.

Certainly the arresters did not constitute the entire police force in the Okayama Prefecture after the abolition of the investigator/detective system. Prior to the institution of arresters, prefectural leaders had taken steps to reform the night-watch system inherited from the pre-Restoration period. In November of 1871, the city was divided into five administrative wards.[81] A few days later, six night-watch stations were established to service the five patrol jurisdictions.[82] On January 20, 1873, the night watch was abolished; and in its place, the City Control Group *(shichū torishimari gumi)* was established. In the rural areas policemen called "rural burglary officers" *(gunchū tōzoku banyaku)* were also established. The men in this group manned small stations scattered throughout the countryside.

Fukazu Prefecture (later renamed Oda Prefecture)[83] to the west of Okayama also adopted the arrester system. All the various types of Tokugawa period policemen serving in that jurisdiction were entirely abolished, and ten arresters were appointed to administer 800 patrolmen called "general control agents." As in Okayama Prefecture, arresters were attached to the Justice Department.[84] The selection of the Fukazu prefectural patrolmen reflects a continued emphasis on Tokugawa period recruitment practices. The district chiefs were ordered to choose one or two men in every small ward who would be responsible for controlling thieves, gamblers, and troublemakers. These appointees were further expected to make inquiries about strangers and to guard criminals when they were being transferred from one jurisdiction to another.

Tokugawa practices were evident in the manner of payment of the control agents by each ward. As was the case with the watchmen *(bannin)*, some were given their salaries in cash and others in rice; in each case it amounted to less than ten yen a year for each man.[85] Contrasting this amount with the forty-two yen per year earned by low-ranking arresters, it is possible to gauge the difference in the living standards of the local and prefectural police officials.

The Fukazu prefectural patrolmen were subject to their respective district chiefs in matters relating to their advancement and retirement. It was the district chief's responsibility to inform the prefectural headquarters of the police personnel who were appointed within his jurisdiction. Though the arresters were primarily responsible for the urban and large village patrols, once each month they were required to visit the rural areas to inspect the quality of work being done by the control agents. Such a level of supervision did not differ significantly from the attention that samurai officials had paid to rural law enforcement. The arresters and general-control-agent system was primarily one designed to keep public peace; however, Fukazu (later Oda) Prefecture continued to have difficulties maintaining order.

In Hōjō Prefecture, which was located north of Okayama in the territory of Mimasaka including old Tsuyama domain, the experimentation with police nomenclature was much more active. As of June 1872, there was an officer called an "arrester" whose name was changed to "burglary inspector" *(tōzoku metsuke)*. The following year, in September, this title was changed to "village inspector" *(mura metsuke)*. Only four months later an official termed *junra*, whose functions were much like those of the arresters in Okayama Prefecture, was established in the prefectural headquarters.

Just at the time when the central government was abolishing the name "constable" *(rasotsu)* in Tokyo, the local prefectures were instituting the title as a vehicle for further unification of police personnel. In Okayama, the arresters, city control group, and rural burglary officers were all unified under the title "constable" on January 9, 1875. This was done in compliance with a central-government directive. A breakdown of the ranks and salaries is as follows:

Rank	Number of Men	Monthly Salary	Yearly Total Expenditure
Constabulary Sergeant	32	5 yen	1,920 yen
Constable First Class (on duty at Prefectural Headquarters)	13	4 yen	624 yen
Constable First Class	50	3.5 yen	2,100 yen
Constable Second Class	147	3 yen	5,292 yen[86]

Along with the innovations in standardization, there were new arrangements in the methods for financing police protection in the prefecture of Okayama. Significantly, by 1875 the central government was investing directly in local law enforcement as opposed to the previous absence of any meaningful financial contribution. Revenue from taxes rather than from traditional ward sources was now employed for payment of the constables who worked in the city as well as in the rural areas. The financial breakdown was as follows:

Central government grant	2,835 yen
City tax	1,990.625 yen
Rural tax	11,292.15 yen (0.15 yen per household)[87]

By providing for police salaries from tax revenues, the government further emphasized the public, as opposed to private, nature of the new law-enforcement organization. However, the depth of the Meiji leadership's interest in institutions of coercive control cannot be gauged solely by the extent of the contribution of the central government, since it was the local-government treasury that bore the heaviest burden.

During the early months of 1875, the prefectural police organization in Okayama reached a point of significant compliance with the structural arrangements decreed by the central government. A totally new concept of the police emerged that replaced the Tokugawa ideas of neighborhood associations providing their own protection. By 1875, the government had taken upon itself the responsibility of policing the cities. The law-enforcement officers on the patrol level were the government's men.

Policing Rural Japan

With the promulgation of the Administrative Police Regulations (*Gyōsei keisatsu kisoku*)[88] in March of 1875, a new phase of development began in which the police officers accepted new roles and fulfilled those roles in the countryside as well as in the urban areas. Having achieved standardized prefectural police organizations, the central administration was ready to use those organizations actively to control the rural areas.

On November 30, 1875, the central government abolished the Local Administration Act, which had been in force since the abolition of the domains in 1871, and established a new organizational structure for the prefectural governments.[89] This new arrangement was effected in Okayama in January 1876.[90] The important element of this reform with regard to police organization was to group all administrative police activities under the direction of one department head, the director of the Fourth Department. The Justice Department continued to be responsible for the administration of the court system. Later during the year, on March 9, the Justice Department was renamed the Prefectural Court.

Between the issuance of the reorganization plan and its adoption, Okayama absorbed Oda Prefecture. The geographical limits of modern Okayama Prefecture were defined in the spring of 1876. On April 18, Hōjō Prefecture was joined with Okayama, while in May, parts of old Oda Prefecture were separated from Okayama and made a part of Hiroshima Prefecture.

On June 19, 1876, the Okayama police system was formally dispersed into the rural areas of the prefecture. The Police Central Office was established in the prefectural headquarters, while five branch headquarters and forty patrol stations were deployed throughout the prefecture. The locations of the branches and the number of stations under the jurisdiction of each was as follows:

Location	Number of Patrol Stations
#1 Branch, Bizen, Okayama City	14
#2 Branch, Bizen, Katayama Village	5
#3 Branch, Bitchū, Tamashima Village	5
#4 Branch, Bitchū, Takahashi City	4
#5 Branch, Mimasaka, Tsuyama City	12[91]

The movement of the police into the rural areas of the prefecture was a process of considerable significance for it represented a radical departure from the Tokugawa period law-enforcement system. Rather than depend primarily upon the continued strength of traditional values and institutions in the countryside, the government in Tokyo directed its prefectural governors to break with the arrangements of pre-Restoration Japan. With the deployment of police stations and patrol boxes beyond the urban centers, the framework for sustained surveillance and supervision of the population was set in place. By 1876, the basic structure of the prefectural police system was firmly in place.

A police force can only attempt to solve as much crime as its organizational capabilities allow it to know. In reality, most crime is made known to the police through citizen complaint rather than through police work. Indicative of the new political order in Japan, the government, through the deployment of its police, sought to make its agents available to receive complaints. To establish the credibility of its extensive claims to sovereignty, the government sought to replace traditional structures of adjudication and, in so doing, to enhance its power at the expense of local and private interests. Complaints that had previously been handled through the five-man group or the village officials were now to be directed to the prefectural police. If the government were going to prohibit traditionally acceptable private acts such as revenge as a means of redress,[92] then new machinery had to be provided through which the victim of a crime could seek amends. The grass-roots element of that new machinery was the network of police stations and patrol boxes.

Conclusion

Tokugawa Japan was an unpoliced society. In such a society individuals with the government's mandate to enforce law and maintain order played relatively passive roles. The citizen was paid to provide the authorities with information about crimes and the whereabouts of criminals. A mutual-responsibility network was arranged, and severe penalties were decreed for the entire group if a criminal act by any one of its members came to the attention of the authorities. Japanese feudal authorities sought to limit the movement of individuals as a further means of preserving the integrity of group surveillance. The various domain governments in the Tokugawa period sought to place the burden of maintaining law and order on the private sector. Even in the few urban areas that existed, the actual number of domain-appointed policemen was small. For the most part, law-enforcement tasks were carried out by outcastes hired either by the domain administrations or by neighborhood associations. The bulk of these police functionaries was primarily concerned with fire warning and only secondarily with deviant behavior.

The law-enforcement arrangements of the Tokugawa period were wholly inadequate for the needs of the Meiji government. This fact became evident soon after the establishment of the Restoration. Evidence is clear that police reform constituted an area of early innovation in the planning of the new system of administration. The leadership did not depend solely upon normative means of social control, nor did they seek for long to convert the Tokugawa control machinery to their own ends. The basic reason was that the ends of the new government were quite different from those of the feudal lords under the previous regime.

The decentralized Tokugawa system that allowed and encouraged large areas of administrative autonomy was precisely what the new leadership aimed at destroying. The restoration of imperial rule soon came to mean centralization in reality rather than simply in name. Effective centralization suggested the need for tools to implement the will of the leadership. The creation of a bureaucratized police system that could be controlled directly from the central government fulfilled the role. The five-man group represented the basic building block for the privilege and responsibility of autonomous adjudication. The emperor's claims to sovereignty penetrated deep into this area of privilege by assuming far more responsibility than the great lords had done. The imperial claims to sovereignty needed to be actualized on the local level. The emperor's policeman, as opposed to the neighborhood's watchman, served as a demonstration of the imperial government's determination to rule rather than simply reign. Men fulfilling police functions were no longer agents of the community; they were agents of the imperial will.

Notes

1. Social control" is understood to be all the means and processes whereby a group or a society secures the conformity of its members to its expectations.
2. Marion J. Levy, Jr., *Modernization and the Structure of Societies: A Setting for International Affairs* (Princeton, N.J., Princeton University Press, 1969), p. 765.
3. Ibid., p. 767.
4. For the purposes of this investigation, the word *police* refers to individuals appointed by the government at its various levels to insure compliance with laws by the use of force if necessary. Police, unlike the military, were limited to domestic activity. In the Tokugawa period a wide variety of men enforced the laws. Some were of such a part-time nature and had such a limited jurisdiction that they are referred to as "police functionaries."
5. Allen Silver, "The Demand for Order in Civil Society: A Review of Some Themes in the History of Urban Crime, Police, and Riot," in *The Police: Six Sociological Essays*, ed. David J. Bordua (New York: John Wiley and Sons, 1967), p. 7.
6. There are several reasons for selecting Okayama Prefecture to represent the local element in this study. During the Tokugawa period, what is now Okayama Prefecture consisted of several types of administrative units: Okayama-*han*, a medium sized *tozama* (outside) domain; provinces of Mimasaka and Bitchū, conglomerations of *bakufu* domains. Such a variety allows comparison of responses to police reform. Secondly, Okayama men played a role in early police work in the nation's capital. Finally, a wealth of research has centered on Okayama since World War II. Hopefully, this study will contribute to the enduring effort to construct an interdisciplinary view of Japanese historical experience as exemplified in Okayama.

7. All individuals in a village were related to one of these groups. Since the orgnization gets its name from the number of household heads assigned to it, the groups actually contained more than five individuals. Such organizational patterns are not uncommon in premodern societies. See Kung-Chuan Hsiao, *Rural China: Imperial Control in the Nineteenth Century* (Cambridge, Mass.: Harvard University Press, 1971), pp. 150–54, for discussions of the contemporary Chinese institution.

8. Hozumi Nobushige, *Gonin gumi seido ron* (Tokyo: Yūhikaku shobō, 1921), p. 163.

9. Ibid.

10. Imagawa Tokuzō, *Hasshū mawari to daikan* (Tokyo: Yūzankaku shuppan, 1974), p. 179.

11. Hozumi, *Gonin gumi*, p. 168.

12. Kōri bugyō sho, "Shoshoku no bu: Gonin gumi gashira," in *Satsuyōroku*, ed. Yoshida Gen, 2 vols. (Okayama: Nihon bunkyō shuppan, 1965), 2:1022.

13. Hozumi, *Gonin gumi*, pp. 171–83.

14. Imagawa, *Hasshū mawari*, p. 141.

15. Hozumi, *Gonin gumi*, pp. 162–63.

16. Okayama shi shi henshū iinkai, *Okayama shi shi: Seiji hen* (Okayama: Okayama shiyakusho, 1964), p. 236.

17. Yokokura Tatsuji, *Yoriki, dōshin, meakashi no seikatsu* (Tokyo: Yūzankaku shuppan, 1973), p. 32.

18. Higuchi Hideo, *Edo no hankachō* (Tokyo: Jinbutsu ōraiosha, 1962), p. 34.

19. Okayama shi, *Okayama shi shi*, p. 237.

20. For a description of the *sankin kōtai*, see George T. Tsukahira, *The Sankin Kōtai System of Tokugawa Japan, 1600–1868* (Cambridge, Mass.: Harvard University Press, 1966).

21. Higuchi, *Hankachō*, p. 34.

22. Yokokura, *Yoriki*, p. 29. Prior to 1713, the *yoriki* and *dōshin* had lived near Ueno.

23. Higuchi, *Hankachō*, p. 34. "Itchō" referred to the way the cut ends of topknot hair were spread to resemble the fan-shaped ginko *(itchō)* leaf. High-ranking *sumō* wrestlers wear a similar style today.

24. Taniguchi Sumio, *Okayama-han seishi no kenkyū* (Tokyo: Hanawa shobō, 1964), p. 244.

25. Higuchi, *Hankachō*, p. 36.

26. Ibid., p. 35. In the Meiji period, revenue from Yoshiwara was used to establish hospitals.

27. Shibata Hajime, *Shibuzome ikki ron* (Tokyo: Yagi shoten, 1971), pp. 6–7.

28. Okayama shiyakusho, *Okayama shi shi*, 6 vols. (Okayama: Okayama shiyakusho, 1937), 3:394.

29. Higuchi, *Hankachō*, p. 36.

30. Naimushō chihōkyoku nai jichishinkō chuōkai, eds., *Fuken seido shiryō*, 2 vols. (Tokyo: Rekishi tosho sha, 1973), 1:19.

31. Marius B. Jansen, *Sakamoto Ryōma and the Meiji Restoration* (Princeton, N.J.: Princeton University Press, 1961), p. 138; and Hirao Michio, "Bakumatsu ronin to sono hogo oyobi tōsei," in *Meiji ishin shi kenkyū*, ed. Shigakkai (Tokyo: 1930), pp. 552–53.

32. Kuroda Shigeo, *Nihon keisatsu shi no kenkyū* (Tokyo: Reibunsha, 1963), p. 215.

33. Keishichō shi hensan iinkai, eds., *Keishichō shi*, 3 vols. (Tokyo: Keishichōshi hensan iinkai, 1959), 1:17.

34. Hiroshima-ken keisatsu shi hensan iinkai, eds., *Hiroshima-ken keisatsu hyakunen shi*, 2 vols. (Hiroshima: Hiroshima-ken keisatsu honbu, 1971), 1:92.

35. Yamamoto Kazuo, *Nihon keisatsu shi* (Tokyo: Shōkado shoten, 1934), p. 144.

36. Katsu Kaishu had been the *bakufu* commander who surrendered Edo castle to Saigō Takamori, the actual commander of the loyalist army, rather than to submit the city to destruction in an attempt to maintain the stronghold.

37. Taniguchi Sumio, *Okayama-han* (Tokyo: Yoshikawa kōbunkan, 1964), p. 294.

38. Tamura Yutaka, *Keisatsu shi kenkyū* (Tokyo: Ryōsho fukyū kai, 1936), p. 188.

39. Tamura Yutaka, "Nihon keisatsu seido seiritsu shōshi," Part 1, *Keisatsu kenkyū*, (May 5, 1930), p. 69.

40. Iwata Masakazu, *Ōkubo Toshimichi: The Bismarck of Japan* (Berkeley, Calif.: University of California Press, 1964), pp. 117–19.

41. Keishichō shi, *Keishichō shi*, 1:18–19.

42. "*Goyō*" refers to the function of arresting criminals by means of an official govern-

ment sanction. During the Tokugawa period, police on night searches used paper lanterns decorated with the characters *goyō*. See Nawa Yumio, *Jute torinawa no kenkyu* (Tokyo Yūzankaku shuppan, 1964), pp. 155–57.

43. Keishichō sōmubu kikakuka, *Keishichō nempyō* (Tokyo: Keishichō sōmubu kikakuka 1968), p. 3.
44. Yamamoto, *Keisatsu shi*, p. 144.
45. Hiroshima-ken, *Keisatsu hyakunen shi*, 1:86. For an English language account of aspects of the crown prince's visit, see Iwata, *Ōkubo*, p. 134.
46. Kuroda, *Nihon keisatsu shi*, p. 207.
47. Keishichō, *Nempyō*, p. 3.
48. Mainichi shimbun sha, ed., *Kanagawa no hyakunen* (Tokyo: Mainichi shimbun sha, 1968), pp. 268–69.
49. Oka Tadao, *Meiji jidai keisatsu kan no seikatsu* (Tokyo: Yūzankaku shuppan, 1974), p. 10.
50. Taniguchi Sumio, "Meiji ishin shi ni okeru Okayama-han no seiji katei," in *Meiji ishin shi mondai ten*, ed. Sakata Yoshio (Tokyo: 1962), pp. 377–400. For an English account, see John W. Hall, "From Tokugawa to Meiji in Local Administration," in *Studies in the Institutional History of Early Modern Japan*, eds. John W. Hall and Marius B. Jansen (Princeton, N.J.: Princeton University Press, 1968), pp. 377–78.
51. Okayama-ken, *Okayama-ken no rekishi* (Okayama: Nihon bunkyō shuppan, 1962), p. 498. Though Mochimasa appears to have resigned due to a conflict of loyalty, during the second year of Meiji, he was appointed as vice-head of the *danjōdai*, the central government's special "political" police agency.
52. Text quoted in Okayama-ken, *Okayama Kenseishi*, 2 vols. (Okayama: Okayama-ken, 1940), 1:133–35.
53. Dajōkan hatsu 676 in Okayama-ken, *Kenseishi* (1940), 1:10.
54. Naimushō, *Fuken seido*, 2:4–5.
55. *Torishimari-ko* were renamed *rasotsu* in the summer of 1872; however, some sources prematurely use the term *rasotsu* for personnel of the *torishimari gumi* in 1871.
56. Tamura, *Keisatsu shi kenkyū*, p. 188.
57. For an example, see Kawaji Toshiyoshi, *Keisatsu shugan* (Tokyo: Keisatsu shugan fukkokukan Kōkai, 1973).
58. Chiba Shūsaku's brother was Sadakichi, who taught Sakamoto Ryōma in the use of the sword. See Hirao Michio, *Kaientai shimatsu ki* (Tokyo: Daidō shobō, 1941), p. 12.
59. Daikakai, *Naimushō*, 4 vols. (Tokyo: Chihō zaimu kyōkai, 1970–71), 2:571.
60. "Memorial by Kawaji Daikeishi on Police Affairs," *Tokyo akehono shimbun*, January 20, 1876, in *Shimbun shūsei Meiji hennenshi*, ed. Nakayama Yasuaki (Tokyo: Zaisei keizai gakukai, 1934), p. 472.
61. Hyogō-ken keisatsu shi hensan iinkai, *Hyogō-ken keisatsu shi* (Kobe: Hyogō-ken keisatsu shi hensan iinkai, 1972), pp. 31–32.
62. See "Keihōryō shokusei oyobi shōtei," Dajōkan hatsu 17, in *Nihon no keisatsu*, ed. Koike Yoshimi (Tokyo: Nihon keisatsu hensanka, 1968), p. 63.
63. Matono Hansuke, *Etō Nanpaku*, 2 vols. (Tokyo: Hara shobō, 1968), 2:118–21.
64. Oka, *Keisatsu kan*, p. 20.
65. Tamura, *Keisatsu shi kenkyū*, p. 193.
66. Daikakai, *Naimushō shi*, 2:577.
67. Keishichō, *Keishichō shi*, 1:40.
68. Oka, *Keisatsu kan*, p. 24.
69. Keishichō, *Nempyō*, p. 12.
70. Iwata, *Ōkubo*, p. 175.
71. Dajōkan fukoku 560 in Naimushō, *Fuken seido*, 2:14–16.
72. "Kenji jōrei," in Dajōkan notice 623, January 7, 1872, in ibid., 2:16–19. For *hobō*, see especially p. 18.
73. See document in Hiroshima-ken, *Keisatsu hyakunen shi*, 1:147.
74. Ibid. During the first year and a half of the Meiji period, a group of ardent modernizers, among whom Ōkuma Shigenobu and Itō Hirobumi were the most prominent, attempted to use their positions in this strategic branch of the bureaucracy to promote reform. In the fall of 1869, the Ministry of Civil Affairs became a part of the Finance Ministry. These men were

able to exert pressure on local administrative procedure. However, their tactics alienated conservatives to the degree that the Ministry of Civil Affairs was made autonomous in the summer of 1870. (See William G. Beasley, *The Meiji Restoration* [Stanford, Calif.: Stanford University Press, 1972], pp. 342–44.) Ōkubo Toshimichi assumed control of the Finance Ministry in 1871, and the ministry of Civil Affairs was again absorbed under the Finance Ministry, thereby explaining the role of the *ōkurashō* in local administrative affairs. See Itawa, *Ōkubo*, pp. 142–43.

75. Hiroshima-ken, *Keisatsu hyakunen shi*, 1:149.
76. Okayama-ken, *Okayama kenseishi* (Okayama: Okayama-ken, 1967), p. 23.
77. Okayama-ken shi hensan gakari, *Okayama-ken shi kōhon*, 2 vols. (Okayama: Okayama-ken chihō shi kenkyū renraku kyōgikai, 1967), 1:149.
78. "Meiji gonen junigatsu shokusei o kimaru," *Shokusei*, 1875, in Okayama-ken, *Kenseishi* (1940), 2:743.
79. "Okayama-ken shokusei," 1873, in Okayama-ken, *Kōhon*, 1:149–51.
80. Keisatsu shi hensan iinkai, Salary schedules, 1872–74, Keisatsu hon sho, Okayama-ken.
81. Okayama-ken, *Kōhon*, 1:66.
82. For the location of the six stations, see Okayama shi, *Okayama shi shi*, p. 399.
83. Oda Prefecture had once been Fukazu Prefecture, which had been created on November 15, 1871, by consolidating eleven prefectures that comprised all of Bitchū and the six eastern districts of Bingo. Kurashiki and Takahashi were the most prominent of the Bitchū prefectures that became a part of Fukazu. On June 7, 1872, Fukazu Prefecture had its name changed to Oda Prefecture.
84. Kibi bunsho kenkyū kai, ed., *Oda-ken shi* (Okayama: Nihon bunkyō shuppan, 1971), pp. 173–74.
85. Ibid.
86. Okayama-ken, *Kōhon*, 2:5.
87. Ibid.
88. Text in Koike, *Nihon no keisatsu*, pp. 65–67. Also see Okayama kenchō, *Genkō ruiju keisatsu hōki honhen* (Okayama: Okayama-ken, 1888), pp. 67–73. Articles 1, 2, 3, and 5 are translated into English in Ōura Kanetake, "The Police of Japan," in *Fifty Years of New Japan*, ed. Ōkuma Shigenobu, trans. Marcus B. Huish (London: Smith, Elder, 1909).
89. Dajōkan Ordinance 203 in Naimushō, ed., *Fuken seido*, 2:54–63. For police, see p. 56.
90. Okayama-ken, *Kenseishi* (1940), 1:753.
91. Okayama-ken keisatsu honbu kyōyoka, "Okayama-ken keisatsu shi nemphō," (an), 1876–1971, Okayama-ken.
92. Revenge was prohibited by a *dajōkan* order in January 1873. The people were required to report murder to the prefectural office rather than engage in unofficial retribution. There were heavy penalties for failure to adhere to the new policy. See Okayama-ken, *Kenseishi* (1940), 1:1123.

Glossary

ashigaru	足軽
bannin	番人
banya	番屋
chōdansho	聴断所
chōshōka	聴訟課
daikeishi	大警視
daimyō	大名
danjōdai	弾正台
dōshin	同心
eta	穢多

fuhei gakari	府兵掛
Fuken kansei	府県官制
gonin gumi	五人組
gunchū tōzoku banyaku	郡中盗賊番役
gunmukan	軍務官
gyōbushō	刑部省
Gyōhō	刑法
Gyōsei keisatsu kisoku	行政警察規則
hatchō-bori ichō	八丁堀銀杏
heibushō	兵部省
hinin	非人
hobō	捕亡
hobōkata	捕亡方
hobōkata shitametsuke	捕亡下目付
hobōshi	捕亡司
jishinban	自身番
junra	巡邏
junsa	巡査
keihōkan	刑法官
keihōryō	警保寮
keishichō	警視庁
kenji jōrei	県治条例
Kenkan jinin narabini jobikin kisoku	県官人員並常備金規則
machi bugyō	町奉行
machi metsuke	町目付
meakashi	目明
mura metsuke	村目付
naimushō	内務省
rasotsu	邏卒
rōnin	浪人
sankin kōtai	参勤交代
shichū torishimari gumi	市中取締組
shihōshō	司法省
Shihō shokumu teisei	司法職務定制
shinsen gumi	新撰組
sozeika	租税課
shomuka	諸務課
taibu	逮部
tōzoku metsuke	盗賊目付
torishimari gakari	取締掛
tsubo	坪
yoriki	与力
yen(en)	円

2   Managing the News:
Fukuchi Gen'ichirō Attempts to Balance Two Worlds

James L. Huffman

It is hardly new to suggest that one of the more distinctive features of Meiji Japan was the highly pragmatic efforts of its leaders to adapt foreign methods and institutions to Japanese society, to balance, as it were, the uniquely Japanese with a number of typically universal features of civilization. Nor was such balancing and adaptation new to Meiji Japan. Similar efforts had occurred at least as far back as the fourth- and fifth-century tomb period, again in Nara and yet again in the days of the Ashikaga. But never before had the determination to balance been carried out with such intensity; never had it been compacted so massively into such a brief period of time.

To read the history of these years is to study a constant series of clashes, sometimes dynamic and sometimes disruptive, sometimes conscious and sometimes less so, between the traditional and the modern, the particular and the universal, the Japanese and the Western. It was a struggle experienced in some measure by every single individual who significantly influenced the period's history. Ōkuma Shigenobu from Hizen, for example, might well have been a strictly Japanese type, given his unwillingness ever to leave his homeland to travel abroad; yet it was this very patriot who in so many ways led the parade of economic Westernization as finance minister in the 1870s.[1] Itō Hirobumi, in contrast to Ōkuma, went abroad several times, but on one of his most publicized trips, the 1882 mission to Europe to study Western constitutional systems, his primary aim was to find a means of legitimizing a distinctly Japanese form of constitutionalism. The very individuals supporting the erection of a social pavilion, the Rokumeikan, for Western-style dances and entertainment in the early 1880s would in those same years help prepare an important set of "Imperial Precepts to Soldiers and Sailors" aimed at reinforcing such traditional values as loyalty and valor. Whether consciously or unconsciously, the Meiji leaders always seemed to be struggling to incorporate both the Japanese and the universal into a single new way of national life.

Sometimes their efforts were cautious, begrudging, or petty, as when Tokyo newspapers suggested that rickshaw men no longer strip to their loin cloths and that proprietors of bath houses put screens before the entrances, so that the Japanese will "not be laughed at by foreigners."[2] At other times the balancing was more dynamic, a fact emphasized by the way in which traditional codes of loyalty provided the primary reservoir of talent and support required for carrying out the Meiji political and social changes.[3] But always the two poles were evident. "Eastern ethics and Western methods" was more than a neat phrase. The ethics employed by Meiji figures may not always have been truly Eastern; nor were the methods wholly Western. But the interaction of the two was unceasing. As one of the figures of the day wrote: "I felt a constant ebb and flow, a constant collision within myself, of both extreme conservatism and extreme progressivism."[4]

A particularly fascinating characteristic of this struggle to balance East and West was the evolutionary manner in which it unfolded. At first glance, the Meiji era sometimes seems a cacophony of simultaneously blaring sounds, a continuous clashing of things Japanese, American, Chinese, Russian, British, Egyptian, and what have you. But as a number of scholars have noted, the cacophony was patterned; though each of the divergent sounds was ever-present, the major motif changed from period to period. Thus we find the pre-Meiji years dominated by antiforeignism, the 1870s by faddish and uncritical Westernization, the early 1880s by increasing skepticism about the West and the period from the late 1880s onward by a relatively conscious effort genuinely to balance the two worlds.

One of the more illuminating examples of this evolution (and, thus, the focus of this study) is Fukuchi Gen'ichirō (1841–1906), the iconoclastic father of Japan's modern press and the most influential, popular exponent of many government policies in the 1870s and 1880s. Born in Nagasaki, his family's first male child in three generations,[5] Fukuchi was a man of diverse talents. (No less a figure than Iwakura Tomomi called him one of the most versatile, talented men of the age.[6]) For that reason one might justifiably analyze his life in terms of its contributions to fields as varied as economics, politics, journalism, history, literature, and drama. But taken in its entirety, his career casts perhaps its brightest light on the nationwide struggle to fit the uniqueness of Japanese traditions into the universal frame of reference forced on Japan by encounters with the new world. It is from that perspective that his life will be viewed here.

Until the age of twenty, Fukuchi Gen'ichirō's world view, like the general intellectual mood of the early Meiji some two decades later, amounted in practical terms to a repudiation of Japanese traditions and a feverish, almost intoxicated pursuit of Western ideas and ways. Like most other samurai born before the advent of Perry, Fukuchi's early education included rote memorization of Confucian classics, drill in calligraphy, and composition of Chinese literary forms. He also was a child of Nagasaki, about the only spot in Japan of the 1840s where a samurai lad might snatch glimpses of the exciting vistas of barbarian learning or, perhaps, even see a few Dutch barbarians themselves on their way to a supervised evening in the town's entertainment district. After his father decided in 1855 that his son, then age fourteen, should begin studying Dutch, Fukuchi largely rejected the old-world, classical learning in favor of the excitement and promise of the new. He even went so far, temporarily, as to agree to adoption into the household of Namura Hachiemon, his Dutch teacher[7]—rather a drastic step for the oldest son in a Tokugawa era family, but nevertheless a striking illustration of Fukuchi's attitudes toward both the old and the new.

At the age of eighteen, Fukuchi carried the break with tradition even further and left his hometown altogether to journey to the Tokugawa capital in Edo, where his ability as a translator seemed more likely to be fully utilized. It was a pivotal move, intellectually as well as physically. No sooner had he arrived there than he began to see the utter incompatability, for himself at least, of Eastern and Western orientations in that city's *bakumatsu* society. Since a number of his father's Edo acquaintances were Confucian scholars, he considered continuing classical studies for a time, more or less as a cushion in case the trend toward Westernization should lose force. However, those same scholars made it clear to the naïve youth that he would be welcome in their circles only if he turned away from Western learning. Faced with that choice, he at once opted to discard Eastern learning instead, to devote all his energies to the study of Dutch and English. The traditionalists denounced him, calling him an "alien barbarian," but he retorted that "not one" of them "was pursuing anything worthwhile." He would not "waste life by advancing with them."[8] Instead, he went to live with the English interpreter Moriyama Tachichirō and within six months had become a *bakufu* retainer as a foreign office (*gaikoku bugyō*) interpreter.

It was not the choice that most young samurai in Edo of the late 1850s would have made; antiforeign (*jōi*) zeal charged the city's atmosphere and involvement with things Western invited ostracism if not bodily harm. Fukuchi's decision seems to have been based on a specific goal orientation, not unlike that of the leaders of the new Meiji government a decade later.[9] He was not anti-Tokugawa and never would be. He was, rather, a young pragmatist convinced that Confucian axioms held no hope for Japan in its confrontation with the modern world. In Nagasaki he had shuddered at the size of Western ships, pondered over the detailed descriptions of world events found in Western newspapers, stirred to the potential of moving Japan in new directions. Now, as a relatively private man unburdened yet by the responsibilities of power, the claims of powerful friends, or the tempering effect of public recognition, he could—and would—pursue his ideals with unquestioned, unhindered zeal. He saw Western methods as essential to national survival and strength. Free of traditional structures, somewhat as the new government would itself be after the demise of the Tokugawa in 1868, he would approach the study of the West with an abandon approaching religious conviction. He read Shakespeare and Gibbon in these years, advocated full-fledged democracy, longed for a chance to travel abroad, and he talked about his ideas without inhibition. The Enlightenment of the early Meiji years has been referred to by Japanese scholars as an "invasion of Western culture."[10] Even so, Fukuchi's own approach to the West during the late-adolescent years was one of sailing blithely with the storm. The winds, to him, were not threatening, only exhilarating.

The all-out pursuit of Western ways and attitudes did not, however, last long. On June 26, 1859, the very day that the first full-fledged Western minister arrived to take up residence in Japan, Fukuchi went to work for the *gaikoku bugyō* and in the process entered a new stage in his intellectual evolution—the stage of "critical Westernization." Almost from that very day, one begins to notice a change in his attitudes toward the West, a change barely perceptible at first, then increasingly obvious as the years passed. In this second stage, he became more and more sensitive to the uniqueness, or at least the centrality, of Japan itself and determined as time passed that Western offerings would have to be evaluated in terms of their relevance to the achievement of certain goals he harbored for his own country. The Western world would continue to be dominant, almost normative on occasion. He would pursue its knowledge with little-abated vigor, but no longer, from mid-1859 on, would Western ways and attitudes exercise an exclusive hold. He would look at them in the light of how they related to Japan's own patterns. His thoughts may not have reached the stage of sophistication of Hashimoto Sanai, who declared late in the 1850s that "we shall take the machines and techniques from [the West], but we have our own ethics and morals."[11] Never, after 1860, would he assert uncritical faith in Western ideals. The years from then until 1874 would be typified, for Fukuchi, by a spirit of Western dominance modified by Japanese traditions.

Superficially, it may seem paradoxical that the onset of this new stage coincided with the beginning of Fukuchi's period of greatest contact with the West, the years in which he read most widely, traveled abroad four times, and opened two different foreign-language schools. However, the paradox is more apparent than real, for direct contact with a fantacized ideal almost always stimulates some disillusionment. Hirata Atsutane's early-nineteenth-century claim, for example, that "people all over the world refer to Japan as the Land of the Gods"[12] could only have been made by a man who had never been "all over the world." Likewise, the early-nineteenth-century writer Kayahara Kazan's adulation of American philosophy and practice turned to scorn once he had journeyed across the Pacific and encountered racial prejudice.[13] Similar attitudinal changes could be cited in the lives of such diverse intellectuals as Tokutomi Sohō, Uemura Masahisa and Nagai Ryūtarō. Ideals tested by reality only seldom maintain all of their original luster.

So it was with Fukuchi. Once he had begun encountering tactless Western merchants in the customs house at Yokohama or intractable diplomats in negotiating sessions, never again would he be willing to accept Western ideas or proposals without question. Merchants ranked at the bottom of the Tokugawa social scale and, hence, owed submission and respect to officials; yet, Western businessmen in Yokohama flaunted Japanese traditions with a hearty brashness born of ignorance and contempt. They refused to learn Dutch, the official commercial language at the time. They proved totally incapable of suppressing outward displays of emotion, whether anger or hilarity; and, worst of all, they allowed even their dogs to wander about in areas designed for officials only. "They made us furious," noted Fukuchi. "They were proud, rude, antagonizing barbarians."[14]

Not that such "outrages" sapped much of Fukuchi's general preoccupation with Western ways and thoughts. Much to the contrary, the West remained central in his life during these years, even if it was now to be scrutinized more carefully. In 1861, for example, he traveled to Europe with the Takenouchi diplomatic mission, immersed himself in such novelties as Western theaters, electricity, politics, and hotels containing "thousands of rooms," then came home convinced that he would henceforth be consulted "in intimate conversation" by officials of the highest rank.[15] Again in 1865, 1871, and 1872–73, he traveled to Europe and America, the last time as a first secretary for the noted Iwakura mission. While abroad, he was always known for the intense zeal with which he pursued new things. Indeed, the major pitfall to his bureaucratic advancement lay in this very fascination with the West, for he loved to talk unreservedly and about all that he knew. After each mission he tended to describe his new encounters to anyone who would listen, not hesitating even to ridicule the "backwardness" of more conservative leaders of the entourages. Unfortunately, he lived in a hierarchical society still dominated in the early 1860s by antiforeign sentiments. It was not an atmosphere in which loquacity made superiors feel comfortable; so Fukuchi often was encouraged to work at home, or even left without work when a diplomatic mission or crisis did not demand his considerable skills. Nor, it should be noted, was the danger implicit in such uninhibited conversation merely a figment of official imaginations. On three separate occasions during the 1860s antiforeign zealots planned or attempted attacks on Fukuchi's life, so obnoxious were his ideas to *jōi* factions. He was, in other words, obsessed in these years with Western ideas and places.

When the *bakufu* fell in 1868, Fukuchi, ever a loyal defender of the Tokugawa family, though not of its "anachronistic" policies, gave further evidence of this tendency by launching one of Japan's earliest attempts at a modern-style newspaper,[16] the *Kōko shimbun*, in order to attack the new government. Several years before, in Paris, he had begun to think about developing Western-style journalism in Japan, and with his old work as a *bakufu* retainer gone, he decided now to fight the Meiji "insurgents" through a newspaper. The paper lasted less than three months, but its influence on Japanese press history was significant as was its dedication to ideas encountered in the West. Like European papers, it attempted a style understandable even to "women and children."[17] Like the Parisian press, it attempted to cover all sorts of news; and Fukuchi's writings bore frequent evidence to the influence of Western political theory. The most influential of his editorials, *Kyōjaku ron* ("On Strength and Weakness"), published on June 24, 1868, for example, not only reviewed the history of Japanese military campaigns, but advocated such innovations as parliamentary government and world-oriented approach to trade.[18] It landed Fukuchi in jail and brought him face to face with possible execution, but it also made him a place in press history and showed clearly the heavy influence of the West on his thoughts. Fukuchi never was to be a systematic, careful student of Western treatises; he followed no particular school; nor did he ever work out a careful, logical approach to Western thought. He read voraciously and the breadth and enthusiasm of his ideas tended to affect readers of the paper with the force of a geyser.

Nevertheless, the decade and a half after Fukuchi's entry into the *gaikoku bugyō* also bore evidence to a growing skepticism about the total applicability of all Western patterns to Japan. Even while his basic approach remained the same, the tone began undergoing a change. While his pursuit had at first been all-consuming and essentially uncritical, it now became more selective, more specifically directed to the perceived needs of Japan. Two decades later, in the middle 1880s, a great number of Japanese intellectuals, men such as Kuga Katsunan and Tokutomi Sohō would begin to question seriously the "Western craze" of Meiji's first decade, worrying that "if the culture of one country is so influenced by another that it completely loses its own unique character, that country will surely lose its independent footing."[19] For Fukuchi, one of the most zealous early pioneers of Westernization, the questioning began somewhat earlier.

For one thing, Fukuchi's approach to the West became more pragmatic after entering the Tokugawa bureaucracy. Partially because he now was involved in the actual day-to-day operations of the foreign office, he stopped simply imbibing and began analyzing: How did Western proposals apply to Japan? Which should be accepted, which rejected? It was in this frame of mind that he advocated an immediate switch in the summer of 1859 to English as the language of diplomacy, despite treaty provisions that only Dutch and Japanese would be allowed until 1864. Western merchants could not use Dutch, he observed, so "stubborn insistence on the treaty would create clear problems for both sides."[20] Even while siding with Westerners on that issue, he would mark a personal departure the same month by arguing against them on the question of where the "Kanagawa treaty port" should be located. The first commercial treaty had called for a port at Kanagawa; but Japanese officials decided instead to open it that summer at a small community several miles away known as Yokohama; and when American and British ministers arrived, they were faced with a fait accompli. Marsh land had been filled, wharves built, merchant shops opened, and an entire new community constructed. Though the foreign diplomats protested vigorously, fearing that the new port site, isolated as it was from major throughfares, would allow the Japanese to maintain too close a watch on foreign development, the *gaikoku bugyō* persisted; and within a year the issue had died a natural death, thanks to the unwillingness of the practical-minded Western merchants to join their diplomatic representatives in quibbling over the matter of location. They simply moved in force to Yokohama, and the diplomats found themselves arguing a moot point. Fukuchi, though not directly involved in decision making, pronounced himself fully sympathetic with Japan's position. He admitted that the primary reason for the choice of Yokohama was political, just as the foreigners suspected. At the same time he feared "much trouble in foreign intercourse" if trade were not carefully controlled and, thus, pledged support to the policies of Foreign Commissioner Mizuno Tadanori, the man responsible for the selection of Yokohama.[21] One reason for this stance undoubtly lay in the fact that Mizuno was Fukuchi's chief mentor. However, that does not alter the fact that with the Yokohama issue Fukuchi's support for the West had entered a new and more pragmatic stage.

A second facet of this changing stance was a new impatience with specific Western practices and individuals. Increasingly, he began separating men and their actions from the general body of Western thought, even though the men and practices did not always fare well in the separation. His contempt for American and European merchants already has been cited. He was equally perturbed by the Western exploitation of Japan's gold reserves and the resultant "gold drain" of 1859. His descriptions of the Western diplomats, though generally charitable, were realistic to the point of occasional sarcasm. Duchesne de Bellecourt of France, for example, was a "nobleman who loved dignity . . . an unsteady person whose feelings fluctuated wildly between joy and rage." Rutherford B. Alcock of Great Britain had "planned to use a policy of bluff and menace toward Japan when he first arrived but had gradually become more conciliatory,"[22] and Minister Polsbroek of the Netherlands "knew Japan's situation well but . . . always followed a threatening policy in collusion with Great Britian and France."[23] Indeed, it was partially to seek redress against what he saw as the high-handedness and unfairness of these diplomats that Fukuchi went to Europe with the Shibata Gōchū mission in 1865. Though ostensibly planning to assist mission leaders in laying the groundwork for a naval yard at Yokosuka, his real motive seems to have been the study of international law. His reasons are best described in his own words: "I intended to study international law so that on my return I could devise some eloquent and superior theses that would confound the foreign ambassadors. . . . I hoped to crush the arrogance of the foreigners, to rob them of their cocky self-assurance and cool them off."[24] It was a vain hope because his French was not adequate to the detailed pursuit of international law, but the rather poignant statement of goals illustrates a marked change in the perspective from which he had come to evaluate Western ways.

Perhaps the most noticeable and, in the long range, most significant aspect of this new, more critical pursuit was Fukuchi's growing identification with Japan and its own traditions during the late 1860s and early 1870s. Until then, Fukuchi's writings showed little awareness of Japan as a country with unique and viable traditions of its own. Even as an official, he fought for its causes but showed little concern with the idea of "Japaneseness" or "particularistic traditions" that would later occupy his attention. As he passed his middle twenties, however, he changed and discussions regarding the maintenance of national traditions began increasingly to rise to the level of consciousness in his thought. This was a significant development; for while the disillusionment with certain aspects of Western culture was almost bound to occur as he fought diplomatic battles, it was the concomitant reassertion of concern for Japanese traditions that would, in the end, most fully undergird and shape Fukuchi's mature efforts to balance the East and the West, the particular and the universal.

It seems clear that the man who most stimulated Fukuchi's growing concern with "Japan and Japaneseness" in the 1860s was his *gaikoku bugyō* mentor, Mizuno. As foreign commissioner at Kanagawa when Fukuchi entered the bureaucracy, and later as an influential man of affairs in Edo, Mizuno became somewhat of an idol to Fukuchi. It was he who had provided lodging during Fukuchi's first days in Edo and who brought Fukuchi into the government. It was Mizuno who, above all others, tutored him in the arts of diplomacy and politics, spending endless off-hours discussing the intricacies of *bakumatsu* officialdom. Though Mizuno was a thoroughgoing pragmatist, a man who believed wholeheartedly in cooperating with the West since that seemed the only viable option at the time, he also was a genuine traditionalist in the more enlightened, historically rich sense of that word. As Fukuchi described him, "though he advocated the abolition of the *bakufu* system and called for reforms, his nature was one of despising radicalism and rejoicing in gradualism, honoring order. . . . He was rich in conservative coloration."[25]

Long hours with Mizuno made Fukuchi into a man proud of being a Japanese by the summer of 1868. Thus, at *Kōko shimbun*, he based his most bitter denunciations of the new Meiji government not on the idea of "imperial restoration" nor on a "modern" view of politics, but on a reading of Japanese history that pictured the Satsuma-Chōshū forces as usurpers out of step with traditional challengers to power and thus predestined to failure.[26] My philosophy, he said of his *Kōko shimbun* efforts, "included not a particle of objection to revering the emperor, nor was I opposed to a restoration of government to the emperor by the shogun. It was simply that power had in fact been returned not to the court but to Satsuma and Chōshū."[27] This rising concern for traditional patterns set precedents in Fukuchi's thinking. Resentment over the Tokugawa overthrow may have caused him to devise anti-Satchō theories of this nature, but it was not a temporary line of reasoning. Concern with national traditions grew increasingly important in his thought, heralding more difficult times for him philosophically, a period when he could not ignore the West; its influence was becoming too pervasive for that. With the growth of a new conviction about Japan's own cultural validity and undeniability, Fukuchi was forced into the tortuous process of actually balancing the two worlds. As long as Western thought had seemed normative or even dominant, the two had lived, for Fukuchi, in easy co-existence: the West teaching, the East learning and adapting. Once sensitivity to Japan's own past pushed the homeland to a position approaching equality, it became necessary for Fukuchi to make both worlds "fit" into a balanced framework, an agonizing process.

Change in that direction had become clearly perceptible by 1873, when the thirty-one-year-old interpreter began growing weary of the long travels of the Iwakura embassy. It was his fourth trip to the West, his second as an official in the Meiji government,[28] and it had to be counted among the highlights of his life. Unlike former trips, when his zeal always amazed colleagues, the travels this time gradually lost their luster, so much so that he was dispatched home ahead of the rest of the embassy in the spring of that year.[29] Just over a year later, in mid-1874, he left the official world to become editor of the newspaper *Tokyo nichi nichi*, a post that would not only earn him a reputation as Japan's foremost journalist but allow him to give full expression to the third stage in the evolution of his inner struggle with universality and particularism. The years at *Nichi nichi* (1874–88) would see the maturation of his conscious, even if sometimes tortured, efforts to balance East and West in his own mind.

A decade and a half later, near the end of the first Sino-Japanese war, an editorialist for the magazine *Kokumin no tomo* described his own generation's awakening conviction that the Japanese must "believe in themselves" with the comment: "If someone stood on London Bridge and shouted that England's independence was in danger, . . . how would Englishmen treat him? . . . No one would take him seriously, because the English have complete confidence in their country's independence. The reason the English are a great nation is not only that they are a great people, but that they believe they are a great people."[30] Yet, already in 1875, Fukuchi had reached a similar evaluation, asserting that Japan possessed intrinsic superiority over England because its emperor had "voluntarily" agreed to set the nation upon the path of popular rights while Englishmen earlier had found it necessary to wrest similar consessions from their monarch by force.[31] Fukuchi, the writer, constantly would urge colleagues to "Know Japan."

During his early years, Japanese ways had often embarrassed Fukuchi. Required by Shibata to wear Japanese kimono during the trip to France in 1865, Fukuchi had "secretly felt stubborn" and ridiculed Shibata's insensitivity to Western customs[32]; yet, by the time he had gained full stature at *Nichi nichi* he would reverse himself, defending his leader's rules as "sensible" and commenting that a nation's "manners should not be changed without good reason." It was an evolution that evinced both a growing maturity and an awakening sense of confidence in his own homeland, a country he had once looked down on.

Fukuchi's *Nichi nichi* years were his best, years in which perceptive editorials and myriad public activities influenced nearly every aspect of Japan's political and economic development. In those years, both his public activities and newspaper writings gave constant evidence of a searching, spirited desire to blend alien ways still seen as necessary for modernization into a domestic tradition newly rediscovered as essential for national strength and order.

This balancing—sometimes evidencing itself more precisely as ambivalence—revealed itself at first in a host of peripheral facets of Fukuchi's personal life-style. His attitudes toward friends, for example, illustrated it: while, on the one hand, he often and bitterly castigated government officials for showing favoritism or falling short of objectivity in making appointments,[33] at the same time he ever remained incapable of acting himself with cool-headed or objective calculation toward fellow human beings or even of countenancing acquaintances who did so. He was accused of being "feudal" in his insistence on maintaining and rewarding personal loyalties. Itō Hirobumi once told him in this regard: "If you would just quit acting so much like a loyal retainer, Fukuchi, you might be named to a post like foreign minister!"[34] The *Nichi nichi* editor's daily habits also highlighted this ambiguity, perhaps, in even more colorful fashion. He was known primarily as a Westernizer, the champion of Western-style editorials and news reporting, the proponent of Western-style banking of stock exchanges, and the advocate of selective adaptation of Western habits. He began wearing Western haircuts very early; and a famous woodblock print shows him in Kyushu in 1873, war correspondent's notebook in hand, nattily outfitted in a plaid suit, black boots, trench coat, and wide-brimmed hat. With a walking cane under his arm, he was very much the Western dandy. Yet Fukuchi was equally well known for preferring Japanese customs and manners in numerous areas of his private life. He owned no fewer than thirty-five, fine-patterned kimonos, which he wore almost nightly to Yoshiwara tea houses; he detested Western-style homes; he spent lavishly to have a custom-made tea house constructed at his Ike no Hata residence.[35] It was not a difficult blend. After all, twentieth-century men do not find it difficult to integrate Italian pizza, Nehru jackets, Japanese rock gardens, and "Southern style" chicken into a single life pattern. As a symbol, however, the contrasts were significant.

On a deeper, more substantial level, the same contrasting traditions again and again shaped or contorted the nature of Fukuchi's public contributions. One observes the contrast especially in his manner of editing *Nichi nichi*. When scholars speak of him as the "father of Japan's modern press," they refer primarily to his introduction of Western concepts. He was one of the first influential Japanese, for example, to see the press's potential as a shaper of public opinion and government policies. Early in the 1870s, most Meiji intellectuals and officials still regarded the press simply as a diversion, a form of entertainment hardly worthy of sustained attention from men of influence; indeed, when Fukuchi announced his intention to enter *Nichi nichi* in 1874, official friends remonstrated that he was throwing his life away, foolishly plunging from a plateau of power to a canyon of obscurity. But he persisted, commenting that, short of being a cabinet minister, he could see no better way to "see my ideas realized in society."[36] "Newspapers," he wrote a year later, "are the eyes and ears of the world, the movers of mankind."[37] His views proved perceptive; by the end of the decade nearly all Meiji leaders had come around to a similar position, partially at least as a result of Fukuchi's influence at *Nichi nichi*.

Fukuchi also proved himself modern in tendency, at least, in his attitudes toward the place of news in a newspaper. Here again, he innovated by insisting that news reporting was itself a valid function of self-respecting journalists. Through the 1870s, all of Japan's newspapers followed the practice of hiring two kinds of staffers, *kisha*, or "writers" who composed highly literate, polished prose, and *tambōsha*, or illiterate "gatherers of news items," whose labors provided the details for the *kisha*'s words. The despised, often poorly motivated *tambōsha* committed frequent errors and resultant stories tended often to be more elegant than reliable. News, as a consequence, was relegated to a secondary role by the editors of Tokyo's major papers and given a position far below that of the political editorials that came to wield such influence after 1875. Fukuchi, on the other hand, led the way in illustrating the fact that objective reporting was indeed a valid function of the respectable press.[38] Unlike most editors, he insisted that news be accurate, he sought scoops, and he made *kisha* themselves go into the streets and government offices seeking news. In fact, he himself went to Kyushu in 1877 to cover the Satsuma Rebellion, thus becoming one of the country's first "war correspondents" and thoroughly scooping all of Japan's other newspapers in the process. Further, he led the way in instituting such other informational devices as the hiring of foreign correspondents and the publication of book reviews and medical news.[39] Space prohibits consideration of his numerous other Western-style contributions at *Nichi nichi*, such as the introduction of daily editorial columns, the unification of management procedures, the articulation of innovative theories of journalistic independence, and the attempt to write for all classes of people. However, the Western orientation of Fukuchi's journalistic philosophy was all-pervasive and thoroughly influential in Japan of the 1870s and 1880s.

Yet, non-Western, traditional Japanese customs constantly modified or impinged on these Western-inspired innovations. Fukuchi provided a new awareness of the press's social, informational, and political potential; but his own interpretation of that potential retained traditional elements that prevented him from keeping abreast of further innovations introduced by others in the middle 1880s, thus, causing a distinct decline in his journalistic career at that time. When he entered *Nichi nichi*, Japan's newspaper world was divided into two camps, *daishimbun*, or "major papers," which dealt mainly with political issues, and *koshimbun*, or "minor papers," generally viewed as scandal sheets because they printed so much of a sensational or erotic nature. The persistence of Tokugawa moral and social norms demanded that "respectable" papers avoid even the appearance of being influenced by the *koshimbun*, and Fukuchi remained "respectable" to the end. Even in the 1880s, when the *koshimbun* began to contribute new ideas to the established press, stimulating new practices such as serializing novels, diversifying the types of news covered, branching out into entertainment news, Fukuchi attacked most of the innovations as "uncultured." He refused even to consider the idea of serializing novels,[40] sneering contemptuously at those well-known journalists who indulged in "the gossip of low class housewives, the crudities of quarreling students." He added: "I always insisted on the high-level conversation of the *bushi* class."[41]

His view of news reporting, though innovative, showed the pull of tradition in much the same way. Though he made *kisha* themselves go out and gather news, he nevertheless continued to employ *tambōsha* for lesser newsgathering jobs, thus insuring the continuation of office class distinctions. He also maintained Tokugawa-nurtured views regarding the kinds of news proper in a paper. Sensational stories about sex or love suicides were as much taboo as the publication of novels. Seeing his paper first of all as a political instrument, he never transcended the tendency to subordinate the news column to editorial opinion. This was a reflection, one might argue, of the fact that he was reared in a country and era where public service was defined not in terms of aiding society, but of assisting the bureaucracy or government. If service were defined in terms of institutions rather than people, it followed that political opinion must take precedence over mere "news," which might be interesting but was not essential to the success of the government.[42]

Thus it was that Fukuchi's *Nichi nichi* devoted most of the first page and often part of the second to editorials. Even when public interest in politics waned sharply after 1883 and a new breed of journalists, men such as Fukuzawa Yukichi at *Jiji shimpō* and Murayama Ryūhei at *Osaka asahi shimbun*, began developing successful nonpartisan, news-oriented papers, Fukuchi refused to change. Locked into traditional Japanese values regarding property and standards of public service, he was unable to alter direction. *Nichi nichi*'s political focus continued; its approach to news, innovative for the 1870s, fell behind the times; and as a result, the paper's circulation declined so drastically that in 1888 Fukuchi was forced out of the newspaper world, a bitter and disappointed man.

Politics, a second pivot of Fukuchi's best years, also illustrated this constant pull between West and East, perhaps with even greater clarity. If *Nichi nichi* served Fukuchi partly as a medium for political expression, it also gave him a platform from which to plunge directly and actively into the political maelstrom itself. He served, for example, as a secretary in the government's first Conference of Local Officials *(Chihōkan kaigi)* in 1875, presided over Tokyo's first prefectural assembly *(fukai)*, and organized the Rikken Teiseitō, Japan's first conservative political party, in 1882. In each of these arenas, the blend of traditional and modern elements lurked constantly beneath the surface, often breaking through in either dynamic or turbulent forms.

His service in the prefectural assembly illustrates this fact particularly well. Organized by the central government in 1878 as a cautious step toward some sort of nationwide representative government, the first assembly included a number of Tokyo's most illustrious citizens, men such as Fukuzawa Yukichi and the industrialist Ōkura Kihachirō, with Fukuchi serving as president from 1879 to 1884. The assembly was, in Fukuchi's mind, a distinct move in the direction of administrative modernization, a major turning point on the road toward constitutional government. As a proponent of both, Fukuchi remained for a decade one of the body's most wholehearted supporters. Yet, if the assembly represented a step toward democracy, it was a most timid, one might say distinctly Meiji kind of step. The local governor, a central-government appointee, decided what the body would discuss and retained veto power over its decisions; its main business was to consult on "the means of raising the local taxes" and on ways to spend tax revenues,[43] and it met for only thirty days a year. A Westerner might have concluded that this was hardly a genuine step toward representative government. Yet the timidity of the approach did not seem to concern Fukuchi; on the contrary, he approved of it. As an advocate of modernization and national strength, he supported representative and constitutional forms; yet as a child of the Tokugawa era's bureaucratism and hierarchical structures, he never seems to have envisioned thoroughgoing, participatory, or direct democracy. The *fukai* instituted a new and Western form, yet maintained the essence of Japan's traditional hierarchical centralization. It was, for him, a most satisfactory blend.

An important question raised by such a mixture of Western and Japanese forms is whether the blending was conscious or simply the result of an inability fully to understand Western concepts, whether Fukuchi actually intended for Japan to adapt Western ways in non-Western fashions or just lost his receptivity to innovation with the advance of years. Obviously, various factors were involved. But it would seem, on balance, that the preponderant numbers of balancing acts were carried out consciously by a man quite aware, indeed acutely aware, of what was traditionally Japanese and what was being either borrowed or adapted from foreign cultures. The best evidence of this fact—and perhaps the most deeply significant area in which this struggle shows up—lies in his writings themselves. Fortunately, there are many available, since Fukuchi wrote over 3,000 editorials at *Nichi nichi* between 1874 and 1888 in addition to a host of other articles and books. For the purposes of this essay, it should be sufficient to glance at three of the products of his brush: the first, an editorial campaign during the nationwide popular-rights debate in the middle 1870s; the second, a series of editorials written during the general discussion of constitutionalism early in the 1880s; and the third, an important imperial document promulgated in 1882.

As noted earlier, Fukuchi's attitude toward Western knowledge was just moving into a balancing stage when he assumed the *Nichi nichi* editorship late in 1874. His first editorial battle, fought over the issue of popular sovereignty, makes that fact amply clear. Although his concern with Japanese traditions had obviously not yet matured, those traditions seem nevertheless to have taken on increasing importance as the debate progressed. Likewise Western models, though far more important for Fukuchi than they would be a decade later, showed a diminishing hold on his thought.

The popular-sovereignty debate was sparked partly by a memorial to the throne by Itagaki Taisuke and his followers early in 1874 calling for the immediate opening of a popular assembly. Throughout 1874 and 1875, most of Tokyo's press became involved in an intellectual war over the advantages and disadvantages of that proposal, with most writers favoring immediate steps toward a parliamentary system and Fukuchi leading the opposition. Labeling his position "gradualism" (*zenshinshugi*), Fukuchi argued that the national transformation since 1868 had perhaps been too rapid and should, as a result, be curbed lest further acceleration endanger either tradition or tranquility.

His basic policy, outlined in over three dozen editorials late in 1874 and throughout 1875, was rather correctly regarded by opponents as a popular justification and rationalization of the existing government's policies, particularly of the ideas of his close ally, Kido Kōin. He agreed with popular rightists' demands for representative government: to meet these would be to fulfill the recognized responsibility of "redeeming the basic natural rights of all the people."[44] However, he felt that steps in that direction should be deliberate, that prior to the opening of a national parliament, people should be trained to manage their own affairs through the creation of local and then prefectural assemblies. Undue rapidity, he asserted, would be a vice. "The farmers, artisans and merchants have lived under oppression for many years. . . . To hurriedly establish a national assembly for such people, weak as they are in the spirit of self government, would not be advantageous."[45] He maintained, moreover, that "popular" government should be defined more broadly than Itagaki and his supporters were wont to interpret it. While the "popular-rights" camp would have included only the old Tokugawa elite (*shizoku* and *kazoku*), Fukuchi proposed suffrage for the nation's thirty-two million commoners (*heimin*) as well. The latter was a policy, he maintained, designed to modernize without endangering "national tranquility."

To his opponents, Fukuchi's arguments seemed a neat rationale devised primarily to consolidate the power of the existing regime, a charge heatedly and rather effectively denied by Fukuchi himself.[46] But the key concern here must be with the method and rationale that undergirded his arguments and the way they illustrated his growing concern with both Western and Japanese ideas. That he was still concerned with a kind of progress acceptable by Western standards seemed clear in every editorial. He used Western examples as proof that "no country which follows radical policies can maintain national tranquility forever."[47] His defense of broad suffrage and parliamentary assemblies grew from ideas encountered on trips abroad, and he sought Western sources whose ideas would buttress his position. Yet the debate bore evidence of deep concern about Japan's own traditions, a concern far greater in quantity and depth than evidenced in any of his earlier works. He wrote with special force about "national tranquility," a major shift from a few years earlier when he had argued with Itō in an American hotel that Japan must democratize regardless of the cost. He worried that overly rapid change would violate the essential "Japaneseness" of Japan, a concern that foreshadowed later *Nichi nichi* writings.[48] He talked in new and proud ways, some of them already noted, about the superior benevolence inherent in Japan's unique brand of imperial rule. This editorial crusade, in short, marked an important personal departure. Western philosophy might have much to offer, but no longer would Fukuchi view the countries from which Occidental ideas sprang as necessarily superior. Rather, he increasingly would attempt to graft specific aspects of Western thought onto a Japanese tradition and culture ever more openly evaluated as being superior.

This tendency seemed to grow apace during each succeeding year at *Nichi nichi*; and by the time Fukuchi's influence had reached its zenith in the early 1880s, it seemed that two powerful, nearly equal rivers had come to rush along almost side by side in his thought. His dedication to incorporating facets of Western law, government, economics, and culture really never waned. At the same time, the assertion and reassertion of Japan's own traditions had become uppermost. Two projects in which he was involved almost simultaneously during 1880 and 1881 illustrate this fact with particular force.

First was the editorial series on constitutional government.[49] Early in 1881, Japan's leading newspapers became involved in a heated debate over a whole range of questions related to sovereignty and constitutionalism, with Fukuchi's major contribution coming during March and April in a fourteen-part draft (with commentary) on the kind of constitution he felt Japan needed. Though adamant in its emotional insistence on imperial sovereignty, most other features of the draft reflected relatively liberal elements of Western political thought. The articles insisted, for example, on popular rights, comparatively broad suffrage, a free and independent judiciary, limited civil liberties, and the creation of an executive responsible to the legislature. It became clear, indeed, on reading the editorials that Fukuchi's commitment to Western political theory was more than a kind of window dressing intended simply to secure respectability among Western powers. His constitution, had it been enacted, would quite likely have assured the spread of genuine parliamentary democracy (though it is unclear whether Fukuchi himself foresaw it as going quite that far).

Yet, as was apparent in his concomitant, if seemingly paradoxical, defense of the idea of imperial sovereignty, another side also had grown large in Fukuchi's thought, a side vividly illustrated by his role that same year in helping draft the Imperial Precepts to Soldiers and Sailors *(Gunjin chokuyū)*, a document often credited with helping propel Meiji Japan down the road to resurgent nationalism.[50] The rescript, prepared at the urging of Yamagata Aritomo, was a call for military men to recognize the absolute and eternal supremacy of the emperor and to practice the five basic precepts of loyalty, propriety, valor, righteousness, and simplicity. Though directed ostensibly at the military, it was in truth a document designed to arouse national sentiments generally in the direction of expressing vigorous support for an imperial institution divine and inviolate from ages eternal. It was Fukuchi's brush that gave the document a polished literary, strongly pro-imperial tone replete with images of national superiority and Japanese uniqueness.⁵¹

Drafting such a document during the very year that he had called for a constitution guaranteeing a strong legislature and relatively broad suffrage would seem, on the surface, a paradox; and in some ways it was. The imperial sovereignty envisioned by Fukuchi sprang from a uniquely Japanese tradition conducive to autocratic or oligarchic rule, while ideas of strong legislatures and independent judiciaries rested on Western concepts of popular control. These two strands, it would seem, could hardly coexist in harmony. Thus some have wondered whether men such as Fukuchi could have been sincere in supporting both.

The answer to the paradox seems to lie, however, in Fukuchi's view of the nature of the imperial institution, a view that represented the final stage in his efforts at balancing East and West. He had, by 1881, become fully and unequivocably convinced of the supremacy of Japan's own culture and of the essential role the imperial institution had always played in that culture. This conviction did not entail a concomitant rejection of Western theory. Rather, for him, the two traditions could be brought together by the particularistic, unique nature of Japan's own emperor. He wrote that Japan's imperial sovereignty differed from that of European nations. There, in the world of the Caesars, the Henrys, and the Napoleons, emperors often had been tyrants; but Japan's experience had been different. Here, in the land of Jimmu, Kammu, and Meiji, imperial rule had always been benevolent, truly divine in nature. How could a genuinely benevolent ruler abrogate, indeed even threaten, the best interests of his beloved subjects? The answer, to Fukuchi, was simple: he could not. In the benevolence of the emperor lay the needed balance, the cement supporting the bridge between Japanese uniqueness and Western universalism. To argue otherwise, he asserted, would be to violate Japanese history.⁵²

By the time Fukuchi resigned from *Nichi nichi* in 1888, bitter and disillusioned over reverses in both his journalistic and political careers, his philosophical evolution had reached a point of completion where the sense of Japanese uniqueness had come to overshadow faintly, but never to obscure, the belief in Western-oriented reforms. It was not an easy coexistence. Logic all too often had to be twisted, stretched, or even ignored in the acts of balancing and bridging. False premises sometimes overlooked historical fact. Fukuchi always, like so many others in the world of Meiji thought, did find it necessary to make the balancing effort. All of which leads to a final question: why was such a balance so important to him? It is not, of course, a new question. Scholars have approached the "universal-particular," "East-West," "modern-traditional" problem from diverse and varied angles.⁵³ However, Fukuchi's case does seem to suggest a few hypotheses worth noting.

First, there is the view that the evolution simply evidenced an opportunistic personality. As Fukuchi grew older and identified more fully with the establishment, his opponents often charged, he became less interested in reform, more concerned with preservation. Since he had been an early friend of men such as Kido Kōin, Yamagata Aritomo, and Itō Hirobumi, competitors sometimes saw him as a pawn or lackey seeking historical justifications for the oligarchy's increasingly autocratic form of rule.[54] Such an argument, though not totally without substance, seems, however, entirely too simplistic. Even though Fukuchi did support most government policies during the bulk of his journalistic career, his concerns as often foreshadowed official views as followed them. Moreover, his support of the balanced "popular rights–imperial sovereignty" position held solid to the end of life, even after he had broken completely with the government. The opportunistic theory fails totally to account for the blending in so many other areas—personal habits, theories of the press, business practices, and the like. Other reasons must be sought.

More to the point is the evolutionary nature of events themselves and the psychological need to account and compensate. Given the pragmatic, ambitious nature of Fukuchi's father, Fukuchi's blind zeal in pursuit of things Western as a youth should hardly come as a surprise. Living in Nagasaki and translating Dutch in the early 1850s was an overwhelming experience, not unlike that of the bright Midwestern farm youth entering the cosmopolitan world of the state university. Confronted by vast and tantalizing new experiences and ideas, he soon rejects the staid conservatism of home and starts almost drunkenly to chase after each new school of thought or strand of experience. Unlike China, where Western knowledge had seeped in gradually across the centuries, it came to Fukuchi's Japan with the suddenness of the farm youth's transfer to the university. Fukuchi's reaction was not unnatural.

Unlike the farm lad, Fukuchi stayed home and the new world came to him. While the new ideas continued to challenge him, the surrounding environment and its native traditions also remained ever-present, constantly reminding him of the world of his forebears. Thus it should seem not at all unusual that in time, as the novelty of Western ways wore off, he would begin to evaluate Western offerings more in the light of traditional values. His earliest teachings, after all, had included the nationalistic concepts of Rai Sanyō; his early employment had been under the deep-rooted traditionalist, Mizuno Tadanori. Thus, as time revealed the fallibility of Western thought, the inapplicability of many of its strands, and the arrogant imperialism of many Westerners themselves, traditional values began to look much better by contrast. Had Fukuchi spent his adult years away in Europe, these early, national traditions might have been washed away by time. But he had stayed home, except to travel, and as a result they persisted. No nation ever sees the full and rapid eradication of centuries-old traditions, regardless of the intensity of efforts to wipe them out. If, as in

Japan's case, that nation is dramatically confronted by a wave of alien influence, stunningly embarassed by the onslaught of foreign ways, the need to reassert old values once the initial attack has subsided is likely to be all the stronger. So, it seems to have been with Fukuchi.

A third important motive for the balancing, in Fukuchi's case, was his personal embodiment of what others have called the achievement or goal orientation of the Japanese.[55] Unlike the nineteenth-century Chinese who so often seemed self-satisfied and confident that theirs already was the world's supreme civilization, a civilization not to be tarnished by the corruptible machines of an industrializing West, Fukuchi's Japan may be characterized as having felt an apparent need to prove itself, to cope with Western barbarians either by driving them out or by playing their own game. Later, Japan sought to enter the community of nations as a first-rate power possessed of "national wealth and a strong army" *(fukoku kyōhei)*. In this approach, Fukuchi was typical. As soon as he entered the foreign office, he began talking about besting foreign diplomats; on trips abroad, he longed for national respectability. At *Kōko shimbun* he wrote about achieving national wealth through trade, and rarely a week passed at *Nichi nichi* that he did not discuss his basic goals for Japan: order and progress. It is beyond the scope of this essay to analyze the reasons for this goal orientation. However, such an orientation necessarily meant that, once Fukuchi had entered the government, he would begin evaluating Western offerings in terms of national interests. Moreover, as his homeland's successes mounted, he would grow proud, increasingly convinced that Japan was inherently superior and decreasingly concerned with the need to emulate the West.

A fourth cause of this resurgent particularism may well have come from Fukuchi's lifelong interest in history. At the age of seven his father had sent him to the Osagawa family of Nagasaki for tutelage in Japanese history. Near the end of life, he wrote *Bakufu suibō ron (On the Decline and Fall of the Bakufu)*, a book widely heralded as the first historical account sympathetic to the Tokugawa family. He constantly spoke of himself as "an historian first of all."[56] One important result of this proclivity for studying the past was that, once the initial intoxication with Western elixirs had lost the aura of superreality, Fukuchi found it exceedingly natural to return to the area of scholarship with which he felt most comfortable and conversant. When he did so, he found in the writings of men such as Rai Sanyō and Hirata Atsutane an imperial tradition and an emphasis on Japanese virtues ready-made for revitalization as an antidote to the ills produced by the gluttonous consumption of Western ways. It has been noted that nearly all members of Japan's "loyalist tradition" across the centuries were "in one way or another avid students of history."[57] So it was with Fukuchi; one could hardly have called him a full-fledged scholar of history during his years of public life, but he was at least a layman widely read and deeply concerned with the past, a fact that made an eventual rebirth of interest in Japanese traditions almost a foregone conclusion from the beginning.

Finally, as years passed and national changes sparked occasional domestic resistance, both violent and nonviolent, it seems to have become apparent to Fukuchi that reassertion of traditional values would provide a certain social cement. It is important to remember that when he first invoked the argument of orderly, gradual change in 1874, national tranquility was indeed under threat from both samurai revolts in western Japan and burgeoning political clubs in the southern and central prefectures. The foundations of the new Meiji order, which appear so skillfully and firmly constructed from the twentieth-century vantage point, seemed shaky at best to Fukuchi and his peers. Threats were real. What better answer could be given the agitators, he reasoned, than the lessons of Japan's own past, the necessity of revering the imperial institution. Such an approach, one might argue, was therefore expedient, a calculating choice of philosophical systems devised simply to insure support for the existing order. In a certain sense, that argument holds weight. It does not, however, argue against the genuineness of the support men such as Fukuchi felt when they reasserted national traditions. Support of national order and tradition had been the chief preoccupation of Fukuchi's friend and mentor, Mizuno. As early as 1868, writing in opposition to the Meiji government, he had proclaimed a convincing brand of allegiance to the centrality of the imperial institution. Thus, to begin reasserting that belief as an answer to the problems of the 1870s was hardly a surprising development. Faith in national traditions already was well rooted; the obvious need for a social balm merely caused him to turn to this faith.

Many other possible reasons for this reassertion of Japanese tradition might be considered: the hierarchical nature of Japan's social structure, which lent itself readily to identification with the emperor and the nation, the sense of separateness and ethnocentricity fostered over the centuries by both Tokugawa isolation and the island nature of Japan, the myth of divine origins and divine protection dating back at least to the Mongols' attempted invasions in the thirteenth century, and the psychological reaction against millenia of frustration in the role of cultural receiver from China and Korea. While the list could continue to great length, most such reasons lie beyond Fukuchi's specific situation.

On July 10, 1888 a *Nichi nichi* advertisement noted that Fukuchi Gen'ichirō had been discharged "due to a nervous disorder." It was a terse announcement, marking the disillusioned end of a newspaper career that had for a decade "dominated society."[58] *Nichi nichi*'s circulation had been on the decline of late, Fukuchi's influence had waned somewhat in public circles, and he had become increasingly cantankerous. Subordinates had launched an office revolt, with Fukuchi's coming out the loser. It was a surprisingly rapid demise. Yet, in a sense, the dismissal was not unlike the paradoxical public career of the man dismissed. It highlighted again the tension and constant contrast between universal and particular, modern and traditional. From the rational or modernistic perspective, Fukuchi's firing was a sensible act. Having failed lately as editor, he had become a liability to *Nichi nichi* and deserved to be let go; dismissal was to be expected. Yet, according to a more Japanese, humane, and traditional way of thought, severance represented an act of tyranny. Fukuchi had made *Nichi nichi* the paper that it was; as an editor he had tutored many of the very journalists who turned against him: he had given too much to be treated in so cavalier a fashion. But time had passed and traditions now were being balanced by the modern ways of a universal age. The balancing was not easy for anyone. Particularistic traditions persisted, sometimes modifying or eradicating the universal, sometimes merely lending an aroma of poignancy to modern alterations by highlighting the contrast. The latter was the case in Fukuchi's journalistic demise, but still the balancing was there. Such had been his life, such the Meiji world in which he lived.

Notes

1. See Joyce Lebra, *Ōkuma Shigenobu, Statesman of Meiji Japan* (Canberra: Australian National University Press, 1973), pp. 135, 145.
2. George B. Sansom, *The Western World and Japan* (first Vintage edition; New York: Vintage Books, 1973), p. 385.
3. See Edwin R. Reischauer, *The United States and Japan* (New York: Viking Press, 1965), pp. 142–77. The point also is illustrated in Nakane Chie's frequent reference to Japan's vertical society. See her *Japanese Society* (Berkeley, Calif.: University of California Press, 1970).
4. Fukuchi Gen'ichirō, *Kaiō jidan*, in Yanagida Izumi, *Fukuchi Ouchi shū, Mejiji bungaku zenshu* (100 volumes projected, 80 now in publication; Tokyo: Echima Shobō, 1966), 11:313.
5. Following Japanese custom, the family line had been carried on in the preceding generations by the adoption of adult male heirs who had taken on the wife's surname. Fukuchi himself was the eighth child in his own family, his birth following that of seven daughters. For early biographical data, see Yanagida Izumi, *Fukuchi Ouchi* (Tokyo: Yoshikawa Hiroshi Bunkan, 1965), pp. 1–17.
6. See Yanagida Izumi, "Fukuchi Ouchi," in *Fukuchi Ouchi shū Meiji bungaku zenshū*, p. 409. Iwakura credited Fukuchi with being capable of accomplishing the work of four "normal men."
7. Actually, the adoption was abrogated in 1858, two years after its inception, when Fukuchi became involved in an acrimonious dispute with Namura's other students and was sent home. Yanagida Izumi, *Fukuchi Ouchi*, pp. 39–41.
8. Fukuchi, *Kaiō jidan*, p. 278.
9. For an evaluation of this tendency to goal orientation, see Robert N. Bellah, *Tokugawa Religion* (Glencoe, Ill.: The Free Press, 1957), pp. 188–97.
10. Ōkubo Toshiaki, "Bummei kaika," in *Nihon rekishi*, 23 vol. (3rd edition; Tokyo Iwanami Shoten, 1967), 15:253.
11. Quoted in George M. Wilson, "The Bakumatsu Intellectual in Action: Hashimoto Sanai in the Political Crisis of 1858," Albert M. Craig and Donald H. Shively, eds., *Personality in Japanese History* (Berkeley, Calif.: University of California Press, 1970), p. 238.
12. Trans. in Ryusaku Tsunoda, William Theodore de Bary, and Donald Keene, eds., *Sources of Japanese Tradition* (New York: Columbia University Press, 1958), p. 544.
13. See Akira Iriye, "Kayahara Kazan and Japanese Cosmopolitanism," in Craig and Shively, eds., *Personality in Japanese History* pp. 373–93.
14. Fukuchi, *Kaiō jidan*, p. 269.

15. Ibid., p. 293.
16. See, for example, Ono Hideo, "'Moshiogusa' oyobi 'Kōko shimbun' no kaisetsu," in Osatake Takeki, ed., *Bakumatsu Meiji shimbun zenshū* (Tokyo: Sekai Bunko, 1934–35), 4:12–13. The word *modern* refers to the fact that the paper attempted accuracy (though not objectivity) in its reporting and aimed to write in the vernacular, both points of contrast with other papers of the time.
17. *Kōko shimbun*, no. 1 (May 24, 1868), reprinted in Osatake, *Shumbun zenshū*, p. 3.
18. Ibid., pp. 61–64.
19. Kuga Katsunan in *Tokyo dempō*, June 12, 1888, quoted in Kenneth B. Pyle, *The New Generation in Meiji Japan* (Stanford, Calif.: Stanford University Press, 1969), p. 75. For an excellent overall analysis of Japanese intellectual development in this period, see Robert N. Bellah, "Intellectual and Society in Japan," *Daedalus*, Spring 1972, pp. 89–115.
20. Fukuchi, *Kajō jidan*, p. 269.
21. See ibid., pp. 266–71, for a detailed account of the entire dispute.
22. Ibid., pp. 283–84.
23. Ibid., p. 284.
24. Ibid., p. 305.
25. Fukuchi Gen'ichirō, *Bakumatsu seijika*, in *Bakumatsu ishin shiryō sōsho* (Tokyo: Jimbutsu Ōraisha, 1968), 8:382.
26. *Kōko shimbun*, June 24, 1868, in Osatake, *Shimbun zenshū*, 4:p. 61. Fukuchi maintained that all previous "unifiers" in Japan had risen in the East. Since Satchō forces came from the West, he argued, the weight of history would mitigate against their success.
27. Fukuchi Gen'ichirō, *Shimbunshi jitsureki*, in Tsurumi Shunsuke, ed., *Jiyanarizumu no shisō* (Tokyo: Echima Shobō, 1965), p. 78; reprinted in its entirety in Yanagida, *Fukuchi Ouchi shū*, p. 326.
28. Fukuchi had entered the Meiji government late in 1870 after almost three rather bitter years as a private citizen. Itō Hirobumi, then in the Finance Ministry, was instrumental in persuading him to join the new government, partially, it seems, through the offer of a chance to accompany him to the United States for a fact-finding study of American economic institutions. See Fukuchi Gen'ichirō, "Ishin no genkun," *Taiyō* 1, no. 4 (April, 1895): 31.
29. Another reason for leaving early was that mission leaders wanted Fukuchi to go through Egypt in order to study the "mixed court" system there. They thought such a system, where foreign and native officials sat together on the judicial bench in cases where foreigners were being tried, might be a halfway solution toward the removal of extraterritoriality provisions from treaties with Western nations. See, for example, Inō Tentarō, *Nihon gaibun shisō shi ronkō* (Tokyo, 1966), 1:232–34.
30. "Idai naru kokumin," *Kokumin no Tomo*, May 23, 1891, quoted in Pyle, *New Generation*, p. 147.
31. *Tokyo nichi nichi shimbun*, April 14, 1875 (hereafter cited as *Nichi nichi*; all *Nichi nichi* citations are found on page 1 of the paper unless otherwise indicated).
32. Fukuchi, *Kaiō jidan*, p. 306. See further comments in Ozawa Ryōzō, *Onnagata konseki dan* (Tokyo: Echima, 1941), p. 53.
33. One of the most incisive examples is "Satchō ron," *Nichi nichi*, January 19–23, 1886.
34. Ozawa, *Onnagata*, p. 50.
35. Zushikawa Chōko, "Ouchi Koji no tsuioku," *Denki* 2 (February 1935): 19.
36. Fukuchi, *Shimbunshi jitsureki*, p. 328.
37. *Nichi nichi*, July 28, 1875.
38. It should be noted that news *was* the major focus of one segment of the early Meiji press, the *koshimbun*, or "minor papers." These, however, were papers that specialized in scandals, a Japanese brand of yellow journalism. As a result, they were not included in the contemporary "respectable" press. Two of the best press histories of the period are Ono Mideo, *Shimbun no rekishi* (Tokyo: Tokyodō Shuppan, 1961) and Nishida Taketoshi, *Meiji jidai no shimbun to zasshi* (Tokyo: Shibundō, 1966).
39. See Sugiura Tadashi, *Shimbun koto hajime* (Tokyo: Mainichi Shimbunsha, 1971), p. 297.
40. Ironically, after leaving the newspaper world in 1888, Fukuchi, driven at least partly by economic necessity, began writing novels for part of his living; and during the 1890s, many of his own works were serialized in *Nichi nichi* and other newspapers.
41. Quoted in Sugiura, *Shimbun koto hajime*, p. 277.

42. A most concise, yet incisive analysis of the structure and concepts undergirding the Tokugawa bureaucracy is found in Tetsuo Najita, *Japan* (Englewood Cliffs, N.J.: Prentice-Hall, 1974), p. 16–42.
43. Quoted in Walter W. McLaren, "Japanese Government Documents," *Transactions of the Asiatic Society of Japan* 42, part 1 (1914): 272. See also Walter W. McLaren, *Political History of Japan during the Meiji Era, 1867–1912* (New York: Russell and Russell, 1965. Reprint), pp. 130–31, 141, for a discussion of the *fuken kai*.
44. *Nichi nichi*, November 19, 1874; see also December 5, 1874, and December 28, 1875.
45. *Nichi nichi*, December 28, 1875.
46. The idea that Fukuchi's view, as well as that of the government itself, was more "liberal" or "popular" at this time than the elitism advocated by the popular-rights camp is supported by numerous scholars. See, for example, George Akita, *Foundations of Constitutional Government in Modern Japan, 1868–1900* (Cambridge, Mass.: Harvard University Press, 1967), p. 23; Maruyama Masao, "Meiji kokka no shisō," in *Nihon shakai no shiteki kyūmei*, comp. by Rekishigaku Kenkyūkai (Tokyo: Rekishigaku Kenkyūkai, 1949), p. 200.
47. See, for example, *Nichi nichi*, December 6, 1874.
48. See *Nichi nichi*, January 6, 1875.
49. *Nichi nichi*, March 30–31, April 1–16, 1881; reprinted in Meiji Bunka Kenkyukai, ed., *Seishi hen*, no. 2, *Meiji bunka zenshū*, 16 vol. (Tokyo: Nihon Hyōronsha, 1956), 10:377–405.
50. See, for example, the evaluation of Roger Hackett, *Yamagata Aritomo in the Rise of Modern Japan* (Cambridge, Mass.: Harvard University Press, 1972), p. 86. The "Precepts" are translated in Arthur E. Tiedemann, *Modern Japan, A Brief History* (Princeton, N.J.: Van Nostrand, 1955), pp. 107–12.
51. Authorship of this document was long in dispute, with most scholars attributing it solely to Nishi Amane. Actually there were five drafts, the fourth one, that which was prepared by Fukuchi, being pivotal in establishing the document's ringing defense of the imperial system, while the fifth draft constituted a final polishing of the prose. See Umetani Noboru, *Gunjin chokuyū seiritsu shi no kenkyū*, *Osaka Daigaku bungakubu kujō*, no. 8 (1961): 112–16, 134–40.
52. This view is articulated in numerous *Nichi nichi* editorials, including especially January 28, 1882, and May 16, 1886.
53. Numerous helpful, provocative interpretations and illustrations of this theme are found in Donald H. Shively, ed., *Tradition and Modernization in Japanese Culture* (Princeton, N.J.: Princeton University Press, 1972).
54. The most damning phrase attached to *Nichi nichi* in later years was that of *goyō shimbun*, or "patronage paper," a phrase employed by the paper itself in the 1870s to indicate that it was being used by the government for reporting official transactions. At the time, the phrase connoted power; but later it was used by opponents to accuse Fukuchi, usually unjustly, of being a "kept editor." In a related vein, a superb analysis of the role "conservative" intellectuals such as Fukuchi often play in not only creating but in carrying and legitimating established traditions is found in S.N. Eisenstadt, "Intellectuals and Traditions," *Daedalus*, Spring, 1972, pp. 1–19.
55. See, for example, Bellah, *Tokugawa Religion*, pp. 188–92.
56. See Showa Joshi Daigaku Kindai Bungaku Kenkyūshitsu, ed., "Fukuchi Ouchi," in *Kindai bungaku kenkyū sōsho*, (Tokyo: Showa Joshi Daigaku, 1958), 8:358.
57. Herschel Webb, "The Development of an Orthodox Attitude toward the Imperial Institution in the Nineteenth Century," in Marius B. Jansen, ed., *Changing Japanese Attitudes Toward Modernization* (Princeton, N.J.: Princeton University Press, 1965), p. 170.
58. Quoted in Kubota Tatshiko, *Ni jūichi daisenkaku kisha den (Osaka: Osaka Mainichi Shimbunsha, 1930), pp. 65–66.

Part 2
Ideas in the Air

Grocery shop. *(Photo permission of Anna Brinton Collection. Reproduction by Masako Imai.)*

Introduction

The Meiji era was a time of intellectual ferment as a new generation of Western-educated and influenced intellectuals sought to devise a new political and social order. The Confucian universe of the Japanese intellectual had disappeared along with the shogunate; yet the Meiji mind, as heir to *shushigaku* (Neo-Confucianism) and the ethics of the *shishi* (patriot), sought to relace the philosophic unity of an integrated ethical, social, and political system with new political institutions based on an alien and "scientific" morality.

While ever-questioning the old and examining the new, the Meiji intellectual was acutely aware of the conflict between tradition and the need for change. He found himself forced to define the areas of the national culture that should be preserved while seeking to purge those aspects which prevented modernization or engendered ridicule abroad. The tension between tradition and reform pervaded Meiji life and politics and led to cultural and philosophical inconsistencies in thought, in government policy, and in all aspects of Meiji life.

The Meiji mind was subject to a bombardment of new ideas from which it had to select concepts, institutions, and technologies most useful to the new age and, most important of all, to preserving national independence. Selective adoption and adaptation and flexibility were, therefore, the keynotes of Meiji. In an environment of confusion and change, the Meiji mind was practical and eclectic, ever ready to try new ideas and techniques and to cast them aside when they proved no longer useful or failed to attain the desired results. Progress was the theme of the time, and the intellectuals of early Meiji were optimistic about their ability to remake society for a better future. The opening of the Diet in 1890 and the revision of the unequal treaties in 1898 symbolized the success of the first period of reform and the end of rapid experimentation. Thereafter, new institutions and ideas would be subject to a more careful and cautious evaluation, tradition would be more highly valued, and moderation and gradualism would be the watchwords at home and improvement of Japan's international stature would be the aim in the international arena.

The Confucian tradition required change to be justified in the words of the sages of the past, and the new intellectuals of Meiji similarly sought to promote reform by using the philosophies of the new sages of the West.

Yamashita Shigekazu shows how both the advocates of democratic rights and the conservative bureaucrats found ammunition for their ideas in the writings of the nineteenth-century British philosopher, Herbert Spencer. Spencer's attack on strong centralized government and his assertion that natural rights were based on natural law were used to support *jiyū minken undō* (democratic-rights movement) demands for a national assembly and constitution. At the same time, government spokesmen used Spencer's theories on social Darwinism as a rationale for conservative change and for a social order based on survival of the fittest. The leading scholars of the West served as mentors and the means to rationalize the new political ideologies and institutions proposed by Meiji conservatives and liberals.

While the reformers of early Meiji concentrated on political and technical modernization, Fukuzawa Yukichi, the outstanding intellectual of the era, called for reform of the thought pattern and system of values as the foundation of progress. Mikiso Hane presents Fukuzawa as an early crusader for women's rights and equality between the sexes and as a rare opponent of masculine arrogance and the double standard characteristic of Japan's male-dominated society. While Fukuzawa's ideas moderated as Meiji society progressed, he was well in the forefront of his own time—and well in advance of the majority of contemporary Japanese men—in his criticism of the role to which women were relegated in Japan and in his call for equal opportunity for men and women alike.

No area of Japanese life was immune from change in Meiji, and Ellen P. Conant reveals Franco-Japanese relations as the catalyst that reawakened the Japanese to the value of the national tradition in the arts and to the development of modern Japanese art. The Meiji government saw the arts as a means of promoting Japan's international image and of earning the foreign exchange needed to finance modernization. "Enrich the country through the arts" *(Bijutsu Fukoku)* was part of "rich country–strong army *(Fukoku Kyōhei)*. As government involvement in the arts and as both sponsor and arbiter of taste increased, so the bureaucatic factionalism characteristic of politics began to pervade the art world as bureaucrats and their artistic protégés sought to promote their own standards of taste and political power.

In an era of rapid reform, all institutions and values were subject to attack and change, reform or oblivion. Restoration *(Ishin)* was the political keynote, and progress was the political theme of the time; but for the mind subject to the intellectual ferment of the age and in search of a new order, the Meiji period was a time of intellectual revolution and genesis.

3 Herbert Spencer and Meiji Japan

Yamashita Shigekazu

The year 1882 was the most memorable in the long, solitary academic life of Herbert Spencer (1820–1903). In that year, he completed part five of his *Principles of Sociology* and then traveled to the United States, where he was welcomed warmly by his many readers and admirers. The climax of his short visit was a banquet on December 9 that many American leaders of science, politics, and business attended. In his speech to the group, Spencer pointed out that his *System of Synthetic Philosophy* was published because of the assistance of American scholars and readers; and he deeply appreciated his "general indebtedness to numerous friends, most of them unknown, on this side of the Atlantic."[1] This speech symbolized Spencer's deep influence in the United States.[2]

Spencer's books also had deep influence in Japan during the same period. He was one of the best-known English philosophers during the early Meiji era. In 1882, when Spencer visited the United States, five of his books and articles had already been translated into Japanese. They were "The Rights of Women" (chapter 16 of *Social Statics*, 1851), the *Social Organism* (1860), *Prison Ethics* (1860), *The Morals of Trade* (1859), and the first volume of the *Principles of Sociology* (1876). In addition, Matsushima Kō completed a very fine translation of *Social Statics* between 1881 and 1883. The first Japanese translation of Spencer's books was an abridged translation of *Social Statics* by Ozaki Yukio, who later achieved fame as a statesman. It was published in 1877. Thereafter, from 1877, the year of the Satsuma Rebellion, to 1890, the year of the first Diet, twenty-three translations of Spencer's works were published, including four translations of *Representative Government* (1857) and three translations of *Education* (1875). This is very unusual, especially when we consider that later translations of his writings during the period 1891 to 1970 number only seventeen.[3]

Spencer's influence on Japan is of particular interest; for "Spencer's ideas were welcomed as a foundation of the principles of the popular-rights movement and, at the same time, were regarded with great importance by the Meiji government, which strongly opposed the popular rights movement."⁴ Thus there appears to be a curious paradox in his influence on Meiji Japan. Some scholars explain this dichotomy very precisely. Shimizu Ikutarō, professor of sociology at Gakushūin University, argues that there were "two souls of Herbert Spencer," that is, "the idea of natural law common to the philosophers of the Enlightenment," and "the Romantic theory of social organism." He writes: "Spencer was imported to Japan as a justification of the principles of the popular rights movement because of his use of the theory of natural law;" on the other hand, "Spencer won the confidence of the Meiji government because of his concept of the theory of social organism."⁵ This point of view has been accepted by several scholars. Miyagawa Tōru, professor of philosophy at Tokyo College of Foreign Languages, states: "The progressive aspects of Spencer's philosophy which emphasized human liberty based on natural law, equality, and natural rights were welcomed by the popular rights front. . . . The conservative aspects of his philosophy which tried to rationalize the existing social order on the basis of the law of survival of the fittest, offers a strong clue to the reactionary bureaucratic ideology of Katō Hiroyuki and others, who endeavored to establish social Darwinism."⁶ In the same vein, Professor Nagai Michio of Sophia University, Tokyo and former minister of education, points out: "We can see the mixture of the ethics of individualism and the theory of social organism in Spencer's thought. In his earlier ideas, the individualistic elements predominant; but in his later thought, the elements of social organism became clearer. . . . In Japan, these two aspects were separated; and each aspect was accepted by a different group. Intellectuals of the popular rights group learned the theory of individual freedom while conservative academicians adopted Spencer's theory of social organism as their own theory."⁷

Some scholars recently have begun to question these clear-cut views of the influence of Spencer on Meiji Japan as seen in the following interesting dialogue between Shimizu Ikutarō and Takahashi Tōru, professor of sociology at Tokyo University:

TAKAHASHI: Your view is that sociology in Japan is based on organology, one of the two souls of Spencer. However, I think you have misread Spencer. Didn't Spencer have only one soul in Japan up to 1887?
SHIMIZU: Which soul?
TAKAHASHI: The soul of atomism or *laissez-faire*. Spencer's thought in Japan functioned not only as the political ideal which led the popular rights movement but also as a social theory which inspired the movement. . . .
SHIMIZU: I now think that my view was oversimplified.⁸

Takahashi's criticism of Shimizu's ideas is keen, but while suggestive,⁹ it does not seem to be a satisfactory explanation of the complexity of Spencer's influence on Japan. This is one of the most difficult and important problems in explaining the influence of European thought on Meiji Japan. To study the influence of Spencer, it is necessary to reexamine both his impact on Japan and the thought of Spencer himself.

As many scholars have noted, there were three primary channels through which Spencer influenced Meiji Japan. These were the popular-rights movement, the Meiji government, and Tokyo University.[10] These three channels are examined in succession and it will be confirmed that their influence was almost simultaneous, though very different in content.

The first important channel was the popular-rights movement from 1874 to 1889. Its political leader, Itagaki Taisuke regarded *Social Statics* as the "text book of popular rights."[11] Itagaki, with an introduction provided by Mori Arinori, personally called on Spencer in London in May 1883. Since Spencer was ill, Itagaki could not discuss politics with him[12]; but he sent Spencer all the Japanese translations of his works after he returned to Japan. In return, Spencer sent Itagaki some of the galley proofs for part of his *Principles of Sociology*, and these were translated into Japanese.[13]

Many young intellectuals of the popular-rights front read Spencer's works in the original English or in Japanese translation since translations were available in the 1870s and 1880s. Spencer's writings were welcomed as a strong weapon against the Meiji government. Several members of the movement translated Spencer's works while others read them with enthusiasm during the period.

The most influential book during the period of the *jiyū minken undō* was the Japanese translation of Spencer's *Social Statics*. An abridged translation had been published by Ozaki Yukio in 1877; and the complete translation was published between 1881 and 1883, during the high point of the popular-rights movement. The translator, Matsushima Kō, was a young scholar of English and geology, who had studied English at Keiō Gijuku under Fukuzawa Yukichi. His translation, entitled *Shakai heikenron*, was one of the major works produced in the early Meiji era; and it had a profound influence on the popular-rights movement. Matsushima himself, in his unpublished autobiography, wrote: "I published the translation of *Social Statics* in six volumes. As it was published when petitions requesting the opening of a new national assembly were rushing to the Meiji government from all points of Japan, my translation was welcomed with unexpected enthusiasm. Letters asking for the next volume lay in piles on my desk. The Risshisha in Tosa, in particular, often ordered many copies by telegraph."[14] He further recalled in 1927: "Orders from every part of Japan lay in stacks. No amount of reprints was sufficient. Booksellers waited at the printer's shop.... I received 2,500 or 2,600 yen instead of the promised 25 yen.[15]

Spencer's strong attack on government power was one factor in the popularity of *Social Statics* with the popular rights movement. Early in *Social Statics*, he criticized the utilitarianism of Jeremy Betham.[16] He did not criticize utilitarianism as an ethical theory, but he attacked Bentham's political implications. Bentham's political ideal was to establish an efficient centralized government based on democratic suffrage.[17] He was a radical democrat, but he was a very different type of democrat from Spencer, who asserted that the least government was the best government. Members of the popular-rights front preferred Spencer to Bentham because they wanted a political theory justifying their opposition to the strong, centralized power of the Meiji government. In this sense, Matsushima's very fine translation of *Social Statics* fitted their aims very well.

One of the main aspects of Spencer's social theory was his unique idea of social organism, a concept that was adopted and interpreted by Baba Tatsui (1850–88). Baba studied in England from 1870 to 1878 and became a leading member of the popular-rights movement, but he later sought refuge in the United States and died in Philadelphia in 1888.[18] He did not translate Spencer's writings, but he wrote an introduction to the abridged translation of *First Principles*, published under the title of *Banbutsu shinka yōron* in 1884. He wrote: "I cannot but recommend Herbert Spencer as the foremost British philosopher because of his breadth of his knowledge and bold speculation. He appeared after John Stuart Mill had greatly advanced European civilization by asserting his important theories. He divided his *First Principles* into two parts, 'unknowable and knowable'; and his theory of the relationship between the absolute and the relative is admired by many of the world's scholars. In particular, his theory of evolution is the object of their attention and admiration."[19]

Spencer's influence on Baba's political thought can be seen in his unfinished article entitled "Honron" ("Fundamental Principles"), published in 1882.[20] The most notable aspect of this article is his theory of social organism. Positing the question of "whether society is an organism or a mechanism," he repies, "The individuals who compose society are organic; thus, society as the collective whole of individuals must be an organism."[21] Baba not only emphasized the analogy between the individual and the social organism but also the differences between these two organisms. He asserted: "The end of society is the welfare of the individuals who compose it. The individual does not exist for society; on the contrary, society exists for the individual. Individuals create a society in order to secure their innate freedom."[22]

Baba's theory of social organism was a reflection of Spencer's idea.[23] Spencer's theory was not totalitarian in the sense of attaching more importance to society as a whole than to the individual. It simply meant a relationship of voluntary cooperation among free and equal individuals. Baba and other intellectuals of the popular-rights front tried to utilize Spencer's theory of social organism as a strong weapon within their attack on the Meiji government.

Sakamoto Naohiro (whose early name was Sakamoto Namio, 1853–1911), the nephew of the famous statesman Sakamoto Ryōma, was another intellectual of the popular-rights front who showed a deep understanding of Spencer's thought. Sakamoto studied English at the Risshi Gakusha, a school in Tosa established by the Risshisha.[24] He was an active member of the *jiyū minken undo*, and he also was one of the youthful intelligentsia who read the books of Mill and Spencer in the original English and wrote many political works.[25]

Sakamoto's political writings during the popular-rights movement reflected Spencer's ideas very clearly.[26] In his long article on politics entitled "Seiron" (1881), he quoted from *Social Statics:* "It is a mistake to assume that government must necessarily last forever. The institution marks a certain stage of civilization. . . . All tyrannical institutions are merely the most vigorous kinds of rule springing out of, and necessary to, a bad state of man. The progress from these is in all cases the same—less government."[27] "Not only does magisterial power exist because of evil, but it exists by evil."[28] Sakamoto's quotations from *Social Statics* were very effective in justifying his opposition to the centralized educational policy and suppression of the popular-rights movement by the government. He wholly agreed with Spencer in asserting "the law of equal freedom," which implied that all members of a state should have equal claim to political power. Sakamoto's theory of governmental functions, emphasizing that it was the government's main duty to protect the life and property of the people and that it must not interfere with the voluntary activities of the people, clearly depended on *Social Statics* (especially chapter 22, "Duty of the State," and chapter 23, "Limits of the State-Duty").[29] He also quoted from Stuart Mill's *Representative Government* (1861) to criticize paternalistic government.[30]

Sakamoto retired from politics rather early in life and became a Christian missionary.[31] His activities as a member of the popular-rights movement are not well known; but his political thought should be held in high esteem because of his deep comprehension of English liberalism and, in particular, the way in which he wielded *Social Statics* as a strong weapon in his political activities during the popular-rights movement.

Tokutomi Sohō (1863–1957) was "the most widely recognized spokesman for the new generation emerging in the 1880s."[32] Tokutomi came to Tokyo in 1886 when he was twenty-three years old. He established the Min-yūsha (Friends of the Nation), which published a new magazine entitled *Kokumin no tomo (The Nation's Friend)*, and achieved fame as a journalist. Though he became an ultranationalist after the Sino-Japanese War, he was a member of the *jiyū minken undō* in his youth; and his concept of *heiminshugi* ("populism" or "democracy") was one of the landmarks of Meiji political thought.

Young Tokutomi had been a teacher at the Ōe Gijuku in Kumamoto from 1882 to 1886. This small local school had a strong tie to the popular-rights movement. In addition to teaching with youthful enthusiasm, Tokutomi read many works in English, including those by Tocqueville, Cobden, Bright, Macaulay, and Spencer.[33] In his pamphlet *Shōrai no Nihon* (*Future of Japan*, 1885), he clearly contrasted the old, militant, aristocratic society with the new, productive, democratic one and pronounced his view of *heiminshugi* for the first time.[34] In this could be seen the important influence of Tocqueville's *Democracy in America* and Spencer's *Principles of Sociology*, both of which he had read with great enthusiasm in Kumamoto.[35]

Tokutomi drew from Tocqueville's comments on the United States a fresh image of a peaceful, productive society based upon the active cooperation of the people; and then he tried to explain its historic inevitability through Spencer's theory of social evolution. As Professor Pierson pointed out, Tokutomi learned from Spencer that "modern democracies had evolved out of militant societies and had developed as a result of the productive forces generated by military need."[36] He severely criticized the old system of Japanese feudalism and its ideology of Confucianism.[37] In the past, he strongly had lamented the backward status of Japanese society in comparison with Western countries. However, thanks to Spencer's sociology, especially his thesis of social evolution "from militant to an industrial type of society" and from compulsory cooperation to voluntary cooperation,[38] he could fit Japan into a universal pattern of social evolution.

Shōrai no Nihon described a clear-cut contrast between the present "world of violence" and the future "peaceful world" and between the "old Japan," the feudalistic military society, and the "new Japan," the democratic, industrial society.[39] Though Tokutomi was rather pessimistic in regard to the state of Japan at that time, he unexpectedly was optimistic as to the Japan of the future.

Tokutomi's drastic "apostasy" to obstinate nationalism and imperialism is well known.[40] His book, *Dainihon bōchōron* (*Expansion of Great Japan*, 1895) was a public declaration of his apostasy. His change in perspective implied the complete breakdown of his optimistic views based on the sociology of Spencer. It was the result of his realization that the world was not moving into a peaceful industrial stage and his awareness of the critical situation faced by a Japan surrounded by strong, western states.[41] While Spencer's influence on Tokutomi's political thought was very strong though short-lived, *heiminshugi* should not be underestimated, as it was one of the major applications of Spencer's theories during the period of the popular-rights movement.

One of the historic contradictions of the Meiji era is that Spencer, whose writings were considered almost as text books of the popular-rights movement, personally offered conservative advice to Japanese statesmen and diplomats. Yet, in truth, this paradox symbolizes the complexity of his influence on early Meiji Japan. Spencer also had a profound effect on Mori Arinori and Kaneko Kentarō, both of whom had close personal contact with the British philosopher.

Mori Arinori (1847–90), the eminent diplomat and minister of education, has been studied extensively by Ivan Parker Hall.[42] Mori served in Washington as chargé d'affaires from 1871 to 1873. His biographer wrote: "Mori, being fond of learning, read extensively while at the legation, placing special emphasis on literature and ethics and reading Spencer on philosophy and J. S. Mill on economics."[43] On his return trip to Japan, he called on Spencer in April or May of 1873. Spencer wrote in an undated notation his diary: "He [Mori] came to ask my opinion about the reorganization of Japanese institutions. I gave him conservative advice—urging that they would have eventually to return to a form not much in advance of what they had, and that they ought not to attempt to diverge widely from it."[44] This short entry is very interesting; for he gave "conservative advice" to Mori in 1873, namely, a few years before his own writings began to inspire the popular-rights movement.

While Mori served as the Japanese minister to London from 1880 to 1884, he often called on Spencer. Spencer, who then was writing part 5 of *Principles of Sociology*, was very interested in the young Japanese diplomat and sought firsthand information on Japanese affairs from him.[45] He gave a dinner at the Athenaneum in Mori's honor on May 19, 1881, which was attended by Professor Alexander Bain, John Morley, and others.[46] Itagaki Taisuke, as was mentioned previously, was introduced to Spencer by Mori.

The most interesting paper written by Mori in London is a pamphlet entitled *On a Representative System of Government for Japan*, which he privately sent to several foreign statesmen and scholars, including Spencer. Spencer wrote in a letter to Kaneko Kentarō on August 21, 1892: "Probably you remember I told you that when Mr. Mori, the then Japanese Ambassador, submitted to me his draft for a Japanese Constitution, I gave him very conservative advice."[47] Hall presumes that this draft was Mori's *Representative System*, and Spencer's conservative opinion might have been reflected in this pamphlet.[48] This pamphlet clearly restated Mori's opinion, which he expressed in an interview with the *Pall Mall Gazette*: "In the Europe of which you [the British] form a part, parliamentarianism with universal suffrage as its ultimate outcome is in the line of your development: You can not avoid it; but I doubt whether we shall find it equally inevitable in Japan."[49] His *Representative System* advocated a kind of parliamentarianism in which the representatives of the people had only advisory functions. It also asserted that people should participate in politics not as individuals but as family units represented by the heads of the household. It is not possible to determine whether this was Mori's original idea or the outcome of Spencer's advice; but it is very probable that Spencer, who was informed of the backward state of Japanese society by Mori, in turn gave very conservative advice to Mori.

Hall, referring to Spencer's letters to Kaneko, suggests: "The simplest explanation of points of resemblance between Mori's essay and the letters to Kaneko, is that Spencer is repeating points he forgot he already had made to Mori. Another possibility, of course, is that Mori originally may have put some ideas in Spencer's head."[50] To this author, the second possibility seems to be the stronger case.

The other important statesman of the Meiji government who had close contact with Spencer was Kaneko Kentarō (1853–1942). He studied in the United States from 1871 to 1878 and graduated from the Law Department of Harvard University. In his unpublished autobiography, he referred to his acquaintance with Henry Wadsworth Longfellow, Charles Norton, and John Fiske. He wrote: "John Fiske, who was once a professor of philosophy at Harvard University, opposed the old schools of philosophy in his lectures on Spencer's philosophy, then he resigned, and propagated Spencer's philosophy. I became close with him and often called on him to study the new theory of evolution. I understood that Maine's theory of the evolution of law and Spencer's theory of social evolution were in the same current. Fiske was a prolific scholar and a good debater. He discussed the philosophy of evolution very well so that the listeners could not but agree with him."[51]

After Kaneko returned to Japan, his ability was recognized by Itō Hirobumi and he participated in the writing of the Meiji constitution.[52] When the constitution was promulgated, he was sent to the United States and to Europe to ask the opinions of many statesmen and scholars about it. In an interesting interview with Spencer on March 2, 1890, he reports that Spencer told him: "If the Japanese constitution and laws have not the same spirit and nature as have Japanese history and customs, future difficulties will be numerous; and you will not attain the aims of constitutional government. I had advised Mr. Mori, the Japanese Minister, to use the principles of gradualism and conservatism. . . . I heartily agree with your opinion that the Japanese constitution has been based on Japanese history and customs. . . . My principle of politics is to reduce government activities and let the people themselves do their own business. . . . But, this presupposes a future perfect world. Instructions to reduce government interference must be gradual. Government interference must cease immediately after the people themselves begin to cultivate the spirit of independence and to discharge their duties without injuring the rights of others and without the guidance of the government."[53]

Two years later, on August 21, 23, and 26, 1892, Spencer sent three very important letters to Kaneko. As previously quoted, the first referred to the "very conservative advice" that he had earlier given Mori.⁵⁴ In the second letter, he discussed his conservative views very concretely. His main points were (1) to utilize "the ancient system of family organization," that is, "the patriachs or heads of groups should be made the sole electors or members of your representative body," and (2) make the representative body merely advisory, namely, "the assembly . . . should be limited in their functions to making statements of grievance."⁵⁵

This advice shows a remarkable resemblance to Mori's pamphlet, *Representative System*. The third letter advocated "keeping Americans and Europeans as much as possible at arm's length," that is, refuse leases on land and property, mining rights, the right to engage in the coastal trade, and intermarriage with foreigners.⁵⁶ It is clear that such advice was far more conservative than the policies of the Meiji government or the Meiji constitution. It clearly was based upon Spencer's theory of social evolution as applied to a backward society, but it must not be forgotten that Spencer's view of Japanese society depended largely upon the information received from Mori.

Spencer's sociology flourished in the academic environment of Tokyo University during the early Meiji era. Tokyo University was established as the first modern university in Japan in 1877. It developed from the former Tokyo Kaisei School and the Tokyo Medical School and had four departments—law, literature, science, and medicine. When the university opened, the theory of evolution was introduced by Professors Edward Sylvester Morse (1838–1925) and Ernest Francisco Fenollosa (1853–1908), both graduates of Harvard University. Morse, as professor of zoology, introduced Darwinian theory in his lectures; and Fenollosa came to Japan through Morse's recommendation.

Although Fenollosa is very famous as a scholar of Japanese art, it is his activities as a young professor of philosophy, economics, and political science from 1877 to 1886 that merit attention here. His lectures at Tokyo University and some public lectures clearly reflected Spencer's ideas. His lecture on religion (1877) and his article on "theory of social evolution" (1879), both published in Japanese translation, were not original in content, but they are a very remarkable introduction to Spencer's sociology.⁵⁷

At Tokyo University, Fenollosa lectured on the history of philosophy (1877–85), political economy (1877–83), political science (1877–80), and logic (1877–85). Fortunately, the contemporary scholar can read several notebooks of his lectures on philosophy and political economy left by his students.⁵⁸ Ichishima Kenkichi's notes on lectures on the history of philosophy given in 1878–79 cover the topic from Descartes to Berkley. Sakatani Yoshirō ranges from Kant to Hegel in the lecture notes of 1880–81. Although the notebooks do not include explicit lectures on Spencer, they often refer to Spencer as in the following passages:

> We must recognize that the narrow limits of nature within which we dispute are not the limits of reality, but that there may be and must be an infinite number of aspects of this universe which we are unable to recognize at all. This is the foundation of the modern doctrine of the relativity of knowledge which Spencer, in quite a Spinozan manner, calls the "unknowable reality" or "substance."[59]
>
> So far as philosophy is concerned, Spencer's philosophy is a new Kanteanism though he is superior to Kant as far as science goes.[60]
>
> If I can unite the doctrine of Spencer's Evolution and Hegel's Philosophy, we will have a complete philosophy, and we believe this will be done within the next thirty or forty years.[61]

Fenollosa's comparison of Spinoza, Kant, Hegel, and Spencer is not very satisfactory; but it is remarkable that he introduced Spencer's thought to Japanese academism not only as a theory of sociology but also as a system of synthetic philosophy.

Notebooks of Fenollosa's lectures on political science have not been found, but it is known that these lectures included sociology and that his textbooks were Spencer's *Principles of Sociology* (volume 1), Bagehot's *Physics and Political Science*, and Lieber's *On Civil Liberty and Self-Government*.[62] Fenellosa was the first professor in Japan whose lectures on political science were based on Spencer's sociology.

In addition to Fenollosa, two Japanese teachers at Tokyo University, Professor Toyama Masakazu and Assistant Professor Ariga Nagao, introduced Spencer's sociology to Japan. Toyama, who had studied in England and the United States, used Spencer's ideas as the starting point of his lectures on philosophy and history.[63] Ariga, who was Fenollosa's first student, wrote a three-volume work entitled *Shakaigaku* (*Sociology*, 1882–83), the first systematic treatise on sociology in Japan.

It is very difficult to estimate the influence that Spencer's sociology had on Tokyo University. Professor Takahashi Tōru points out that Fenollosa inspired reflections on the radical interpretation of Spencer and his emphasis on the "moderateness" of his theory of social change. Thus, he prepared the way for the popular theory of "Spencer as a guidebook of state sovereignty."[64] This seems to be too simplistic an interpretation. It is true that Fenollosa and Toyama were not radical thinkers. Fenollosa criticized his former students, Takada Sanae, Ichishima Kenkichi, and others, who participated in the establishment of the Rikken Kaishintō.[65] Yet, at the same time, his lectures on political science offered material used in the Kaishintō platform written by Ono Azusa. Toyama emphasized the gradualism of Spencer's theory of social evolution when he criticized the radical popular-rights movement, but he also criticized Katō Hiroyuki's extreme social Darwinism.

Katō Hiroyuki, the rector of Tokyo University from 1880 to 1893, severely attacked the theory of natural rights in his *Jinken shinsetsu* (*New Theory of Human Rights*, 1882).[66] His denunciation was based on his unique interpretation of the theories of the struggle for existence and the social organism. He wrote in his autobiography: "Soon after I read the books of contemporary European scholars, I began to realize that the theory of natural rights was groundless; and when I read the works on evolution of Darwin and Spencer, when I was forty years old, I realized that mankind was not a special being but has become what it is by evolution."[67] It is, however, a mistake to overemphasize Spencer's influence on Katō. As far as this author can ascertain, Katō read only seven chapters of *Principles of Sociology*, volume 2, part 5 ("Political Institutions") in German translation.[68] His *Jinken shinsetsu* depends entirely on German social Darwinists and not on Spencer. His extreme use of social Darwinism and his organic theory of the state cannot be said to be the result of the influence of Spencer's sociology.

Spencer's influence on Meiji Japan flowed through three channels: the popular-rights movement, the Meiji government, and Tokyo University. To examine the process in more detail, it is necessary to analyze several main characteristics of Spencer's thought, especially the element of dissent, his theory of social organism, and his gradualism. For this, his short memoir, titled *The Filiation of Ideas*,[69] is very useful. In it, he wrote of his boyhood and emphasized how little he was swayed by authority: "This natural trait operated throughout life, tending to make me pay little attention to established opinion on any matter which came up for judgment and tending to leave me perfectly free to inquire without restraint."[70] In regard to his first political article, "The Proper Sphere of Government," which was published in the *Nonconformist* in June 1842, he pointed out that its emotional leaning generated from his "dissenting family."[71] He was born and reared in the atmosphere of opposition to government, and this provided the foundation for his extremely laissez-faire views on government.

Sir Ernest Barker has pointed out that Spencer's thought originated from three major areas: English radicalism, his study of natural science, and the German idealism of Schelling and Schlegel. He emphasized the first point and noted: "He [Spencer] sprang from a family essentially dissenting and, as such, [was] opposed to authority; and his Nonconformist instinct, and the Nonconformist training of his youth, left on [him] an abiding mark."[72] He was educated by his uncle, Thomas Spencer, an evangelical minister. In addition to working as a railroad engineer, he actively participated in the radical political movement and joined the Anti-Corn Law League, and Complete Suffrage Union, and the Anti-State Church Association. As Professor Peel has noted, he was reared among the "urban, provincial, and dissenting experience of the Industrial Revolution"; and "the common thread was the opposition of radical provincial opinion to the traditional state, dominated by the aristocracy and an alien church."[73]

Spencer's first book was *Social Statics*, which appeared in 1851. It "opposed the cult of the state and the cult of the individual."[74] It strongly opposed government intervention and claimed the right of individual autonomy. It was translated into Japanese by Matsushima Kō. Many leaders of the popular-rights movement welcomed it because of its apparent opposition to utilitarianism. Born into samurai families, they were instinctively averse to utilitarianism. However, Spencer did not criticize utilitarianism per se as an ethical doctrine, but rather attacked the idea of the concentration of power in the government that was implied in Bentham's ideas. He pointed out that "the doctrine of expediency" presupposed a strong government and asserted: "Government is an institution originating in man's imperfection."[75] His criticism of utilitarianism was a polemical preliminary to his laissez-faire doctrine. He was not an anarchist, but his view was that "the state is a joint-stock protection company for mutual assurance."[76]

Spencer's general proposition was that "every man may claim the fullest liberty to exercise his faculties compatible with the possession of like liberty by every other man."[77] When this view of human liberty was combined with his ideas on state power as a "necessary evil" and his highly optimistic perspective for "the evanescence of evil" based on his theory of evolution, a distinct concept of minimum government emerged. In this, he asserted many kinds of rights: the right of life and personal liberty, the right to the use of the soil, the right of property, the right of exchange, the right of free speech, political rights, and the right to ignore the state.[78] He limited state power to "the protection of rights" and emphasized that "whenever the state begins to exceed its office of protection, it begins to lose protective power."[79] He excluded from the functions of the state not only religion and colonization but also the establishment of a national system of education. He asserted state-controlled education meant that "government ought to mold children into good citizens, using its own discretion in setting up what a good citizen is, and how the child may be molded into one."[80] His criticism of state education clearly verified that his liberalism was based on the Dissenter's experience. English Dissenters, who had been excluded from higher education, established their own academies by which they provided themselves better than the privileged universities and schools. They emphasized the principle of independence and autonomy not only in education but also in all other aspects of society. In economics, they sharply opposed state interference and demanded an economic policy based on the principle of laissez-faire. Spencer's liberalism reflected "the culture of middle-class provincial radicalism between 1832 and 1851," and this radicalism "goes back to the seventeenth century, [with] its origins in [the] market society and Dissent."[81]

One characteristic of the Dissenters was confidence in the voluntary cooperation of autonomous individuals. Spencer's liberalism was more secularized, but its origin was strongly religious and the result of English religious history. Therefore, it is dubious as to how well Spencer's thought was understood in early Meiji Japan. Furthermore, in order to examine the influence of his laissez-faire liberalism in the early Meiji era, it is essential to look at this theory of social organism, which is erroneously regarded as very conservative but in reality is the other side of his unique liberalism.

The most systematic exposition of Spencer's theory of social organism occurs in his article "Social Organism," which was written in 1860. This was the result of his growth between 1850 and 1860: the first being the date at which in Social Statics, there had occurred the primary recognition of the analogy between an individual organism and a social organism."[82]

In "Social Organism," Spencer summarizes the similarities and the differences between individual and social organisms. The similarities were: both commence as small aggregates and increase in mass; both develop a more complex structure as they grow; with maturity, functionally distinct parts become more independent; and the life of both is independent of and larger than the life of any one of their units. The differences are that society has no external forms; that the units of society are not physically contiguous with one another; that the units of the social organism are spatially mobile, and that all units of a society are endowed with consciousness as opposed to the one conscious part of an organism.[83] He specifically emphasized the last point and noted: "While, in individual bodies, the welfare of all other parts is rightly subservient to the welfare of the nervous system, . . . in bodies-politic the same does not hold. . . . This is an everlasting reason why the welfare of citizens can not rightly be sacrificed to some supposed benefit of the state, and why, on the other hand, the state is to be maintained solely for the benefit of citizens."[84]

In the *Principles of Sociology*, volume I (1876), Spencer again asserted that "society exists for the benefit of its members, not its members for the benefit of society."[85] He summarized his idea of social organism in *The Filiation of Ideas*. "Under peaceful conditions, when corporate action is no longer needed for offense and defense, the highest types of society are those in which the coercive governmental organization was dwindled, and corporate action, with its correlative structures, gives place to individual action, having directive structures of a relatively non-coercive kind."[86] Thus, it is evident that his theory of social organism does not imply exalting society as a whole over the individual. His idea of social organism was not a *substantive* conception but a *relative* conception. His main assertion is that as society develops, it differentiates more and more, and its component members become more organic; that is, mutual dependence increases. There is no room in his philosophy for the concept of a society that transcends its component individuals.

In "Specialized Administration" (1871), Spencer replied to his friend T. H. Huxley's criticism of his theory of social organism. Huxley wrote, "If the analogy of the body politic with the body physiological counts for anything, it seems to me to be in favor of a much larger amount of governmental interference than exists at present."[87] Spencer responded that as industry develops, society becomes more "organic," that is, more mutually dependent, and, thus, strong regulative machinery becomes unnecessary.[88] This replay was dearly dependent on his confidence in the harmonious, voluntary cooperation of developed industrial societies.

Shimizu Ikutarō writes: "If we consider the organic system of society, it must be found in the militant type of society or the primitive society which is centrally controlled. The industrial type of society is a coexistence of free individuals, so it has the least degree of organ structure. What Spencer called social evolution or progress must be evolution or progress for the individual but for society this must be devolution. Is this not a paradox?"[89] This criticism seems shortsighted. Spencer's theory of social organism implies that the militant society is an immature type of social organism. As the developing industrial society promotes individual liberty and the voluntary cooperation of independent individuals, the social organism matures. His theory of social organism was not only consistent with his criticism of the power of the centralized state and governmental interference, but it also supported his assertion of laissez-faire policy by insisting on the organic, or self-governing, voluntary nature of industrial society. These two principal characteristics of Spencer's thought must be recognized as the unique outgrowth of the industrial revolution and non-conformism in England.

Sakamoto Naohiro and Baba Tatsui clearly understood Spencer's ideas and utilized them in their activities in the popular-rights movement. However, it must be recognized that they were in the minority. Sakamoto, who comprehended Spencer's liberalism correctly, lamented the "informal feudalism" of his colleagues in the popular-rights movement, men who were too narrow-minded to cooperate for their great cause.[90] In a severe rebuke of the popular parties *(mintō)*, he said: "We tend to form groups around particular persons rather than on principle. . . . We tend to be jealous of each other. . . . We tend to unite locally but not nationally. . . . We have a bad habit of intolerance of different opinions."[91] This candid self-criticism was very rare in the popular-rights front. Baba, who introduced Spencer's theory of social organism, strongly opposed Itagaki's foreign travel and, as a result, left the Jiyūtō in 1882.[92] Sakamoto retired from politics and became a Christian missionary, and Baba left Japan to seek refuge in the United States. The final isolation of Sakamoto and Baba, as well as Tokutomi Sohō's later "apostasy" to ultranationalism symbolized the failure of Spencer's ideas to penetrate deeply into the philosophy of the popular rights front.

Spencer's gradualism, his assertion that a different policy and social system is necessary for each stage of social evolution, were utilized for conservative purposes. Spencer's gradualism differentiated from other utilitarians. "His insistence on progress as a process passing through inevitable stages according to inevitable laws"[93] appeared very early in his thought. In 1843, he wrote to a friend: "I look upon despotisms, aristocracies, priestcraft, and all other evils that afflict humanity, and I believe that every people must pass through the various phases between absolutism and democrcy before they are fitted to become permanently free, and if a nation liberates itself by physical force, and attains the goal without passing through these moral ordeals, I do not think its freedom will be lasting."[94]

Spencer's policy of laissez-faire was not a universal principle, but it presupposed a highly developed, industrial society. He wrote in his postscript to *Man versus the State* in 1884:

> The restriction of governmental power within the limits assigned, is appropriate to the industrial type of society only; and while wholly incongrous with the militant type of society, is partially incongrous with the semi-industrial type, which now characterizes advanced nations. . . . In the primitive man and in man but little civilized, there does not exist the nature required for extensive voluntary cooperation. . . . The implication is that, during long stages of social evolution there needs, for the management of all matters but the simplest, a governmental power great in degree and wide in range with a correlative faith in it and obedience to it. Hence the fact that, as the records of early civilizations show us, and as we are shown in the East at present, large understakings can be achieved only by state action.[95]

Here we can see those elements of Spencer's thought which influenced Japanese academism and the Meiji government. Fenollosa pointed out the several stages of social evolution from primitive anarchy to despotic government and then to constitutional government when he wrote:

> Liberty as an essential element of civilization can not be expected to exist in the barbarians. It appeared in later ages. But, had despotic government not controlled the barbarians and reared their custom of obedience, liberty would not have found the chance of expression. It would be no exaggeration to say that despotic government is the cradle of liberty. Then, we must understand these two stages to inquire into the causes of the process of civilization. The first stage was one where after a long series of struggles for existence, at last despotic government appeared; and the next stage was one where people began to cultivate the spirit of liberty and to assert their independent thought under [conditions of] domestic peace, and at last destroyed

the uniform customs reared by despotic government and claimed their independence and individuality.[96]

This passage clearly reflects Spencer's theory of social evolution in its emphasis on gradualism.

Professor Toyama Masakazu of Tokyo University closed his long poem, which served as the introduction to the Japanese translation of *Principles of Sociology*, volume 1, with these lines:

> Today's world is in the midst of a wild whirlwind. . . . It is an essential skill of the helmsman not to drive his ship into the whirlwind. I sincerely hope those who are at the helm of government and those who are leaders of public opinion, study sociology and not be imprudent in their activities.[97]

Fenollosa and Toyama, both at Tokyo University, were certainly not ultranationalists who exalted the state above individuals. Fenollosa influenced the leaders of the Rikken Kaishintō (Progressive party) through his lectures on political science, and Toyama criticized the ultraconservatism of Katō Hiroyuki. However, by emphasizing Spencer's gradualism, they opposed the radical liberals of the popular-rights movement. They accepted Spencer's political gradualism, that is, his moderate conservatism, more than his laissez-faire liberalism.

It also is evident that intellectual statesmen of the Meiji government such as Mori Arinori and Kaneko Kentarō utilized Spencer's gradualism to promote a more conservative ideology. It is notable that Spencer's advice to them was unexpectedly conservative, but this followed Mori's detailed description of Japanese society. Spencer viewed Tokugawa Japan as a perfect example of a militant type of society and held contemporary Japan in low esteem. His advice was based, therefore, on Mori's information and views and on his own principle of gradualism.[98]

Notes

1. Herbert Spencer, "The Americans, A Speech on November 9, 1882," *Essays: Scientific, Political and Speculative* (Osnabruck: Otto Zeller, 1966), 3:481–82.
2. See Richard Hofstadter, *Social Darwinism in American Thought* (Boston: Beacon Press, 1955).
3. See Yamashita Shigekazu, "Bentham, Mill, Spencer hōyakusho mokuroku," *Sankō Shoshi Kenkyū*, no. 10 (Tokyo: National Diet Library, October 1974), pp. 29–35.
4. Shimizu Ikutarō, *Nihon bunka keitairon* (Tokyo: Sairen Sha, 1936), pp. 47–48.
5. Ibid., pp. 65–70.
6. Miyagawa Tōru, *Kindai Nihon no tetsugaku* (Tokyo: Keisō Shobō, 1961), p. 61.
7. Nagai Michio, *Kindaika to kyōiku* (Tokyo: Tokyo Daigaku Shuppan Kai, 1969), p. 163.
8. Shimizu, Ikutarō, "Comte and Spencer," *Seikai no meicho;* 66 vols. (Tokyo: Chūō Kōron Sha, 1970), 34:10–11.

9. Takahashi Tōru, "Nihon ni okeru shakaishinrigaku no keisei," *Shakaishinrigaku no keisei* (Tokyo: Baifū Kan, 1965), pp. 414–449.
10. See Shimizu, *Nihon bunka*, pp. 37 ff. Takahashi, "Nihon ni okeru," pp. 374 ff. Nagai, *Kindaika*, pp. 162 ff.
11. John D. Pierson, "The Early Liberal Thought of Tokutomi Sohō," *Monumenta Nipponica* 24 (Summer 1976): 200.
12. Mori Arinori informed Itō Hirobumi in early May 1883 of the curious interview Itagaki had with Spencer: "Itagaki went into it as though approaching the Emperor," but in the actual discussion, master and pupil traded places, with the disciple doing all the sermonizing and putting forth his usual empty and unfounded theories. Finally, the central idol lost his patience, got up in the middle of the interview muttering 'no, no, no,' and took his leave of Itagaki." Kimura Kyō, *Mori sensei den* (Tokyo: Kinkōdō, 1899), p. 96.
13. Herbert Spencer, *Shūkyō shinkaron*, translated by Takahashi Tatsurō, with introduction by Itagaki Taisuke (Tokyo: Itagaki Taisuke, 1886).
14. Quoted from Matsushima Kō's unpublished autobiography written in 1926. National Diet Library, no pagination.
15. Yanagida, Izumi, *Meiji shoki honyakubungaku no kenkyū*, (Tokyo: Shunjūsha, 1961), pp. 364–65.
16. See Herbert Spencer, "Introduction" and "The Doctrine of Expediency," *Social Statics* (London: John Chapman, 1851), pp. 1–16.
17. See my article, "Jeremy Bentham no seiji shisō," *Kokugakuin hōgaku* 3, nos. 2, 3 (Tokyo: Department of Law, Kokugakuin University, 1965–66).
18. See Hagihara Nobutoshi, *Baba Tatsui* (Tokyo: Chuō Kōron Sha, 1967). This book is the best biography of Baba Tatsui. Baba's main writings are included in Ienaga Saburō, ed., *Meiji bungaku zenshū*, (Tokyo: Chikuma Shobō, 1973), 12:201–315.
19. Introduction to *Banbutsu shinka yōron*, trans. Matsumoto Kiyotoshi and Nishimura Gendō (Tokyo: Mintoku Kan, 1884).
20. "Honron" was published in *Jiyū shimbun*, no. 2 to no. 27 (July 1–August 27, 1882).
21. "Honron," *Meiji bungaku zenshū* 12:204.
22. Ibid., p. 206.
23. Takahashi, "Nihon ni," pp. 419–20.
24. The Risshi Gakusha was a school established in 1875 by the Rissisha, the most famous political body of the popular-rights movement. In this local school, several graduates of Keio Gijuku taught English using the books of Mill, Spencer, and others. See my article, "Jiyūminken undō to Igirisu seiji shisō," *Kokugakuin Daigaku Tochigi Tanki Daigaku kiyō* 9 (1975): 116–32.
25. Sakamoto Naohiro's writings were published by his grandson, Doi Haruo. See *Sakamoto Naohiro chosaku shū*, 3 vols. (Kōchi: Kōchi City Library, 1970).
26. See Yamashita Shigekazu, "Sakamoto Naohiro ni okeru seiyō seiji shisō no juyō," *Kokugakuin Daigaku kiyō* 8 (1971): 119–28.
27. "Seiron," *Sakamoto Nachiro chosaku shū* I:14. See *Social Statics*, p. 13.
28. Ibid., pp. 45–46; *Social Statics*, p. 201.
29. Ibid., p. 59.
30. Ibid., p. 67. See J. S. Mill, *Considerations on Representative Government*, 3rd ed. (London: Longman, Green, 1863), p. 41.
31. For Sakamoto's autobiography, see "Waga shinkō no keireki," *Chosaku shū* 3:83–190.
32. Kenneth B. Pyle, *The New Generation in Meiji Japan* (Calif.: Stanford University Press, 1969), p. 25. This book includes very fine section on Spencer's influences on Tokutomi (pp. 36–42).
33. For young Tokutomi, see Kano Masanao, "Ichi minken shijuku no kiseki," *Shisō* 536 (February 1969): 54–74. Wada Mamoru, "Wakaki Sohō no shisōkeisei to heiminshugi no tokushitsu," *Shisō* 585 (March 1973): 68–92, and John D. Pierson, "The Early Thought of Tokutomi Sohō," *Monumenta Nipponica* 24 (Summer 1974): 199–224. Wada Mamoru, "Jiyūminken: Ūndō to Sohō," *Yamagatadaigaku Kiyō* 5, no. 2 (Yamagata: Yamagata Daigaku, February 1975): 99–126.
34. In the preface to *Shōrai no Nihon*, Tokutomi emphasized his belief in the inevitability of the peaceful, industrial society that he called *heimin shakai*. See Ueto Michiari, ed., *Meiji bungaku zenshū* 34 (Tokyo: Chikuma Shobō, 1974): 50.

35. Tokutomi's copy of *Democracy in America* is held in the City Library of Minamata, Kumamoto Prefecture, and his copy of part 5 of *Principles of Sociology* is held in the library of Shufu no Tomo Shuppan Sha in Tokyo. I have examined both of these copies. Both copies were read by young Tokutomi very minutely, and they are full of underlinings and insertions.
36. Pierson, "Early Thought," p. 215. Cf. Wada Mamoru, "Jiyūmin Ken," pp. 82–84.
37. See Tokutomi's earlier article "Jiyū dōtoku oyobi jukōshugi," *Meiji bungaku zenshū* 34:32–49 ff.
38. In *Principles of Sociology*, 2, part 5, "Political Institutions," Spencer explained his thesis of social evolution very clearly. Young Tokutomi read this book with enthusiasm.
39. *Shōrai no Nihon*, pp. 57–80.
40. Pyle, *New Generation*, pp. 172–73.
41. Pierson, "Early Thoughts," pp. 220–23.
42. Ivan Parker Hall, *Mori Arinori* (Cambridge, Mass.: Harvard University Press, 1973).
43. Kimura Kyō *Mori sensei den*, p. 62.
44. David Duncan, *The Life and Letters of Herbert Spencer* (London: Methuen & Co., 1908), p. 161.
45. For example, Spencer referred to the Japanese guild system, commenting, "As I learn from the Japanese minister, a kindred state of things once existed in Japan." See *Principles of Sociology* (New York: D. Appleton, 1900), 2:466.
46. Hall, *Mori Arinori*, pp. 290–91.
47. Quoted in Duncan, *Life and Letters*, p. 319.
48. I. P. Hall, "Introduction," *Mori Arinori zenshū*, ed. Ōkubo Toshiaki, (Tokyo: Senbundō Shoten, 1972), 3:30.
49. Hall, *Mori Arinori*, p. 301. Quoted from *The Pall Mall Gazette*, 26 February 1884, no pagination.
50. Ibid., p. 319.
51. Quoted from Kaneko's unpublished autobiography. National Diet Library, no pagination.
52. See Kaneko Kentarō, *Kenpō seitei to ōbeijin no hyōron*, (Tokyo: Keneko Hakushaku Koseki Kenshō Kai, 1938), pp. 1–176.
53. Ibid., pp. 252–54.
54. Duncan, *Life and Letters*, p. 319.
55. Ibid., pp. 319–21.
56. Ibid., pp. 321–23.
57. Ernest Fenollosa, "Shūkyō ron," *Geijutsu soshi* (1877), nos. 26–40, and "Seitai kaishin ron," *Gakugei shirin*, nos. 36, 37, 39 (1880), See Yamashita Shigekazu, "Fenollosa no Tokyo Daigaku kyōju jidai," *Kokugakuin hōgaku* 12 no. 4 (1975): 121–63.
58. A notebook written by Ichijima Kenkichi on Fenollosa's lectures on philosophy is in the Waseda University Library and several notebooks written by Sakatani Yoshirō on philosophy and political economy are in The National Diet Library. See Sugihara Shirō, "Fenollosa no Tōkyō, Daigaku kōgi," in *Kikan shakai shisō* 2 no. 4 (1972): 189–205, and my article on Fenollosa.
59. From Ichishima Kenkichi's notebook of Fenollosa's lectures on the history of philosophy.
60. From Sakatani Yoshirō's notebook.
61. Ibid.
62. See *Tōkyo: Daigaku nenpō* (1879–80), 1:257–58.
63. Sakatani Yoshirō's English language notebook on sociology includes the summary of Spencer's *Principles of Sociology*, vol. 1. This is from a lecture by Professor Toyama.
64. Takahashi, "Nihon ni," p. 428.
65. Kurihara Shin-ichi, *Fenollosa to Meiji bunka* (Tokyo: Rikugei Shobō, 1968), pp. 118–21.
66. See my article on Fenollosa, pp. 158–59.
67. Katō Hiroyuki Keirekidam, *Nihon no meicho* (Tokyo: Chūō Kōron Sha, 1970) 34:488. Cf. Matsumoto Sannosuke, "Katō Hiroyuki no tenkō," *Kindai Nihon no seiji to ningen* (Tokyo: Sobunsha, 1966), pp. 61–92.
68. Katō's copies of the German monthly *Kosmos* are now held in the Tokyo University Library. They include German translations of Spencer's *Sociology (Staatliche Einrichtungen)* with many underlinings and insertions by Katō.
69. Duncan, *Life and Letters*, Appendix B, pp. 553–76.

70. Ibid., p. 534.
71. Ibid., p. 537.
72. Ernest Barker, *Political Thought In England, 1848–1914* (London: Oxford University Press, 1947), pp. 72–73.
73. *Herbert Spencer on Social Evolution*, ed. J. D. Y. Peel (Chicago: The University of Chicago Press, 1972), pp. xi–xii.
74. Barker, *Political Thought*, p. 82.
75. *Social Statics*, p. 14.
76. Barker, *Political Thought*, p. 87.
77. *Social Statics*, p. 78.
78. Ibid., pp. 112 ff.
79. Ibid., p. 278.
80. Ibid., p. 333.
81. J. D. Y. Peel, *Herbert Spencer, the Evolution of a Sociologist*, (London: Heinemann, 1971), pp. 56–57.
82. *The Filiation of ideas*, p. 554.
83. "Social Organism," in *Essays*, 1:271–76.
84. Ibid., pp. 276–77.
85. *Principles of Sociology*, 1:461–62.
86. *The Filiation of Ideas*, p. 570.
87. T. H. Huxley, "Administrative Nihilism," *The Fortnightly Review* 16 (November 1, 1871): 535.
88. "Specialized Administration," *Essays*, 2:413.
89. Shimizu, *Nihon bunka*, pp. 64–65.
90. Sakamoto Naohiro's article in *Aikoku Shinchi* (March 15, 1881), *Sakamoto Naohiro chosaku shū*, 1:41.
91. Sakamoto's speech on May 13, 1882, ibid., 2:50–52.
92. Hagihara, *Baba Tatsui*, pp. 169–78.
93. J. W. Burrow, *Evolution and Society* (Cambridge, Mass.: Cambridge University Press, 1970), p. 187.
94. Duncan, *Life and Letters*, p. 41.
95. Herbert Spencer, *Man Versus the State* (New York: Appleton and Company, 1892), pp. 412–15.
96. Fenollosa, "Setai kaishinron," *Gakugei Shirin* 40, no. 34 (1880): 313–14.
97. Introductory "Shintaishi" (new-style poem) by Toyama Masakazu, preface to the Japanese translation of *Principles of Sociology* (Tokyo: Tokyo Keizaigaku Koshū-Kai, 1882), 1.
98. The influence of Western political thought on Japan. See Ishida Takeshi, ed., *Nihon ni okeru "Seiō seiji shisō"* in 1975 issue of *Nihon Seijigakukai nenpo*. (1976). In this volume, seven writers wrote about the influences of English, German, and French political thought on Japan, including the Japanese version of this article. See also Yamashita Shigekazu, "Meiji shoki ni okeru J. S. Mill no juyō," *Shisō* 594 (December 1973): 55–75.

4   Fukuzawa Yukichi and Women's Rights

Mikiso Hane

> The great foundation of human relations consists of husband and wife. The relationship between husband and wife emerged before that of parents and children or brothers and sisters. From the beginning of time when Heaven created human beings there has been an equal number of men and women. Many million years have passed but this ratio of one man to one woman has not changed. Whether a person is a man or a woman he or she counts for only one between Heaven and Earth. There is no justification for making distinctions of superior and inferior.[1]

These words were written in 1870 by Fukuzawa Yukichi (1835–1901) only three years after the Tokugawa regime was overthrown and a new order was established. Fukuzawa was the first influential advocate of women's rights in modern Japan and the most prominent and persistent champion of the movement to liberate Japanese women from the fetters of traditional ideas and practices. Nor was he the only advocate of women's rights among the early Meiji exponents of liberal reforms. Many of his friends in the Meirokusha, an association of men dedicated to the propagation of Western concepts and knowledge, shared his desire to improve the status of women. Among them was Mori Arinori (1847–89), who published several articles in the *Meiroku Journal* calling for equality between men and women and in particular attacking the practice of concubinage. When he married in 1875, he and his wife signed a marriage contract in which they pledged to love and respect each other, and consult each other on matters relating to property. Fukuzawa served as a witness upon this occasion.[2] Nakamura Masanao (1832–91), the translator of John Stuart Mill's *On Liberty* and Samuel Smiles's *Self Help*, also favored improving the lot of Japanese women. He was especially interested in furthering their education because the character and mode of thinking of children are molded by their mothers. "If we wish to see," he wrote, "mankind in general attain the highest and purest state possible, both men and women must be provided with the same king of training, and they must be made to move forward together."³ In accordance with his convictions, Nakamura devoted much of his life to the education of women.

Not all men of the Meirokusha circle agreed with the advocates of women's rights. Tsuda Mamichi (1829–1903), who was among the early advocates of Westernization, did not believe it was necessary to give equal legal or political rights to women, although he believed that there should not be any social discrimination. He pointed out that women did not possess such rights even in the West.⁴ Katō Hiroyuki (1836–1916), who was an advocate of liberal political reforms before he turned to conservatism and German statism, expressed his opposition to any move to change the status of women, and asserted that he did not wish to see Japanese men fawn over women as Western men did.⁵ Even younger liberals such as Ono Azusa (1852–86), a student of English Utilitarianism, though disapproving of the strong patriarchal system that prevailed in Japan, did not believe that husband and wife should have equal rights, for unless one led the other, there would be constant conflict in the family and eventually it would disintegrate.⁶

The primary concern of the Meiji liberals was political reforms; social reforms were placed, so to speak, on the back burner. By the 1880s the initial enthusiasm for Westernization abated somewhat and a period of political conservatism and cultural nationalism was beginning to set in. Many early Meiji liberals were caught up in this trend also. But the one person who remained loyal to liberal ideals was Fukuzawa, who fought for the improvement of women's plight throughout his life. In this sense he was a true pioneer in the feminist movement in Japan and was far in advance of most of his fellow countrymen. In fact, he was not very far behind Western liberals of his age. John Stuart Mill was among the early champions of women's rights in England, but he did not turn his attention to this problem until late in his life. He wrote *The Subjection of Women* in 1861, but did not publish it until 1869. Incidentally, this essay by Mill, like his other works, was imported into Japan and had a considerable influence on the Japanese feminist movement. It was used as the source for a book on women's rights in 1876 and, in 1878 it was translated into Japanese.⁷

Fukuzawa first broached the problem that was to vex him throughout his long crusade to improve the status of Japanese women, that is, the prevalence of polygamous practices in Japan, in his *Seiyō Jijō (Conditions in the West)*, which was published in 1866. This book consisted mainly of translations from Western works, but of course, he choose to translate those aspects which he believed would be illuminating for the Japanese and serve as examples that could be followed by them. Taking a passage from William and Robert Chamber's *Social Economy*, he wrote, "It is in accordance with the Way of Heaven that there should be one husband and one wife in the house. This constitutes what is called a family."⁸

In 1870 he submitted a statement to a friend in his hometown (from which the quotation at the head of this essay was taken) concerning human relations and criticized the practice of polygamy and the oppression of women. Then in 1874 he published chapter 8 of his *Gakumon no Susume (Encouragement of Learning)* and inveighed against the practice of the strong oppressing the weak. As a prime example of such abuses, he cited the domination of women by men in Japan. He wrote: "Men are human beings; so are women. . . . The only difference is that men are stronger than women. If a huge man fights with a woman naturally he will win. In the society at large if someone takes away another person's possessions or humiliates him by force, he is punished as a criminal. Why is it then that in the home, a person can openly humiliate another person and not be censured at all for his behavior?"[9]

He then proceeded to criticize Kaibara Ekken's (1630–1714) *Onna Daigaku (Great Learning for Women)*, whose teachings still governed the way of life of the Japanese woman. The entire thrust of Ekken's teachings was that women must subordinate themselves to men and be completely self-abnegating. Fukuzawa also criticized the Buddhist notion that women are born with an evil karma, that they are born sinners. These ideas, Fukuzawa contended, merely served the interests and convenience of men, and had been imposed on women because they were physically weaker than men. He then proceeded to attack the practice of concubinage as being contrary to the principle of Heaven; a practice fit for birds and beasts, not human beings.[10]

Gakumon no Susume covers a wide range of issues and does not place great stress on women's rights, but Fukuzawa produced a large number of books and articles that dealt specifically with this topic. His production of such works increased noticeably in the mid-1880s. Evidently he felt compelled to take up this issue with a greater sense of urgency because, after the initial wave of enthusiasm and interest in Western concepts, institutions, and practices subsided, a reaction had set in. There was now a revival of interest in traditional ways and values. Some progress had been made in the political arena (in 1881 the government had agreed to draft a constitution and convene a Diet in 1890) and, despite the rise of cultural nationalism, many of the ideals propagated by the advocates of "civilization and enlightenment" had penetrated the society. But the one area where hardly any progress had been made was in feminine rights. If traditional values were to become reentrenched, the Japanese woman would continue to be fettered by the oppressive values and practices that were epitomized in Ekken's *Onna Daigaku*. Perhaps for this and other reasons, Fukuzawa as well as others began to pay greater heed to this issue in the 1880s.[11]

In 1885 Fukuzawa published his *Nihon Fujinron (On Japanese Women)* and its sequel, as well as *Hinkōron (On Proper Conduct)*.[12] In the following year he published his *Danjyo Kōsairon (On the Association of Men and*

Women). This was followed in 1888 by *Nihon Danshiron (On Japanese Men)*. Then for about a decade he ceased publishing any major essays on the subject. He may have felt that he had made his point sufficiently. But his attention was also drawn more toward international affairs, especially Korean affairs, an area that he was greatly interested in. As Sino-Japanese relations became strained over their rivalry in Korea and eventually resulted in war, Fukuzawa's attention came to be devoted largely to this conflict. He was in fact extremely hawkish and chauvinistic and supported the war effort vigorously, going so far as to raise money for the war effort, and in the editorial pages of his newspaper advocated the imposition of tough peace terms on China.[13]

After the war ended and normalcy returned, Fukuzawa, in the last years of life, turned his thoughts again to the plight of women. In fact his last major writing efforts consisted of *Onna Daigaku Hyōron (A Critique of Onna Daigaku)* and *Shin Onna Daigaku (A New Onna Daigaku)*. The fact that this subject weighed heavily on his mind to the end of his life is indicated by his insistence on working on the manuscripts even though he had suffered a stroke soon after he had completed the drafts. The two books were published in 1899, two years before his death. He wrote numerous other essays on the topic, but those mentioned above were his major publications on the subject of women's rights.

In his *Nihon Fujinron* he described the restricted status of the Japanese women as follows: "At home she has no personal property, outside the home she has no status. The house she lives in belongs to the male members for the household, and the children she raises belong to her husband. She has no property, no rights and no children. It is as if she were a parasite in a male household."[14] This situation had to be rectified, he said, for the foundation of the family consists of the husband and the wife. There should be equality between the two, and love and respect, rather than domination of one by the other, should characterize their relationship. In order to signify the equality of relationship, he suggested that upon marriage a new family name be adopted by the couple by taking portions of their surnames. For example, if the husband's name is Yamahara and the wife's is Itō, they should take "yama" from the former and "tō" from the latter and adopt the name Santō.[15]

Another topic discussed in the *Nihon Fujinron*, and it was certainly a matter that disturbed the sensibilities of those Japanese who believed that women should never consider such matters, was the thesis that it was necessary to allow women to satisfy their passions and desires. Fukuzawa pointed out that in Japan men were allowed to have as many wives and concubines as they pleased. Moreover, they unabashedly frequented houses of prostitution, while women were expected to adhere strictly to the ideals of continence and chastity. If a woman was widowed, she was not permitted to remarry. In Japan, then, women's natural desires were smothered. This created all sorts of emotional and psychological problems, causing many women to fall into a state of neurosis. Just as the body needs food for its sustenance and well-being, Fukuzawa asserted, a person's sexual needs must be fulfilled in order for him/her to have an emotionally healthy and vigorous life.[16]

In the 1880s government officials were preparing a new civil code. In doing so, they must, Fukuzawa insisted, make certain that equality of women was provided for. Specifically, he asked that their property rights be guaranteed and that they be protected from the husbands' arbitrary right to divorce them at will.[17]

In the sequel to the *Nihon Fujinron*, Fukuzawa reiterated the need to maintain equality of husband and wife, but he added other points. One is struck by how far in advance of his time he was. For example, he called for equality of job opportunities for women. Women, he pointed out, were as capable as men in performing a given task, and they should be allowed to hold any job they wished. As he frequently did when he advocated specific reforms, he cited examples from the West. There, and in particular in the United States, all sorts of jobs were being opened to women.[18] He may have overestimated nineteenth-century America, but comparatively speaking, what Fukuzawa said was true.

In his work, Fukuzawa also criticized the Chinese practice of equating women with *yin* and men with *yang*. This notion was a fantasy dreamed up by the Confucians and had no basis in reality, Fukuzawa contended.[19] In fact, the Confucians were responsible for fostering "respect for men and contempt for women" *(danson jyohi)*. Confucianism, he argued, was a philosophy that taught proper conduct to the weak but not to the strong.[20] Ekken's *Onna Daigaku* was a crystallization of this philosophy which extended all sorts of rights and privileges to men but denied them to women. As a result, women came to be treated no better than dogs by their husbands, and came to be looked upon merely as devices to produce children. He bemoaned the fact that the arrogant attitude harbored by the samurai male had permeated through the entire society.[21]

In his *Hinkōron* Fukuzawa concentrated his attack on the licentious sexual behavior of the Japanese men. But, being a pragmatist, he did not believe that their mode of conduct could be transformed overnight. It would be, he remarked, like trying to force a lame person to run. But, he pleaded, if men were incapable of refraining from promiscuous conduct, they could at least be discreet about it instead of openly flaunting their profligacy. One aspect of civilization, he asserted, consisted in covering up whatever is vulgar and ugly. So Japanese men must keep their licentiousness hidden.[22] In a way his position on this matter may strike us as being somewhat hypocritical, but he was merely following an old Japanese adage, "If it smells, keep it covered." But one of the reasons he gave for asking the Japanese men to curb their profligacy makes us wonder if practical considerations rather than basic principles governed much of Fukuzawa's thinking on this matter. In admonishing Japanese men to refrain from licentious behavior, he constantly gave as an important consideration the opinion of Westerners. He contended that, unless the Japanese curbed or at least put a veil over their loose sexual conduct, Westerners would criticize, ridicule, and scorn them. He was appalled in particular by the fact that the leaders of Japan such as Prince Ito were patrons of the geisha. Such behavior by the nation's leaders, he asserted, was bringing shame to Japan.[23] One of the reasons that he consistently refused to serve in the government, Fukuzawa claimed, was because he did not wish to work with licentious government officials.[24] Upon occasion, then, he seemed more concerned about appearances and the opinion of the West than the moral issues involved. He was certainly not a moral crusader against legalized prostitution. Unless these outlets existed, he contended, sexual crimes would become widespread.[25]

Like a true nineteenth-century liberal, Fukuzawa was relatively unconcerned about the social conditions that bred prostitution. He tended to place the blame on the shoulders of those who had fallen into their miserable plights. Prostitutes, he argued, were the lowest of the low, and should be cast out of human society. But in Japan, Fukuzawa noted, such people were not held in total contempt as they deserved to be, but instead, were held up as paragons of filial piety for having sold themselves to the brothels to help their families. Such an attitude, he argued, encouraged other girls to follow the same path without any sense of shame. And some girls entered the brothels because of the idealistic and glamorous ways in which courtesans were depicted in old stories and plays. In order to correct this situation, Fukuzawa contended that girls and women who follow such a course should be defamed and ostracized. Men of the better classes must stay away from them.[26] Of course, he cannot be faulted for trying to keep members of the "gentleman" class away from the brothels, but in castigating the inmates of the brothels as if they had freely entered these houses and in condemning them as lowly outcasts, he neither displayed much sympathy or compassion toward them nor manifested much understanding of the socioeconomic conditions that pushed them into what in effect was a life of enslavement.

By and large, Fukuzawa remained more unsympathetic to the plight of the poor and the economically underprivileged than one might expect of a man of progress. He tended to place the blame on them rather than the society or the objective circumstances. In his *Gakumon no Susume* he condemns the poor for rioting and demonstrating because they had fallen into a state of poverty and near starvation because of their own ignorance. Instead of blaming themselves, they resent the rich and covet their wealth. He remarks "A poor person should realize the reason for his poverty and humble station in society; he should realize that the cause is to be found in himself."²⁷ Of course, he was aware that this was not strictly true and later he observed that the poor could argue back that ignorance is not the cause of poverty, but rather poverty is the cause of ignorance.²⁸ But Fukuzawa remained a firm adherent of laissez-faire philosophy and did not believe that the government should intervene to redress the imbalance in wealth between the rich and the poor. He professed to prefer "inequality of wealth to equality of poverty."²⁹ In explaining the principle of equality in his *Gakumon no Susume*, he remarks that he was advocating equality of rights, not equality in social or economic conditions.³⁰ So his harsh attitude toward prostitutes was not an aberration, but a natural product of his general social philosophy.

In his *Danjyo Kōsairon* Fukuzawa points out that Japanese men tended to regard the relationship between men and women mainly in terms of physical relations and ignored the emotional, psychological aspects. Consequently the husband neither loved nor respected his wife. When a rare couple did establish close emotional ties, the society, in particular, the in-laws, fought to quash such tendencies. So in Japan men were educated and conditioned to have little respect for their wives.³¹

Fukuzawa continued his discussion of the relationship between husband and wife in his *Nihon Danshiron* and emphasized the point that this relationship constituted the fountainhead of morality. There are, he asserted, two aspects of morality, private and public. The relationship between husband and wife belongs to the former and is founded upon feelings, while the latter is based upon logical principles. But public morality, he contended, cannot be perfected without upright private morality. He also related the acquisition of individual (legal) rights to the perfection of private morality. When private morality is perfected, individual rights will be fortified, and when individual rights are strengthened, public (political) rights will be secured, he maintained.³²

In linking the private and public aspects of morality in this way, Fukuzawa, despite his contention that he was an all-out opponent of Confucianism, was following the Chu Hsi mode of thinking, in which private morality (*shūshin saika*—cultivation of personal life and regulation of the family) and public morality—politics (*chikoku heitenka*—order in the state and peace in the world) were linked together.³³ His propensity for linking private and public aspects is seen in such statements as "loyal subjects emerge from [the ranks of] filial sons," "the foundation of the nation is rooted in the family," and "husband and wife constitute the foundation of the family. Hence the relationship between husband and wife constitute the foundation of the society and nation."³⁴

According to Fukuzawa, the traditional thinkers failed to differentiate clearly between the private and public sectors and tended to emphasize the latter at the expense of the former. This meant, he argued, the politicization of all aspects of life. The overpowering of the private sector by the public, we might justifiably conclude, contributed to the decline of private morality and the ascendancy of licentious and polygamous practices. Contrary to common belief, the prevalence of such behavior, Fukuzawa contended, indicated that the family system in Japan was not strong, but actually very weak.[35]

As we noted above, Fukuzawa did not devote much time to the question of women's rights for about a decade, but a few years before his death he turned his full attention to the problem again. In his *Onna Daigaku Hyōron* he made a point-by-point criticism of Ekken's teachings. The main thrust of his argument was that the rules of conduct laid down by Ekken for women were unfair and unnatural. If such rules were necessary for women, they were also necessary for men. It was unjust to make such stringent demands only of women. In fact, men misbehaved much more brazenly than did women, so there was a greater need to compose a code of conduct for men in order to regulate their behavior.[36] The *Onna Daigaku*, Fukuzawa asserted, was designed simply to serve the interests and convenience of men. It was based upon the notion that women were merely vassals or servants of men.[37] In his *Nihon Fujinron* he had written:

> If women were to follow the teachings [in the *Onna Daigaku*] they would be unable either to sleep and rise, or drink and eat as they pleased. They would not be able to see plays or listen to music, wear fancy clothes, or step outside the house or associate with anyone. Moreover, they can be divorced at the whim of their husbands. They may be considered a member of a household but they are as insecure as a person treading on thin ice or crossing a deep ravine. When they lift their heads and survey the world of men, they see them saturated with arrogance and pride as if they were their lord and master. All things within and without their homes are bent to their will.[38]

Although the *Onna Daigaku* was written for women of the samurai class during the Tokugawa period, women's plight had not really changed very much during the three decades that followed the end of Tokugawa rule. The ideal woman was still expected to follow the spirit and dicta of the *Onna Daigaku*. Shidzue Ishimoto (1897–) in her *Facing Two Ways* writes that among the three things left to her as legacies from her grandfather around the turn of the century was "a manuscript bound with a purple silk cord, bearing the title *On-na Daigaku*." And she writes, "I have watched my mother conduct herself all through her life in a literal following of what is written in this great book of morals."[39] Her mother's behavior was not untypical of middle- and upper-class women of the Meiji period. So Fukuzawa was not indulging in a futile act of beating a dead horse.

After having denounced Ekken's *Onna Daigaku*, Fukuzawa composed his own book, spelling out what he regarded to be the proper code of conduct for women. In it he emphasized the importance of maintaining equality between husband and wife. In conducting their affairs, there is to be a division of labor, with the husband's managing the affairs outside the household and the wife's managing domestic affairs. Although normally the wife is expected to behave in a gentle and docile manner, where matters of basic principles are concerned she is not to be blindly submissive, Fukuzawa insists, but she must be prepared to defy even her parents and husband.[40] He again urges that widows be allowed to remarry, and that wives and daughters be granted the right to own property independently. This would enable wives to be independent of their husbands should the latter begin to misbehave.[41]

Though enlightened for its time, Fukuzawa's *Shin Onna Daigaku* is still conservative and, in some ways, even traditionalist. Moreover, in light of some of the statements he had made earlier, he appears to be hedging or even backsliding somewhat. This may be explained partly by the fact that, when he first launched his campaign for women's rights, society had to be given a dramatic shaking up. That is, the "cake of custom" had petrified to such an extent that the only way to loosen it up would have been to use a sledgehammer. And this is what Fukuzawa and some of the early Meiji advocates of reforms initially did. They may have written and said things that were much more radical than they themselves would have been willing to accept in reality. By the time he wrote his *Onna Daigaku Hyōron* and *Shin Onna Daigaku*, he had been pleading the case for women's rights for three decades. Others had also joined the movement and some limited progress had been made. Nonetheless, politically women suffered a severe setback when in 1890 the government enacted a law prohibiting them from partaking in any political activity. They were prevented from organizing or sponsoring any political groups or meetings, and were enjoined from joining any political party. But the new civil code of 1898 did strengthen women's rights to some extent. It provided for monogamy; concubines were no longer accorded legal recognition as second-degree relatives of their patron's family.[42] Led by Christian reformers, the move to ban houses of prostitution, though unsuccessful, was becoming more active. Some women were beginning to join the small circle of socialists. Higher education for women, after suffering many setbacks, was beginning to make some headway. In 1899 the government issued an ordinance to establish higher schools for women. After the turn of the century a few women's colleges, including a medical college, came into existence.[43]

Perhaps it was for these reasons that Fukuzawa began to tone down his remarks about equality for women to some extent. Moreover, it appears that as soon as someone went one step beyond him toward radicalism in whatever area, Fukuzawa pulled back and started to urge moderation. For instance, although he was an early and vociferous advocate of popular rights, when the movement began to gain wider support and started to turn in a more radical direction, he commenced to counsel moderation.

Eventually he began to condemn the radicals as "vulgar advocates of popular rights."[44] Aside from his basically moderate temperament, he always seemed to avoid following the pack. It appears that by temperament he was an outsider and a streak of contrariness runs through his life.

In his *Shin Onna Daigaku,* then, there are strains of traditionalism. For example, although in developing physical fitness Fukuzawa maintained that there should not be any differentiations between men and women, in their comportment women should be polite, gentle, restrained, and courteous. They were not to speak up aggressively or vociferously or argue in a heated manner. They were to be mindful of preserving their refined and graceful qualities and abstain from using coarse or vulgar words.[45] He even went so far as to argue that they should not waste their time reading novels, plays, or poems because such works frequently aroused a person's passions, especially in young girls, who were most susceptible to sensual stimulation[46] Instead, they were to be encouraged to read practical books. His position on this matter, however, cannot be regarded simply as evidence that he was biased about feminine education. "In matters of learning," he wrote in the *Shin Onna Daigaku,* "there should be no difference between men and women. The first step in education must be the laying of the foundation by studying the physical sciences. Then one may proceed to various specialized areas." He acknowledged that women were unable to pursue learning so freely and extensively as men could because they were preoccupied with household affairs and the task of rearing their children. For the time being, he contended, the Japanese had to resign themselves to the fact that women's education would be more limited than men's.[47] As far as his emphasis on practical education for women is concerned, it was not out of tune with his general educational philosophy. He consistently took a negative stance toward what he considered "impractical" subjects among the arts and letters. In his *Gakumon no Susume* he wrote:

> The impractical custom of learning difficult words, reading abstruse old writings, composing and enjoying Chinese and Japanese poems, etc. is not learning. These literary activities are very useful in entertaining people but they do not deserve the honor and respect that scholars of Chinese classics and Japanese literature are wont to pay them.[48]

When a group of students at his school, Keiō Gijuku, printed a collection of poems, he got extremely upset and stopped its circulation immediately. "When physical science is still unpopular despite our efforts to arouse people's interest in it," he explained, "it would indeed be outlandish for our students to publish a collection of poems. When I heard of this matter I almost died of shame."[49]

Thus Fukuzawa favored practical education for both men and women.

But he did agree, perhaps again for practical reasons, that women need not pursue advanced learning. He noted that many educators were advocating the advancement of female education as a means to redress the inequality between the sexes, but it would be more effective, he contended, to focus on specific issues, such as the banning of polygamy rather than promoting higher education.[50]

Another strain of traditionalism that is discernible in Fukuzawa's *Shin Onna Daigaku* is his class consciousness. The book was clearly designed to serve as a guide for upper-class ladies. He condemned geishas and prostitutes as vulgar creatures unfit to sit beside well-bred ladies, but he advised ladies not to express overtly their contempt for them. Nonetheless, they must keep them at arm's length.[51]

The reason he spoke so harshly of geishas and prostitutes was, as we noted earlier, the fact that many prominent Meiji leaders were patrons of geishas. But his low regard for the lower classes was reinforced by the growing emphasis in Western scientific circles on heredity as a factor that determined one's character and ability. Fukuzawa was particularly impressed by the theories of Francis Galton (1822–1911), the founder of the science of eugenics. As a result, he began to insist upon the moral and intellectual superiority of the descendants of the samurai class over the commoners. In order to preserve their inherited superiority, members of the *shizoku*, Fukuzawa insisted, must abstain from marrying members of the common classes; he upbraided those who did so merely because they found some commoner girls physically attractive.[52] In choosing one's mate, he insisted that three factors—genealogy, health, and brains—had to be given special consideration. Because physical and moral characteristics are inherited, a prospective mate's family background must be checked through four to five generations, and the family's occupation, tradition, life-style, and intellectual qualities must be investigated, he claimed.[53] This is a far cry from his statement in *Gakumon no Susume:* "Heaven does not create a person and place him above or below anyone else, it is said. Thus at birth everyone is equal and there are no distinctions of high and low, noble and base."[54]

During the last years of his life, Fukuzawa seemed to be hedging somewhat about the equality of husband and wife in all phases of their lives. "Affairs outside the house," he wrote, "are not matters with which the wife is intimately involved. And there are differences in ability and intelligence among women. So I am not necessarily arguing that the husband and wife should work together in all things." The only point he wanted to make, he explained, was the need for the husband to keep his wife informed.[55] And now he began to assert that the status of Japanese women was not so bad as it appeared on the surface. Although superficially it may seem that "respect for men and contempt for women" was prevalent in Japan, this was not an accurate picture of what obtained behind the scenes, he asserted. In fact, the wife exercised a great deal of authority in the family. She controlled much of the household affairs, and her authority over the children was very strong. He then criticized the advocates of women's rights for making immoderate demands.[56]

Even when he was championing the cause of women vociferously, Fukuzawa did not advocate granting suffrage to them. He favored, he said, equality but not equal political rights. Again practical considerations may have been the underlying reason for his position on this question. When he began espousing women's rights, no one had the franchise, and when the Diet was established in 1890, only a small number of male property holders were given the franchise. Being a realist, Fukuzawa no doubt concluded that universal suffrage could not be introduced in Japan in one fell swoop. But his tardiness in espousing universal suffrage does not bespeak well of him, because others, such Ueki Emori (1857–92) and an early feminist leader, Kusunose Kita (1836–1920), began calling for female suffrage as early as the 1870s.[57]

Despite these mild signs of tergiversation, Fukuzawa continued to believe in the basic principle of equality between the sexes. Among the many liberal causes that he championed from the early Meiji years, women's rights remained a matter of major concern for him. Over the years he consistently inveighed against male profligacy, concubinage, tyrannical husbands, suppression of women's emotional needs, and championed the right of women to be treated with respect and dignity, to remarry, to own property, to step ouside the house and have an independent social and professional life. Looking back from today, one sees limitations in his thinking on these matters, but he was far in advance of his nineteenth-century Japanese contemporaries. Even compared to his Western contemporaries, he emerges as a truly progressive thinker on this question.

One may wonder how well Fukuzawa lived up to these ideals himself. Nineteenth-century Japan was full of theoretical liberals who, in their personal lives, behaved as despotically and tyrannically as their feudal forebears. According to Fukuzawa's own account, he treated members of his family, regardless of age or sex, with love and respect. An air of informality prevailed in his family. "Perhaps to the men of the old school," he wrote in his autobiography, "my family appears lacking in the proper etiquette between young and old, high and low."[58] Certainly he did not follow the licentious life-style of many of his contemporaries and remained faithful to his wife.

Ironically his children were not brought up in as liberal a manner as might be expected from this. This may have been consequence of his conviction that the wife should have full responsibility in managing the affairs of the house. He appears to have left the education of his daughters in the hands of his wife, who was very conservative and believed in maintaining the traditional distinctions between the sexes. One of his daughters recalled being brought up in the traditional manner in which women were taught to know their place in relation to men. She was not allowed to have any voice in her marriage, which was arranged for her by her parents when she was eighteen.[59]

In his *Danjyo Kōsairon,* Fukuzawa held that parents should not force their daughters to marry against their will, and bemoaned the fact that because young men and women were not allowed to associate with each other and become acquainted, they were unable to make any judgments about choosing their mates. So, in fact, they had little to say about their marriages.[60] But later he came to assert that Japanese parents usually did not compel their daughters to marry against their will. Although they took the initiative in finding mates for their children, the marriage was arranged only with their consent. Foreigners who say that Japanese marriages are arranged according to the wishes of the parents are mistaken, he claimed. They arrive at such erroneous conclusions because they see only the surface of things.[61] Either Fukuzawa was not very observant or he was engaging in the same kind of sophism that the upholders of traditionalism were using in insisting that Japanese women were in fact free and equal.[62] He was, as we have seen, aware of the fact that social conventions precluded the possibility of young people's getting acquainted with members of the opposite sex so they were not prepared to make their own decisions. He knew that they had only a limited choice in the matter even if they were consulted. Undoubtedly, if his daughters had rejected his and his wife's choice, he would have respected their wishes.

Why, it may be asked, was Fukuzawa more progressive than his contemporaries on the question of feminine rights? What led him to become an early and ardent advocate of equality of the sexes? No doubt the answer lies in the complex of factors that went into the formation of his mind and personality. But one of the most influential factors must have been his mother. Fukuzawa's father died when he was only a year and a half. Consequently, he knew only one parent. There were five children in the Fukuzawa family, two boys and three girls. His brother was the eldest and he was the youngest of the siblings. Although there is insufficient evidence in his autobiography to draw a full portrait of his mother, what evidence there is gives us reason to believe that she was a remarkable person. She had the burden of raising five children and managing the household with a small stipend that the family received from Nakatsu-han, a feudal domain in Kyushu. Watching her run the household and raise the children single-handedly must have fostered in Fukuzawa a deep-rooted conviction that women were as strong and capable as men in managing the affairs of life.

Difficulties and hardships confronted the family, but the atmosphere at home, Fukuzawa claimed, was relaxed and warm. He could not recall, he wrote in his autobiography, witnessing any quarrels or conflicts in the family. His mother was not strict and left the children relatively free of supervision. But a sense of honor and rectitude prevailed in the household. His mother associated freely with members of the lower classes, including beggars and outcasts. She used to clean the lice-ridden hair of a local beggarwoman periodically. She was also unorthodox in other respects. For instance, she declined to go to the Buddhist temple to pray like other women of her community because, she said, she felt silly doing so. On the other hand, she never neglected the task of taking care of the family grave.[63]

When Fukuzawa was twenty-one, his brother died and he had to return from Osaka, where he had gone to study, to his home in Nakatsu. But he was unable to abandon his plan to continue his studies in Osaka. When he asked his mother's permission to do so, she readily agreed to let him go despite the fact that everything of worth in the house had to be sold to pay his way back to Osaka and she was left to live alone in Nakatsu with a tiny grandchild.[64]

Fukuzawa's ability to empathize with women must have been strengthened further by the fact that the Fukuzawa household, when he was growing up, was predominantly feminine. He had three older sisters, and he, being the baby of the family, was undoubtedly pampered and spoiled with affection by the others. There seems to have been nothing in his family environment to foster the kind of masculine arrogance that prevailed in most Japanese families.

Another factor that might explain his unorthodox stand on women as well as on other important issues of his age was the fact that he was by nature and upbringing a maverick, an outsider. This aspect of his personality may also have been molded by the circumstances of his family and early childhood. His father was a financial officer of the Nakatsu-han and had been stationed in Osaka. All the Fukuzawa children were born and raised there. When his father died, the family returned to Nakatsu, but the children felt like outsiders and were unable to meld into the Nakatsu social milieu because they spoke and behaved like Osaka-ites. This not only drew the family members closer together but gave them a sense of being estranged from the community.[65] Fukuzawa's sense of estrangement may have been reinforced by the fact that he had to engage in activities that were regarded as unbecoming to members of the samurai class. Since the family stipend was meager, he did handicraft work—making and repairing things—to supplement the family income. Moreover, because his family belonged to the lower ranks of the samurai hierarchy, he was subjected to the inconveniences and humiliations that low-ranking samurai families had to endure. He wrote in his autobiography:

> The thing that made me most unhappy in Nakatsu was the restriction of rank and position. Not only on official occasions, but in private intercourse, and even among children, the distinctions between high and low were clearly defined. Children of lower samurai families like

ours were obliged to use a respectful manner of address in speaking to children of high samurai families, while these children invariably used an arrogant form of address to us.[66]

These circumstances no doubt sharpened Fukuzawa's ability to look at the existing order of things with critical eyes as only an outsider is capable of doing.[67]

That Fukuzawa was able to turn away rather readily from traditional values and attitudes may have also been influenced by the fact that his early education was neglected somewhat because his father was not present and his mother was too busy to oversee his education closely. As a result he did not get down to studying seriously until he was thirteen or fourteen. This meant that he was not conditioned to accept blindly and uncritically established beliefs and concepts like other youngsters, who had traditional ideas pounded into their heads from early childhood. By the time Fukuzawa began to study Confucianism earnestly, he was old enough to make critical judgments about what he was studying.

Also there was a Confucian scholar who had influenced traditional learning in Nakatsu, Hoashi Banri (1778–1852). Banri was regarded as one of the top three scholars of his age and was known for the breadth of his learning. Unlike many Confucian scholars of his age, he was not a narrow moralist, but was interested in practical subjects such as mathematics, natural sciences, and economics. Moreover, the teacher under whom Fukuzawa studied as a youth was Shiraishi Tsuneto (1815–83), also an independent-minded scholar. So well before Fukuzawa turned to Western learning, his thinking was inclining toward pragmatism, rationalism, and scepticism.

It would be difficult to assess the impact Fukuzawa had in improving the lot of Japanese women. But in light of the fact that very little progress was made in the Meiji period—or for that matter until the end of World War II—the practical results were probably relatively insignificant.[68] But he did play a major role in thinking about the problem and getting some involved in the feminist movement. Women interested in improving their status were aware of and appreciated what Fukuzawa had done for their cause. Upon his death in 1901 one woman asserted that she had worshiped him more than any deity because of what he had done to improve the status of women.[69]

Notes

1. *Fukuzawa Yukichi Senshū*, ed. Fukuzawa Yukichi Chosaku Hensankai, 8 vols. (Tōkyō, 1951–52), 5:320.
2. Ota Masataka, *Chōnin Yukichi* (Tōkyō, 1927), pp. 261–62 and *Meiji Bunka Zenshū*, ed. Yoshino Sakuzo, 24 vols. (Tōkyō, 1927–30), 17:93, 110, 127, 153, 184.

3. *Meiji Bunka Zenshū*, 18:212.
4. Ibid., pp. 226–27.
5. Ibid., pp. 202–3.
6. *Ono Azusa Zenshū*, ed. Nishimura Shinji, 2 vols. (Tōkyō, 1936), 1:62–66.
7. Shidzue Ishimoto, *Facing Two Ways* (New York, 1935), p. 360; Kada Tetsuji, *Meiji Shoki Shakaikeizai Shisōshi* (Tōkyō, 1937), p. 912.
8. *Fukuzawa Yukichi Senshū*, 5:378.
9. Ibid., 1:151.
10. Ibid., p. 152.
11. Among the works on women's rights published in this period, aside from Fukuzawa's, were Dohi Koho, *Great Civilized Learning for Women* (1876), Yumoto Hokichi, *Women's Rights in the Western Countries* (1882), Fukama Naiki, *On Mill's Equality* (translation of Mill's *Subjection of Women*, 1884), Inoue Nao, *Japanese Women* (1886), Tatsumi Kojiro, *History of Women's Rights in the West and in Japan* (1887), Yoda Ko, *Monogamy* (1887), and Nakayama Seiu, *Japanese Women of Tomorrow* (1888). See Ishimoto, *Facing Two Ways*, p. 360.
12. These and many others of Fukuzawa's works first appeared as series of articles in his newspaper, the *Jiji Shinpō*.
13. *Zoku Fukuzawa Zenshū*, ed. Jiji Shinpōsha, 7 vols. (Tōkyō, 1932), 6: 453, 526–27. See Erwin Baelz, *Awakening Japan* (New York, 1932), pp. 104–5.
14. *Fukuzawa Yukichi Senshū*, 5:10.
15. Ibid., p. 29.
16. Ibid., pp. 16–23.
17. Ibid., p. 31.
18. Ibid., p. 44.
19. Ibid., p. 45.
20. Ibid., pp. 92–93.
21. Ibid., pp. 52–54, 57–58, 61, 76.
22. Ibid., p. 111. In his *Nihon Danshiron* he asserted that Western men misbehaved too, but they try to hide their misconduct because they would be censured by others. Ibid., p. 175.
23. Ibid., pp. 85, 89, 209, 219.
24. Yukichi Fukuzawa, *Autobiography*, tr. Eiichi Kiyooka (New York, 1966), p. 310. Prince Ito was renown as a patron of geishas and came to be known as the *kōshoku kōshaku*, "the lascivious Marquis." *Nihon no Hyakunen*, ed. Tsurumi Shunsuke, et al., 10 vols. (Tōkyō, 1961–64), 7:244.
25. *Fukuzawa Yukichi Senshū*, 5:109.
26. Ibid., 119–20, 126.
27. Ibid., pp. 188, 192.
28. *Fukuzawa Zenshū*, ed. by Jiji Shinpōsha, 10 vols. (Tōkyō, 1925–26), 10:165–66.
29. *Zoku Fukuzawa Zenshū*, 1:438.
30. *Fukuzawa Yukichi Senshū*, 1:97.
31. Ibid., pp. 148, 150.
32. Ibid., pp. 169–70, 182–83.
33. He drew a closer analogy when he asserted, "When an individual gains his independence, the family becomes independent. When the family gains its independence, the nation becomes independent. When the nation becomes independent the world becomes independent." Ibid., pp. 319–20.
34. Ibid., pp. 169–71. It would appear that in stressing the importance of the husband-wife relationship as the cornerstone of the family, Fukuzawa was challenging a stronger tradition than he could have suspected. According to a contemporary (1970) study of Japanese society, "Most Japanese wives adopt the role of mother rather than wife to their husbands; this is the traditional pattern, little affected by post-war change. The core of the Japanese family, ancient and modern, is the parent-child relationship, not that between husband and wife." Chie Nakane, *Japanese Society* (Berkeley, Calif., 1970), p. 128.
35. *Fukuzawa Yukichi Senshū*, 5:188.
36. Ibid., pp. 242, 249.
37. Ibid., pp. 252, 276.
38. Ibid., pp. 48–49.
39. Ishimoto, *Facing Two Ways*, pp. 38, 278. Shiduze Ishimoto divorced Baron Ishimoto

and married Katō Kanjū, a prominent labor and socialist leader. She became one of the first women to win a seat in the Diet, in 1946, and is currently a member of the House of Councilors.

40. *Fukuzawa Yukichi Senshū*, 5:308.
41. Ibid., p. 313.
42. See Ronald P. Dore, *City Life in Japan* (Berkeley, Calif., 1958), p. 160.
43. Karazawa Tomitarō, *Meiji Hyakunen no Kyōiku* (Tōkyō, 1968), p. 100.
44. *Fukuzawa Zenshū*, 5:271.
45. *Fukuzawa Yukichi Senshū*, 5:292–93, 305.
46. Ibid., p. 307.
47. Ibid., pp. 291–92.
48. Ibid., 1:88.
49. *Zoku Fukuzawa Zenshū*, 6:151.
50. *Fukuzawa Yukichi Senshū*, 7:79.
51. Ibid., 5:307–8.
52. *Fukuzawa Zenshū*, 5:403–9.
53. *Fukuzawa Yukichi Senshū*, 7:48–49.
54. Ibid., 1:87.
55. Ibid., 7:54–55.
56. Ibid., p. 82. Fukuzawa's attitude in this regard was not out of step with other progressive thinkers of his time. At the turn of the century Nitobe Inazo, a leading Christian educator and an exponent of Westernism, criticized an American advocate of women's rights for saying, "May all the daughters of Japan rise in revolt against ancient customs." He wrote, "Can such a revolt succeed? Will it improve the female status? Will the rights they gain by such a summary process repay the loss of that sweetness of disposition, that gentleness of manner, which are their present heritage?" Inazo Nitobe, *Bushido, the Soul of Japan* (Tokyo, 1904), p. 137.
57. Tanaka Sumiko, *Jyosei kaihō no shisō to kōdō (Thought and Action in Women's Liberation)* (Tōkyō: Jiji-tūshin-sha, 1975), pp. 49 ff.
58. *Autobiography*, p. 320.
59. Carmen Blacker, *The Japanese Enlightenment* (New York, 1964), pp. 157–58, note 44.
60. *Fukuzawa Yukichi Senshū*, 5:147–48.
61. Ibid., p. 295.
62. Shidzue Ishimoto, in writing about the marital arrangements of her clasmates at the Peeresses' School at the end of the Meiji era, noted that "these marriages and engagements were arranged by their families regardless of the girls' individual interests." "Marriage for the Japanese girl meant losing individual freedom." Ishimoto, *Facing Two Ways*, p. 79.
63. *Fukuzawa Yukichi Senshū*, 6:8, 17–19 and *Autobiography*, pp. 14–15.
64. *Fukuzawa Yukichi Senshū*, 6:46 ff and *Autobiography*, p. 43 ff.
65. *Fukuzawa Yukichi Senshū*, 6:5–6 and *Autobiography*, p. 2.
66. *Autobiography*, p. 18.
67. Fukuzawa cherished his status as an outsider and after the Meiji Restoration deliberately stayed out of government service of any kind. He criticized other scholars of Western learning for "abandoning their independence" by taking government posts or by teaching in government-operated schools. See *Fukuzawa Zenshū*, 8:96–97, and *Fukuzawa Yukichi Senshū*, 1:115 ff. He shunned any action that would link him with the established authorities and even refused to accept the degree of *hakase* (doctor of letters) when the government indicated its plan to grant him the degree. Ishikawa Kanmei, *Fukuzawa Yukichi-den*, 4 vols. (Tōkyō, 1932), 1:575–78.
68. Writing about the early twentieth century, Shiduze Ishimoto said, "In spite of the tide of liberalism that had been breaking over Japan with the new social order, influencing literature, men's education and other aspects of culture, women's world remained true to the conception which survived from the feudal age. 'A good wife' and 'a good mother'! How well these words sound! Indeed, there could seem to be no objection to them in any society or age. But when we peel off the skin from this perfect fruit of feudalism, we expose the bondage to husbands and subjection to the tyranny of the family system as a whole." Ishimoto, *Facing Two Ways*, pp. 77–78.
69. Asataro Miyamori, *A Life of Mr. Fukuzawa* (Tōkyō, 1902), p. 139.

5 The French Connection: Emile Guimet's Mission to Japan, A Cultural Context for *Japonisme*

Ellen P. Conant

France has always been adroit at utilizing its cultural attainments to advance its strategic interests. Thus the French government expeditiously sought to channel mounting preoccupation with all aspects of Oriental civilization by convening in Paris in 1873 the First International Congress of Orientalists. The precedence accorded Japan at this congress was indicative of French determination to strengthen their relations with the Japanese by fostering cultural ties whose full significance has yet to be probed. One such venture sanctioned by the French government as an aftermath of the congress was a scientific mission to study the religions of India, China, and Japan, undertaken by a Lyonnaise industrialist, Emile Guimet (1836–1918). The Japanese segment of this mission discloses the activities of a number of French and Japanese officials and students whose role and influence upon each other's culture merit study.

The reciprocal nature of these influences has not been dealt with adequately in either the literature on *Japonisme* or on Japanese art of the corresponding period. Whether by intent or default, Western scholars of *Japonisme* have focused on stylistic issues with scant regard for the cultural context. At the conclusion of a comprehensive review of five recent publications on *Japonisme*, Henry Adams notes that "it is remarkable how many directions of inquiry remain to be pursued and how many basic questions remain unanswered and even unasked."[1] The questions most relevant to this study are: "To what degree was *Japonisme* brought about by social and political circumstances? How was it connected with the evolution of imperialism and with the growth of a network of international trade?"[2] Similar issues are skillfully dealt with by Linda Nochlin in her article, "The Imaginary Orient,"[3] concerning the related art of French Orientalist painting. She contends that this art "cannot be confronted without a critical analysis of the particular power structure in which these works came into being."[4] Moreover, she raises methodological issues that are just as apropos the study of *Japonisme* in all its ramifications, as well as one of its major sources, Japanese art of the *bakumatsu* and Meiji periods (1854–1912).

I

France did not become active in the Far East until the 1830s, by which time England already had vital political and economic interests in this region. During the following decade, French naval officers, diplomats, missionaries, and merchants tried to establish commercial ties and to extend France's influence and prestige in this area, but their repeated efforts to establish relations with Japan were steadfastly rebuffed. Distracted during the period from 1848 to 1854 by her own political upheaval, France did not turn her attention to the East again until after the opening of Japan by Perry and the outbreak of the Crimean War. Baron Gros succeeded in signing a treaty with the Japanese on October 9, 1858. The French sought from the outset "to demonstrate to Japan the superiority of French culture" while "acquiring trade advantages for the future," and soon convinced the *bakufu* that "France is one of the most influential nations in Europe."[5]

The first French envoy, Duchesne de Bellecort, arrived in Japan on September 6, 1859. According to Haga Tōru,[6] he lacked the resiliency and astuteness of his British counterpart, Sir Rutherford Alcock. Bellecourt pursued a policy of close cooperation with the British consonant with the cordial relations that existed between them during the first decade of Napoleon III's reign. There was some rivalry over trade but it did not amount to much. French wines, liquors, perfumes, and jewelry were subject to stiff tariffs, and her silk, luxury wares, and other goods did not meet Japanese taste or needs. Bellecourt managed to secure some reduction in tariffs, but by the time he was recalled in 1864, France controlled a bare 3 percent of Japanese foreign trade, most of it transported in British ships, as contrasted with England's share of over 80 percent.[7] Despite this trade imbalance, France was determined to establish closer relations with Japan.

France's primary preoccupation, according to Meron Medzini, was the maintenance and extension of her national prestige. She could not stand by while England expanded its influence worldwide and became the major power in the Far East. Thus she had no alternative but to follow British leadership, while seeking to conceal it. Although so often bellicose, France was determined to avoid the use of force since England was certain to be the beneficiary. She therefore assumed the role of mediator, a not incompatible one for a nation that was favorably disposed toward the Japanese. Baron Gros considered them "une race supériere," and they were often referred to as "the French of the East."[8]

France's policy toward Japan became increasingly independent of England about 1863 because of her vital interest in the Japanese silk trade.[9]

France and Italy were the only nations in Europe then engaged in all phases of silk production. During the 1850s half a million French workers were employed in this industry, which was centered in the departments of Rhône, Isère and Drôme, whose prefectural seats were Lyons, Grenoble, and Valance, with Marseilles as their principal port. Both silk production and exports were increasing rapidly when the industry sustained two severe blows in 1861. The American Civil War drastically curtailed exports to the Southern states and the silkworms were decimated by two dread diseases. The Lyons Chamber of Commerce asked the Foreign Minister, Drouyn de Lhuys, honorary president of the Société Impériale d'Acclimatation, to help them obtain samples of a strain of Japanese silkworm that nourished on oak leaves. When experiments with the *bombyx yamamai* silkworms selected by a French merchant in Yokohama, Louis Bourret, proved them able to acclimatize, Japan suddenly became of utmost importance to France.[10] By December 1861 there were six French firms and many independent merchants in Yokohama engaged in the silk trade.[11] The sudden demand for silkworms and cocoons sent prices soaring and led the Japanese to restrict their export lest it disrupt domestic markets. As soon as it became apparent that Japanese silkworms could revive their industry, the silk lobby began to pressure the foreign minister to secure them a sufficient supply of both silkworms and silk.

The silk industry was fortunate in the appointment of the new envoy to Japan, Léon Roches (1809–90), a military officer and career diplomat who had served in North Africa for thirty-two years.[12] He was born in Grenoble, maintained close ties with his native region, and was sympathetic to the plight of his friends in sericulture in Grenoble and Lyons. Roches was not wealthy, educated, and well-born, as were many French diplomats, but he was experienced and "determined to win for his Emperor leadership over British diplomacy in Asia."[13] He had the full confidence of Drouyn des Lhuys, who allowed him considerable latitude in determining French policy toward Japan. Roches was responsible for making unswerving support of the *bakufu* the keystone of French policy at a time when the British, particularly after the arrival of Sir Harry Parkes, nominally accorded the shogunate such recognition while simultaneously seeking relations with Satsuma, Chōshū and other feudatories. Roches' policy eventually proved his undoing, but it brought him immediate success. His determination to expand France's trade with Japan was also extremely effective in the short run.

Roches proceeded to accomplish a series of stunning coups. He had been in Japan barely a year when he persuaded the shogunate to build a foundry and dockyard at Yokohama and an arsenal at Yokosuka. The Japanese agreed to engage a naval engineer from Toulon, Francois Léonce Verny, to head the project. An additional forty French administrators and technicians were recruited to supervise and train some two thousand Japanese supervisors and construction workers. Roches obtained permission to establish a school in Yokohama in February 1865, headed by Mermet de Cachon, that enrolled forty-seven Japanese to study French and other subjects, ostensibly so they could serve as interpreters. The *bakufu* empowered his attorney, Paul Fleury-Hérard, to purchase equipment for a mint and to hire the necessary personnel. Roches was also asked to help secure arms and supplies for their expedition against Chōshū[13] and the services of French officers to train the Japanese military. In the course of these negotiations, Roches elicited their agreement to participate in the Paris Exposition of 1867.

Roches proposed to have the *bakufu* pay for these costly enterprises by their establishing a monopoly that would channel all of Japanese silk exports to France. The funding was handled by a French company established by Roches' friends and headed by Fleury-Hérard, who was appointed Special Consul General of Japan. In return for his moderating the terms of indemnity imposed under the Shimonoseki Convention, the shogunate agreed in the fall of 1864 to lift the restrictions on the sale of silk. Roches then obtained their consent to purchase twelve thousand cartons of silkworm eggs of superior strain selected by a M. Berlandier, a French expert who was then in Japan. Through additional purchases and a "gift of fifteen thousand cartons of silkworms of the highest quality" to Napoleon III,[14] Roches assured his friends of an adequate supply of silkworm eggs and cocoons needed to restore France's faltering sericulture. The largest steamship company in France, Messageries Impériales, extended their Marseilles-Shanghai route to Yokohama in the summer of 1865 to handle the burgeoning silk trade, thereby freeing French merchants from relying upon British firms and carriers and channeling a greater portion of silk exports directly to Marseilles. The vigorous objections of other powers forced the cancellation of this monopolistic scheme, but Roches nonetheless had enabled France by 1866 to cope with the silk crisis. He also secured a further reduction in tariffs and an increased share of trade with Japan.

When the Marquis de Moustier became Foreign Minister in the fall of 1866, he queried Roches' policies and advocated, because of the recent fiasco in Mexico and mounting strains with Prussia, a more cautious policy. He counseled Roches to establish relations with the southern *han* as a hedge against the possible defeat of the *bakufu*, but Roches remained confident to the very end that the shogunate would survive. Following the Meiji restoration, he thought it best to withdraw but remained at his post until the arrival of his successor, Maxime Outrey, on June 7, 1868. After his return to France, Roches retired and settled in Tain, near Grenoble. His policies may have failed, but his projects had established a strong French presence in Japan that was not repudiated by the Meiji government.

To Outrey fell the task of renegotiating Roches' ventures with the new authorities.¹⁵ Work on the Yokohama and Yokosuka projects was delayed until funds were secured to settle the outstanding debt and new contracts could be signed with Verny and other French personnel. When the Yokosuka arsenal and docks were completed in 1871, they were placed, along with part of the Yokohama foundry, under the authority of the Navy Ministry, as were the remaining fifty French employees. The first vessel was launched in 1875 and the following year Verny left after having built a major naval base for the Japanese. The French military mission of sixteen officers and enlisted men under the command of Capt. Charles Chanoine came to Japan in January 1867 under a three-year contract to train the *bakufu* troops. Too little had been accomplished to affect the outcome of the restoration, during which they remained neutral. Outrey acquiesced to the partial cancellation of their contract and their return to France early in 1869, but he attached Captain Chanoine and Lt. Albert Charles Du Bousquet to the French Legation in Tokyo. The Meiji government reversed itself in 1870 and adopted the British model for the navy and the French for the army. From 1872 until the end of the 1880s, French officers trained the cavalry, artillery, and infantry and taught callisthenics and music. Until their arrival, Du Bousquet also served as advisor to the Military Affairs Ministry; from 1871 until his death in 1882, he also served as interpreter, translator, and consultant, first to the Council of State and then to the Genrōin, Senate.¹⁶ Thus even the projects that were aborted proved to be of lasting influence.

Because of the close ties that had developed between Japan and the silk industry of Lyons, Itō Hirobumi and Shibusawa Eiichi asked Du Bouquet to help them locate a spinning expert. He recommended Paul Brunat,¹⁷ who had been employed since his youth in the silk industry. He had been sent by a wholesale dealer of Lyons to work for a French merchant in Yokohama who was their agent. In 1870 Brunat signed a three-year contract and drew the plans for a new spinning mill at Tomioka that was built by Edward Auguste Bastien, an assistant of Verny at Yokosuke. Brunat went to Lyons in 1871 to purchase machinery and returned in February 1872 with three engineers and four spinners. The plant was operating by early 1873, and the silk thread spun there won a prize at the Vienna Exposition. This in turn may have led to the employment of C. de Boinville, the first Frenchman to be engaged as an architect, who came to Japan in 1872. Nothing is known of his background and training or his activities in Japan other than that he utilized the design of T. J. Waters to build the Printing Office, completed in 1876; he both designed and built the Technological College Auditorium, completed in 1877; and designed and built, with the assistance of an Italian architect, Giovanni Vincenzo Cappelletti, the Foreign Office, completed in 1881.¹⁸ Similarly, military ties undoubtedly account for the presence of a French artist by the name of Abel Guerinau, of whom likewise nothing is known other than that he was employed by the Military Affairs Ministry in 1874 to help Kawakami Tōgai organize and teach a special course in drawing and painting for the personnel of the Officers' Training School.[19]

Exposure to French philosophical and legal principles led talented young Japanese, such as Mizukuri Rinshō, who had accompanied the Japanese delegation to the Paris Exposition of 1867, to recommend that the Meiji government engage French legal experts to revise the Japanese legal codes and judicial institutions. The first law instructor hired by the Ministry of Justice was George Bousquet, who taught from 1872 to 1876 and thereafter published some interesting accounts of his stay in Japan.[20] In 1873 Emile Gustave Boissonade de Fontarabie, the former vice-rector of the University of Paris, was engaged to revise the civil and penal codes. Despite his independent nature and violatile temperament, he remained adviser to the Justice Ministry until 1895. He laid the foundations of legal education and the judicial system, initiated the abolition of torture in Japan, and propagated the French school of law.[21]

Of the approximately two hundred technical and language teachers employed by the Japanese during the *bakumatsu*, "More than eighty were French, more than sixty were Dutch, about thirty were British, and Americans and Germans constituted the remainder."[22] The dominant role of Great Britain, following the Meiji restoration, is reflected in the ranks of *oyatoi*, government foreign employees. The number had risen by 1872 to 213, of which 119 were British, 49 French, 16 American, 8 German, and 21 of other nationalities.[23] By 1874 their numbers peaked at 503, with a similar ratio of 269 British to 108 French.[24] The French government was keenly aware that its failure to anticipate the restoration and its defeat in the Franco-Prussian War had diminished its prestige and influence in Japan, and the French therefore were determined to refurbish their image and bolster their relations with the Meiji government. It was to these ends that they convened the First International Congress of Orientalist.

II

The moving force behind the first International Congress of Orientalists was the pioneer scholar of Japanese studies in Europe, Léon de Rosny (1837–1914),[25] who achieved this capstone of his career with the aid of his former pupils. He entered the Ecole des langues orientales vivantes in 1852, majored in Chinese under Stanislaus Julien, and taught himself Japanese with the aid of Abel Remusat's *Elemens de la Grammaire japonaise*, published in 1825.[26] He was attached to the first Japanese mission to Europe in 1862, astonishing them by his ability to speak and read Japanese. In the course of accompanying them to England, Holland, Germany, and

The French Connection: Emile Guimet's Mission to Japan

Russia, he became acquainted with these officials and their interpreters, particularly Fukuzawa Yukichi, Fukuchi Gen'ichirō, Kurimoto Jōun and Narushima Ryūboku. While serving as a commissioner of the Paris Exposition of 1867, he also assisted the large Japanese delegation headed by the younger brother of the shogun that came to celebrate their nation's first participation in an international exposition.

De Rosny began to teach Japanese in 1863 and to publish prolifically. In 1868 he was appointed to a chair in Japanese at the Ecole des langues orientales vivantes, a position that until 1907 afforded him the opportunity to play a seminal role in the development and diffusion of Japanese studies in Europe.[27] This aspect of his career is ignored by the French Japanologist Bernard Frank, who deems him "a scholar more endowed with imagination than with scholastic exactitude," and dismisses all but two of his publications.[28] De Rosny undoubtedly attempted too much and at too great a distance. He never had the advantage of long residence in Japan that nurtured the early English scholars. He visited Japan only once for a few months in 1872 while working on the agenda for the congress. It was published in the *Yūbin hōchi shimbun* of September 19 and cited the need to develop a method of transcribing Japanese in Western languages, to compare the civilization of Japan with that of the Occident, to evaluate their relative stage of scientific development, and to initiate scholarly cooperation between Japan and the West. The Meiji government responded to this challenge by sending a group of noteworthy officials to participate in the proceedings.

The opening sessions of the First International Congress of Orientalists were held in the Hall of Theology of the Sorbonne on the morning of September 1, 1873. Presiding over the first two sessions that dealt with formalities was the president of the congress, de Rosny, followed by Admiral Roze, who had served with Roches in Japan during the trying years that culminated in the restoration. The first working session, held that afternoon, was chaired by the twenty-six-year-old Japanese Minister to France, Samejima Naonobu. This former Kagoshima samurai had been sent to England when he was eighteen and studied there for three years before being posted to France in 1870. His opening remarks reveal an acute awareness of the political ramifications of cultural relations:

> "The research you pursue, Gentlemen, will echo in Japan; not only will it be known, but I am convinced that, directly or indirectly, it will further the national development that my government is so eagerly promoting. . . . Your presence here today marks the first public recognition in Europe of Japan's entrance into the comity of Occidental nations, and the consonance of our aims and future aspirations. We have already established political and commercial ties but today, for the first time, we initiate intellectual ties."[29]

The remainder of that session was devoted to a series of papers on Japanese art and archaeology. The only paper by a Japanese was Imamura Warau's discussion of an inscription from Hasedera. European scholars covered such subjects as the ancient monuments of Japan; stone age Japan, including a discussion of *magatama*, some actual examples, and reference to other such objects collected by a Dr. Sabatier while in the employ of the arsenal at Yokosuka; ancient mirrors; ancient gold coins; Chinese and Japanese antiquities, with reference to objects displayed in the exhibition held in conjunction with the congress; Japanese use of color, and the nomenclature of pigments. It is noteworthy that Japanese art should have been given such precedence. Furthermore, the content of these papers, the ensuing discussion, and accompanying plates (including that of a silver vase in the possession of Hōryūji)[30] published by the congress confirms that the Japanese of early Meiji were by no means indifferent to their ancient monuments and that the Europeans exhibited a greater degree of interest, knowledge, and appreciation of the early periods of Japanese art than has hitherto been realized. The first day's activities concluded with a reception held that evening for the members of the congress.

Five more panels on Japan occupied much of the next three days. The morning of September 2 centered on a discussion of problems involved in transcribing Japanese in European languages, led by such pioneers as de Rosny's Italian disciple, Anselmo Severini, and the Viennese scholar, August Pfizmaier.[31] The afternoon session included two papers by Madier de Montajau, a banker who had served in China and Japan; two on Japanese religion, one by the Sanskrit scholar, Emile Louis Burnouf, and another by Du Bousquet and de Rosny; a paper on the revenues of the Japanese government by de Rosny's native language assistant and a Japanese delegate to the congress, Imamura Warau, who also led a discussion on the subject of the Japanese feminine ideal; and the session concluded with a paper on the recent Meiji restoration, written by the Vice Minister of Education, Tanaka Fujimaro, who was not able to attend the congress. Anthropological subjects, including a paper on the Ainu, were considered during the morning of September 3, followed by papers on the introduction of Chinese characters to Japan, their pronounciation, and early Japanese poetry. That afternoon was given over to scientific subjects of such immediate interest as Japanese silkworms, indigo dye, and minerals. A dinner was held that evening at the Grand Hotel, possibly to accommodate Samejima and other Japanese officials who were unable to remain for the duration of the congress.

The morning of September 4 the delegates attended two exhibitions held in conjunction with the congress at the Palais de l'Industrie. The Italian banker, Enrico Cernuschi,[32] organized a major display of art and all manner of artifacts, including armor and musical instruments, from India, China, and particularly Japan, much of which he had acquired during his recent tour of the Orient with the noted writer, Théodore Duret.³³ A former curator of the Louvre, J. Geslin, acted as guide and lectured informally on Oriental art and specifically that of Japan.³⁴ For his part in organizing this extremely influential exhibition which was considered a highlight of the congress, Cernuschi was awarded a medal. In an adjacent room was a special exhibit of Japanese sericulture and sample fabrics assembled by the Inspector General of Sericulture, Guérin-Méneville, that confirms the importance that the French attached to this industry and their trade with Japan. De Rosny compensated for the lack of a morning session by chairing one that evening which dealt with his own major area of interest, the translation of Japanese texts.

The afternoon of September 4 and the whole of the next five working days were devoted to one panel for each of the following studies: Chinese, Tartar and Indo-Chinese, Oceanic, Egyptian, Assyrian, and Semitic archaeology, Semitic, Iranian, Dravidian, Sanskrit, Buddhist, and Armenian and neo-Hellenic—in short, all areas that could possibly be subsumed under the heading of Orientalism, a discipline that the French and British had dominated since the late eighteenth century. The morning of the final day, September 11, was reserved for an overview of Orientalism, a cultural phenomenon whose Islamic etiology has been anatomized recently by Edward Said.³⁵

The final session held that afternoon was presided over again by de Rosny. His willingness to make short shrift of fields of study in which the French were preeminent and to allocate more than one-third of the sessions to a culture that they had just begun to master underscores the political orientation of the congress and its intent to enhance relations with Japan. It explains why he (rather than one of the more eminent French Orientalists) was chosen to head the congress, and why he sought to enlist the prestige of their fields to promote a scholarly interest in Japan. He placed Japanese studies within the wider orbit of Orientalism, and created a new forum for all those concerned with the Orient. The frequency with which the congress was convened thereafter is testimony to de Rosny's accomplishment, and it is ironic that his name was not mentioned at the centenary held in Paris in 1973.³⁶

III

The list of members of the congress includes the name of Emile Guimet, who was certain to attend because of his keen interest in Egypt. Guimet relates that he first went to Egypt in 1865 as a tourist, visited the famous monuments and the new archaeological finds housed in the museum at Bulaq, and avidly read the catalogue of the museum prepared by Auguste Mariette.³⁷ He returned with the usual assortment of curios that he housed in a cabinet that he had specially built on the third floor of his home. He found himself drawn to objects of religious significance and began to frequent curio shops where he purchased amulets, statuettes of deities, stele and before long, a mummy. He grew increasingly curious about the civilization that had produced these works and particularly about the religious and philosophical concepts they embodied. The pace of his collecting quickened as he began to read the rich tradition of French scholarship on Egypt, dating back to Napoleon's campaign of 1798 that included 165 French scientists, artists, and writers who produced a monumental work, *Description de l'Égypte*, published in Paris from 1809 to 1828, which awakened European interest in ancient Egypt and inspired the study of Egyptology and of Islam. Among the authors Guimet cites are J. F. Champollion, who in 1821 first deciphered the hieroglyphics on the Rosetta stone, and other noted authorities such as H. K. Brugsch, E. de Rouge, and F. J. Chabas. He gradually began to collect on a grander scale, purchasing entire collections as they came up for sale, while at the same time widening his range to include Greek, Roman, and Etruscan antiquities. He then wanted to compare these cultures with the ancient civilizations of India, Chaldea, and China, purchasing objects as well as the books to elucidate them, but this too did not long suffice. He soon felt compelled to come into direct contact with these cultures and decided to tour Japan, China, and India since he had already visited Egypt and Greece.[38]

The foregoing has the ring of an oft-told tale, the urbane response of the founder of the Musée Guimet to the inevitable question of how he began to collect, but it sounds more like a rationalization than an explanation. There is, in fact, a curious dearth of biographical material concerning a man as active and prominent as Emile Guimet. What little is known of the family derives from an article honoring his father, Jean-Baptiste Guimet (1795–1871),[39] who was born in Voiron, in the department of Isère, where the family had lived since the early sixteenth century. He became an engineer like his father, graduating from the Ecole Polytechnique in Paris in 1816, and went to work for the arsenal in Paris. A government offer of six thousand francs for the invention of a synthetic ultramarine blue dye with the properties of lapis lazuli spurred him to produce one that was awarded the prize in 1828. He was then transferred to Lyons and so liked this ancient and cultured city, whose major industries at that time were silk, textiles, dying, chemicals, and banking, that he resigned from government service and established at Fleurieu a dye factory that prospered. He became a prominent citizen and was frequently decorated for his work as a research chemist. He had married, in 1825, a young painter, Zélie Bidault, the daughter and niece of artists.[40] Little is known of the family apart from a son, Emile, to whom he relinquished control of the factory in 1860 because of ill health.

Only twenty-three and a half when he took over the plant, Emile

Guimet lived to celebrate his fiftieth anniversary as director on January 1, 1910.[41] He seems to have been an enlightened industrialist and humane employer who was concerned about the welfare and even the spiritual well-being of his workers. He inherited considerable wealth but must have been an extremely able businessman in his own right to afford to collect so extensively and to undertake such costly projects. He does not appear to have had his father's training or aptitude for engineering and chemistry, but shared rather his mother's fondness for art, literature, and music. He evidently received extensive training in music and is known to have studied with teachers in Vienna, Berlin, and Dresden.[42] The public lecture that he gave on the occasion of his admission to the Académie des Sciences, Belles-Lettres et Arts de Lyon on December 21, 1860 was on *Musique populaire,* and another paper that he presented to this organization in 1882 was on *Chants populaires du Lyonnais.* He composed trios, quartets, oratorios, and an opera, *T'ai Tsung,* about a noted Chinese emperor, with a libretto by his friend, Ernest d'Hervilly, which was presented at a theater in Marseille on April 11, 1894. He was also a patron of ballet and sponsored performances at the Théâtre Bellecourt, which he established in Lyons despite the vexation and financial loss it entailed.

Why he began to travel is not known. His first book, *A travers l'Espagne—Lettres familières,* published in 1862, shows him to be a facile writer of popular travel literature. During the next fifteen years he published, in chronological order, books describing his visits to Dresden, the Near East, Egypt, Scandinavia, and North Africa.[43] Why he began to collect is another indeterminate factor. One can only surmise that the many excavations, both official and clandestine, than under way in Egypt, Greece, and the Near East guaranteed a steady stream of antiquities at the same time that the publication of superb excavation reports with splendid plates stimulated the acquisitive instincts of collectors. It would be intriguing to know what he collected at the outset, how discerning he was, and how he displayed these objects in his own home.

Guimet acknowledges that it was due to the influence of French Egyptology that he began to collect and to study Egyptian antiquities. He appears to have derived the intellectual framework for his activities from the remarkable advances that were made in the late eighteenth and early nineteenth centuries in the field of philology, "whose major successes include comparative grammar, the reclassification of languages into families, and the final rejection of the divine origins of language." Edward Said[44] goes on to note that "the study of Sanskrit and the expansive mood of the later eighteenth century seemed to have moved the earliest beginnings very far east of the Biblical lands." He further observes that "What Renan's generation—educated from the mid-1830's to the late 1840's—retained from all this enthusiasm about the Orient was *the intellectual necessity of the Orient for the Occidental scholar of languages, cultures, and religions"* (emphasis added), and that in keeping with advances in the natural sciences, "libraries, laboratories, the museums could serve as its place of exhibition and analysis." This was, in fact, the course that Guimet, who was educated in the 1840s to 1850s, followed.

The development of philology is too complex to be dealt with here, but certain relevant contributions of the French are worth noting: Father Coeurdoux perceived the kinship of Sanskrit and European languages in 1767 and thereby fostered the study of linguistics; the publication in 1786 of Abraham-Hyacinthe Anquetil-Duperron's translation of four *Upanishads*, based on a Persian text; the establishment in 1795 of the first course in Sanskrit at the Ecole des langues orientales vivantes and the first university chair at the Collège de France in 1814; the founding of the Société Asiatique in Paris in 1822 and its publication, *Journal Asiatique*, which helped to disseminate information about the Orient. Sanskrit studies assumed new significance in 1816 when Sylvestre de Sacy's pupil, Franz Bopp, traced the common origin of Sanskrit and the classical languages of Europe. This gave rise to the study of comparative philology. His pupil, Max Müller,[45] was impelled by Eugène Burnouf at Paris in 1845 to undertake the study of comparative religion and to edit the *Rigveda*. Müller's *Introduction to the Science of Religion*, published in 1873, may have had a direct influence upon Guimet's decision to study the religions of India, China, and Japan.

The expulsion of the French from India in 1763 led them to concentrate on linguistics, and it was left to the British victor to lay the foundations of Indology.[46] The first members of the British East India Company in Bengal to master Sanskrit, Charles Wilkins and Sir William Jones, helped to found the Asiatic Society of Bengal in 1784, and they published translations of the Sanskrit classics in the journal of that organization, *Asiatic Researches*. It was not until the early nineteenth century that the British turned their attention to the material remains of India's past. The father of Indian archaeology was a young officer of the Royal Engineers, Alexander Cunningham who, from the time of his arrival in 1831, devoted all his spare time to the study of the Indian remains. When the Archaeological Survey was established in 1862, he was named director and supervised the publication of exemplary reports of the major Indian sites. Publications of this nature could only have whetted Guimet's desire to visit India.

China had loomed large in the imagination of the French since Louis XIV had dispatched missionaries there in the late seventeenth century. By the eighteenth century, knowledge of the country had so expanded that the French Jesuits, Father du Halde and Father de Mailla, could issue encyclopedic histories of China that were milestones in Sinology.[47] These Jesuits tended to view Confucianism as a system of ethics and political morality rather than as a religion. Thus the French philosophers of the Enlightenment thought that China could shed new light on the crucial question of the age in Europe, namely, on the relationship of morality to religion. The study of Chinese was introduced in Europe in the early nineteenth century and aficionados began to look beyond the "Vision of Cathay" and the art of Chinoiserie that it had inspired.[48] After the Opium War, diplomats, missionaries, traders, and technicians were permitted to reside in China, but political instability hampered travel and study. Still Guimet was tempted to seek the tenets of Confucianism and Taoism at their source.

Japan was of more immediate concern to Guimet, the director of a dye factory. As previously noted, the bulk of Japan's exports to France during the 1860s consisted of silk products that helped to revitalize the French silk industry, and hence the economy of Lyons which was then the controlling center for the silk trade of the world. As the critical need for silkworm eggs and cocoons abated in the early 1870s, the Meiji government took measures to increase the export of raw silk, the principal source of foreign credit needed to finance their industrialization.[47] Silk spinning factories such as the pioneer one built by Brunat at Tomioka produced a fine even thread that was much sought after. The quality and quantity of raw silk available for export rose rapidly in volume and value and this, in turn, led to an expansion of the textile and dying industry in Lyons and neighboring areas. Much of this burgeoning trade in silk products was handled by Lyonese firms that may well have included in their shipments an assortment of prints, curios, and bibelots that were increasingly in vogue. Some of Guimet's associates in the Lyons' Chamber of Commerce could boast of firsthand knowledge of Japan. This nextus of trade likewise attracted to Lyons a few of the young Japanese sent to study in France in early Meiji.[50]

The First International Congress of Orientalists afforded Guimet an ideal opportunity to learn more about Japan and to meet members of her delegation. He would have found the papers on sericulture, indigo (which the French had tried to cultivate unsuccessfully in the 1830s), and government revenues no less relevant than those on religion and antiquities. The exhibitions held in conjunction with the congress and particularly the objects acquired by Cernuschi during his recent tour of the Far East may have encouraged Guimet to consider a similar voyage in pursuit of his own interests, the study of comparative religion and the assemblage of ritual objects and representations of deities and religious legends. The prospects were heightened by the critical acclaim lavished on the Japanese objet d'art and artifacts displayed at the International Exposition which was then being held in Vienna.[51] There was, by way of further enticement, a spate of publications such as Aimé Humbert's *Le Japon illustré*[52] that an inveterate traveller such as Guimet was tempted to emulate, and we can be certain that he was familiar with the invaluable books on Japan written by former members of the Dutch East India Company stationed at Deshima during the Edo period.[53] All this contributed to Guimet's determination in 1876 to visit Japan, China, and India.

Guimet relates that when he discussed his impending trip with friends who had recently returned from the Orient, they stressed the difficulties of traveling in China without a diplomatic passport and advised him to ask the Minister of Public Instruction and Fine Arts to commission him to undertake a study of the religions of the Far East which he would fund.[54] Guimet writes that he was hesitant to ask the government to intervene on his behalf, but eventually overcame his reluctance and obtained from the minister official credentials authorizing him to lead a scientific mission to the Orient. He left via the United States in the spring of 1876, accompanied by Félix Régamey (1844–1907),[55] an artist and well-known correspondent for illustrated journals in Paris, London, and New York. While crossing the United States, Guimet observed the museums that were recently established there, and was particularly impressed by the Smithsonian Institution in Washington, D.C. which, in addition to its collections, sponsored lectures, publications, and other programs.[56] They set sail from San Francisco and arrived in Yokohama where they could count on the assistance of Lyonese friends resident there.

IV

No sooner did Guimet call on an official he had met in Paris, Kuki Ryūichi (1852–1931),[57] than he found that the official accreditation, which he claims he had not intended to use, was essential to the realization of his goals. He was, moreover, remarkably fortunate in his choice of a contact. For close to a decade, Kuki occupied a position of such influence within the Ministry of Education that, according to Miyake Setsurei, people mockingly referred to it as "Kuki's Ministry." The son and adopted son of samurai from two minor *han* that are now part of Hyōgo prefecture, he studied English under Fukuzawa Yukichi at Keiō and Dutch under Dr. Guido Verbeck. He entered the Ministry of Education when it was formed in 1871 and rose rapidly. In 1873 he was sent to Europe and the United States to evaluate the achievements of Japanese studying abroad. Although he is not known to have attended the First International Congress of Orientalists, it is quite possible that Guimet met him there.[58] On his return, Kuki recommended, allegedly for reasons of economy but actually to lessen the domination of Satsuma and Chōshū in the appointment of students for foreign study, that foreign teachers be engaged to provide basic training. He thus came to wield considerable influence over the selection of foreign teachers as well as the selection of Japanese subsequently sent abroad for advanced study or special training. Since he was acting Minister of Education during the absence abroad of Tanaka Fujimaro, he handled all arrangements for Guimet's tour of temples and shrines.

Guimet had arrived at a most opportune time. Japan was on the verge of recovering from a period of religious strife that occurred following the restoration.[59] In order to reaffirm the principle of imperial sovereignty, the Meiji government set about revitalizing Shintō and in 1870 declared it the national religion. They issued an edict in 1868 to separate Shintō from Buddhism which had enjoyed quasi-national status and had served as an administrative organ of the *bakufu*. Further measures taken to rescind the economic, legal, and social advantages previously granted Buddhism were seen inadvertently as a drive to exterminate Buddhism and culminated in a movement known as *haibutsu kishaku*, "exterminate the Buddhas and abandon the scriptures," that resulted in wanton destruction of temples and images, the secularization of priests, and a denunciation of Buddhism itself as an obstacle to progress. Enlightened priests realized that Buddhism would have to undergo thorough renovation if it were to meet the demands of a new era and the competition posed by Christianity, which was legalized in 1873. Their efforts to achieve a spiritual awakening brought into question many traditional religious and social concepts that further stimulated the intellectual ferment kindled by the introduction of Western ideas. The two principal branches of the Shin sect in Kyōto, Higashi, and Nishi Honganji, seized the opportunity offered by the government to send Buddhist scholars abroad to observe Western religious organizations as a basis for institutional reform and the adoption of new programs. A member of the group from Nishi Honganji that toured Europe in 1872, Shimaji Mokurai, was instrumental in convincing the government to separate Buddhism and Shintoism in 1875, thereby creating a semblance of parity and religious tolerance which Kuki was eager to convey to Guimet. The various religious denominations were no less eager to explain their religious tenets and observances.

Kuki arranged for Guimet to visit the great temples and shrines of Tokyo, Nikkō, Ise, and Kyōto, as well as the major ones along the Tōkaidō. A special ceremony was held in his honor at Nikkō, replete with a procession and floral offerings. He had some initial difficulty securing the cooperation of the Shintō authorities at Ise, but succeeded in gaining their confidence, elicited the information he desired, and was even permitted to view a ritual dance. The Vice-Governor of Kyōto, Makimura Masanao, arranged for him to confer with Shintō dignitaries and with representatives of six Buddhist sects. Each of these councils, he reported, had all the solemnity of religious and official ceremonies and were held at temples or official quarters. He was particularly impressed by the receptions tendered him by the Zen and Nichiren sects, as well as his meeting with Shintō priests that terminated with a ceremony in honor of Tenmangu. The highlight of his trip was a day-long grand council of the Shin sects convened in his honor at the Hiunkaku of Nishi Honganji.[60] Régamey was always on hand to record the sites and events while Guimet, with the aid of his interpreters, attempted to explore the dogma of the various Buddhist sects and to assemble a coherent account of Shintō beliefs.

Guimet could not have pursued his studies so effectively had it not been for the assistance and able interpreters provided him by Léon Dury (1822–91),[61] who contributed so much to the success of his mission. Dury was born in Lambesc in Bouches du Rhône, obtained the degree of Doctor in Medicine in Marseilles, and served for three years as a physician in the Crimean War. He came to Japan in 1862 to join the staff of a hospital that the Japanese were planning to establish at Hakodate. When the scheme fell through, Bellecourt arranged for him to stay on as French Consul in Nagasaki. His home leave happened to coincide with the departure of the Japanese delegation to the Paris Exposition of 1867, and he agreed to accompany them. During the course of the trip, he came to know some of the leading government officials responsible for the development of foreign trade and the promotion of the arts and handicraft industries such as Shibusawa Eiichi, Sano Tsunetami, and Yamataka Nobuakira. He also became acquainted with the some the problems and potentials that confronted them.[62] These contacts were to prove invaluable to Guimet.

Dury returned to his post in 1868, but when the consulate was closed in 1870 because of the Franco-Prussian War, he chose to remain in Nagasaki as a teacher of French at the Kōunkan, where he numbered among his pupils such future leaders as Prince Saionji. When the French course was discontinued, the former British Consul in Nagasaki, Abel A. J. Gower, recommended that Makimura engage Dury in October 1871 to teach at the French School that was being established in Kyōto.[63] He taught French, history, geography, and general science, and subsequently also taught Latin at a hospital that had just been founded by the city. In addition, his wife, whom he had married in Nagasaki, taught French and sewing at a school for women that had been set up to train ex-geisha and other women for suitable employment. When the school was closed in 1875 for want of funds, the vice-governor, Makimura Masanao, tried to find other employment for Dury in Kyoto, and when this failed, he interceded with the Minister of Education, Tanaka Fujimaro, to obtain for him a position teaching French literature and history at the Kaisei gakkō in Tokyo. Dury signed a two-year contract to teach there, beginning April 1875, and from September 1876 he also taught at the Tokyo gaikokugo gakkō. Some of his students followed him once again to Tokyo and he is said to have helped a few of them financially. Thus when Guimet arrived, Dury was conveniently situated in the capital, extremely well informed, and had at his disposal a group of able pupils who could assist him and act as his interpreters. He contributed greatly to the success of Guimet's activities in Kyoto because of his close association with a leading official, Makimura Masanao (1834–96).[64]

Makimura was the second son of a lower samurai of Yamaguchi *han*. Nothing is known of Makimura's education and experience prior to 1868 when he joined the Kyoto government. He assisted the first governor of Kyōto, Hase Nobuatsu,[65] set up an effective prefectural administration and took steps to allay the fear of the Kyoto populace who protested the shift of the capital and court to Tokyo. They used the parting gift of 150,000 yen from the emperor to assist the traditional industries to modernize, and they also established a wide range of new educational and industrial projects that paralleled, and even anticipated, those initiated by the national government, thus belying the common view that Kyōto was then a center of traditionalism that failed to adapt to the demands of a new era.

Makimura believed that the immediate economic viability of the city depended upon helping the major traditional industries adapt to a rapidly changing market domestically and new markets internationally. In order to increase textile production, which was the major industry, Makimura sought the advice of Dury and authorized him to purchase six Jacquard looms in Lyons in 1872. Dury also arranged for two Kyōto weavers, Sakura Tsuneshichi and Inoue Ihei, together with a skilled toolmaker, Yoshida Chūschichi, to be sent there in 1872 to spend a year mastering the use of the looms and observing the methods of production of the silk weavers who lived atop Croix Rousse, in the northern part of Lyons. These young craftsmen were greatly impressed by the famous textile museum in Lyons and brought back a study collection of sample fabrics; a far more extensive one was assembled by the noted Nishijin weaver, Date Yanosuke IV, who visited Lyons after attending the exposition in Vienna. The looms bought in Lyons were displayed at the Kyōto Exposition in the spring of 1874 and then were installed by Sakura and Inoue in a textile factory set up at Nijō Kawaramachi to experiment with new methods of production and the manufacture of sample textiles. In January 1875 they began to teach the techniques that they had learned in Lyons to local craftsmen. Dury thereby forged a bond between the textile industry of Kyoto and Lyons.

Also of great interest to Guimet were Dury's efforts to help the staff of the Industrial Research Laboratory experiment with ways of improving the materials and dyes used in the production of textiles, pottery, and other handicrafts. Dury worked directly with the leading potters of Kyōto and is known to have helped the Awata kiln operated by Kinkōzan Sōbei improve their wares and market them in France.[66] While encouraging the potters to develop foreign outlets, Dury repeatedly cautioned them not to let the demands of the export trade violate their sense of design and good taste. He appears to have contributed to the remarkable progress made during the 1870s by such noted Kyōto potters as Kinkōzan Sōbei, Seifū Yohei II and III, Takahashi Dōhachi IV, Kiyomizu Rokubei III and IV, Kanzan Denshichi, Eiraku Wazen, and others. Dury must have introduced Guimet to these potters, whose works appear in the *Catalogue du Musée Guimet*, and interested him in Japanese ceramics. Dury made arrangements for him to visit, in the course of his travels, the major kilns and centers of ceramic production. Guimet relates that he queried the potters regarding the means by which traditional techniques were passed on from father to son, as well as their methods of manufacture and distribution. Guimet was so impressed by what he saw that he decided to assemble a collection of Japanese and Chinese ceramics to parallel his collections of religious objects.

The experience he gained while attending the exposition in Paris in 1867 enabled Dury to help Makimura give substance to his slogan *Bijutsu fukokuron*, "enrich the country through the arts," by assisting him to organize a full-scale industrial fair that was held on the grounds of Nishi Honganji, Kenninji, and Chionin in the spring of 1872.[67] Some forty thousand Japanese, including the Meiji Emperor, attended this First Kyoto Exposition, as well as 770 foreigners who, for the first time, were granted special permission to visit the ancient capital. So successful was this fair, which included a large art exhibition, that one was held annually and subsequently semi-annually thereafter, and not only helped to promote trade but also offered the contemporary artists and craftsmen a means of exhibiting their work and solicitng new patronage. Prizes began to be awarded in the spring of 1875 as a means of encouraging competition and stimulating new ideas, products, and markets. Dury may have also been consulted by Sano Tsunetami, Yamataka Nobuakira, and other officials he knew when they took charge of the Japanese exhibits sent to the international expositions held in Vienna in 1873, in Philadelphia in 1876, and in Paris in 1878. Hence he was extremely well acquainted with the contemporary art scene and could arrange for Guimet to call on artists such as Kawanaba Kyōsai. He was also familiar with the craftsmen and art dealers and must have helped Guimet assemble and ship the material he purchased for his new museum, and organized as well a network of people who could continue to supply Guimet's needs.

Dury decided to return to France at the conclusion of his contract in March 1877. He evidently told Guimet of his desire to help some of his pupils continue their studies in France. Guimet invited the two ablest interpreters, Tomii Masaaki (1858–1935) and Imaizumi Yūsaku (1850–1931) to come to Lyons to help him organize his material, and he promised to help Dury place the others in Lyons. Dury broached his plan to Makimura who welcomed this opportunity to send some Kyōto craftsmen abroad for practical training under the aegis of Dury and Guimet. The Kyōto Industrial Development Office agreed to fund, for a period of three years, four of Dury's former pupils—Kondō Tokutarō, Imanishi Naojirō, Yokota Manjunosuke, and Utahara Juzaburō. The four younger students selected by the Kyōto government—Inahata Katsutarō, Nakanishi Yonesaburō, Yokota Jūichi, and Satō Tomotarō—were given an extra year in which to master French before pursuing one of a number of stipulated fields of study.[68] Dury received the sum of six hundred yen a year for acting as academic mentor, bursar, and *parentis-in-locus*. He also agreed to assist members of Kyōto industry when they visited France and to reply to the government's requests for advice. Thus he initiated a new phase in Kyōto's relations with Lyons.

V

On his return to France, Guimet promptly submitted a report to the Minister of Public Instruction summarizing what he had accomplished in each of the three countries he visited.[69] He wrote that he had obtained, during the three months he spent in Japan, important documents concerning religion there and that he had also brought back three hundred religious paintings, six hundred statues of divinities, and a collection of over one thousand volumes of Chinese, Japanese, and French works that needed to be catalogued. He acknowledged his indebtedness to Kuki, Makimura, Dury, and Dury's pupils who had interpreted for him. He concluded with an account of the institutions that he planned to establish in Lyons: first, a museum of religion that would contain representations of "all" the deities of India, China, Japan, and Egypt[70] (and noted that the last two were already complete); second, a library of Sanskrit, Tamil, Sinhalese, Chinese, Japanese, and European books pertaining to religious subjects which already numbered close to three thousand volumes; third, a school where young Orientals could come to learn French and French youths could study the ancient and modern languages of the Orient, which would not be geared solely to philosophical and philological interests but also to those of young Lyonese who planned to engage in business in the Orient.

Since his museum was still under construction, Guimet offered to exhibit some of his material at the Exposition universelle that was held in Paris in 1878. He was allotted an area in the Trocadéro where he exhibited thirty-three paintings and drawings by Régamey that vividly depicted the highlights of their travels, as well as a selection of the material that he had collected.[71] That same year he published a glowing account of their visit to Japan entitled *Promenades japonaises* that was illustrated by Régamey and published by G. Charpentier, a proponent of *Japonisme* and a patron of Monet and Renoir. A companion volume, *Promenades japonaises Tokio-Nikko*, which appeared in 1880, contains an engaging account of a visit to the studio of Kawanabe Kyōsai. The frontispiece of the book leaves little doubt that the facile and eccentric Kyōsai was the victor of a "duel" with Régamey in which the two artists simultaneously sketched each other.[72] It is worth noting that the arch tone of these books, so characteristic of the popular literature on Japan of that era, is nowhere evident in his scholarly works. These activities brought Guimet into the mainstream of *Japonisme*, which was then at its peak of popularity and becoming an ever more pervasive influence on the contemporary art of Europe and America.

Guimet's participation in the exposition brought him to the attention of the Japanese delegation, which included Kuki Ryūichi. He reciprocated Kuki's favors by appointing him an honorary member of the Provincial Congress of Orientalists that he presided over in Lyons from August 31 to September 7, 1878, prior to the convening in Florence of the Fourth International Congress of Orientalists.[73] Kuki could not come because of illness, nor did Maeda Masana, the head of the Japanese delegation. Guimet elicited a broad cross section of support and participation. For the first time since the congress of 1873, there was extensive coverage of Japan.[74] As might be expected of Lyons, the first working session was on "Commerce and Industry," and included several papers on Chinese and Japanese sericulture, as well as some on trade with the Orient, and Japan in particular. One of Dury's pupils whom Guimet had brought to Lyons, Tomii Masaaki, discussed the products of Hokkaidō and their export. Japan, however, did not figure as prominently as India and China in the two sessions on "Science, Philology, History, and Fine Arts." In keeping with Guimet's interests, the remainder of the program consisted of one panel each on ancient Egyptian, ancient Persian and Assyrian, Indian, Chinese, and Japanese religion. Imaizumi Yūsaku, another of Dury's pupils, presented several papers at these last two sessions that Tomii translated into French and delivered for him. Still another Japanese who had come to assist Guimet and hoped thereafter to attend the military school at Saint Cyr, identified only as M. Harada,[75] spoke about the different types of characters used in writing Japanese. Guimet emerged from the congress as a leading proponent and patron of Oriental studies in Lyons.

The congress concluded with a preview and an inauguration of the Musée Guimet, which was formally dedicated by the Minister of Public Instruction, Jules Ferry, and other dignitaries on September 30, 1879, and donated to the city. Guimet had selected a handsome site on the boulevard du Nord, near the Parc de la Tête d'Or (containing a lake, a zoological collection, and fine botanical gardens), in the wealthy residential district of Brotteaux. It was on the left bank of the Rhône where the university and prefectural offices were located. The architect, Jules Chatron of Lyons, had designed an impressive neo-classical structure that covered an area of 3,500 meters.[76] The centrally located main entrance, framed by a Grecian-style portico, provided access to the galleries on the ground floor where Guimet displayed his marble statuary and ceramic collection. An imposing central staircase led to the main galleries on the next floor where his collection of religious art was exhibited, as well as the paintings made by Régamey during the course of their travels. At one end of the building was a monumental tower that had a second-story circular room reserved for the library, which was surmounted by an enclosed observation deck containing a diorama representing the ruins of the temple of Karnak as viewed from the summit of the central pylon. Guimet was so pleased with the architectural design that he virtually reproduced it when he established his new museum in Paris in 1889.

While it is impossible to reconstruct the original contents of the museum, it is apparent from the catalogue that he acquired much of his Asian material in Japan.[77] For example, there was only one room that contained ancient and modern Chinese ceramics, some of which may have been purchased in Japan, in contrast to three rooms that featured all manner of Japanese pottery, including Banko, Seto, Oribe, "Ninsei" (Kyōto wares), Awata, Imari, Satsuma, Bizen, Kutani, etc., as well as works by leading contemporary potters. This same imbalance characterized what Guimet regarded as his main collection. His Indian, Tibetan, Cambodian, and Siamese objects fit into one room that also contained a Chinese statue of Kuan-yin, some jades, and historical material—in short, the overflow of the one room devoted to Chinese buddhist, confucian, and taoist art. By contrast, his Japanese collection filled a full four rooms. Few of these works purported to be older than the Edo period, and most of them dated from the eighteenth and early nineteenth centuries. A considerable number were unabashedly listed as modern or copy, obtained or ordered to fulfill his iconographic requirements or didactic program. Since Guimet's definition of "religious art" was broad enough to include objects depicting Japanese legends, such popular themes as the "Seven Gods of Good Fortune," *netsuke*, armor, historical objects, Kanō paintings, and a variety of modern decorative objects such as tapestries, bronzes, and lacquers, his collection could not have been radically different from that of his French contemporaries. Scholars of *Japonisme*, therefore, can ill afford to ignore what was undoubtedly one of the major collections of Japanese art in France at that time.

The second of Guimet's projects, the library, was catalogued and installed in the museum by the same group of Japanese who helped to edit the first and second editions of the *Catalogue du Musée Guimet* and the first three volumes of the *Annales du Musée Guimet*.[78] His two principal assistants were Tomii Masaaki and Imaizumi Yusaku, who came to Lyons at his behest in the spring of 1877 and remained there until 1883. Tomii had studied with Dury in Kyōto and Tokyo and was evidently the most fluent in French.[79] Moreover, his father, Tomii Masatune, was affiliated with one of the Kyōto temples and he therefore had entrée to Buddhist circles. While working for Guimet, Tomii attended the University of Lyons and was awarded the degree of Doctor of Law in 1883. Following his return to Japan, he became a professor and later dean of the Law School of Tokyo University. After retiring in 1901, he served as president of Kyoto hōsei semmon gakkō, the forerunner of Ritsumeikan University, until 1927. During this period, he was active in Francophile circles dominated by Ueda Bin at Kyōto University.

Imaizumi's choice of a career was directly influenced by his association with Guimet.[80] The son of an Edo samurai family, he attended the Confucian College in Edo, taught Chinese literature for several years, and subsequently studied French with Dury at Tokyo gaikokugo gakkō. His thorough training in Chinese and Confucian studies was invaluable to Guimet. He had planned to specialize in linguistics, but supposedly was so impressed by the esteem and high prices paid for even mediocre works of Japanese art in France that he decided to major in art and archaeology. He thus became the first Japanese to study the ancient art of India, Egypt, Greece, and Rome, and is believed to have learned some Sanskrit and Egyptian. When he returned to Japan, Guimet may have interceded with Kuki to obtain Imaizumi a position in the Ministry of Education where he worked alongside Okakura Kakuzō, who is certain to have tapped his knowledge of European art. He helped Okakura and Ernest Fenollosa establish the first art magazine, *Dai Nihon bijutsu shimpō*, and worked with them in the Tokyo Art School and the art department of the Tokyo National Museum. From 1894 to 1898 he served as director of the Kyōto Art School and during his tenure promoted a group of younger artists who, together with their pupils, dominated Kyōto art circles for half a century. He then went back to Tokyo and was appointed a professor at the Tokyo Art School and one of the chief curators of the National Museum. His significant contribution to the development of Meiji art has been obscured by the renown of his flamboyant colleague, Okakura.

It has only recently been possible to trace the career of another of Guimet's assistants, Yamada Tadazumi (1855–1917),[81] who proves to have a pupil of Dury's at the Kōun-kan in Nagasaki. He was then employed as an interpreter at the Ikuno Mines where Jean François Coignet was chief engineer and thereafter at the Arsenal. It was evidently with the aid of Dury and the prospect of employment with Guimet that Yamada made his own way to Lyons in 1878. He attended a technical school of which Guimet was a trustee and, after graduating, worked for the Chemical Research Institute attached to the university and then for a chemical fertilizer plant. In 1885 he was hired by the Japanese Consulate in Lyons and because he married a young Frenchwoman from there in 1893, managed to remain with the consulate until 1908, when he was recalled to Japan and assigned to a position in the Ministry of Foreign Affairs. He probably continued to assist Guimet during the 1880s while the museum was still in Lyons.

Tomii, Imaizumi, and Yamada helped Guimet to launch his third project, the School of Oriental Languages, on February 3, 1879.[82] The Ecole de Commerce provided the facilities and Guimet the native teachers who offered courses in regular and commercial Japanese, based upon the texts and methods followed in Japanese primary schools. About sixty students registered but only eighteen completed the first term. The second semester began October 20, 1879 with thirty pupils and most of the twelve who remained were interested in commerce, although a few wished to study philology and learn to translate Japanese. Guimet believed that the students of Oriental languages in Paris, to quote Guimet, "ne *poussent* pas" (failed to develop),[83] were too few in number, and had no other ambition than someday to succeed their professors who themselves had difficulty deciphering Japanese texts. Guimet maintained that he was of a more practical bent and hoped that his young Japanese assistants would train interpreters capable of reading the usual range of material, thereby facilitating the commercial needs of Lyons. To what extent he achieved these goals remains to be determined.

VI

In the decade following his return from Japan, Guimet was busy enlarging and refining his collection, publishing his material, and making plans for the new museum that he intended to establish in Paris. He was in constant contact with Japanese officials, scholars, priests, artists, and dealers; some of them, in turn, sought his advice and assistance. He was somehow involved in the pet project of Makimura after he became governor of Kyōto in 1877, namely, the establishment in 1880 of the Kyōto Art School. This was the first government school to offer training in the various branches of the traditional arts as well as Western art. The idea supposedly originated with a prominent *nanga* painter, Tanomura Chokunyū, who submitted a proposal in 1878 that was endorsed by Kose Shōseki and Mochizuki Gyokusen, heirs to old, established schools, and by Kōno Bairei and Kubota Beisen, two mavericks in Kyōto art circles.[84] The idea actually had been conceived by Makimura himself as a means of soliciting the cooperation of artists to produce designs and train craftsmen and artists necessary to insure the continued excellence of the handicraft industries so vital to the prosperity of Kyōto. Makimura had relied previously on Nyounsha, an organization of artists, scholars, antiquarians, and collectors founded by Shiokawa Burnin soon after the restoration. Mori Kansai assumed leadership following the death of Bunrin in 1877 and rapidly transformed Nyounsha into a social gathering that had no concern for such seemingly mundane matters.

Makimura is known to have drawn upon the expertise of one of his foreign employees, a German chemist by the name of Gottfried Wagener[85] who was working then at the Chemical Research Laboratory. Makimura is believed to have sought also the advice of Dury, who was technically still in the employ of the Kyōto government. One can safely assume that he consulted Régamey, who was for many years an inspector of drawing for the schools of Paris and the author of many articles on art education, including that of the United States and Japan. He illustrated and published numerous books about Japan and Japanese art, and throughout his lifetime was an active member of the Société Franco-Japonaise in Paris.[86] Makimura must have likewise consulted Guimet, who could have written him about the Ecole des Beaux-Arts in Lyons which produced such famous painters as Puvis de Chavannes, Paul Chevenard, Paul Flandrin, Ernest Meissonier, and others, while at the same time training the designers and craftsmen that brought Lyons' silk damasks and brocades world renown. Guimet must have played a significant role because a portrait of him was presented to the Kyōto Art School by Makimura in February 1881.[87] It hung for many years in a place of honor in the entryway of the school, indicative of a relationship that has yet to be explored.

The religious art of Asia that Guimet exhibited at the Trocadéro may have alerted Kuki Ryūichi to a dimension of Japanese art not hitherto perceived by officials responsible for Japan's participation in international expositions. Here were objects that possessed antiquity, monumentality, religious or legendary or historical content—criteria for the Fine Arts as opposed to the decorative or industrial arts; they were of sufficient import that even copies were acceptable; and they were lent by, in addition to Guimet, men of means and social stature. Kids also noted the importance that the French attached to the arts and to the preservation of their national culture, specifically, the adroit use they made of it politically. He returned to Tokyo convinced that the government was foolish to promote Western art, apart from its purely technical applications, when Japan possessed an artistic tradition that could serve as a source of national pride and international prestige.

Kuki became an active participant in all that pertained to the arts. He was one of the founding members of Ryūchi kai (renamed Nihon bijutsu kyōkai in 1886), an organization formed in Tokyo in 1879 by a group of government officials to stimulate Japanese interest in their native arts, both ancient and modern with a view to improving the contemporary arts and the quality of artifacts produced for export, and to raise the level of public taste. Ryūchi kai sponsored annual exhibitions and also sent two exhibits of Japanese paintings to Paris in 1883 and in 1884 to acquaint the French with this lesser known aspect of Japanese art.[88] Kuki used his position in the Ministry of Education, as Minister to the United States from 1884 to 1888, and as Director of the Tokyo Imperial Museum from 1889 to 1900 that thwart the development of Western art; to investigate, classify, preserve, and protect works of art belonging to temples and shrines and to prohibit their export; to help establish the Tokyo Art School and accord it a dominant role, to influence what was exhibited in national and international expositions; and finally, to foster an art that would be compatible with the national aspirations of the Meiji government. Guimet is certain to have maintained his relations with so influential a figure.[89]

Some of the objects that Guimet exhibited at the Trocadéro were lent by "M. Vakaï," i.e., Wakai Kanezaburō who, after taking part in the Vienna Exposition, helped organize a quasi-official trading company, the Kiritsu kōshō kaisha,[90] to handle these international ventures and the trade they generated. The company opened a shop in New York in 1877 and Paris in 1878, where they sold off the remains of the exhibits and attempted to satisfy, on a continuing basis, the foreign demand for Japanese wares. Unfortunately their factories in Japan had difficulty meeting both the popular demand for inexpensive trinkets and the more discriminating desire for reasonably priced objects of better quality and greater utility, as well as the growing demand for works of art. The enterprise was a financial failure and the company was disbanded in 1891. Its name appears as one of the contributors of objects to the Musée Guimet.

It is difficult to determine why the Kiritsu kōshō kaisha was unable to convert this fascination with *Japonisme* into a protfitable trade, as was the French enterpreneur, Samuel Bing,[91] who also became a successful art dealer. Wakai, who was originally a Kyōto antique dealer of whom little is known, followed Bing's example. He joined forces in the early 1880s with Hayashi Tadamasa,[92] a personable young man who had been hired by the Kiritsu kōshō kaisha as an interpreter during the Paris Exposition of 1878, and for a period of some fifteen years they were one of the leading art dealers in Paris. Their specialty was *ukiyo-e* prints and paintings, ceramics, decorative arts, and finely wrought miniatures such as *inrō*, *netsuke*, and sword fittings so eagerly sought after by collectors that included such prominent artists, writers, publishers, and industrialists as Manet, Monet, Degas, Fantin-Latour, Tissot, Alfonse Hirsch, Bracquemond, Jacquemart, M. L. E. Solon, Burty, Duret, Zola, Charpentier, the de Goncourts, Régamey, Barbedienne, Christolfe, Bouilhet, Falize, and others too numerous to mention. Louis Gonse, the de Goncourt, and other noted writers on Japanese art all acknowledged their indebtedness to Wakai and Hayashi. Guimet too is certain to have consulted them and they may well have assisted him in enlarging his collection of Japanese art.

Serious collectors of the like of Guimet and Cernuschi seem to have had difficulty upgrading significantly the artistic quality of their Japanese collections. The quantity and quality of *ukiyo-e* prints, pottery, and decorative arts acquired by French collectors seemed proof that the Japanese, indeed, had ceased to appreciate their native arts. The economic and social upheaval resulting from the dissolution of the *han* and the abolition of hereditary ranks supposedly had made it possible to purchase the entire collections of former nobles for a mere pittance, particularly when one considers the favorable exchange rate. Coming so soon after the disestablishment of Buddhism, Guimet should have been able to acquire marvelous ancient statues of Buddhist and Shintō dieties. But *ukiyo-e* apart,[93] when one seeks to identify in extant collections the masterpieces that were acquired from the 1860s to 1870s, they prove to be surprisingly few in number. This is partly attributable to a lack of appreciation and discrimination, but there were other constraints as well. It was not any sudden shift in taste, but economic necessity and altered styles of living that accounted for most of the art and furnishings that appeared for sale. The dislocation of the art market, however, was of brief duration because the available works were purchased by canny antique dealers and wealthy merchants from areas such as Kanazawa that had been less adversely affected by the restoration.[94] Important works of art were accepted as collateral for loans, or else found ready buyers, but admittedly at deflated prices inevitable during periods of political and social disruption. This acted as a restraint upon sales, as did legal prohibitions governing the disposal of *daimyō* property. Another negative factor soon surmounted was the provincial taste, pro-Western orientation, and Confucian outlook of the early Meiji bureaucrats who nonetheless were quick to perceive the potential for profit and social aggrandizement, and thus became avid art collectors.

A set of documents kept in the archives of the Japanese Ministry of Foreign Affairs in Tokyo reveals how difficult it was to obtain works of art that the Japanese themselves esteemed.[95] The same French Minister of Education and Fine Arts who presided over the dedication of the Musée Guimet, Jules Ferry, began negotiations in July 1882 with the Japanese Minister of Foreign Affairs, Inoue Kaoru, for an exchange of French works of art of superior quality in return for Japanese works of a comparable nature which were to be displayed in a specially designed "Salle Japonaise" in the Louvre. The Japanese conceivably should have been eager, during this heyday of Westernization that gave rise to the Rokumeikan, to obtain examples of French art that could serve as models for their artists and craftsmen, and they should have welcomed the opportunity to dazzle the French with their artistic prowess. Inoue, in fact, was an appreciative and reputedly rapacious art collector, and the two men he delegated to deal with the matter, Shioda Shin and Yamataka Nobuakira, were knowledgeable art administrators. Negotiations reached an impasse because the French wanted examples of the brilliantly bold and decorative art of the Momoyama and early Edo periods which Japanese officials contended belonged to temples and shrines or private collectors, rarely reached the art market, and were in any event beyond the means of the government to purchase. Their offer to furnish photographs and fine copies of such works was dismissed by the French as unworthy of the Louvre, as were also unspecified "original works of art of the ancient period." The correspondence continued until 1885 when the project was finally abandoned without resolution. By the mid 1880s Japanese officials and industrialists were

The French Connection: Emile Guimet's Mission to Japan

vying to assemble their own collections, and a decade later the wealthy shipbuilder, Kawasaki Shūzū, was erecting his own private museum in Kobe.

Despite his manifold efforts, Guimet soon realized that he could not create a center of Oriental studies in Lyons. The scholars, archaeologists, philosophers, and philologists whom he needed to consult rarely visited Lyons but were bound to come to Paris because the libraries, academic institutions, museums, and professional organizations were all centered there. His offer to establish a new museum in Paris and to present his collection, which had grown in size and scope, to the French State was accepted by the government in August 1885.[96] The city of Paris provided a plot of land on the Place d'Iéna and Guimet agreed to share the cost of construction. One of the men who helped to insure that the project proceeded as planned was Léon Roches. The new Musée Guimet was inaugurated on November 20, 1889 by the President of the Republic, Sadi Carnot. Guimet served as director during his lifetime, and once again he created a center for learning. He placed his private library which had grown to some thirteen thousand volumes at the disposal of scholars and the public. He sponsored lectures, continued to publish the *Annales du Musée Guimet*, and founded a journal, *Revue de l'Histoire des Religions*. He reappointed Léon de Milloué as his curator, and engaged a trained staff whom he closely supervised to run the museum, while he continued to reside in Lyons and to manage his factory at Fleurieu, until shortly before his death in 1918.

In 1925 the Musée Guimet became part of the Réunion des musées nationaux de France. Guimet's original collection was gradually reclassified and upgraded, and in time much of the Japanese material disappeared from view. A more profound transformation occurred in 1945 when it was decided to shift the Asian collection of the Louvre to the Musée Guimet and to transfer Guimet's Egyptian objects to the Louvre. Thus the Musée Guimet became so identified with Paris and with the treasures acquired by French archaeologists, scholars, and private collectors in Afghanistan, Pakistan, India, Indonesia, Indo-China, Tibet, Chinese-Turkestan, China, and Japan that the public, and even specialists, have lost sight of Guimet's original intent to found a museum of comparative religion in his native Lyons and the extensive cultural relations that resulted from his "mission" to Japan.

The transformation of the Musée Guimet into a national museum of Asian art in Paris has all but effaced its original character, apart from a vestigal concern with religious iconography, and an active educational and research program.[97] The Muśe Guimet in Lyons is now a museum of natural history, and the records pertaining to its founding appear to have been lost in the transition to Paris. Little remains of Guimet's collection of Japanese art and even Régamey's paintings can no longer be found. The archives of the Musée Guimet yielded no information concerning the young Japanese who had assisted Guimet. The Japanese art brought back by Cernuschi has been as effectively eliminated from the Musée Cernuschi and it is doubtful how much of it survives in storage. It is important to comprehend the evolution in taste that led to the withdrawal and dispersal of most of the Japanese art collected by Guimet and Cernuschi during the 1870s and 1880s, and the related but no less pertinent issue of why Japanese art now constitutes such a minor proportion of the possessions of both these museums of Oriental art. This, however, should not be permitted to obscure the major contribution that both these men made to the development of *Japonisme*.

Guimet himself remains elusive and, despite his many publications and role as a collector, it is difficult to gauge his personal proclivities, his aesthetic criteria, and his artistic sensibility. Yet the range of his activities reveals how essential it is that scholars of *Japonisme* look beyond considerations of style and the concerns of a circle of artists, writers, and collectors that have been the focus of their attention and consider the larger political, economic, and cultural forces that enabled *Japonisme* to have so profound an influence upon European and American art in the second half of the nineteenth century. This will necessitate directing their attention, at long last, to its source—a contemporary Japan in the throes of transformation. They inevitably must come to understand what an even more profound effect the West had upon the modern evolution of Japanese art, and how this in turn influenced the course of *Japonisme*.

Notes

1. Henry Adams, "New Books on *Japonisme*," *The Art Bulletin*, vol. 65, no. 3 (Sept. 1983), pp. 495–502; citation, p. 502.
2. Ibid.
3. Linda Nochlin, "The Imaginary Orient," *Art in America* (May 1983), pp. 119–89 passim.
4. Ibid., p. 119.
5. Ardath W. Burks, "A 'Sub-Leader' in the Emergence of the Diplomatic Function: Ikeda Chōhatsu (Chikugo no Kami), 1837–1879," Bernard S. Silberman and H. D. Harootunian, eds., *Modern Japanese Leadership: Transition and Change* (Tucson, 1966), pp. 303, 312.
6. Haga Tōru, "The Diplomatic Background of *Japonisme*: The Case of Sir Rutherford Alcock," The Society for the Study of Japonisme ed., *Japonisme in Art* (Tokyo, 1980), pp. 28–32.
7. Meron Medzini, *French Policy in Japan during the Closing Years of the Tokugawa Regime*, Harvard East Asian Monographs 41 (Cambridge, 1971), p. 21.
8. Ibid., p. 179.
9. Ibid., pp. 50–57.
10. J. J. Rein, *The Industries of Japan* (New York, 1889), pp. 200–211, describes the diseases that decimated the European silk industry and its gradual recovery through the importation of "silk seeds, or *graines*," from Japan. He differs with Medzini regarding the duration of the crisis and claims that attempts to cultivate the *yamamai* in France in 1861 were unsuccessful.
11. The largest of these companies and the one that employed Bourret, Rémi Schmidt & Cie., contributed some of the objects exhibited by Sir Rutherford Alcock at the exposition held

in London in 1862, thus furnishing evidence that the French companies engaged in the silk trade in Yokohama were also importing Japanese artifacts. See Sir Rutherford Alcock, *Catalogue of Works of Industry and Art, Sent from Japan, International Exhibition* (London, 1862).

12. Medzini, *French Policy in Japan*. Chapters 8–15 refer to Léon Roches and his policies; another major source not cited by Medzini is R. L. Sims, "French Policy towards Japan, 1854–1894," (Ph.D. diss., University of London, 1968), pp. 67–114.

13. Marius Jansen, *Sakamoto Ryōma and the Meiji Restoration* (Stanford, 1961), p. 214.

14. Medzini, *French Policy in Japan*, p. 110.

15. Hazel Jones, *Live Machines: Hired Foreigners and Meiji Japan* (Vancouver, 1980), pp. 24–48.

16. Ibid., p. 96.

17. Yoshida Mitsukuni, *Oyatoi gaikokujin*, 2, *Sangyō* (Tokyo, 1968), pp. 53–73.

18. Kumamoto Kenjirō, *Kindai Nihon bijutsu no kenkyū* (Tokyo, 1964), pp. 142–47.

19. Ibid., pp. 24, 52.

20. David Bromfield, *The Art of Japan in Later Nineteenth Century Europe: Problems of Art Criticism and Theory* (Ph.D. diss., University of Leeds, 1977), has located seven articles and books by Bousquet, whom he refers to as a journalist. Philis Floyd, *Japonisme in Context: Documentation, Criticism, Aesthetic Reactions* (Ph.D. diss., University of Michigan, 1983), found one more article by Bousquet, whom she identifies as a critic. Both these authors have thoroughly researched French and English sources and found much valuable new material, but have not always been able to identify the individuals and artists cited.

21. Jones, *Live Machines*, pp. 104–5; L'Institute nationale des langues et civilisations orientales, *Le Japon et la France: Images d'une Recouverte* (Paris, 1974), pp. 107–13.

22. Jones, *Live Machines*, p. 1.

23. Umetani Noboru, *Oyatoi gaikokujin*, 1, *Gaisetsu* (Tokyo, 1968), p. 69.

24. Ibid., p. 71. Scholars of *Japonisme* have failed to consider the role of these *oyatoi* and are therefore unable to identify them or evaluate their observations on Japan and Japanese art.

25. Henri Cordier, "Nécrologie, *T'oung-pao* 15 (1914): 553 and Larousse, *Dictionnaire Universel du XIXe Siècle*, 13 (Paris, 1875): 1399 provide only the barest biographical information.

26. This book, which was published by the Société Asiatique in Paris, is essentially a translation of a Japanese grammar originally published in Nagasaki in 1604 by the Jesuit Father Rodriguez.

27. *La Japon et la France*, pp. 83–84, is the only recent publication to accord him some recognition.

28. Bernard Frank, "Japanese Studies in France," *The Japan Foundation Newsletter*, III, 3–4 (December 1975), p. 3. The two books are *Anthologie japonaise, Poésies anciennes et modernes des insulaires du Nihon* (Paris 1871), and *Zitsu-go-kyau-Dō-zi-kyau*, "*L'enseignement de la vérité. . . , l'enseignement de la jeunesse*" (1876). The former contains a woodblock print.

29. Congrès International des Orientalistes, *Compte rendu de la première session Paris 1873* 1 (Paris, 1874), pp. 60–61.

30. Ibid., p. 104.

31. Pfizmaier published in 1847 a meticulous reproduction and translation of an illustrated *ukiyo-e zōshi* in the possession of the Imperial Court Library in Vienna, entitled *Ukiyo-e gata rokumai byobu* by Ryūtei Tanehiko, with illustrations by Utagawa Toyokuni, that was first published in 1822. This pioneer work immediately attracted scholarly interest. An English translation of the text was published by William A. Turner, "Acount of a Japanese Romance, with an Introduction," *Journal of the American Oriental Society* 2 (1851): 27–54. It was translated into Italian by Severini, *Uomini et Paraventi: Racconto Giapponese* (Firenze, 1872). A French edition by F. Turrettini, *Komats et Sakitsi ou la Recontre de deux Nobles Cours dans un pauvre Existence* (Genève, 1875) contains a transcript of the Japanese text and reproduces six of the illustrations.

32. Cernuschi was an Italian revolutionary who escaped to France and later became a naturalized citizen. He left Paris in October 1871, to avoid the Commune, and returned in the summer of 1872. Bromfield, in *The Art of Japan*, and Floyd, in *Japonisme in Context*, have had but limited success identifying the contents of the exhibition, which was predominantly Japanese and featured bronzes, ceramics, and lacquer. In 1874 Cernuschi engaged Bouwens van der Boyen, the architect of the Crédit Lyonnais, to design the mansion that served as his home and later as the Musée Cernuschi, which he presented to the government. See Maurice Demaison, "Le Musée Cernuschi," *La Revue de l'Art* 2 (1897): 251–66.

33. Duret published an account of their trip, *Voyage en Asie* (Paris, 1874), which shows Japan to have been the highlight of his travels. While there he collected prints and illustrated books that had attracted his attention at the Paris exposition of 1867, and it likely that they were included in the exhibition. He is also the author of important studies on Japanese art, impressionist painting, and the avant-garde.

34. J. Geslin, "Question sur l'Art Oriental en général et en particulier sur l'Art au Japon," Congrès International des Orientalistes, *Compte rendu* 1, pp. lxii–lxvi.

35. Edward Said, *Orientalism* (New York, 1979). Unfortunately he does not include Japan and China.

36. *Le Japon et la France*, p. 83.

37. Auguste Mariette (1821–81) was a pioneer archaeologist in Egypt. He joined the Egyptian department of the Louvre in 1849, was sent to Egypt in 1850 to purchase manuscripts and, during the four years he spent there, discovered the remains of the Serapeum at Memphis and excavated other sites. In 1858 he was appointed conservator of Egyptian monuments, excavated at Karnak, Medinet-Habu, Deir al Bahri and other sites and founded the museum at Bulaq, Cairo, to house his discoveries. He published *Catalogue du Musée de Boulaq*.

38. *Le Jubilé du Musée Guimet: vingt-cinquième anniversaire de sa fondation, 1879–1904* (Paris, 1904), pp. i–v.

39. E. Mulsant, "Notice sur Jean-Baptiste Guimet, 1795–1871," *Mémoires de l'Académie de Sciences, Belles-Lettres et Arts de Lyon* 19 (1871–72): 160–72.

40. Her father was Jean Pierre Xavier Bidault (1745–1813); he was the teacher of his brother, Jean Joseph Xavier Bidault (1758–1846), who became a member of the Académie des Beaux-Arts in 1823 as a replacement for Proudhon, and along with Ingres, was decorated by Louis XVIII in 1825.

41. Emile Guimet, *Cinquantenaire, 1er janvier 1860–1er janvier 1910* (Lyon, 1910).

42. Henri Cordier, "Nécrologie," *T'oung-pao* 15 (1914): 380, states that he studied with Den in Vienna, Lindau in Berlin, and Reichel in Dresden.

43. Ibid., p. 382. *Catalogue général des Livres imprimé de la Bibliothèque nationale* 66 (Paris, 1916): 870–78 contains a more complete list of his publications.

44. Said, *Orientalism*, pp. 135–41.

45. Friedrich Max Müller (1823–1900) was an Anglo-German orientalist and comparative philologist who contributed to the study of linguistics, mythology, and religion. He studied Sanskrit with Hermann Brockhaus at the University of Leipzig, comparative philology with Franz Bopp at the University of Berlin, and Zend with Burnouf. He went to Oxford in 1846 to oversee the publication of the *Rigveda* and remained there. In 1868 he was elected to a newly established chair in comparative philology and taught until 1875, when he became editor of *The Sacred Books of the East*, 51 vols. Articles by him and his leading Japanese pupil, Nanjō Fumio, were published in the *Annales du Musée Guimet*. He was in close communication with Japanese scholars, and after his death, his library was acquired by the University of Tokyo.

46. A. L. Basham, *The Wonder that was India* (New York, 1959), pp. 4–8.

47. Father du Halde, *Description géographique, historique, etc., de l'empire de la Chine* (Paris, 1735); and Father de Mailla, *Histoire générale de la Chine*, 13 vols. (Paris, 1777–85).

48. Hugh Honour, *Chinoiserie, The Vision of Cathay* (New York, 1973); and Michael Sullivan, *The Meeting of Eastern and Western Art* (New York, 1973), chap. 3.

49. J. J. Rein, *The Industries of Japan*, pp. 544–45.

50. Ishizuki Minoru, *Kindai Nihon no kaigai ryūgaku shi* (Kyoto, 1972), pp. 301–39, lists the students sent to France during the *bakumatsu* and early Meiji, but rarely specifies where they studied. Nakae Chōmin is known to have studied in Lyons from the summer of 1872 until about June 1873. He is said to have acted as an interpreter for the Japanese division of an industrial fair held in Lyons in 1872; see *Bulletin Officiel de l'Exposition universelle de Lyon*, no. 37 (April 28, 1872).

51. For a contemporary evaluation, see Carl von Lützow, *Kunst und Kunstgewerbe auf der Wiener Aufstellung 1873* (Leipzig, 1875), as compared with a centennial retrospective, Wien, Osterreichisches Museum fur angewandte Kunst, *Japan auf der Weltausstellung in Wien 1873* (Wien, 1973).

52. This book, which was written in 1868 by the Swiss Minister to Japan, was published in Paris in 1870 and contains many plates by contemporary photographers, particularly Felix Beato.

53. Deborah Johnson, "Japanese prints in Europe before 1840," *The Burlington Magazine* (June 1982), pp. 343–48, lists the major publications and tentatively tries to trace the collections brought back by Engelbert Kaempfer, Carl Peter Thunberg, Isaac Titsingh, and Philipp Franz von Siebold.

54. *Le Jubilé du Musée Guimet*, p. v.

55. Emile Guimet, *Promenades japonaises Tokio-Nikko* (Paris, 1880), pp. 189–192, relates that he was the son and brother of artists and helped to create the new art of chromolithography. His brother Guillaume was a painter of military subjects and his work was exhibited in numerous museums. His brother Frédéric was a painter, engraver, and lithographer. Félix was taught by his father and then attended the Ecole des Beaux-Arts where he obtained a medal for his work on anatomy. He began to exhibit in 1865 when he was still a student. At the time he accompanied Guimet, he was a teacher at the Ecole nationale des Dessin and also at the Ecole spéciale d'Architecture. There is a fine portrait of him by William Morris Hunt in the Museum of Fine Arts, Boston. Fortunately he is to be the subject of a forthcoming article by David Bromfield, now at the University of Western Australia.

56. In 1846 the Congress of the U.S. accepted the bequest of an English scientist, James Smithson, and his mother "to found at Washington, under the name of the Smithsonian Institution, an establishment for the increase and diffusion of knowledge among men." The enabling act also provided for a library and for a museum to contain "objects of art and of foreign and curious research, and objects of natural history, etc.," belonging to the U.S.; the latter was designated the United States National Museum. The first secretary was Joseph Henry, who established an international exchange of scientific literature and published a series of reports, special treatises, monographs, and other special papers. *Encyclopedia Britannica* 20 (Chicago, 1970): 698–700.

57. A recent, but by no means adequate source, is Kōzu Zenzaburō, "Hyōden Kuki Ryūichi," Nagano ken tanki daigaku jimbun shakai kenkyūkai ed., *Gendai e no shikaku* (Nagano, 1980), pp. 3–80.

58. According to Hiroko T. McDermott, who is now preparing a more complete biographical account of Kuki and his activities while in the employ of the Ministry of Education, he arrived in London June 14, 1873, and sent a letter to the Minister of Education which was dated Paris, August 21. There is no accurate data concerning his movements in Europe and his return to Japan via the United States.

59. Kishimoto Hideo, *Japanese Religion in the Meiji Era*, trans. John F. Howes. Japan Centenary Culture Council Series 2 (Tokyo, 1956), chaps. 1–3 provide a comprehensive résumé of these complex developments.

60. *Annales du Musée Guimet* 1 (Paris, 1880): 335–73.

61. There are two early, limited accounts of Dury's career: Takanashi Kōji, "Meiji shoki no Keihan bunka to Futsujin Leon Dury," *Kamigata* 68 (August 1936): 532–39, and Inahata Katsutarō, *Inhata Katsutarō kunden* (Osaka, 1937), pp. 109–39; a more recent source is Shigehisa Tokutarō, *Oyatoi gaikokujin*, V. *Kyōiku, shūkyō* (Tokyo, 1968), pp. 114–37, but he fails to link him to Guimet.

62. These officials were impressed by the widespread esteem for Japanese artifacts, although dismayed by its indiscriminate nature. They were determined to exploit this potential for foreign trade since the government was in dire need of foreign currency to finance the importation of Western technology and armaments vital to Japan's industrialization and national security. Their concerted efforts to succeed in the export market and concomitantly to win recognition at international expositions were to have a profound effect upon the development of Meiji arts and crafts.

63. Shigehisa, *Oyatoi gaikokujin*, pp. 138–40.

64. *Nihon rekishi daijiten* 17 (Tokyo, 1961): 63 and Honjō Eijirō, *Kyōto* (Tokyo, 1966), pp. 174–76 provide only meager biographical data.

65. *Dai Nihon jimmei jisho* 2 (Tokyo, 1919): 2084, provides few details concerning Hase. For additional information regarding him and those who assisted him to establish new institutions in Kyōto in early Meiji, see my forthcoming article, "Kyoto, A Critical Century, 1790–1890."

66. A surprising number of foreign employees collected Japanese art and are known to have helped individual artists and craftsmen, but this aspect of their careers has not yet been

adequately explored. Metropolitan Museum of Art, *19th Century America: Furniture and other Decorative Arts* (New York, 1970), fig. 212, features a blond maple bedroom suite with inset porcelain tiles by Kinkōzan that was made by Herter Brothers between 1877 and 1880 for Lyndhurst, the Hudson River mansion of Jay Gould. Although the tiles clearly bear his signature, no effort was made to identify this noted potter, whose work has once again commanded high prices at recent Sotheby auctions.

67. Kōbe Genemon et al., *Kyōto hakurankai shuppin mokuroku* (Kyōto, 1872) list the objects shown at a fair that was held on the grounds of Nishi Honganji in October 1871. Since it was little more than an exhibition of paintings, ceramics, armor, coins, and some Western objects lent by the foreign teachers, it was not regarded as an industrial fair, a designation which was reserved for the one held the following spring. For details, see Kyōto hakurankai kyōkai comp., *Kyōto hakurankai shiryaku* (Kyoto, 1895), pp. 11–39.

68. Dury's former pupils went to study weaving, thread spinning, flax (or jute or hemp) spinning, respectively but nothing is known of Utahara, other than that he and Kondō interpreted for Guimet when the reception was held at the Hiunkaku in Kyōto. The first three of the new students were drawn by competition from the ranks of Kyōto fu shihan gakkō; the first, Inahata, spent eight years in Lyons studying dyeing and on his return opened a plant for dyeing military uniforms; the profession of the next two is not known, and Sato studied pottery. Kondo, Imanishi, Yokota, and Inahata all contributed to the monument erected in honor of Dury, near Nanzenji, in Kyōto in October 1899.

69. *Rapport au Ministère de l'Instruction publique et Beaux-Arts sur la mission scientifique de M. Emile Guimet dans l'Extrême-Orient* (Lyon, 1878).

70. It neglects to mention his Greek and Roman statuary.

71. Exposition Universelle: Galeries Historiques—Trocadéro, *Notice Explicative sur les objets éxposés par M. Emile Guimet et sur les peintures et dessins faits par M. Félix Régamey* (Paris, 1878). The catalogue shows that he organized the material iconographically rather than according to country, chronology, or medium.

72. Chap. 29 of this book tells of Guimet's visit to the home of Kawanabe Kyōsai (1831–89) who came of a samurai family, studied Kanō painting but in 1858 decided to become independent and settled in the Hongō district of Tokyo. A brilliant draftsman and incisive caricaturist, he had great powers of invention and a mordant wit. He was also a printmaker and illustrator. The English architect, Josiah Conder, studied painting with him and acquired a large collection of his works. His paintings were exhibited at the Vienna Exposition, and there are excellent examples of his work in Western collections. Chapter 30 describes their duel.

73. Congrès Provincial des Orientalistes, *Compte rendu de la troisième session de Lyon 1878* (Lyon, 1880).

74. The Second International Congress of Orientalists, which was held in London in 1874, did not have any papers on Japan; there was only one, on the first Russian expedition to Japan, included in the program of the third congress held in St. Petersburg in 1876. The Congrès Provincial des Orientalistes first met at St. Etienne in 1875 and focused on France's outstanding branch of Orientalism, Egyptology. Guimet presented a paper on Chabas. Its president, Baron Textor de Ravisy, submitted an ambitious agenda—to formalize their basic principles; to promote two new branches of study, Khymer art and the ethnography of Cambodia; to encourage commerce and industry to avail itself of knowledge of the Orient as well as the needs and aspirations of French Orientalism. The second provincial congress was held in Marseilles and was led by Ferdinand de Lesseps; one of the sessions was chaired by the first President of the Republic, Adolph Thiers.

75. It is difficult to trace the careers of lower-ranking military officers in early Meiji, and the only clue to his identity is Shigehisa, *Oyatoi gaikokujin*, p. 131, which lists Harada Terutarō (alternate reading Kitarō?) as one of three pupils from Nagasaki who accompanied Dury to Kyōto and acted as his assistant and interpreter, particularly since he notes that Harada later became a colonel. Harada also appears as one of the contributors to Dury's monument.

76. Congrès Provincial des Orientalistes, *Compte rendu* 2, pl. 10, furnishes one of the earliest reproductions of the museum.

77. Léon de Milloué, *Catalogue du Musée Guimet* 1 (Lyon, 1880).

78. Ibid., (Lyon, 1883), p. xi, refers to Japanese and Indian collaborators "MM. Ymaizoumi, Tomii, Yamata, Harada, Panditeleke et Da Sylva de Colombo."

79. *Dai jimmei jiten*, vol. 4. See also Sugiyama Naojirō ed., "Hommages à la mémoire du Baron Masaakira Tomii," *Bulletin de la maison franco-japonaise*, 7, 3–4 (Tokyo, 1936), pp. 1–53.

80. *Dai jimmei jiten* 1:302–3, and Mombushō, *Tokyo bijutsu gakkō rireki sho: Imaizumi Yūsaku.* (unpublished), mistakenly notes that he went to Paris and that the Musée Guimet was located there. See Mori Senzō, *Meiji jimbutsu itsuwa jiten* 1 (Tokyo, 1965): 114, regarding his decision to study art in France.

81. Yajima Midori, *La Japonaise: Kiku Yamata no isshō* (Tokyo, 1983) provides the first biographical material concerning Yamada Tadazumi, the father of this well-known Franco-Japanese writer.

82. *Annales du Musée Guimet* 1 (1880): 375–84. Bernard Frank, "Japanese Studies in France," p. 5, mistakenly claims that Guimet "organized Japanese courses at the Ecole de Commerce which were taught by the Buddhist monks whom he had introduced from Japan." He cites as his source P. Demieville, "L'Extreme-Orient dans l'oeuvre de Sylvain Levi," *Bulletin de la Maison franco-japonaise*, 8, 2–4 (1936), p. 51, where the author quite correctly states that Imaizumi and Yamada, who had published translations of Buddhist texts in the first two issues of the *Annales*, could not be considered *ryūgakusei*, foreign students, because they had been brought to France by Guimet to classify his collection and to teach Japanese at the Ecole de Commerce in Lyons.

83. Congrès Provincial des Orientalistes, *Compte rendu* 2, p. 150.

84. See *Kyōto ichiritsu bijutsu kōgei gakkō enkaku ryaku* (Kyōto, n.d.), pp. 1–3 for the text of the proposal.

85. Ever since his arrival in Japan in 1868, Wagener had been involved in various projects related to the arts. He assisted San Tsunetami organize the Japanese exhibit at the Vienna Exposition of 1873, the Philadelphia Exposition of 1876, and the first National Industrial Exposition held in Tokyo in 1877. After the Vienna Exposition, he accompanied Sano on a tour of the leading museums of Europe and consulted their directors regarding the establishment of a museum and auxiliary art school in Japan. Although the proposal Wagener submitted was rejected by the national government, Makimura considered his recommendations pertinent to Kyōto. A Japanese translation by Asami Tadamasa of Wagener's report appears in Ōkoku hakurankai jimukyoku, *Ōkoku hakurankai hōkokusho: hakubutsukan bu ni* (Tokyo, 1875). Ko Wagener hakase kinen jigyō kai, *Wagener sensei tsuikai shū* (Tokyo, 1938), pp. 169–85 contains a fine, brief biography of Wagener by his intimate friend, the Swiss diplomat Rudolf Lindau. See also Yoshida, *Oyatoi gaikokujin*, pp. 75–95.

86. Régamey published two more books in collaboration with Guimet, *Okoma* (Paris, 1883) and *Le Théâtre au Japon* (Paris, 1886). With regard to art education, he published *L'Enseignement du Dessin aux Etats-Unis: notes et documents* (Paris, 1881) and *Le Dessin et son Enseignement dans les Ecoles de Tokyo* (Paris, 1899). He issued a catalogue, *Catalogue de son Exposition* (Paris, 1888). Of particular interest is *Le Japon pratique* (Paris, 1891) which appeared in an English translation by M. French-Sheldon and Eli Lemon Sheldon, entitled *Japan in Art and Industry* (New York, 1892). More popular books on Japan include *Le Cahier Rose de Mme. Chrysantheme* (Paris, 1894), *Le Japon en Images* (Paris, 1903) and *Japon* (Paris, 1905). Because of publications of this nature, he was approached, during his tenure as Secretary-General of the Societe Franco-Japonaise, by Japanese who considered engaging him to "start a monthly review 'specially destined for advocating the cause of Japan.'" See Robert B. Valliant, "The Selling of Japan: Japanese Manipulation of Western Opinion, 1900–1905," *Monumenta Nipponica*, XXIV., 4 (Winter 1974), pp. 429–30. Shigehisa, *Oyatoi gaikokujin*, p. 143, reproduces a handsome sketch of Makimura, signed "Regamey, Kyoto Nov (?) '76," which he presented to Makimura. It is now in the possession of the Kyōto University of Fine Arts, formerly the Kyōto Art School.

87. See *Kyōto ichiritsu bijutsu kōgei gakkō enkaku ryaku* (February 11, 1881).

88. Union centrale des Arts décoratifs, Palais de l'Industrie, *Salon annuel des Peintres japonais*, Première Année (Paris, 1883), Deuxième Année (Paris, 1884). These catalogues were discovered by Dr. Gabriel P. Weisberg, who kindly furnished me a copy.

89. Scholars have been reluctant to study Kuki because of complications resulting from his wife Hatsuko's affair with Okakura Kakuzō and his insistence upon keeping her confined to a mental institution. A full account of the affair has been made public at last by Matsumoto Seichō, "Okakura Tenshin to sono teki: rivaru monogatari," *Geijutsu shinchō*, serialized from January 1982 to February 1983.

90. Katori Shūshin, "Kiritsu kōshō kaisha," *Nihon bijutsu kyōkai hōkoku* (October 1931), pp. 11–27; Hasegawa Sakae, "Kiritsu kōshō kaisha," *Museum* 232 (July 1970), pp. 22–31. Some additional information is to be found in Segi Shinichi, "Nihon bijutsu ryūshutsu shi," *Taiyō*, Bessatsu, 21 (Winter 1977), pp. 109–40.

91. Gabriel P. Weisberg, "L'Art Nouveau Bing," *Arts in Virginia* 20, 1 (Fall, 1979), pp. 2–15, surveys his career and lists pertinent bibliography.

92. Segi, "Nihon bijutsu ryūshutsu shi," pp. 119–20, which also appeared in English, Segi, "Hayashi Tadamasa: Bridge Between the Fine Arts of East and West," The Society for the Study of Japonisme ed., pp. 176–72.

93. Concerning the Japanese attitude toward *ukiyo-e* and its export, see Segi, "Meiji izen ni okeru ukiyo-e no kaigai ryūsutsu shi," *Ukiyo-e geijutsu* 24 (1969), pp. 15–33 and Segi, *Ukiyo-e: Edo bigaku no saikentō* (Tokyo, 1972), pp. 215–62.

94. Takahashi Yoshio, *Kinsei dōgu idōshi* (Tokyo, 1929), pp. 8–79, describes the art market during the *bakumatsu* and the first decade of Meiji.

95. Gaimushō Zōhan, *Nihon gaikō bunsho* (Tokyo, 1952), vol. 15, pp. 301–6; vol. 16, pp. 346–52; vol. 17, pp. 400–405; vol. 18, pp. 397–407.

96. Jeanine Auboyer, in the introduction to Asia House Gallery, *Rarities of the Musee Guimet* (New York, 1975), pp. 11–18, traces the evolution of the museum.

97. Omoto Keiko, "Guimet Tōyō bijutsukan to Emile Guimet," *Cahiers d'études françaises* 9 (1980), pp. 90–101, places the present activities of the museum in a historical context.

Part 3
International Treaties and National Security

Moat around Emperor's Palace, Tokyo. *(Photo permission of Anna Brinton Collection. Reproduction by Masako Imai.)*

Introduction

The Meiji mind developed in the shadow of the unequal treaties and during the high tide of Western imperialism in Asia. The first thirty years of Meiji were devoted to strengthening the nation in the face of the militarily and industrially dominant West in order to end the humiliation of the unequal treaties and regain full sovereignty. The Restoration was a response to the Western threat that the "barbarian-expelling" (jō-i) shogunate could not meet. Every aspect of the modernization process was conditioned by the need to attain treaty revision, whether the haste to develop modern industry and a strong military or the more cautious approach to judicial and legal reforms and the creation of a new social order. Power lay in the industrialized and industrializing nations of the West, whose standards Japan would have to meet to attain the end of its unequal status and whose drive for imperialism Japan would soon emulate.

The treaties concluded by the *bakufu* and inherited by the Meiji government limited Japanese sovereignty through extraterritoriality, the most-favored-nation clause, and loss of tariff autonomy. Extraterritoriality, first established in the convention with Great Britain in 1854, removed foreign nationals from Japanese law and jurisdiction and left them subject only to the law of their home country as administered by consuls and other diplomatic representatives. Unable to control the foreigners residing in Japan or have them subject to the judicial system, the *bakufu* and Meiji governments restricted them to the treaty ports and prevented foreign ownership of land and travel outside these areas until the unequal treaties were ended. The most-favored-nation clause, first used in the Treaty of Kanagawa of 1854 between Japan and the United States, unilaterally granted to the Western treaty power those rights and privileges granted to all other nations and severely limited Japan's freedom of action in the field of diplomacy. The tariff rate was set by treaty; and by 1866, the average rate was set at a low of five percent, which would fail to provide revenue in a time of acute financial need and afford no protection to developing industries. Lastly, the treaties contained no termination date, only the provision for revision.

The treaty powers were determined to keep Japan in a status of inequality, a relationship emphasized by the power demonstrated by the combined fleet bombardment of Kagoshima in 1863 and Chōshū in 1864 and by the presence of their gunboats in the ports of Japan. The Japanese soon realized that international equality was limited to Western, Christian states; others were not equal. The aim of both the Japanese government and its opponents in the democratic-rights movement was to rid Japan of the unequal treaties and to regain full sovereignty. Only thereafter would efforts be concentrated on attaining recognition as an equal among the world powers.

Sandra T. W. Davis illustrates the overwhelming concern of the Meiji mind with the issue of the unequal treaties and its concern with the schizoid nature of Japanese diplomacy. The Meiji intellectual Ono Azusa could document Japan's case for treaty revision while justifying the Japanese "murder" of the Ryūkyū kingdom and interference in Korean politics from the standpoint of national security. Yet, while calling for regional cooperation to stem the Western onslaught in East Asia, this *mintō* spokesman in a prophetic vision argued for a peaceful settlement to the problem of Korean independence to forestall Japanese military intervention and ultimate expansion.

The continued resistance of the treaty powers to Japanese attempts at treaty revision and their contemptuous treatment of Japan led to the rise of a new idea on revision: unilateral denunciation. Richard T. Chang documents the development of the idea of unilateral denunciation of the treaties by Japanese foreign ministers and their foreign advisers from 1882 to 1892 and the cautious response of a Meiji leadership that feared Western retaliation, perhaps excessively.

The irony of history is that, while seeking to end the humiliation of the unequal treaties and bitterly attacking the arrogance of the treaty powers, Japan acted in the same big-power fashion toward China and Korea and imposed upon the "Hermit Kingdom" similar unequal treaties. Hilary Conroy shows the importance of Western, especially American, influence in promoting and encouraging Japanese expansion through the acquisition of the Ryūkyūs and Taiwan and the failure of Great Britain, Russia, and the United States to exert sufficient pressure to prevent the Sino-Japanese War and the beginning of Japanese imperialism. The Meiji leadership operated within an internationally defined area, which set the terms of Japan's relationship to the West in detail but failed to delineate the outlines of acceptable Japanese-East Asian relations or to condemn Japanese actions during the initial stages of Japanese aggression in China, and thereby, by default encouraged Japanese expansion.

The three essays are related in showing the ways in which the actions of Meiji leaders were circumscribed by the environment in which they operated.

6 Treaty Revision, National Security, and Regional Cooperation: A *Mintō* Viewpoint

Sandra T. W. Davis

The search for treaty revision dominated much of the thought and activity of public officials and the leaders of the *mintō* (popular parties) during the first three decades of the Meiji era. Because the treaties exerted a grave influence on the legal and economic structure of the nation, changes were essential to end the disadvantages imposed by extraterritoriality and lack of tariff autonomy, to avoid the perils of foreign domination, and to establish a framework for peaceful international relations.

To the Japanese, the unequal treaties exposed the nation to the continual danger of foreign imperialism. The treaties controlled the character of the Japanese market. Once opened to the outside world, advanced industrial countries came to view Japan as a market for their manufactured goods and as a source of raw materials. Justifying their activities by the doctrine of free trade and the legal guarantees written into the treaties, foreign merchants moved into and came to dominate certain sectors of the Japanese economy, particularly foreign trade and shipping. The five-percent ad valorem duty set by the Tariff Convention of 1866 meant that customs duties supplied only a small portion of revenues and forced the government to rely on the land tax as a major source of funds. Lack of protection against foreign imports directly affected developing domestic industries and prevented capital accumulation. Industry was, therefore, forced to rely on the government for funds. The rapid growth of imports created an unfavorable balance of trade; and the resulting loss of specie led to inflation, prevented currency stabilization and the establishment of stable fiscal policies. Inflation created a continual feeling of crisis in the government, which met the situation by issuing convertible paper notes.

Extraterritoriality restricted national sovereignty and was a serious obstacle to political unity. Decisions made by the consular courts were regarded as biased and inequitable and placed the Japanese at a serious disadvantage in international trade. In cases tried under consular jurisdiction, there was no recourse to appellate review and the courts operated according to Western law and judicial procedures, a situation detrimental to Japanese litigants. Revision of the treaties depended upon reforms that would enable Japan to improve its standing with the powers and create a more advantageous international position.[1]

In October 1871, Prime Minister Sanjō Sanetomi suggested to Iwakura Tomomi, vice-president of the Council of State and foreign minister, that a special mission be sent to countries having treaty relations with Japan to study their laws, customs, and institutions and to recommend those which should be adopted. His letter illustrated Japanese sensitivity to what was regarded as a position of international inferiority and to the injustices received at the hands of foreign nations as well as the realization of the need for radical change in order to get revision.[2] The return of the Iwakura mission in 1873 marked the advent of a major program of modernization through the adoption of selected aspects of Western technology and institutions and the beginning of the debate on the methods needed to revise the unequal treaties, promote national security, and enable Japanese-Chinese-Korean cooperation against the advance of Western imperialism in East Asia.

Treaty revision as an issue involving national sovereignty and international status, and as a means of attacking the *hanbatsu* (the Satsuma-Chōshū clan group that dominated the government) occupied a key place in the thoughts and policies of the new Meiji intellectuals and politicians. Concern over the adverse effect of the treaties and Japanese weakness vis-à-vis the West were based not merely on political opportunism but on a sincere concern for the future of the nation and on a deep commitment to modernization. This sense of urgency and dedication can be seen in the speeches and writings of the chief organizer and spokesman for the Rikken Kaishintō (Constitutional Progressive Party), Ono Azusa (1852–86), a youthful leader of the movement for constitutional and parliamentary government on the British model and moderate political reform. Ono, a native of Tosa, had studied law in New York for one year and economics and law in London for two years and was a scholar and disciple of Jeremy Bentham's and John Stuart Mill's utilitarian theories.[3] Although an advocate of increased popular participation in government through representative institutions and of British political parties and methods, his admiration was tempered by realism, by fear of colonial domination and cultural imperialism, and by the ever-present question of selective modernization to enable Japan to survive as an independent nation while preserving its own traditions and institutions. Within this context, his ideas reflect much of the early Meiji view on treaty revision and on Japan's position in East Asia.

In October 1882, before an audience of 2,000 at the Meiji Hall in Tokyo, Ono asked: "What do you think of the present situation of Turkey? The Western powers always interfere in the government of Turkey, which no longer can maintain its autonomy. The flag of the crescent has lost its light and the sultan is exalted no longer." According to Ono, shortsighted diplomacy was the reason why Turkey declined and was now despised by foreign countries. Diplomacy was the most important aspect of foreign policy. The harm caused by suppression of freedom of speech or communications, while great, can be reversed; but the damage caused by diplomacy can not be cured by a change of government or cabinet. Its effect is long-lasting and changes require the approval of other countries. The Turkish Empire once spread over Europe and Asia, but Turkey's fate is now determined by the Western powers. Was this example irrelevant to Japan?

Ono continued by answering his own question. Recent Japanese history proved what kind of treaties the *bakufu* (clan government) had concluded. These treaties were the result of careless and disgraceful diplomacy. The fault of the shogunate was, considering the situation at that time, permissible; but the collective treaties with England, France, the United States, the Netherlands, and Russia were so damaging that it was just like the Turkish case. If not revised, Japan would follow the path of Turkey. Rather than run the risk of interference from the combined powers, the government should conclude separate treaties with each power as the interests of nations differ.

Italy and the United States had agreed to revision. Why did the government not conclude revised treaties with them? The government had to revise the treaties on two points: abolition of extraterritoriality and restoration of tariff autonomy. The first point was necessary to save national honor, but it was lack of tariff autonomy that did the most harm, as it resulted in a heavy land tax and prevented increased productivity and monetary reform. Tariff autonomy was indispensable if the nation was to become strong. The government had to concentrate on this point first. Extraterritoriality would not be ended until government reform was complete. The government should not allow foreign nationals to reside outside the treaty ports ("mixed residence") as this was not advantageous so long as extraterritoriality continued. Thus, Ono concluded, even the proposed treaty with Hawaii that, though negotiated on the basis of equality, would allow foreign residence in the interior should be rejected because it would set a precedent for other states to demand similar rights.[4]

Tariff autonomy was the most immediate aspect of treaty revision; and Ono, normally an advocate of laissez-faire, expressed the popular viewpoint when he wrote in 1881:

> Those who produce cotton ask for protection, which would close the country [to imports] and prohibit the import of cotton from foreign countries. Those who produce sugar ask for protection and the imposition of a tax on imported sugar to promote the production of sugar in Japan. Those who deal in silk, leather, paper, umbrellas, hats, soap, wines, beer, and tobacco seek protection.[5]

The demand for treaty revision was motivated not by mere opposition to the oligarchy, but by a deep sense of patriotism and concern for the welfare of the nation. Etō Shimpei had demonstrated this earlier in 1870, when he pointed out the need to compile new legal codes and a constitution and to modernize the military in order to get the Western powers to agree to revision. Only when the nation was prosperous would it attain a position of equality with foreign countries.[6]

Ono Azusa represented the intellectuals of the second decade of the Meiji era. Unlike the generation of Etō and Fukuzawa Yukichi who called on the *jinmin*, the people, Ono's generation began to use the word *kokumin*, the nation, to arouse patriotism and make the people aware of the threat from hostile foreign countries. Like others who had been abroad, his attitude toward the West was realistic, and he recognized that "the public law of the nations of the world does not mean that the law is followed and maintained by governments to keep peace in the world. Therefore, if there is a country which is strong enough to break the law, it will do so because of its growing desire [for power]."[7] Cognizant of Japanese technological and military unpreparedness and faced with foreign gunboats in their harbors, Ono and his contemporaries called on their countrymen to forget sectional and clan differences and to unite to save the nation.[8]

As the political scene calmed and public attention focused on problems of treaty revision, especially the issue of mixed residence or foreign residence outside the treaty ports in 1884, Ono told his followers in the Kaishintō that the people had not progressed intellectually. They were absorbed in the treaty revision and had become so aroused as to try to drive foreigners away. However, if this led to opening up the interior to foreigners and to higher customs duties, the people would suffer even more. The most important thing was to end extraterritoriality and to restore tariff autonomy. Although those in government were competent, he feared they would make mistakes, and so he had written an essay entitled *Jōyaku kaisei ron (Discussion on Treaty Revision)*, which he planned to submit to the Foreign Minister. Regardless of whether one was an official or a commoner, since all were subjects of the emperor, it was essential not to make an error in judgment in such a critical moment in Japanese history.[9]

Jōyaku kaisei ron is a representative critique of the Meiji view of the unequal treaties. Ono began it with a discussion of the nature of the treaties and a claim that they should have been revised twelve years before, in 1872. The treaties were concluded when a majority of Japanese were ignorant of foreign affairs. The *bakufu* was forced to sign them because of the military supremacy of foreign countries. As a result, national independence was forfeited and the nation was gravely injured. These unequal treaties had to be abolished at once. Treaty revision had to include the following six points: (1) abolition of extraterritoriality, (2) restoration of the right of tariff autonomy, (3) conclusion of separate treaties with each nation, (4) separation of the articles on commerce from those on amity, (5) elimination of the most-favored-nation clause, and (6) placement of a time limit on each treaty.

There were two types of extraterritoriality, Ono said. One was carried out in Europe and the other in the Far East. Extraterritoriality was the right of a foreign government to execute its orders in other countries, but it does not mean foreign governments possessed unlimited rights abroad. Those who live in foreign countries do not have the right to issue orders as do their governments. Although a foreign ambassador has many special privileges, he is punished if he disturbs the peace of the host country. The right of extraterritoriality is regarded as limited to the monarch and government officials of other countries, ambassadors and their families, and military and naval personnel passing through or along the coast of a nation in Europe. The basic rule of extraterritoriality is respect for other countries, but extraterritoriality is carried out quite differently in the Orient. The special rights usually applicable only to foreign officials, diplomats, and the military are extended to ordinary citizens of foreign nations. Certain conditions are essential prerequisites for national independence. A nation must be equal in status to other countries and its government must be able to rule without foreign interference. Theodore Dwight Woolsey, an American political scientist, said a sovereign state is independent and free from outside intervention and has the power to establish and enforce the laws of the country. However, when foreign countries interfere in domestic affairs and enforce their laws, a nation is no longer independent. This is the reason that the Japanese are eager to abolish extraterritoriality, Ono argued.

Continuing, he said that tariff autonomy must be restored in order to increase production. In Europe, national revenues come from direct or indirect taxes; but the Japanese government is forced to depend on direct taxation because of the lack of industry. Yet, since the beginning of the Meiji era, enormous sums have been spent for modernization. If Japan had the right to levy duties on foreign imports, the people would not have to bear such a heavy tax burden and more funds would be available for new public works. Inexpensive imported goods have replaced domestic items, and it is necessary to revise the treaties to allow for tariff autonomy in order to increase national income and help Japanese industry. It is best to conclude treaties with each country on an individual basis, not with the powers collectively. The treaties concluded at the beginning of the Ansei era (1854–59) are a disgrace to Japan's national rights. The Tokugawa *bakufu* is to be blamed for this; but since it no longer exists, the only thing to do is to correct the situation. Each nation has specific interests, and so it is best to conclude new treaties one by one. Treaties of commerce should be separated from the treaties of amity. The terms for friendly relations seldom change even though a hundred years may pass, but the terms of commerce must change at least every ten years. The same treaty need not be concluded with each nation but should be concluded according to the status and interests of the signatories. The most-favored-nation clause is the type of agreement made between victor and vanquished in war and must be stricken from the treaties. It is necessary to set a time limit on the treaties as the demands of history change. If a treaty continues unchanged for many years, it causes many problems, said Ono.

The first time the Meiji government tried to negotiate on treaty revision was in 1870. In November 1871, Iwakura Tomomi, Kido Kōin, Ōkubo Toshimichi, Itō Hirobumi, and Yamaguchi Naoyoshi were sent to Europe not to negotiate new treaties, but to cultivate friendly relations with Western nations. Ono noted that at the time he was studying in the United States and had the chance to see them and personally to look at the message sent from the Emperor Meiji to the American government. It said that Iwakura, Kido, Ōkubo, Itō, and Yamaguchi were sent to America as a demonstration of friendship and to improve relations. Furthermore, as the treaties were to be revised in one year, it was hoped that Japan would attain equality with other nations even though it differed from them in many ways. Japan did not hope for immediate revision, but only wanted to learn more about the customs of Western nations and to select those that would be suitable in order to improve its policies and customs. By these efforts, the Japanese were sure that they would be able to attain a position equal with that of Western nations.

Following the return of the Iwakura mission, treaty revision could have been attained if the government had concentrated on negotiations. However, the cabinet changes over the issue of Korea, the Saga and Satsuma rebellions, and the trouble over Taiwan occupied the attention of the administration until after 1872. In 1878, the treaty with the United States was amended on ten points. The Japanese government was given the right to levy duties on imports from the United States, equal to those levied on goods from other countries, and to control and regulate trade along the Japanese coast. Both the United States and Japan could tax exports shipped from their respective countries. Shimonoseki and one additional port were opened for American trade, and American merchant ships were allowed to trade in any Japanese port provided they observed tariff regulations. Americans violating the revised treaty were to be tried by an American consular court. The treaty was to be ratified within fifteen months.

Ono continued to discuss the revised treaty in *Jōyaku kaisei ron* and noted that it did not abolish extraterritoriality but only provided for the restoration of tariff autonomy between the United States and Japan. Thus, in 1880, the government invited all foreign ministers to a secret meeting on the issues of extraterritoriality, mixed residence, mixed courts, and reform of the legal code and police. The meeting had no positive results; and from what Ono himself had learned, treaty revision would take a longer time than expected.

Since 1878, the government had discussed changes in customs duties with the powers five separate times. The first negotiations on the tariff were held in 1858 with the United States; and the resulting agreement was just and fair for the time, though not to Japan's advantage. A similar treaty was concluded with Great Britain. In 1858, the United States, the Netherlands, and Russia pressured the *bakufu* to accept the most-favored-nation clause, which placed Japan in a very unfavorable position. The tariff schedule was revised in 1866 (Keiō decision) and 1869 (Meiji new plan), and the importation of opium was prohibited in 1866. The 1858 tariff was set at an average of 10 percent with 3 items duty-free. The 1866 level was cut to 5 percent with 18 items duty-free. In 1869, the tariff was set at 5 percent ad valorem with gold and silver, coins, fertilizer, raw wool, and ships duty-free. Ono then presented a detailed listing of the rates to support the contention that the Meiji new plan was in many ways an imitation of the first tariff convention.

Ono declared he would never deceive his readers, but he was indignant over the situation. The government revised draft was fair compared with the present rate, but its policy of continuous concession and retreat had no results. It should not have yielded an inch and should have tried to recover the right of tariff autonomy. At the fifth and latest trade negotiations, the Western powers demanded the inclusion of foreign judges in Japanese courts and freedom of travel. "We Japanese cannot approve such a selfish request!" Allowing foreign officials to participate in court trials was foreign intervention in Japanese internal affairs and was an indignity against national independence. It was opposed to any concept of sovereignty. Such "mixed courts" would not end extraterritoriality. The idea was similar to closing the front door to prevent a tiger from entering, but opening the back door to allow a wolf to come in. The distinction between extraterritoriality and the use of foreign judges was that the former permitted foreign laws to be used in governing the country and the latter allowed foreigners to intervene in domestic law. Mixed courts would increase extraterritorial rights as seen in the case of Egypt, which is "nothing but a colony of both Britain and France." Western judges would not be under the control of the Japanese government, but of a diplomatic conference and could not be considered in the same category as foreign advisers, who are appointed and discharged by the government. As seen by the Egyptian example, which was explained in detail, once advisers were appointed by foreign governments, even as a result of diplomatic agreements, the Egyptian monarch lost the power to dismiss them and ultimately forfeited control over his own administration.

Articles by two contemporary writers who favored opening the interior to foreign travel and residence because of the inevitability of close contact between Japanese and foreign nationals were then quoted by Ono in detail. They claimed the coming of the railroad would simplify travel throughout the country; and once the people became accustomed to associating with Westerners, they would learn to live in peace, do business, and talk together. The more quickly this happened, they declared, the better. While not disputing the value of foreign contacts, Ono feared that mixed residence would attract many foreigners to Japan. This would increase the number of civil suits and employment problems. If not subject to Japanese law, the establishment of foreign communities would create "countless independent states" in the interior of the country. Mixed residence would not result in treaty revision. Japan was constantly giving up rights to the treaty powers but receiving nothing in return. Mixed residence in the interior should not be allowed until the country regained its national power and dignity. The foremost interest of the Japanese people was to maintain their independence permanently. Even if the treaty powers refuse to amend the treaties, the demands made at the fifth commercial conference should not be accepted by any means.

How then were the treaties to be amended? The key issue in treaty revision, Ono noted in *Jōyaku kaisei ron*, was the abolition of extraterritoriality. Revision would be possible if each of the treaty powers were dealt with separately, taking its specific interests into consideration. Before instituting this method of negotiations, preparations were needed. Revision would be meaningless unless the most-favored-nation clause was removed from the treaties of amity as this gave all the treaty powers something for nothing. If each power in consultation did not agree to drop this article from the treaty and to meet Japanese demands, then the government should state that customs duties were to be imposed on its goods equal to that placed on all other imports and no special benefits will be permitted. If no agreement is reached, the Japanese negotiator should propose an article stating that special rights given to Japan by one treaty power must be provided by all other powers, a form of reverse most-favored-nation clause threat. Only after a state agrees to accept Japanese demands, namely, to end extraterritoriality and to recognize the right of tariff autonomy, should Japan grant it special benefits, mixed residence in the interior, or allow its nationals the right to own land in Japan. If a power offers only to acknowledge the right to set tariff rates, but not the end of consular jurisdiction, Japan should promise only to reduce customs fees on imports. If a nation is so obstinate as to refuse all Japanese demands, the government should cease to negotiate and wait patiently. Thus, Ono concluded, "I believe that such a country will soon realize the disadvantages of such stubborn disagreement and in less than ten years will give in and come to accept our demands." This strategy should be kept secret, but should not be so rigid as to preclude changes when necessary. "If we are too impatient over the issue of ending extraterritorial rights and go about it in a careless way, our children surely will suffer greatly for our mistakes. So, we should always remain calm and patient in order to succeed in this most difficult task."[10]

Jōyaku kaisei ron was a representative work of popularly held views on the subject of the unequal treaties. As such, it was similar in content but much less vehement in tone than numerous articles and editorials in the press. Ono eschewed violence and was the spokesman of moderation, and he showed the work to the Kaishintō president, Ōkuma Shigenobu, who twice read, corrected, and discussed it with him. Yet, because of the sensitive nature of the contents, the essay soon involved Ono in a continuous battle with the government as he sought to avoid censorship and get it published. On May 24, he applied to the home minister for a copyright; and six days later was told to submit a copy of the work with his application, which he did at once. On June 19, he urged the government to grant a copyright. Nine days later, the copy was returned with a note telling Ono to apply to the Foreign Ministry for permission to publish. "Where," he wrote in his diary on June 28, "is freedom of the press?" Ono immediately wrote to Foreign Minister Inoue Kaoru but received no response. On July 23, he again wrote to Inoue and pleaded to see him on the grounds that as a private citizen he, too, was deeply concerned over treaty revision and wanted to explain his proposals. The next day Inoue replied and invited Ono to meet him at his house in Kasumigaseki on July 28.

Inoue began the conversation by stating that he did not intend to remain silent about negotiations with the treaty powers, but he would be very embarrassed if news about the talks was released at this time. He would discuss the negotiations only if Ono promised not to publicize his views. Ono agreed and stated he had come only to discuss the issue of treaty revision, which "actually concerns the glory and shame of our country. I only want to do my best to help our government achieve it." He agreed not to act against Inoue's wishes but only asked him to tell the truth.

Inoue informed Ono that his proposals on revision were not suitable as meetings were currently being held to discuss trade and the opening of three additional harbors. Officials appointed at the harbors would handle criminal cases and civil suits, both under the jurisdiction of Japanese courts. Other officials would be in charge of laws relating to the police, sanitation, hunting, and local taxes. While the public might say that this was too small a gain in return for opening three harbors, it was a precedent for extending jurisdiction over foreigners. Yet, the foreign minister recognized that if the powers would not agree to this plan, no compromise could be reached. Ono feared this policy meant an end to attempts to revise the treaties, but noted that the government alone could not attain revision. The support of the entire Japanese nation was essential, and Inoue concurred. Ono stated that, although the difficulties over treaty revision originally stemmed from the haughty attitude of the foreigners, yet the fact that domestic affairs were not in order prevented revision. For example, neither the police nor judges satisfied the people, let alone foreigners. Here, too, Inoue agreed and added he continually informed the Home and Justice Ministries that, if the police and judiciary were not well run, revision could not be accomplished. Ono then presented *Jōyaku kaisei ron* to the foreign minister, noting that it was essential to conclude separate treaties with each country. Inoue remarked that this was not possible because of the previous treaty. He promised to read the work and then to discuss it with Ono.

On August 14, Ono wrote to Inoue to urge that they meet again. There is no record of a second meeting; and although *Jōyaku kaisei ron* was revised and ready for the printer by September 3, it was not published during Ono's life time.[11] Refused permission to publish by the Home Ministry, he resorted to lecturing on the work at Tokyo Senmon Gakkō, the predecessor of Waseda University, and began by telling his audience of 300 students:

> How dangerous are the current treaties to the independence of our country? I have worried about them for a long time. I have often seen foreigners behave audaciously. I have been angry and saddened as our national rights have been neglected. Therefore, I have tried to restore them for many years. You, who have gathered here today to meet with me, are the brothers of our 35 million countrymen. I am sure you are all as angry as I over this issue. Hence, we rejoice and sorrow over the same things. Who does not hope to realize treaty revision as soon as possible so that our great country will be able to participate in diplomatic relations as do other nations? But, on the contrary, I have heard that the government is going to permit foreigners to live in our country wherever they want without abolishing extraterritoriality. Don't you think this is very unusual? Because I can no longer remain silent, I wrote a treatise entitled *Jōyaku kaisei ron* in order to appeal to all the people. In this way, I wanted to save Japan from the shame into which it has fallen; but the government will not allow it to be published. . . . However, once a man stands up, he must be well prepared for any great difficulty. I know I would sacrifice myself for this country however seriously ill I may be, for I am a Japanese. You . . . are, so to speak, the children of the Emperor Meiji; and so you are all responsible for the restoration of our national rights. . . . I want you to use your education to every extent possible for our national welfare.[12]

Denied the right to publish his views, Ono called upon the youth of Japan to make treaty revision a mark of patriotism and self-dedication.

Jōyaku kaisei ron was Ono's most explicit statement on how to attain treaty revision. Much of his career, both as an official in the Ministry of

Justice from 1876 to 1881 and later as a politician, had been devoted to promoting reforms that would hasten revision. As secretary to the Genrō-in (Senate) in June 1879, he made, in his own words, a "most splendid speech on the abolition of torture."[13] In support of the cabinet's decision to discuss the topic he said:

> Traditionally, torture has been adopted as part of criminal law; however, there are accusations that this cruel practice has been used to obtain false confessions from offenders. On the other hand, in regard to international relations, the existence of this tradition has interfered with the negotiations and attempts to amend the treaties. There has been a general trend toward the abolition of this tradition since 1872 or 1873. . . . Even among judges, . . . there are not a few who state it is not necessary to judicial procedures. Therefore, now is the time to abolish it.

Ono then proceeded to discuss various cabinet and ministerial rulings in favor of ending the use of torture in criminal cases. While pointing out that the interpretation of the law was influenced by the general atmosphere and political structure of the time, he emphasized that early Meiji criminal law was based on Chinese legal principles and on the traditional ways of the warrior class. However, the political system had changed, national prosperity had improved greatly, and many governmental methods had been adopted from Western civilization. The criminal codes were anachronisms in the present condition of reform and grave obstacles to national progress and prosperity. In order to revise them, torture had to be abolished. Since the Revised Codes require all legal judgments be made after obtaining confessions, offenders are first forced to confess; and brutal torture is used to obtain the confession. On moral grounds alone, Confucius said the father may protect his son and the son, his father, but the law does not allow for this and is contrary to human reason and feelings. It is written in the American constitution that an individual cannot be forced to make statements damaging to himself. The Ministry of Justice should allow judges to consider material and documentary evidence and to hear witnesses when it is apparent the accused has committed a crime. All articles in the new draft of the criminal code permitting torture should be repealed to show that this country has taken another step toward improvement.[14]

Ono believed that Western ignorance of Japan, especially of the fact that "it has been united under one ruler for over 3,000 years and had never been invaded or defeated by foreigners," was a major factor in the failure of negotiations leading toward treaty revision. To correct Western misconceptions about Japanese culture, he began to write a history of Japan in

May 1883 for distribution abroad. The work, unfortunately left unfinished, was to show that "Japan is now proud of its leading position in the development of Oriental civilization" and "is a progressive country."[15]

Treaty revision was but one aspect of the search for national security. Secure and defensible borders were essential in an age of modern naval power and Western expansion. Yet, the government's decision to assert Japanese sovereignty over the Ryūkyūs in 1879 presented the Meiji liberal with the basic contradiction between the right of the islands to independence and the need for Japanese security, issues directly related to relations with China. In early 1879, Ono noted in his diary: "In my opinion, [control of] Korea is out of the question; but by all means, the Ryūkyūs should belong to Japan. If this is rejected [by China], relations will not improve." The dichotomy between opposition to the use of force by the Western powers in Asia and acquiesence to the forceful takeover of the Ryūkyūs was expressed in an essay entitled *Ryūkyū saku* ("Policy toward the Ryūkyūs") written in April 1881.[16]

> The recent diplomatic policy of our country toward the Ryūkyūs is like a case of murder in which the victim has been attacked but is still alive. When our government attacked the Ryūkyūs and made it our domain, the people of the Ryūkyūs were too astonished at the force used by the murderer to realize that their time was drawing near and, therefore, did not have the chance to feel bitter toward our government. However, they are like a person whose wounds so pain him that he realizes the end of his life is drawing near. If, at this time, the murderer feels pity on the victim who is about to expire, the victim will feel more bitter against him; and at the same time, other people will accuse the murderer for his great cruelty. Our country killed the Ryūkyūs because our government had reason to do so; and at the same time, due to circumstances, the Ryūkyūs were not allowed to die but made our domain. However, this was only a temporary measure and not a final one. The final step should be taken peacefully.

Ono continued and noted that some people say there is no problem in allowing the Ryūkyūs to be independent as the area would be subordinate to both China and Japan. These critics point out there is no profit in having such a backward area as part of the nation. Others say Japan should protect the islands and help them attain independence, for circumstances will not permit Japanese domination. These opinions were not convincing to Ono, who felt the Ryūkyūs lacked sufficient national power to be self-governing. Furthermore, since the islands were directly related to the national interest of Japan, there was no reason to help them become independent. If the Ryūkyūs were free and subordinant to both Japan and China, it would do more harm than good. Some rationalized Japanese claims on the basis of linguistic similarities. Even if such similarities did not exist, the geographic position of the islands was important for diplomatic considerations, trade, and commerce, and possession of the area was directly related to the nation's well-being. Why should the Ryūkyūs not be solely under Japanese control? Because of its geographic position, no European nation regarded control of the islands as important to its welfare.

Thus, the Ryūkyūs were less important to China and Korea than to Japan.

> Geographically, they are closest to Japan. If a foreign nation should conquer the Ryūkyūs and, taking advantage of its unprotected state, station a navy and shipping facilities there, our diplomatic position, trade, and commerce would be adversely affected.... To avoid such grave consequences, there is only one path for us to follow. That is to protect the Ryūkyūs by force and to prepare for the invasion of other nations into the Pacific Ocean. Therefore, even if their language and geographic names were not the same, we have to protect the Ryūkyūs to maintain our national power. Furthermore, they have been subordinate to Japan for a long time. It is natural for Japan to do something to improve the situation. My opinion is that our government should apply the measure abolishing the clans and establishing prefectures in the Ryūkyūs as soon as possible and should notify the treaty powers of this.... objections from China are inevitable. Nevertheless, the danger to China cannot be compared to the threat to Japan if a foreign power should gain control of the Ryūkyūs.... We should point out the great danger to our country. If, at the same time, we explain that cooperation between Japan and China is the first prerequisite for peace in Asia and what is dangerous to Japan is also dangerous to China, the Chinese will realize how meaningless it is to raise objections to this policy. There is no doubt that this is the best policy in regard to the Ryūkyūs, which has already been killed. I suggest we make the Ryūkyūs a prefecture of Japan in order to protect Japan and to contribute to the maintenance of peace in Asia. I dare advocate murder but this murder does not harm our virtue in the least.[17]

Protection of the southern approach to Japan, therefore, required that the Ryūkyūs be incorporated into the empire. Protection of the nation as a whole required unity and patriotism. In 1875 Ono wrote in the *Kyōzon zasshi* that the great powers ignored international law and made their own laws. Japan was surrounded by countries that could be regarded as potential enemies; and if divided and weak, "the white bear will take advantage of an unguarded moment and seek a bloated prize."[18] Only unity and strength would preserve the nation's territorial integrity and boundaries; and only institutional, technical, and military modernization would provide the wealth and power that were believed to be the prerequisites for equality with the treaty powers. The reforms essential for survival in an age of European expansion and colonization meant a reorientation of outlook from East to West, a movement from a world order dominated by China toward a system theoretically based on relationships among equal, independent nation-states. Reorientation meant rejection of the preeminence of China in East Asia and of the assumption of dominance over traditional tributary states, especially the Ryūkyūs and Korea. The changes undertaken by the Meiji regime were essential to national survival, but moved Japan away from traditional relationships and toward those nations which had inflicted the unequal treaties on Japan and China and militarily defeated the once powerful Middle Kingdom.

In the process of consolidating its power, the Japanese government ignored Chinese claims of sovereignty and asserted control over the Ryūkyūs. The island of Tsushima, which during the Tokugawa period had maintained tributary relations with Korea while its ruler was at the same time vassal to the *bakufu*, was also brought under the control of the new regime. Relations with both the Ch'ing and Yi dynasties were embittered, and Seoul's refusal to acknowledge the restoration of imperial power and to address the emperor accordingly almost led to war. In 1876, after eight years of unsuccessful negotiations, a show of force off the Korean coast, and negotiations between Tokyo and Peking, the Treaty of Kanghwa inaugurated diplomatic relations between Japan and Korea and opened three ports to Japan. The treaty referred to Korea as an "independent" or "self-governing country" enjoying sovereign rights and was followed by treaties with the United States and other Western powers. The implementation of the treaty, admission of foreigners, and struggle for power among court factions led to anti-Japanese riots in Seoul, an attack on the Japanese legation, and the murder of several Japanese in 1882. When negotiations for redress failed, a Japanese warship and troops were sent to Inchon. This led to Chinese military and diplomatic intervention and a negotiated settlement of the issue. The Korean regime agreed to pay an indemnity to the families of the deceased and to injured Japanese and the sum of 500,000 yen in ten yearly installments to the Meiji government, which, after two payments, canceled the indemnity.[19]

Ono reacted to the news of the anti-Japanese riots in Korea by stating privately that the Chinese army in Korea agitated the Korean troops to attack and kill Japanese. "I do not hate Koreans, but I feel sorry for their naïveté." Japan should demand a formal apology, reparations "to consol the bereaved, and a promise to reform the Korean administration in the near future." The most important thing was to have Korea become conscious of its independence and to enable the government to rule the country by itself. These factors were related to Japanese security and to the security of the Orient as a whole. "We also accuse China as well as Korea because it looks down on Korea as a subject state and keeps troops in Korea unnecessarily. We should demand China recognize Korean independence, stop interfering [in Korean affairs], withdraw all essential troops from Korea, punish the Chinese general who caused the incident, and offer some reparations." Unless China accepts this demand, Japan will have to resort to arms to maintain its prestige, national welfare, and for the sake of the whole Orient. Now that the ambassador who is to take charge of negotiations has been decided upon, the government should be ready to use as much force as it can employ if negotiations fail.[20] He further asserted that "now we should show our dignity. Having heard of the recent incident in Korea, what we should do is to express our nation's indignation and then indirectly help the party in Korea which favors opening the country to establish Korean independence. Our purpose should be to break the Chinese spirit of arrogance."[21]

In a more thoughtful, prepared speech written after the anti-Japanese rioting in Seoul in 1882, Ono proposed that the government work to end Chinese mistrust and Korean animosity against Japan and not allow the Western powers to interfere in the Far East. India was controlled by England and Indochina by France, and the only independent countries in the Orient were Japan and China. Japan was the leader of the Orient. Japan was important. The Western powers were expanding in the Orient, and the situation was tense. Japan, as the leader of the Orient, had to overcome its differences with China and Korea. Since Sino-Japanese relations were not good, resolution was necessary. Korea concluded a treaty with the United States of America. Rioters in Korea attacked the Japanese legation; and the minister, who was rescued by an English ship, managed to return to Japan. Korean ill will had not ended. Chinese officials tried to interfere in the negotiations between Japan and Korea. Ono hoped that the government would not misinterpret the situation in the Orient. Japan was fortunate to end the conflict with Korea through the virtue of the emperor and the power of the people, but the situation was not advantageous for the Orient. It was Japan's responsibility to improve the situation. A half-million yen reparation was not a satisfactory settlement, but this could not be helped. Ono hoped the government would make beneficial use of this money in order to eliminate both Chinese and Korean distrust of Japan. It should be used to enlighten Korea by promoting progress in the form of post offices, telephones, and other means. Then Korean and Chinese enmity would be resolved to the advantage of the Orient. If the issue of reparations was pursued further, problems with Korea and China would never be resolved.

> Whether Korea is an independent country or a dependent of China is a current problem. There are some who would call on Western countries to normalize relations with Korea. Great Britain is going to interfere, and this is not to the advantage of Japan or China, the only independent countries in the Orient. If the treaty powers intervene, we will be in the same position as Turkey. Western nations are trying to interfere in Eastern problems. Japan, China, and Korea

should normalize relations. Whether Korea should be independent or semi-independent should be decided according to the views of Oriental nations. The prosperity of the Orient is not only to our advantage but also for the Western powers. They will agree with my opinion. Diplomacy is the heart of a country. Once mistakes are made, the injury has a long-lasting effect. Diplomacy requires broad vision.[22]

Upon learning of his government's decision to cancel the indemnity payments and return the amount paid to Korea, Ono noted approval of the policy in his diary on November 25, 1884, but stated he did not know how the money would be put to use. He not only hoped the money would be used "to promote enlightenment," but also proposed that the Japanese government point out how to use the money and then enforce its use accordingly. This would be preferable to having the funds go into the pockets of a few officials. If the money was used for modernization, then Korean and Chinese mistrust of Japanese motives would end and the Koreans would remember "the good deeds" of the Japanese.

Relations with China and Korea continued to occupy Ono's attention in 1884 and 1885 and were a factor in his decision to write *Jōyaku kaisei ron*.[23] The failure of the Seoul incident of December 1884, in which the reform-oriented Independence Club with aid and encouragement from the Japanese legation attempted to overthrow the conservative Min faction, once again focused Ono's attention on events in Korea. After reading news reports on December 14 and 15 of the Korean uprising and fighting between Japanese and Chinese troops, Ono felt the government "should demonstrate its power in order to suppress Chinese arrogance." Several days later, he mentioned that the Chinese had reacted very quickly to events in Seoul, but that Li Hung-chang, who had been responsible for handling Chinese relations with Korea since 1880, was desirous of making peace. On December 22, he noted that Foreign Minister Inoue had left for Korea with several warships. "It is good to practice both a hard and a soft foreign policy at the same time." Four days later, after learning that 4,000 Chinese troops had been sent to Korea, he wrote that developments led to the inevitable suggestion that Korea had to be independent in order to be rid of Chinese influence. To Korea, any suggestion of independence was equivalent to interference in domestic affairs; but within the Meiji government, there had been discussion over the question of sending Inoue to Korea and on Korean independence.

Ono saw 1885 as an inauspicious year, and the first comment in his diary reflected his anxiety over foreign relations:

> It is going to be a very troubled year. As long as contradictions exist among the people, they will not be unified. Overseas [in Korea], events did not turn out as we expected. Sending ambassadors abroad still has not ended these incidents. However, incidents [such as those

in Korea] need not be a disadvantage to a nation. The worse thing is for a country to be "static." This leads to corruption, and corruption leads to destruction. We should make use of this opportunity. In regard to the Korean incident, both advance and retreat will be disadvantageous. According to present conditions, if we want to take the lead among Oriental nations, we have to make use of this opportunity and act effectively. However, this will lead to the expansion of the army and expenditures. It may also lead to militarism.

Following the publication on January 15 of the Japanese-Korean treaty, Ono discussed the need to focus public attention on foreign relations in order to help establish government policy with a colleague in the Kaishintō. He noted that lack of popularity for administration actions could be seen in the fact that Foreign Minister Inoue did not receive a warm welcome from the public when he returned to Japan on January 19. Ono wrote that, if the government decided to go to war over Korea, it should act slowly; but if it intended to use a show of force as a means of making peace, it should act quickly. In a letter sent on January 27 to his brother-in-law, Ono Gishin, a former associate of Ōkuma's and then adviser to Mitsubishi, he suggested Japan should meet with representatives of the Western powers to decide the issue of Korean independence. He mentioned that it was said that the Japanese minister in Seoul tried to persuade the foreign ambassadors there to force China to withdraw its troops from Korea. However, this would not be a permanent solution to the problem, as it must be resolved by the Oriental countries themselves without foreign intervention. Two days later, Ono noted in his diary the rumor that Itō Hirobumi feared the danger of a war with China but that the military were impatient to act. Furthermore, money was in short supply, and people were beginning to show dissatisfaction with the government.

> In my opinion, if we start a war with China, the development of militarism and a shortage of currency will be inevitable. However, if we can not make China fulfill our expectations [i.e., agree to Korean independence and to reforms], then these two trends are inevitable, too. Therefore, if we cannot attain a diplomatic victory over China, the military will have an excuse for expansion and will require a great deal of government money. Itō understands these two problems; yet, he does not try to achieve any diplomatic accomplishments to show to the military. This indicates he is a politician who is concerned only with keeping peace now [but not with the long-range effects of his policies].

During February, Ono's diary contains numerous references to Korean problems and to visits of Korean diplomatic missions to Tokyo. Once again he expressed his concern over the reaction of the military, who were dissatisfied with the slow pace of government actions. Despite a cabinet meeting before the emperor on February 1 and at Prime Minister Sanjo's residence on February 5, the public remained uninformed of policy decisions regarding China. In noting that the third Korean mission since 1876 had arrived to apologize for anti-Japanese activities, Ono remarked that "we have suffered three times and received apologies three times. We had better be more careful because our neighbor Korea is in a period of political darkness and is easily stirred up by the other country [China]."

On learning that an official would be sent to China, Ono wrote that it was necessary to select a person with patience and a strong personality who should be subject to specific instructions in regard to the proposed negotiations. At the same time, the army should prepare for war. When the press confirmed that Itō was to be the minister sent to Peking, Ono pointed out that eighty days had passed since the demonstration in Seoul and the appointment had come much too late. The government had acted too slowly in this crisis. Nonetheless, Ono sent a farewell message to Itō on February 26 and took note of the fact that on February 27, Kuroda Kiyotaka was sent to China unofficially. Itō left for Peking on February 28, and Ono wrote that it was not too much to ask Japan and China to withdraw their troops and to have the Korean army reorganized under Western direction to avoid future Sino-Japanese conflict. The Chinese should also reprimand Yuan Shih-kai, the Chinese resident in Seoul, although this was not a major point. Agreement with China over any future aid to Korea was essential. The important thing in foreign policy was not reparations for past losses but to plan for the future. Korean sovereignty should be made clear-cut as this would calm a tense situation. It was essential to think not merely of gaining momentary advantage for one's country or of momentary comforts, but of the future.

As he studied press reports on the negotiations with China in early March, Ono remarked in his diary that the Chinese minister plenipotentiary, Li Hung-chang, was the most powerful man in China and "it will be good to have him in charge." However, he cautioned on the amount of power Li really exercised, namely, whether he could make decisions on his own or was subject to the views of the leading officials in Peking. If Li had complete power over the course of the negotiations, he would not have to wait for the court's decision on the site for the talks. Then Itō would not have to visit Peking first. If Li's power were limited, then the meetings in Tientsin would be most inconvenient. Subsequent reports on the site were confused and left Ono wondering if Itō had failed in his assignment. News in early April that China was holding concurrent talks with France on a treaty of friendship was regarded as detrimental to the Japanese position. Earlier, in 1884, Ono had written that when China was on bad terms with Russia, "a promise was made to give Okinawa to us; but after resuming friendly relations with Russia, the promise was broken." Good relations with France could directly affect the outcome of negotiations with Japan. On April 18, Ono learned that an agreement had been reached by Li and

Itō, but he was not aware of the contents of the treaty. "The word 'peace' can be very valuable or without value. A peace without value is not to be praised, but I do not know what kind of peace Itō is getting." The failure of the government to release the contents of the treaty immediately was "proof of not having [concluded] a satisfactory treaty as it is human nature to exaggerate if one has satisfied one's hopes."

On April 20, the main points in the Tientsin Treaty or the so-called Li-Itō Convention, namely, the withdrawal of troops from Korea and prior notification of any decision to send troops to the peninsula, was released to the press. Ono wrote that one of the points mentioned was that the uprising of 1884 had occurred because of the "carelessness of Chinese officers" and those responsible would be reprimanded. "It was not bad for both countries to withdraw their troops, but the future safety of Japanese in Korea will be in doubt. Who will protect them? Thus, Itō's work cannot be regarded as successful." Ono decided to reserve final judgment until he had seen the text of the treaty, but disagreed with newspaper reports that the decision on troop withdrawals constituted recognition of Korean independence. Itō returned to Tokyo on April 29. Newspaper accounts on April 30 stated that the treaty provided for Chinese officials to be sent to Korea to check on improper conduct by Chinese soldiers. However, Ono privately questioned if this was any different from an agreement that Chinese officers in Korea be subject to official reprimand or was just a condition for agreement on the treaty. If the officers were reprimanded, the investigation would not be necessary; but since it was under way, would those guilty of misconduct be punished? What would be done, under the treaty, if no punishment were meted out? Itō had signed a treaty that was not secure, and he had not carried out his instructions. Ono had sent his opinions on the treaty to the press; but once again, the Foreign Ministry prohibited publication.

Not until May 27 were the terms of the Tientsin Treaty and the accompanying letter of apology from Li Hung-chang announced to the public. In regard to the issue of troop withdrawals, Ono felt that neither side had gained or lost anything, and this was due to the failure of the negotiator. Second, he felt that Korea had been afforded the right to protect itself; but this also augured neither good nor bad for the future. Since no definite plans had been made, it was not good. Finally, the point that "China cannot send troops into Korea without Japanese approval was most practical, but undermined Korean sovereignty. The reprimand to be given to Chinese officials in Korea had become only a written apology from Li Hung-chang. Thus, the treaty was not sufficient as the wording was too mild. However, this was not an important point and should not be regarded very seriously." Nonetheless, Ono was dissatisfied with the document. On April 30, he had secretly doubted whether the treaty was necessary, but felt the Chinese officials should be reprimanded and punished, for they had insulted Japanese women and killed Japanese citizens. This was known from testimony given by the women involved. On June 11, Ono took note of newspaper reports stating that Korea secretly had sent a minister to Russia to ask for protection. He questioned if this was true and wrote: "I feel very sad about events in Korea." Four days later, after reading in the press the text of the treaty that ended the Sino-French War, Ono wrote that the document was primarily favorable to France and would lead to French domination even in Tokyo. "European control is slowly moving East, and the people of the Orient must pay more attention to this."[24]

To the Meiji mind, international relations in the second half of the nineteenth century were based on a predatory system of might. In the eyes of Ono and many of his contemporaries, international law was followed only insofar as it benefited a nation to do so and the strong ignored the law when it was to their advantage. The imposition of the unequal treaties on a weak and secluded Japan was the most flagrant example of this. In a world dominated by military power, strength and unity were the only means to restore national independence and tariff autonomy. Border areas such as the Ryūkyūs had to be brought under direct control, for Western nations would take advantage of a power vacuum in the area to seize control over unclaimed territory. The maintenance of Japanese independence and territorial integrity justified the assertion of sovereignty over the islands. A weak and semi-independent Korea incapable of reform or of protecting itself invited intervention from the Western powers, and Chinese activity in Korea was seen as preventing change and the assertion of independence as well as instigating anti-Japanese activities. China was incapable of providing leadership in Asia. Japan alone was progressing along the path toward modernization and parliamentary government. Japan alone could lead the Orient into the cooperative action needed to prevent Western dominance. To do this, it was necessary to end the hostility that had developed between Japan and China and Korea. Unity was essential to protect the nation and the Far East and positive leadership had to be demonstrated. East Asian unity could be attained by the resolution of differences through negotiation, and negotiations were preferable to force, even though Japanese citizens had been injured and national honor insulted. Force was to be eschewed, though a show of military power was an acceptable tactic in difficult negotiations, for it was unity in the face of Western expansion that was sought as the best means of protection against the European onslaught. Cooperation among East Asian countries was the means of survival and modernization in an age of imperialism.

Yet, while his public statements constantly advocated moderation, Ono's diary reveals a continual vacillation between the realization that negotiated settlements are most conducive to the long-range attainment of objectives and a willingness to resort to either a show of force or the threat of military intervention when fellow countrymen or national "dignity" were threatened or Chinese intransigence appeared insurmountable. The "honor of the nation" was a constant concern to the Meiji politician, but not the prime issue in Sino-Japanese relations nor an issue on which the nation should go to war. In approving a simultaneous "hard" and "soft" approach to foreign policy, Ono does not reveal at which point the "hard" would devour the "soft," if at all; but he recognized the danger of the situation. His fear of a military solution to the Korean problem and of the resulting danger of militarism was, in retrospect, prophetic. He favored the withdrawal of foreign troops from Korea; and although his national pride was offended by the Chinese failure to reprimand those responsible for anti-Japanese activities, he conceded that this was a minor point that could be dropped. He was willing to have Western specialists train the Korean army as a temporary expedient to avoid war with China, but he recognized the danger inherent in this. Ono's opposition to the Tientsin Treaty of 1885 was that its provisions were too weak to prevent future conflict between Japan and China. It did not guarantee Korean independence. It was a measure of expediency that did not provide for a permanent solution to the Korean problem and could easily be negated. The subsequent decade and the Sino-Japanese War proved his analysis to be correct. Diplomacy had to provide long-range solutions that dealt with the essence of the problem.

Ono described himself as a *shishi*, a patriot, and his private papers reveal a sense of national pride and an emotional undercurrent of nationalism kept under control by his ability to analyze a situation objectively, by his aversion to force, and his espousal of moderation. Whether this control would have vanished during wartime cannot be known, for Ono's lifetime saw Japan beset by repeated crises but not involved in a major war. Ono was sincere in his liberalism and his fear of the military as detrimental to political freedom and economic development. However, he was equally committed to the search for equality with the treaty powers and the maintenance of Japanese independence and territorial integrity. Whether, like other liberals and advocates of popular rights, he would have allowed liberalism to become subordinate to nationalism cannot be ascertained. He died in 1886, and the historian must deal with facts and not conjecture.

Ono's frame of reference in regard to foreign policy was Japanese security and independence in an age of imperialism. This justified the takeover of the Ryūkyūs, domestic change to attain treaty revision, and the promotion of reforms in Korea, whether or not desired by the Koreans. Japanese leadership of East Asia, though never clearly defined, did not mean the political and military hegemony envisioned in the 1930s and 1940s. It envisioned a unified foreign policy toward the West based on a consensus of opinion among China, Korea, and Japan. Such a policy would serve to prevent further encroachments on national independence and territory. Leadership also implied aid in the implementation of institutional and technical modernization. It did not imply a coprosperity sphere or military control. At no time did Ono discuss the export of political liberalism to Korea or China, for the issue that concerned him was not the extension of popular rights abroad but survival as independent national units. National independence was the main issue; reform was secondary and a means to maintain independence. Secure border regions thus justified the takeover of the Ryūkyū islands, and Ono's emphasis on the importance of the Ryūkyūs to Japanese security and his fear of a potential Russian threat to Japan's northern regions had a remarkably modern tone. His concern with Korea and China was based on the fear that weak, divided, and feuding Asian states were easy prey to foreign imperialism. Such a situation placed Japan in a weak position in relation to increased demands by the treaty powers and held, in his view, the potential of outright foreign domination. The failure of all attempts at treaty revision, the ever-present sight of foreign warships in the treaty ports, the military and diplomatic humiliation of China, the former center of the East Asian cultural world, and the spreading cancer of Western colonialism were continual reminders of the foreign menace that required concentrated efforts to attain international equality through new treaties, maintain national independence, and cooperation among China, Japan, and Korea in the early Meiji era.

Notes

1. Ukai Nobushige, *Kōza Nihon kindai hō hattatsu shi*, 14 vols. (Tokyo: Keisō Shobō, 1958–1962), 2:185–88; Mukai Ken and Toshitani Nobuyoshi, "The Progress and Problems of Compiling the Civil Code in the Early Meiji Era," *Law in Japan*, 1 (1967): 32.
2. Joseph Pittau, *Political Thought in Early Meiji Japan, 1868–1889* (Cambridge, Mass.: Harvard University Press, 1967), p. 40.
3. The most complete biographies on Ono Azusa are Nishimura Shinji, *Ono Azusa den* (Tokyo: Fuzanbō, 1935) and Sandra T. W. Davis, *Intellectual Change and Political Development in Early Modern Japan: Ono Azusa, A Case Study* (Cranbury, N.J.: Associated University Presses, 1980).
4. Ono Azusa, "Gaikō o ronzu," in *Ono Azusa zenshū*, ed. Nishimura Shinji, 2 vols., (Tokyo: Fuzanbō, 1936), 1:469–81. This speech was written on October 1–2, 1882 and shown to Ōkuma Shigenobu on October 13. See Ono Azusa, "Ryūkakusai nikki," in Nishimura, ibid., 2:410–12.
5. Ono Azusa, "Hogo o kou no kaisei," *Tōyō zacho*, unpublished manuscript dated March 17, 1881, in the Ono Collection, National Diet Library, Tokyo.
6. Osatake Takeki, *Nihon kempō seitei shi* (Tokyo: Ikuseisha, 1938), p. 61.
7. Minamoto Ryōen, "Kokumin teiki toitsu no rinen to sono kyokun—Meiji nashiyonarizumu no isan no saikentō o tō shite," *Ushio* 88 (October 1942):117. For example, Ono used *kokumin* in the essay "Kokumin nanzo kore o omowazaru" ("Why Do the People Think This Way?").
8. For example, see Ono Azusa, "Tada Nihon ari," *Ono Azusa zenshū*, 2:27–31, and "Kokumin nanzo kore o omowazaru," ibid., 2:13–16.
9. Yamada Ichirō, *Tōyō Ono Azusa kun den*, 2 vols. (Tokyo: Dōkōkai, 1886), 2:16–17.
10. Ono Azusa, "Jōyaku kaisei ron," *Ono Azusa zenshū*, 1:137–212.
11. Ono Azusa, "Ryūkakusai nikki," *Ono Azusa zenshū*, 2:495–506.

12. Nishimura Shinji, *Waseda no hanseki* (Tokyo: Waseda Daigaku Shuppanbu, 1932), pp. 102–3.
13. Ono Azusa, Document no. 18, Ono Collection (n.d.).
14. Ono Azusa, "Gojin haishi no enkaku," *Ono Azusa zenshū*, 2:255–63.
15. Nishimura, *Ono Azusa den*, pp. 92, 289–90; Ono, "Ryūkakusai nikki," *Ono Azusa zenshū*, 2:447–49, 458–59; Ono Azusa, "Nihon rekishi," *Ono Azusa zenshū*, 2:211–225.
16. Ono, "Ryūkakusai nikki," *Ono Azusa zenshū*, 2:318–19, 322, 343.
17. Ono Azusa, "Ryūkyū saku," *Ono Azusa zenshū*, 2:281–83.
18. Ono Azusa, "Kokumin nanzo kore o omowazaru," ibid., pp. 13–16.
19. Hilary Conroy, *The Japanese Seizure of Korea* (Philadelphia: University of Pennsylvania Press, 1960), pp. 22–29, 63–68, 101–6; Inoue Kiyoshi, *Nihon no rekishi*, 3 vols. (Tokyo: Iwanami Shoten, 1963–66), 2:180–81, 195; Gaimushō Kanshū, *Nihon gaikō hyakunen shōshi* (Tokyo: Yamada Sho-in, 1959), pp. 33–34.
20. Ono Azusa, "Shin Kan no shochi o ronzu," in Nagata Shinnosuke, *Ono Azusa* (Tokyo: Fuzanbō, 1897), p. 269.
21. Ibid., p. 275.
22. Ono, "Gaiko o ronzu," *Ono Azusa zenshū*, 1:478–81.
23. Ono, "Ryūkakusai nikki," *Ono Azusa zenshū*, 2:506, 512, 528.
24. Ono, "Ryūkakusai nikki," *Ono Azusa zenshū*, 2:518–41.

7 The Question of Unilateral Denunciation and the Meiji Government, 1888–92

Richard T. Chang

The thirty-year-long attempt by the Meiji government (1868–99) to shake off the fetters of the unequal treaties was a significant human endeavor, for this attempt represented the supreme national quest by the proud, sensitive Japanese for equality of status with the West. One of the lectures I give in my modern Japanese history course is, therefore, devoted to this topic. In response to this lecture, brief as it is, many students over the years have raised one question: "Why did the Meiji government put up with the unequal treaties? Why didn't they unilaterally denounce the treaties?" This chapter is an attempt to answer this persistent question. Specifically, I shall deal with three interrelated questions: (1) Did the Meiji government deliberate on the feasibility of undertaking a unilateral denunciation of the unequal treaties? (2) If so, why did they not take this course of action? (3) What does historical analysis suggest would have been the result of taking this option?

Before dealing with these questions, however, it will be helpful, for a full understanding of what unilateral denunciation involved in the context of nineteenth-century Japan, to discuss the following: the characteristics of Japan's treaties with the Western powers; the nature of the inequality of the treaties; the methods whereby treaties or treaty obligations in general may be terminated; and two rules of customary international law, *pacta sunt servanda* and *rebus sic stantibus*.

In the second half of the nineteenth century, sixteen Western nations—Great Britain, the United States, France, Germany, Russia, Italy, Portugal, Spain, the Netherlands, Belgium, Denmark, Sweden-Norway, Austria-Hungary, Switzerland, Hawaii, and Peru—maintained treaties with Japan. These treaties had four characteristics in common. First, all the treaties provided unilateral extraterritoriality for the Western treaty powers alone. Second, they deprived Japan of the sovereign right to fix her own tariff. Third, the most-favored-nation clause was unilateral, unlimited, and unconditional. Finally, the treaties were interminable in that they contained no provision for termination, only for revision.¹

The unilateral nature of the first three of these characteristics constituted the inequality of these treaties. (The reason that the fourth characteristic of Japan's unequal treaties, the absence of a fixed term for their termination, is not viewed as constituting part of their inequality is the fact that this feature was not unique to the unequal treaties of Japan. Many other treaties concluded in the nineteenth century also did not provide for a fixed term. They were, and still are, often called "permanent treaties.") In Japan a national of a treaty power could be sued not in a territorial court of Japan, but in a consular court of his own country in Japan, there to be tried according to the law of his country. Such a privilege was not conferred upon Japanese subjects in the territories of the Western treaty powers. Similarly, while Japanese goods imported by the treaty powers were subject to tariff schedules determined solely by the governments of these powers, their goods imported into Japan were subject to low tariff rates unalterable except by the consent of the powers. Likewise, the Western treaty powers, while enjoying most-favored-nation treatment in Japan, did not accord the same trade arrangement to Japan.

For all practical terms, the unilateralness of the most-favored-nation clauses turned the sixteen bilateral treaties into a single bipartite treaty, a treaty in which one contracting party was composed of one state and the other party, of two or more states. Most of the treaty powers had little at stake in trade with Japan; however, the treaty arrangements were commercially so advantageous that they were determined to preserve them as long as they could. They therefore followed the lead of Great Britain, whose economic stake in trade with Japan was incomparably greater. For her part, in her attempt to maintain the unequal treaty system, Great Britain was, vis-à-vis Japan, able to speak much of the time for virtually all the treaty powers on treaty-revision matters.

This British-inspired cooperative policy was to be a stumbling block to any Japanese effort to revise the unequal treaties. In the words of the late J. L. Brierly, one of "the most difficult and practically important questions of the law of treaties relates to the termination of treaties which contain, at any rate in their expressed terms, no provision for that purpose."² Speaking of the problem of revision, William W. Bishop, Jr., has observed: "In case all parties concerned wish to bring about the change [revision], existing procedures are not inadequate. The trouble arises when one or more of the states involved is unwilling to agree to the change desired by another."³ Bishop's observation pertains to the present, where the sovereignty of the state is no longer so sacrosanct as it was in the nineteenth century. Since virtually all the treaty powers refused to accept the change she desired, Japan encountered seemingly insurmountable difficulties.

Out of the stupendous struggle that her attempt to overcome them entailed came the consideration of resorting to unilateral denunciation.

Unilateral denunciation is but one of the many methods whereby treaties or treaty obligations may be terminated. These methods include (1) notice given by a contracting party in accordance with the terms of the treaty; (2) fulfillment of the provisions of the treaty; (3) expiration of the period of time for which the treaty was entered into; (4) extinction of one of the parties—in the case of bilateral treaties—or of the subject matter of the treaty; (5) agreement of the parties; (6) the conclusion of a subsequent agreement covering the same subject matter or one wholly inconsistent with the earlier treaty; or (7) denunciation by one party and acquiescence by the other.[4] It will be seen that what made exceedingly agonizing the evaluation by the Meiji government of its possible resort to unilateral denunciation, the last of the seven methods mentioned, is the fact that Great Britain, the foremost treaty power, insisted on the fifth method cited, the mutual consent of the parties.

The norm that any modifications or termination of the treaty required the consent of all the parties involved is derived from the rule of *pacta sunt servanda*—treaties are made to be kept and must be observed in good faith. This fundamental principle of international law was clearly expressed by the Protocol of the London Conference, signed January 17, 1871. The Protocol asserted: "The plenipotentiaries of North Germany, Austria-Hungary, Great Britain, Italy, Russia, and Turkey . . . recognize that it is an essential principle of the law of nations that no power can liberate itself from the engagement of a treaty, nor modify the stipulations thereof, unless with the consent of the contracting powers by means of an amicable arrangement." No assent of all the parties, no modification. This rule has been reaffirmed by several international compacts, the last of which is the 1969 Vienna Convention on the Law of Treaties.[5]

Certainly there would be an end of all stability in international affairs if any state were free to repudiate its treaty obligations whenever it thought fit. But though these obligations are perpetual if no time limit is stipulated, it is also clear that treaties cannot remain unchanged. As circumstances alter, international compacts made to suit them go out of date. This brings us to another rule of customary international law by virtue of which the Meiji government weighed the possibilities of unilaterally denouncing the unequal treaties: the doctrine of *rebus sic stantibus*. Simply defined, the doctrine says that a treaty ceases to be binding when an "essential," "fundamental," or "vital" change of the circumstances in which it was concluded has taken place. Stated still another way, the idea common to most concepts of the doctrine is that "a treaty becomes legally void in case there occurs a change in the state of facts which existed at the time the parties entered into the treaty."[6] An obvious question may arise: "What constitutes a fundamental change?" There is no hard and fast answer to this question. One authority has stated that when and under what conditions it is justifiable to denounce a treaty is a question of morality rather than of law.[7] The several examples of the invocation of the doctrine of *rebus sic stantibus* cited in this chapter alone, however, suggest that the question has been one of strength rather than of morality. To be sure, those powers which successfully invoked the doctrine to terminate their treaties, such as the United States and France, did so because the treaties thus terminated contained no provision for their termination; and in all probability the powers believed that they were unlikely to be able to secure the consent of the other parties for that purpose. On the other hand, had it not been for their military strength or their standing in international relations, which virtually insured acquiescence by the other parties, these powers could not have successfully invoked the doctrine.

We now turn to the first of the three specific questions raised at the outset of this chapter: Did the Meiji government deliberate on the possibility of undertaking a unilateral denunciation of the unequal treaties? The government certainly did for a period of four years, 1888–92. This deliberation evolved in three stages. First, within the government Ōkuma Shigenobu, who was foreign minister from February 1888 to late December 1889, alone advocated resort to unilateral denunciation. Second, other government leaders, while reacting against Ōkuma's advocacy, nevertheless were exposed to the idea of termination, and eventually were convinced by their foreign legal advisers that Japan had the sovereign right to denounce the unequal treaties unilaterally. Third and finally, once convinced of this right, the leaders wrestled with the question of whether or not to exercise that right. In the end they reached the conclusion that such an action was impracticable, but that something had to be done to revise the treaties. Out of this dilemma came a contradictory proposal that Japan seek the consent of the Western treaty powers to invoke her "sovereign" right to denounce the treaties. Each of these stages will be examined.

After Foreign Minister Ōkuma was installed in office, he launched the fourth attempt of the Meiji government to revise the unequal treaties, and in the summer of 1889 his negotiations were encountering resistance from Great Britain. Ōkuma confided in the German minister in Tokyo that he intended to denounce the treaties if two or three powers refused to accept his revision plan.[8] He also informed the Meiji emperor that, should Great Britain refuse to accept the plan, there could be no alternative for Japan but to denounce the existing treaties unilaterally.

Ōkuma's strong stand on the issue of unilateral denunciation created consternation among the top leaders of the government. Itō Hirobumi, for example, wrote Inoue Kaoru concerning Ōkuma's stand as follows: "For sixteen years, ever since I began to participate in the deliberations of state affairs, I have made every effort to meet the exigencies of the state. But I have never witnessed such a difficult time as the present."[9] Finance Minister Matsukata Masayoshi urged Prime Minister Kuroda Kiyotaka to decide on a course of action beforehand in case Great Britain refused to accept Ōkuma's revision plan.[10]

There were three reasons that unilateral denunciation began to command the attention of the Meiji government in the late 1880s. First, the government was disposed to welcome any new, fresh approach to treaty revision, for it had already made three unsuccessful attempts to revise the treaties. Second, this disposition of the government coincided with the coming of an "away from" phase of what could be called a "toward and away from things foreign" syndrome of Japanese history. This phase represented a nativistic reaction against what some felt to be the overzealous, government-inspired Westernization policy of the Rokumeikan period (1883–87). The intellectual climate of the Meiji 20s, *kokusui shugi* (the principle of national essence), criticized the wholesale borrowing of Western institutions and ideas, laying stress on the uniqueness of Japan. Out of such national reactions arose a popular clamor for unilateral denunciation of the unequal treaties.[11] Finally, the personality of Foreign Minister Ōkuma aided in focusing the attention of the government on the question of unilateral denunciation. Overconfident, immodest, boastful, and even defiant, he was an optimist who undertook serious matters with little deliberation. Some of his political failures stemmed from his lack of careful, political calculation.[12] Given this temperament, reinforced by his earlier experience as the first Meiji leader to stand up to such an overbearing Western diplomat in Japan as Sir Harry S. Parkes, it is quite understandable that Ōkuma seriously entertained a resort to unilateral denunciation, a drastic measure to which no other decision makers of the time seem to have given serious consideration, let alone contemplated actually undertaking.

Turning to the second stage of the Meiji government's deliberation on the issue of unilteral denunciation, one finds that probably at the request of Foreign Minister Ōkuma three foreign advisers of the Meiji government in the fall of 1889 wrote their opinions on the issue, and that these views convinced the Meiji leaders that Japan as a sovereign state was entitled to denounce the existing treaties under certain circumstances.

One such adviser was Alessandro Paternostro, an Italian adviser of the Ministry of Justice. Sometime during Ōkuma's foreign ministership, Paternostro brought out a treatise declaring that Japan by international law had the right to denounce the existing treaties. Yet he advised the country against exercising that right, since he believed that to do this would bring about serious consequences.[13] He reiterated this view in an interview with Inoue Kowashi that took place probably on October 15, 1889. Also, in that interview that Italian jurist expounded a pivotal idea in the doctrine of *rebus sic stantibus*. In response to Inoue's inquiry, he explained that all treaties are ephemeral; that the expression "permanent treaty" should not be taken literally, since it simply referred to a treaty of indefinite duration, in contradistinction to one of definite duration. Moreover, Paternostro advanced an interpretation that was to impinge greatly upon the Meiji government's weighing of the issue of denunciation: because of their revision clauses, the unequal treaties were not of indefinite duration. He construed these revision clauses as meaning that each contracting party had the right to demand a revision from 1872 onward; that one-year notice had to be given; and that all modifications had to be made by mutual consent. Hence if a party failed to reach an amicable accord by such a means, then it would be entitled to resort to unilateral denunciation.[14]

Another adviser who influenced the Meiji leaders to accept denunciation as a norm for termination of the treaties was Herman Roesler, the German instrumental in drafting both the Meiji Constitution of 1889 and the Commercial Code of 1890. In a memorandum dated September 25, 1889, he stated that the right of a state to denounce its international compacts was well recognized by many authorities on international law, documenting his statement by quoting from eight treatises on international law by such prominent jurists as Henry Wheaton, Johann Kasper Bluntschli, and William Edward Hall. Roesler then went on to cite several instances of effective unilateral denunciation: (1) the 1856 Paris Treaty by Russia in 1870 with respect to the neutralization of the Black Sea; (2) the 1852 London Protocol by Russia in 1864 regarding the Schleswig-Holstein question; (3) the 1850 Clayton-Bulwer Treaty by the United States in 1882; and (4) the 1868 Sino-American, or more commonly known as the Burlingame, Treaty by the United States owing to the subsequent legislative prohibition of Chinese immigrants.[15]

Roesler was in complete accord with Paternostro on the question of under what circumstances Japan would be justified in denouncing the existing treaties, notwithstanding all the changes wrought in Japan over a period of two decades—namely, that the right of denunciation would accrue to each party to a treaty only when both parties had failed to reach an amicable agreement on revision. This construction implied that, as a rule, the application of the doctrine of *rebus sic stantibus* was restricted to treaties of indefinite duration. The construction was not, however, a prevalent one, for writers on international law made this restriction only occasionally.[16] In one respect, Roesler markedly differed from both Paternostro and another adviser to be mentioned: although Roesler affirmed the state's sovereign right of denunciation, he stated nothing whatever about the practicability of such a recourse by Japan.

The third foreign adviser who facilitated the Meiji government's subscription to unilateral denunciation as a legitimate method of treaty termination was Henry Willard Denison, who served the Tokyo Foreign Office as a legal adviser with dedication and distinction from 1880 until his death in 1914. His lengthy memorandum, probably submitted about the same time as Roesler's, was intended to show that at the time "Japan has the right, in accordance with the principles of international law and practice of nations, to annul the existing commercial and jurisdictional treaties." Though unabashedly pro-Japanese and sharply critical of the treaty powers, Great Britain in particular, the Denison memorandum showed evidence of clear thinking, close reasoning, and careful writing. Like the Roesler memorandum, the Denison memorandum too cited several authorities on international law to support the right of denunciation, and then proceeded to mention a few instances in which that right had been exercised by several powers "under circumstances that would justify Japan in adopting similar measures"—for example, the unilateral denunciation both of the two Franco-American treaties of 1878 by the United States in 1798 and of the Clayton-Bulwer Treaty by the United States in 1882. From these instances Denison induced two circumstances—which still are held valid today—justifying a state in denouncing its international compacts: (1) breach or failure by the other state to execute the stipulations of the treaties; and (2) a change of circumstances that rendered the treaties unreasonably onerous or inapplicable to the new situation. Did the Japanese government, in view of the above circumstances, have the right to free itself, either in whole or in part, from its "ancient" treaties? Denison's answer was a resounding yes. At length he cited several instances of treaty violation, such as the refusal of Westerners to obey the laws of Japan, and a large number of changed conditions, both external and internal, in Japan. Because of the contraventions and "radical and far-reaching changes" cited, maintained Denison, if those principles of "public right and justice which have been drawn from the writings of eminent Publicists and the conduct of other countries, are honestly and intelligently applied to Japan in her present situation, it will be found that history affords no instance in which the right of denunciation was clearer or more perfect than in the case of Japan."[17]

As a result of the views so strongly expressed, the notion common to them, that Japan as a sovereign state had the right to denounce the treaties, was firmly implanted in the minds of the leaders of the Meiji government. Proof of this was the fact, although none of them, except for Ōkuma, seem to have advocated an unreserved exercise of that right, they readily conceded it. For example, in a memorandum warning against such a unilateral denunciation, Itō Hirobumi stated: "It is an established theory of the authorities on international law that these treaties [of commerce and navigation in force at the time] are by nature of definite duration; a party to each of the existing treaties has the right to denounce it. Since this has been closely examined and established by foreign jurists serving our government, it may be stated that there is no room to doubt that this right exists."[18]

How frequently, if ever, the "uncommon measure" *(ijō no shudan)* of unilateral denunciation was seriously considered by the government during Ōkuma's foreign ministership, no one knows. But there is evidence to suggest that the government was prepared to consider a resort to unilateral denunciation, dependent upon the big treaty powers' receptivity to the Ōkuma revision plan. By mid-June 1889 the United States and Germany had already entered into new treaties embodying the plan. At the cabinet meeting of August 2, 1889, it was decided that, if any of the big treaty powers were to refuse to do the same, either by the scheduled date of the treaties' taking effect, February 11, 1890, or during the six months following that date, the government would consider whether or not to liberate itself from its treaty obligations.[19] But this decision came to naught, for when a fanatic threw a bomb at Ōkuma on October 18 he lost a leg and eventually was obliged to resign. Consequently, he never had a chance to try to carry out the daring measure he had so freely spoken of, to the anguish of other leaders such as Itō Hirobumi and Matsukata Masayoshi. It is doubtful, however, that these opponents would have allowed the hawkish Ōkuma to implement that risky option had he tried to do so.

It should be clear that Foreign Minister Ōkuma left a legacy to the third stage of the Meiji government's deliberation on the issue of denunciation. Partly because of Ōkuma's advocacy of denuniciation, the other Meiji leaders came to know that unilateral denuncation was not only a norm for termination of the treaties but also a possible alternative to revision. The central question of the third stage was whether the Meiji government should simply denounce the treaties or first secure the consent of all the other treaty powers.

Aoki Shūzō, who on December 24, 1889 succeeded Ōkuma in the post of vice foreign minister, entertained the measure of unilateral denunciation as an alternative to his revision plan. This plan envisioned that both consular jurisdiction and the conventional tariff would remain in effect for six years after all new treaties went into operation; that from the seventh year onward consular jurisdiction would be abolished and tariff autonomy restored; and that all other provisions derogatory to the sovereignty of Japan would also be wiped out. Should this plan fail to receive support both in and out of the government, Aoki planned to break the fetters of the unequal treaties by means of unilateral denunciation. On the ground—a ground proposed by H. W. Denison—that consular jurisdiction was totally incompatible with constitutional government, Aoki hoped to persuade the treaty powers to confirm Japan's right of denunciation several years in advance of the actual time of denunciation. Aoki's "Plan for the Peaceful Denunciation of the Treaties" *(Heiwa teki jyōyaku haiki ron)*, as it has been called, was molded by two considerations. One was, as already alluded to, that Aoki wished to have some time to prevail upon the expected domestic opposition to accept his revision plan. The other consideration was his belief that since armed intervention or some such threat consequent to unilateral denunciation of the existing treaties was a possibility—neither a certainty nor an impossibility—the best way to execute that extraordinary diplomatic measure peacefully, that is, to insure that no intervention would likely follow, would be to build up Japan's armaments. In order to do this, Japanese needed some time.[20]

It is evident that in Aoki's mind denunciation would be feasible only after a period of negotiation. From hindsight, one can scarcely deny that Aoki's denunciation plan was an impossible dream, for if negotiations had been capable of confirming the right of denunciation they should have been able even more easily to effect a revision. The denunciation plan therefore must be understood within the desperate context of the repeated failures his predecessors had suffered. The plan manifested the acute sense of those failures, and tells us something about the earnest, relentless efforts made by the Meiji government for treaty revision.

Once again, an untoward incident cut short a foreign minister's tenure. Before Aoki had time to present his two plans to Matsukata Masayoshi, who on May 6, 1891, had succeeded Yamagata Aritomo as prime minister, on May 11, the czarevitch of Russia, the future Nicholas II, who was then visiting Japan, was attacked by an escorting policeman while riding through the city of Ōtsu. This incident produced a nationwide shock. Advised by the elder statesmen to assume responsibility for the insult heaped upon the foreign guest, Aoki resigned on May 29.[21]

But Aoki's resignation did not bury the ideas he had of unilateral denunciation. Instead, they found their champion in Elder Statesman Inoue Kaoru, who submitted a memorandum to Yamagata's first cabinet in August 1891. Labeled as "An Opinion Concerning Treaty Revision" (*Jyōyaku kaisei ni kansuru iken*), the memorandum embodied the most serious proposal ever made for unilateral denunciation. After having witnessed the three-year-long labor by his two successors, Ōkuma and Aoki, as well as his eight-year endeavor, come to naught, Inoue concluded that there was no use in initiating hopeless negotiations, and that there was no other way to effect the revision of the existing treaties than to terminate them all. Hence, he proposed that, with the consent of the treaty powers, the treaties be made those of definite duration, and that at the expiration of the duration Japan terminate them all unilaterally.

Various doubts were expressed in government circles concerning the wisdom of carrying out this proposal. The question was asked: "Would it not be difficult for Japan to terminate the treaties once the proposal in question were turned down by the powers? In other words, if the proposal were rebuffed by the powers, would it not set a precedent that Japan could not even invoke her right of denunciation but for the prior consent of the treaty powers?" The seriousness with which this question was debated may be gauged by the fact that Inoue devoted a substantial portion of his proposal to answering this question.

Inoue's answer was threefold. First, since the existing treaties were not of indefinite duration, they should be terminable after a certain duration; therefore, Japan had the right to denounce them as it thought fit without the prior consent of the treaty powers. (Here one may note that the first half of the argument conformed to Roesler's and Paternostro's interpretation of the revision clauses; the second half did not.) For this reason, Inoue asserted, to seek the prior consent amounted to "being particular about priority" *(rei wo atsukusuru)*—a Confucian notion of etiquette that was out of harmony with the reality of nineteenth-century international affairs. Second, Inoue based his proposal on the doctrine of *rebus sic stantibus*. He stated that it was generally accepted by Western authorities on international law that a treaty became null and void when there occurred a great internal political change that rendered it onerous for the party so affected to continue to fulfill its treaty obligations. Third and finally, Inoue made a shrewd analysis of the Protocol of the London Declaration of 1871, portion of which has been quoted earlier in this chapter. By the Treaty of Paris of 1856 the Black Sea was declared to be neutralized, and Russia, which had been defeated in the Crimean War, agreed not to fortify the Black Sea coast or to maintain a fleet. On November 20, 1870, Russia took advantage of the Franco-German War to repudiate the obligations of the Black Sea clauses, and issued a circular declaring herself to be no longer bound by those clauses. Great Britain protested against this action, and the powers that had been parties to the Treaty of Paris agreed in the London Conference of 1871 to free Russia from the restriction, and solemnly reaffirmed the principle that, unless otherwise provided, a treaty could not be modified or terminated through the agreement of less than all the parties concerned. The reality of power politics behind the London Conference did not elude Inoue. In his memorandum under discussion, Inoue was quick to point out that the principle contained in the protocol had nothing to do with the right of denunciation itself. Rather, the principle simply defined how that right should be exercised. So Inoue argued that all that the principle stated was that when a contracting party saw fit to declare itself freed from the obligations of a treaty, it should so apprise the other parties and secure their consent. Failure to secure unanimity in no way nullified the right of denunciation, for the party concerned could still exercise that right. Inoue went on to say that, even if the London Conference had failed to accept the Russian denunciation of the Black Sea clauses, all the same, Russia would have insisted on her right to denounce them.

Evidently Inoue's arguments prevailed upon Matsukata's first cabinet to accept the Inoue proposal and to seek Roesler's opinion on the feasibility of the proposal. On the basis of the Inoue proposal, the Foreign Office drafted a memorandum called "A Theory Concerning the Termination of the Treaties in Force" *(Genko jyoyaku wo haiki suru so setsu),* the gist of which was that at the expiration of whatever term was agreed upon by all the treaty powers, Japan should terminate the treaties. To this end two alternatives were suggested in the memorandum: (1) to insert termination clauses into the existing treaties; or (2) to have all the treaty powers confirm in advance Japan's right to termination. In a revised version, however, the first alternative was deleted and the second alternative was concretized as follows: at the expiration of a certain length of time (for example, six years) Japan had the right to terminate (*haishi*) the existing treaties at any time upon giving one year's notice. In return for such a termination, the interior of Japan was to be opened to the unrestricted travel, trade, and residence of foreign residents. It is interesting to note that in the texts of both versions the word *haishi* (termination), which is less assertive and therefore was perhaps considered less offensive to the treaty powers than the word *haiki* (denunciation), was used in reference to denunciation.

The second version was transmitted to Roesler for his comments. He was not only the most influential of the three foreign advisers whose views on the question of unilateral denunciation had been solicited by the Meiji government; he was also the only one who had scrupulously refrained from expressing any opinion concerning the feasibility of Japan's exercising its soverign right to denunciation. Furthermore, with Denison and Paternostro arrayed pro and con on the issue respectively, perhaps the Foreign Ministry wished to have a third opinion. If so, the Ministry was not disappointed.

In a memorandum dated September 14, 1891, Roesler gave his evaluation of the Foreign Office proposal. In so many words, he acknowledged, as he had done earlier, the right of Japan to terminate the existing treaties by means of unilateral denunciation, and praised the proposed request to the treaty powers as being ingenious. But he went on to say that it was not practicable for Japan to carry out the request. Japan, he argued, should not execute the proposal all of a sudden, as this would "hurt the feelings" of the treaty powers, nor should it do this without a reasonable chance of success. Further, he doubted that Great Britain, which ranked first among the treaty powers, would agree to the proposal.

A copy of the Japanese translation of the Roesler memorandum was duly forwarded to Inoue Kaoru.[22] How disappointed Inoue must have been in Roesler's reservations about his earnest proposal! Nevertheless, the idea of unilateral denunciation was not yet dead in the minds of the Meiji leaders.

Enomoto Takeaki was the last of the few foreign ministers who dealt with the question of unilateral denunciation. Under his instructions, Denison, the strong advocate of denunciation, and Nakada Keigi, both of the Foreign Ministry, drew up alternative plans that in the fall of 1891 Enomoto approved and submitted to the Matsukata cabinet for consideration. These plans were virtually the same as the two Aoki plans. The first plan was for revision and the second, for denunciation. Enomoto, who believed that denunciation "can be more easily said than done," recommended the adoption of the first plan, but this recommendation failed to receive endorsement from the cabinet partly because it was divided on the recommendation and partly because it was preoccupied with the question of how to deal with the Second Diet, due to convene. Beyond this, there was another reason that Enomoto could not carry much weight in the government dominated by Sat-Cho men: he was an ex-*hatamoto*, not a Satsuma or Choshu man. In March 1892, after having consulted Itō Hirobumi and Aoki Shūzō, Enomoto resubmitted his two previous plans to the cabinet. The outcome was that on April 12 the Committee for Investigation of the Treaty Revision Plan (Jōyaku Kaisei An Chōsa Iinkai) was established under Enomoto's chairmanship. The other members of the committee were Interior Minister Soejima Taneomi, Communications Minister Gotō Shōjirō, and Itō Hirobumi, president of the Privy Council, and three privy councilors, Kuroda Kiyotaka, Terashima Munenari, and Inoue Kowashi. For reasons not as yet fully known, the committee held its first and only meeting on April 13, and five days later was advised by the emperor to suspend its work. Even though the committee never again met as a body, throughout April and May Itō, Terashima, and Enomoto, and especially Inoue individually studied various aspects of the subject of treaty revision, and submitted to the committee a dozen written opinions. Thereafter, nothing further was heard of the committee.[23] Mutsu Munemitsu, who succeeded Enomoto in August, never tried to weigh any form of unilateral denunciation as a viable option and instead single-mindedly pushed treaty revision through by means of negotiation. This suggests that Enomoto was the last foreign minister to treat the "Plan for Peaceful Denunciation" as an alternative to revision, and that by the summer of 1892 the Meiji government threw the idea of denunciation out of the window.

We now turn to the second specific question raised at the outset of this chapter: Why did the Meiji government choose not to undertake a unilateral denunciation of the unequal treaties? Of the dozen written opinions mentioned, two, by Itō and Inoue respectively, dealt exclusively with the question of denunciation. From these statements plus other extant records, one can glean two interrelated reasons that the Meiji leadership in the end decided against unilateral denunciation.

One reason was that the Meiji leadership was fully persuaded by the practical advice given by Roesler and Paternostro not to try to denounce the existing treaties and warning, "You probably will get nowhere." It may be recalled that both advisers construed the revision clause as meaning that a contracting party was entitled to demand a revision of the other party from 1872 on, that the demanding party must give one-year notice, that no modifications or termination could be made except by mutual consent, and that only as a result of the failure to reach a mutual accord could the right to denunciation accrue to a party. This was precisely the way Inoue Kowashi, probably the most versed in law of all Meiji political leaders of the time, argued, as did Itō Hirobumi, the most influential political leader of the time.[24] The conception common to Inoue's and Ito's arguments iterated against unilateral denunciation was that Japan should try to denounce her treaties unilaterally only when she had failed to negotiate new treaties with treaty powers.

The second reason that the Meiji government decided against unilateral denunciation—inextricably related to, but more fundamental than, the first reason—is what may be called the anxiety orientation of the Meiji leaders. One source of anxiety, or fear, say psychologists, is a perception of danger in the external world. "Anxiety, in this sense, acts as a signal to the individual that he is in danger. The origin of the signaling function of anxiety lies in the individual's past experience with traumatic situations. He learns to anticipate trauma by applying attention to the incipient anxiety which the perception of danger initiates."[25]

In the early 1860s the future political leaders of Meiji such as Itō Hirobumi and Inoue Kaoru, like virtually all samurai intellectuals of the time, hated Westerners; for example, the two men were among those swashbuckling samurai who raided and British Legation in Edo. Nevertheless, before the decade was over, these and other future leaders witnessed a number of traumatic situations that broke their audacity and caused them to fear the West. For instance, the killing of an Englishman named Richardson by Satsuma samurai in 1862 resulted in the bombardment of Kagoshima by a British flotilla and the payment of £10,000 to Great Britain. The Choshu bombardment of Western vessels in the Shimonoseki Straits in 1863 brought about an attack on Shimonoseki by an allied fleet of Great Britain, France, Netherlands, and the United States, in addition to the exaction of $30,000,000 to be paid in installments. In these and other incidents Western retaliations followed Japanese provocations on an eye-for-an-eye, tooth-for-a-tooth basis, decisively, swiftly, and unfailingly.

This predictable pattern of retaliation made a deep, lasting impression on the future political leaders of Meiji Japan. One illustration of this effect of their early traumas may be found in the reactions of the Meiji government to the Ōtsu Incident, which forced Foreign Minister Aoki's resignation. An American missionary who witnessed the incident observed: "It is impossible for those who were not on the ground to understand what a shock this [incident] produced. The *Tenshi* [here the Meiji emperor] with his cabinet made a hurried journey of two hundred and fifty miles to Kyoto, went in person to the hotel where the wounded prince was lying, and apologized for the insult offered him. The governor of the province, who had held office but five days, was removed; the chief of police was removed and degraded."[26] Interior Minister Saigō Tsugumichi, who removed the two officials mentioned, said in July: "I know nothing about the legal arguments, but should the accused be punished in that way [life imprisonment rather than capital punishment], we could never tell when a

Russian fleet would appear off the coast of Shinagawa [part of present-day Tokyo] and pulverize our country by one shot."[27] That a Russian intervention might result from the unthinkable attack on the Russian prince was very much on the minds of the Meiji leaders.[28] On the recommendation of Saigō and Aoki, Prime Minister Matsukata contemplated sending Prince Takehito to the Russian court, but the plan was dropped since the court did not welcome the visit and, instead, assured Tokyo that Japan had done all to satisfy Russia and that she would make no demands on Japan.[29] Moreover, the selection of Enomoto as successor to Aoki stemmed from the consideration that, since Enomoto, a former envoy of Japan to Russia, had the confidence of St. Petersburg, he would be able to bring Russo-Japanese relations under control.[30]

The anxiety orientation of the Meiji leaders was also reflected in the Aoki scheme of treaty revision. It has already been noted that, of the two choices of revision and denunciation, revision was his first choice, for denunciation involved a high risk, a view shared by most Meiji leaders. Denison had this in mind when in 1889 he wrote in his denunciation memorandum:

> If Japan should see fit to exercise her right to annul the treaties with those Powers that refuse a fair and just revision, it is doubtless true that the act will be followed by written protests, but not a soldier will be moved nor a gun fired to perpetuate those treaties. The wholesale denunciation by Mexico in 1867, of her perpetual treaties with European Powers, for reasons less powerful than those that could be assigned for similar action on the part of Japan, did not precipitate war, but on the contrary trade pursued its accustomed channels and European merchants for years conducted their business operations in Mexico without any conventional protection whatever, and so would it be in Japan.[31]

No other foreign adviser of the Meiji government, with the possible exception of the French adviser, Emile Gustave Boissonade, has been remembered by many Japanese with greater esteem and gratitude than Denison, by 1889 already a highly trusted adviser. Therefore, it is another measure of the strong grip their anxiety orientation had on the Meiji leaders that they seem to have had no difficulty turning a deaf ear to the unequivocal stand taken by Denison in support of the unilateral denunciation of the unequal treaties.

Given the anxiety orientation illustrated above, it is not hard to see how readily Roesler's and Paternostro's advice, that denunciation should be resorted to by Japan only when she had failed to effect a revision by means of mutual accord with all the treaty powers, struck a responsive chord among such leaders as Itō Hirobumi, Matsukata Masayoshi, and Inoue Kowashi.

So much as to why the Meiji government did not exercise the right of denunciation. In the historical context of the time what probable result if Japan had unilaterally denounced her unequal treaties? One thing that can categorically be stated is that Great Britain, and undoubtedly all the other treaty powers as well, would never have recognized Japan's unilateral denunciations but would have continued to insist that the treaties could only be abrogated by mutual consent. Throughout the nineteenth century and the early twentieth century Great Britain's usual policy was to regard a treaty as of perpetual duration and hence incapable of unilateral termination, unless, expressly or by implication, the treaty accorded this right to the powers involved, or otherwise provided for its termination.[32] It has already been observed that the Protocol of the London Conference of 1871, was a product of this very policy. One more example will be cited. By the 1834 treaty agreement between Great Britain and Venezuela, these two countries adopted and confirmed the Treaty of Amity, Commerce, and Navigation of 1825 between Great Britain and Columbia. In 1841, 1843, 1879, 1897, and 1909, the Venezuelan government gave notice thatit desired to terminate the treaties of 1825 and 1834, but on each occasion the British refused to accept the notice and successfully maintained that the treaties could be abrogated only by mutual consent. In February 1903, on the cessation of the British blockade of Venezuelan ports, notes were exchanged between the two countries whereby Venezuela was forced to reconfirm the two treaties mentioned.[33] As in the Venezuelan crisis, it is likely that Great Britain would have refused to recognize Japan's right to unilateral denunciation of the treaties, and all the other Western treaty powers would have followed suit.

No one, however, can provide a simple, unequivocal answer to the question of what, if anything, the treaty powers might have done had Japan attempted to terminate the treaties unilaterally, beyond denying that she had the right to take this action. Instead, two quite different responses seem equally conceivable. One of these is the very course Denison was predicting in 1889: in all probability the Western treaty powers would have protested the unilateral denunciation, but, contrary to the expectation of the Meiji leaders, would not have taken any military action; as a result, for most of these countries trade with Japan would have been carried on as usual. This type of response to unilateral renunciation might be called acquiescence. The other type of response might be labeled intervention, where, for instance, Great Britain and a few larger treaty powers might have taken joint action in the form of a naval blockade of certain ports of Japan, or military occupation of such centers of foreign trade as Yokohama or Kobe, or both actions simultaneously.

To determine which of these two types of response was more probable in Japan, one needs to look to historical examples. An outstanding case of acquiescence was the one referred to by Denison, i.e., the peaceful relations that existed between Mexico and several Western treaty powers even after Mexico's 1867 unilateral denunciation of her commercial treaties with these powers. From 1867 to 1883 Mexico had no commercial treaties with Belgium, Germany, Great Britain, Italy, and Spain, and none with the United States until 1884. Yet during this seventeen-year period foreign trade flourished as before, and even more remarkably, there was no armed intervention by any of the big treaty powers.[34] This sharply contrasts with the 1902–3 intervention in Venezuela by Great Britain, Germany, and Italy, a classical and well-known example of the intervention-type response.

The basic difference between the two cases cited seems to have been whether or not Western residents and investments were protected. In Mexico, Europeans received adequate protection to their persons and property even though no treaties were in effect.[35] In Venezuela, however, the disorders prevailing under the dictatorship of Cipriana Castro proved ruinous to foreign investors; for example, his courts would not give aliens justice, nor in some instances even hear their cases. This attitude led some of the European powers, particularly Great Britain, whose financial stake was five times greater than that of Germany, to consider the use of force to secure justice for their own nationals. When demands for the payment of European claims were refused by Castro, intervention followed.[36]

The foregoing suggests that an armed intervention might have ensued in Japan only if her unilateral denunciation had occasioned loss of life or property in the Western mercantile communities, especially those of the British. During the period concerned, 1888–92, there was little likelihood that denial of justice or outright attacks would have accompanied the denunciation, for Japan was already a highly centralized, orderly country. Unilateral denunciation, however, might well have resulted in a loss of profit for Western treaty powers, with the lifting of the low 1866 tariff schedule, the maximum rate of which was five percent. This outcome, however, even though it might conceivably have led to intervention, must be weighed against other factors that might have counterbalanced it, for example, Great Britain's need for the good will of the Empire of Japan for checkmating Russia in the Far East. Therefore, one may tentatively conclude that armed intervention, while possible, would have been unlikely.

Nevertheless, the 1892 decision of the Meiji leaders to set aside unilateral denunciation as a viable option was a right decision, not only for their own time, but also in the years that followed. Although the Meiji leaders, with the single exception of Ōkuma Shigenobu, never appear to have considered as feasible an outright exercise of Japan's right of unilateral denunciation, they did seriously consider the possibility of requesting the treaty powers to confirm that right in advance. If this right were conceded, the plan called for Japan to terminate the existing treaties at the end of a six-year period. This plan was never put into action, but had it been, Japan's request would have been turned down by the treaty powers. In the first place, Japan was not as yet regarded by the treaty powers as a "civilized" nation. In 1890 the *Times* observed: "The Japanese people are not quite yet as advanced as they fancy themselves."[37] But, on July 17, 1899, on the occasion of the end of the unequal treaties, the *Times* noted: "Japan takes her place to-day as an equal amongst the civilized Powers of the world."[38] The next year, in a decision, an American judge referred to the Empire of Japan as "the last state admitted into the rank of civilized nations."[39] In the second place, in both the works of Western publicists and the practice of Western nations, the rules of international law were regarded as regulating the conduct of "civilized," Christian states only; they were construed as applying *not* to the "uncivilized," heathen states of the Orient. As late as 1925, an authority on international law wrote: "In our day there is a great gulf fixed between the views of civilized Europeans and Americans on the one hand, and those of backward and barbarous peoples on the other. . . . International Law, as we know it, is a system of rules for the guidance of civilized powers."[40] That international law was inapplicable to the "backward and barbarous" peoples was not only a theory but also a practice. One of the treaty revision proposals made by Foreign Minister Inoue Kaoru in 1882 stipulated that the proposed treaties should be valid for twelve years, and that at the expiration of this duration each party should be free to denounce its treaty if it were so inclined. This proposal to accord Japan the right of denunciation excited serious misgivings with some of the European delegates.[41] In view of the image the Western treaty powers held of Japan before 1899 and their construction of the limited applicability of international law, it is safe to assume that in the eyes of these powers, regardless of what they might have done in response to the Japanese request entertained first by Aoki and then by Inoue, the request, if made, might have been viewed as daring, rash, and even vexing; that such an attitude could have certainly impeded subsequent negotiations for treaty revision. As a result, the critical breakthrough that actually came only two years after the Meiji government had abandoned unilateral denunciation as an alternative to revisions would have occurred substantially later.

In summary, on the whole, the Meiji government always backed away from serious consideration of an outright unilateral denunciation of the unequal treaties. Rather, from 1890 to 1892 the government considered the meek measure of requesting the treaty powers to confirm Japan's right to denunciation, a sovereign "right" of the state in customary international law, so that she might in due course terminate the treaties in force. Here one may be struck by a recurrent pattern in the early Meiji government's conduct of diplomacy: a heavy reliance on its foreign legal advisers for obtaining full information about all possible options before reaching a decision. It was these advisers who convinced the government that Japan as a sovereign state had the right to denunciation. It was also they—the excep-

The Question of Unilateral Denunciation

tion's being Denison—who advised the government not to try to exercise that right. The Meiji leaders, who avidly sought advice from their foreign advisers, did not always follow it. As far as the question of denunciation was concerned, the leaders were psychologically well prepared to accept the negative advice discussed. While still young, especially in the 1860s, they had experienced enough traumas to learn that Western retaliation followed Japanese provocation just as surely as night follows day. They also believed that Japan was not as yet militarily strong enough to exercise Japan's sovereign right of denunciation by virtue of the doctrine of *rebus sic stantibus*, and therefore could not expect acquiescence on the part of the Western treaty powers. Consequently, the Meiji leadership elected not to resort to any form of denunciation. And this election was a realistic, wise, and statesmanlike decision.

Notes

1. For standard, full-length works on treaty revision, see Yamamoto Shigeru, *Jyōyaku kaiseishi* (Tokyo: Takayama Shoin, 1943); [Kawashima Shintarō], *Jyōyaku kaisei keika gaiyo*, vol. 6 of *Jyōyaku kaisei kandei Nihon gaikō bunsho*, 8 vols. (Tokyo: Nihon Kokusai Rengō Kyōkai, 1948–56).
2. J. L. Brierly, *The Law of Nations* (5th ed.; Oxford: Oxford, Clarendon Press, 1955), p. 256.
3. William W. Bishop, Jr., *International Law* (3d ed.; Boston: Little, Brown & Co., 1971), p. 223.
4. Green H. Hackworth, *Digest of International Law*, 8 vols. (Washington: Government Printing Office, 1940–44), 5:297.
5. Bishop, *International Law*, pp. 141ff., 144.
6. Draft Convention on the Law of Treaties, prepared by Research in International Law of the Harvard Law School, Supplement to the *American Journal of International Law* 29 (October 1935): 1097. (hereafter cited as Harvard Research).
7. T. J. Lawrence, *The Principles of International Law*, rev. Percy H. Winfield (7th ed.; London: Macmillan, 1925), p. 303.
8. National Diet Library, Kensei Shiryoshitsu (KS), Kenseishi Hensankai Shushu Bunsho (KHSB), 764.9B, Inoue Kowashi to Itō Hirobumi, September 28, 1889.
9. National Diet Library, KS, KHSB, 764.19.2, Itō Hirobumi to Inoue Kaoru, August 18, 1889; 764.19.3, Inoue Kowashi to Itō Hirobumi, September 28, 1889.
10. National Diet Library, KS, Matsukata Ke Monjyo, 52.15, Matsukata Masayoshi to Kuroda Kiyotaka, August 1889.
11. See, for example, Kenneth B. Pyle, *The New Generation in Meiji Japan* (Stanford, Calif.: Stanford University, 1969), chapter 5.
12. Nakamura Naomi, *Ōkuma Shigenobu* (Tokyo: Yoshikawa Kobunkan, 1964).
13. F. C. Jones, *Extraterritoriality in Japan* (New Haven, Conn.: Yale University Press, 1933), p. 123.
14. *Hisho ruisan: Gaikōhen*, comp. Ito Hirobumi, 3 vols. (rep. ed.; Tokyo: Hara Shobo, 1969), 1:515–21. (hereafter cited as *HR: Gaikōhen*).
15. Ibid., 1:525U; National Diet Library, KS, Sanjō Sanetomi Monjyo, 35.4.
16. Harvard Research, Supplement to the *American Journal of International Law*, 29 ‹101.
17. Gaikō Shiryōkan, Tōkyō, "Denison oyatoi kikō jyōyaku haiki ron," [1889].
18. *HR: Gaikōhen*, 1»5.
19. National Diet Library, KS, Matsukata Ke Monjyo, 56.22, May 6, 1892.
20. Yamamoto, *Jyōyaku kaiseishi*, pp. 434f; Aoki Shuzo, *Aoki Shūzō jiden* (Tōkyō: Heibonsha, 1970), pp. 186–89.

21. Aoki, *Aoki Shūzō jiden*, pp. 265ff., 189.
22. National Diet Library, KS, Inoue Kaoru Monjyo, Shorui no Bu, 37.5, Inoue Kaoru to the Cabinet, August 1891; 10.5, August 1891; 10.1, September 14, 1891, Roesler to Foreign Office.
23. Japan, *Nihon gaikō bunsho* (1951): 7–10 (hereafter cited as *NGB*); Ino Tentaro, "Meiji nijūgonen ni okeru Jyōyakyu Kaiseian Chōsa Iinkai ni tsuite," *Chūō Daigaku Bungakubu kiyō* 72 (March 1974): 1–33.
24. *NGB*, 25 ›9–31; Ino, *Chūō Daigaku Bungakubu kiyō* 72:20; *HR; Gaikōhn*, 1 ø0; National Diet Library, KS, Mutsu Monjyo, 92.1, Minutes of the Cabinet Meeting, July 8, 1893.
25. *The Handbook of Social Psychology*, ed. Gardner Lindzey and Elliot Aronson, 2 vols. (2d ed.; Reading, Mass.: Addison-Wesley, 1968), 1:266.
26. M. L. Gordon, *An American Missionary in Japan* (Boston: Houghton, Mifflin & Co., 1892), p. 248.
27. Quoted in Miyake Setsurei, *Dō jidai shi*, 6 vols. (Tōkyō: Iwanami Shoten, 1949–54), 2:443. Under the Penal Code, the attempted murder of a Japanese imperial prince was a capital offense. The punishment of the same crime against an ordinary person was life imprisonment. The code, however, made no mention of offenses against foreign royalty. Hence, such offenses would logically be treated the same as those against ordinary persons. As is well known, the Meiji government desired to see the assailant of the Russian prince executed. But Chief Justice Kojima Iken of the Daishinin resisted the pressure and prevailed upon the Ōtsu District Court to adjudicate the case according to the law. As a result, the attacker was sentenced to life imprisonment. This episode has long been praised as signaling the independence of the judiciary. Of late, however, this interpretation has come under attack. See Ienaga Saburō, *Shihōken tokuritsu no rekishiteki kōsatsu* (rev. ed.; Tōkyō: Nihon hyōronsha, 1971).
28. Itō Hirobumi, who was apprised of the incident by Matsukata's telegram while eating breakfast in Hakone, dropped his chopsticks, so great was his concern over what unreasonable demands Russia, the greatest land power on earth, might make of Japan. Communications Minister Gotō Shojirō suggested the assassination of the assailant in his prison cell, saying that, once he was done away with, this would once and for all remove all pretext of intervention by Russia. Aoki, *Aoki Shūzō jiden*, p. 246.
29. National Diet Library, KS, KHSB 542, pp. 32–44.
30. Yamamoto, *Jyōyaku kaiseishi*, p. 448.
31. See note 17.
32. Sir Arnold Duncan McNair, *The Law of Treaties* (New York; Columbia University Press, 1938), p. 351.
33. Ibid., p. 366.
34. Hubert Howe Bancroft, *The Works of Hubert Howe Bancroft*, 39 vols (San Francisco: The History Co., 1883–90), 14:415, 455.
35. Ibid., p. 358.
36. Samuel Flagg Bemis, *The Latin American Policy of the United States* (New York: Harcourt, Brace & Co., 1943), p. 146.
37. *The Times* (London), April 12, 1890.
38. Ibid., July 17, 1899.
39. Quoted in Bishop, *International Law*, p. 29.
40. Lawrence, *The Principles of International Law*, pp. 3ff.
41. Jones, *Extraterritoriality in Japan*, p. 100.

8 Western Parameters of Sino-Japanese Relations

Hilary Conroy

[A preliminary version of this paper was read at the Social Science Research Council's conference on "China and Japan: Their Modern Interactions," at Portsmouth, New Hampshire, June 1976.]

In their "modern interactions" China and Japan have had a great deal to quarrel about. Basically, of course, this derived from the two countries' rapidly changing positions in the later nineteenth century, as China became the sick, though still pretentious old man of East Asia and Japan became the increasingly cocky and bellicose youth pushing ahead in the modern world.

China had been accustomed to respect, if not obedience, in the East Asian world and it was difficult enough for Chinese leaders to swallow their time-honored pride in the face of Western diplomacy; how much more so in the face of Japan. Also, with Japan's leaders ebullient in their new feeling of savoir faire in the wider world, it would not be easy for them to resist the temptation to exploit China's increasingly obvious weakness and ineptitude.

It is not the purpose of this paper to show that Westerners caused Sino-Japanese hatred, tensions, and wars. Rather, it is to indicate occasions and circumstances in which what Westerners did, or sometimes failed to do, contributed to the intransigence of one side or the other, or both. But the importance, or at least the potential importance of Western influence peddling should not be underrated. The general history of modernization is a sufficient reminder. By the late nineteenth century the advances made in science, technology, and trade in the West had "opened" the East Asian area in such multitudinous ways that all countries there were vulnerable to Western inroads if not helpless to resist them. This is well understood in the case of China. But remarkable modernization obscured the fact that from 1840 to 1875 Japan was as vulnerable as China to such inroads.[1] Indeed, had Western power zeroed in on Japan rather than on China in the two or three decades following the opening by Perry, there might well have been a propped-up shogunate presiding over the disintegration of Japan into spheres of influence, not unlike Manchu China.

As indicated in the bombardments of Kagoshima (1863) and Shimonoseki (1864), whatever samurai heroics might have taken place, there was no possibility of real resistance. And though much has been made of the Japanese response to such demonstrations of Western power, trying to copy, sending missions abroad, and the like, it has been observed that the main avenue to settlement of incidents between Japanese and Westerners even in the early Meiji era was *seppuku* (suicide by disembowlment) for the Japanese individuals involved and payment of indemnity by the Japanese government. Nor was the samurai right to suicide secure; Western pressure was so strong that beheading was accepted by the Meiji government as proper punishment for attacks on foreigners.[2]

Ōkubo Toshimichi's cautious "Reasons for Opposing the Korean Expedition" (1873) was well taken. There he argued that, if Japan became involved in Korea, Russia would "fish out both the clam and the bird" and warned that Great Britain was "watching with a tiger's" eye. . . . Look at India . . . observe carefully the process by which India became a colony."[3]

That the Japanese leadership continued to recognize Japan's vulnerability to Western inroads, if not takeover, is clear at least as late as 1895, when, even in the flush of victory over China, it accepted the triple intervention demands of Russia, France, and Germany. The nervous, almost frenzied conferences in the Japanese diplomatic establishment on that occasion show clearly the extent to which Japanese leadership was sensitive and responsive to almost every nuance of Western diplomacy.[4] The point to be made here is that, up to 1895 at least, Western advice clearly and firmly given could have been decisive in staying Japanese designs on China. It is in this light then that we review three early Meiji incidents that set the stage for future Japanese power plays against China.

The first was the Formosan expedition. It is ironic that after the Japanese themselves had seen the wisdom of calling off *Seikanron* ("Conquer Korea" advocacy) in 1873, two Americans, Charles E. DeLong (U.S. Minister to Japan, 1870–73) and General Charles LeGendre, who is probably best classified as a diplomat-adventurer, with the accent on the latter part of that hyphenated phrase, contributed in no small way to restimulating Japanese chauvinism and in convincing the Okubo-Iwakura "peace" faction that flexing Japan's military muscles in Formosa would produce favorable results.

We include DeLong, the American minister at Tokyo, along with LeGendre in responsibility for this because his "shirt-sleeves"[5] style diplomacy encouraged Japanese nationalistic attitudes not only generally but specifically.

DeLong did not like the Sino-Japanese Treaty of 1871, which was actually a good start toward amicable relations between the "new" Japan and an "old" China struggling to modernize her diplomacy. It was a remarkably equal treaty, which saw China curtail her old Confucian pretentiousness and Japan restrain her potential rapaciousness. But DeLong feared it would likely allow Japan "to drift into an alliance with China" (against Western nations), a possibility he regarded as "calamitous."[6]

Payson J. Treat, in his old but still useful analysis of the diplomacy of this period, regards DeLong's efforts to impede the Sino-Japanese treaty as being "in a well intentioned way" and notes that Secretary of State Hamilton Fish approved his analysis as "statesmanlike." (DeLong had also said that Japan was "a power that should be welcomed as an ally" [of the U.S. and other "civilized states"] should "trouble occur with China or our troubles with Korea enlarge and increase.")

However, DeLong did not stop with analysis. He recommended LeGendre to the Japanese foreign office to stimulate Japanese nationalism against China. And after the latter was employed there as counselor in 1872, DeLong and he frequently discussed approvingly with Foreign Minister Soejima Taneomi (one might almost say conspired with him) on ways to implement Japanese expansion to Formosa, Korea, the Liu-ch'ius and even China.[7]

DeLong very actively negotiated the arrangements by which LeGendre, who was visiting Japan enroute home from his post as U.S. consul at Amoy, accepted employment by the Japanese government, not only as counselor at the Foreign Office, but with the understanding that he would be a general of the Japanese army to conquer Formosa in the (likely) event that China refused to concede that island as well as the Liu-chius to Japanese sovereignty without recourse to arms.[8]

The State Department reprimanded DeLong for his excessive zeal,[9] but did not seek to block LeGendre's appointment, and the results were much as DeLong had hoped and intended. Even though Soejima relinquished office in the aftermath of the abortive "Conquer Korea" scheme of 1873, LeGendre was able to convince his successor at the Foreign Office, Terashima Munenori, as well as the effective heads of government, Ōkubo and Iwakura, of the feasibility of a military expedition to Formosa.

The expedition was a near fiasco, both militarily and diplomatically. DeLong's successor, Judge John A. Bingham, and Dr. S. Wells Williams, American chargé d'affaires at Peking, took such a dim view of the proceedings that they forced the recall of an American ship and two American officers whose participation in the affair LeGendre had arranged, and LeGendre himself was briefly detained under arrest by the American consulate at Amoy when he persisted in promoting the affair.[10]

However, the U.S. State Department ordered the release of LeGendre,[11] whereupon he proceeded to Peking, where he assisted Japanese negotiators Ōkubo and Yanagiwara not only to save face but to extract an admission from China that Japan had been protecting wronged Japanese subjects (Liu-ch'iu islanders) and an indemnity for the cost of the expedition.[12]

The end result was that Japan got away with her first expansionist coup. Though it was not internationally solemnized until four years later, when ex-President Ulysses S. Grant put his foot in the affair, Japan proceeded on this basis to claim and seize the Liu-ch'iu islands, make their king a Japanese peer, and convert them into Okinawa Prefecture. Grant's involvement came at the end of a round-the-world trip by him and his wife when her anxiety to get home made his sally into East Asian diplomacy even more gullible than might be expected of him. Grant, who had been approached by Prince Kung and Li Hung-chang in Peking, tried to present China's case as a need for a "wide channel" to the Pacific. And he urged direct negotiations by Japan with China lest the European powers involve themselves to the "humiliation of Asiatic people."[13]

Grant's effort led the Japanese to offer to leave the two southernmost islands of the Liu-ch'iu chain to China on condition the rest be ceded to Japan. When China failed to respond favorably to this, Japan could then, in good international conscience, simply incorporate them all. It was rather symbolic that thereafter Grant was considered a fine friend of Japan, to the extent that representatives of the Japanese legation in Washington visited him four times during his final illness in 1885.[14]

The second case will require only brief discussion, as it came to nothing very quickly. But it did represent, if only momentarily, an opportunity for the possible removal of Korea as a field for Japanese expansionist activity. This opportunity came in 1882 when Japanese inroads there were in their infancy and China was in the process of tightening up her "dependent country" relationship with Korea. The Japanese minister at Peking, Admiral Enomoto Takeaki, who had formerly been an advocate of Seikanron, approached American Minister John R. Young with the proposal that a congress might be convened among the several powers, Great Britain, Russia, France, Germany, the United States, and Japan, with a view to guaranteeing the independence and neutrality of Korea. "He said," reported Young, "he would like to see Corea politically another Belgium." However, Young presented the proposition to Washington negatively, noting that Japan's motive was probably to get into a situation whereby "she would act and deliberate with Western Powers as an equal."[15]

Secretary of State Freylinghuysen did not reply until March 16 (1883) and then only to say that he had read Young's comments "with interest."[16] Meanwhile, Korea was linked with Siam, which was given primary consideration as the place where Chinese pretensions to suzerainty had to be watched. A report on Korea would be awaited from the newly appointed minister, Lucius H. Foote from Seoul, but as the editors of the Korea documents on this period have pointed out, "Seldom, if ever, in the critical years that followed, was the Department [of State] to issue instructions to Seoul that were of value or perception."[17]

Thus the idea of neutralizing Korea, at a time when Japan was willing to do so, was lost from view.

The third case I wish to discuss lies somewhere between the aggressive involvement of DeLong-LeGendre and the negative noninvolvement of Minister Young in Sino-Japanese affairs. It seems on the surface to be an admirable even-handed neutrality, with good offices tendered, toward quarreling, then warring parties. But underneath, it seems to me it was something else, and worse, namely, a go-ahead to Japan (and to China) to fight the Sino-Japanese war (1894–45) from Western powers who could easily have stopped it.

Of course, the documentation on the Sino-Japanese war is so voluminous, from all sides, that one can work in it for years and not see the forest for the trees. In an earlier study of the *Japanese Seizure of Korea*, the author went through most of the Japanese documentation, as well as quite a bit of the Western, and came to the somewhat ambivalent conclusion that "Various Unexpected Happenings"[18] (such as the murder of Kim Ok-kiun, the Tonghak rebellion, China's ill-timed dispatch of troops to Korea, and the need to get popular and Diet support for cabinet policies in Japan) rather than a deliberate Japanese scheme for war were the causes.

It would seem that this analysis remains in general correct. However, reconsidering the situation from the angle of this paper, it could be said that one fact was not stressed sufficiently in the earlier study. Namely, the major powers concerned, Great Britain, Russia and (to a lesser extent) the United States, all gave their permission for the Sino-Japanese war to occur. Japan especially was attuned for signals of such approval and it was only after she got them that she allowed the "various unexpected happenings" to set the course toward war and whatever territorial gains she could obtain therefrom.

From December 1893 to July 16, 1894, the primary concern of the Japanese Foreign Office, Foreign Minister Mutsu, and, indeed, the whole Japanese cabinet was treaty revision, specifically the negotiation of a new and equal treaty with Great Britain, which would break the stranglehold of unequal treaties. (As the previous essay by Richard Chang indicates, these had shackled Japanese sovereignty since the Perry-Harris and other treaty settlements of the 1850s.) The Japanese draft of an equal treaty was presented to the British government by the minister to London, Viscount Aoki Shūzo, on December 27, 1893, and thereafter, until July 1894, there ensued a long and complicated exchange of redrafts, discussion, and arguments, which from Japan's point of view was seemingly crowned with success in mid-July 1894, when Aoki was authorized to sign the treaty in English to prevent further delay (July 13).[19]

However, at that auspicious moment events in Korea, where Sino-

Japanese tension was mounting, sent Aoki into depths of despair: "By imprudence reported [Japanese demand for dismissal of a British naval instructor in Korea] my arduous work of four months is upset," he wired Mutsu from London.[20] There were at least two other Anglo-Japanese tension points in Korea that could certainly have given the British a rationale for delaying or canceling altogether the treaty signing, had they wished to warn off Japan on war with China. But they did not. Mutsu's hasty reassurances were accepted and, to Aoki's relief and delight, the treaty was signed as scheduled on July 16.[21]

The British one was Japan's icebreaker on Treaty revision, but it should be noted that negotiations with other Western powers, France, Italy, Germany, Russia, and the United States, were soon under way. The new American treaty was signed on November 22, while the Sino-Japanese War was raging.[22] Though it cannot be considered to be a direct approval of Japan's going to war, as in the British case, the fact that negotiations progressed through the opening and escalation of the war certainly did not indicate serious disapproval.[23]

With Russia there were some false starts, but negotiations got under way in earnest on August 17, 1894, and proceeded slowly through the early months of the war.[24]

The strange career of the so-called mediation efforts of the three powers is a further and, the author would argue, conclusive indication that they did not seriously attempt to deter Japan from this war of conquest. Again the British case is the most obvious. On June 24, 1894, Aoki was called in by British Foreign Secretary Lord Kimberley and told that the British government was "extremely anxious" to prevent war between Japan and China, "because it might invite third parties interfering."[25] On June 29 he warned Aoki of possible "great complications" if Japan went to war with China, while informing him that Li Hung-chang had already invited Russia to intervene.[26]

It should be noted, however, that the British warning against war, being predicated on the proposition that Russia might interfere, was something less than definitive. In addition, what may be described as a "sideshow at Shanghai" further weakened the force of the British no-war advice. On June 27 the Japanese consul at Shanghai, S. Okoshi, inquired of Mutsu whether he might agree that Shanghai be declared a neutral port in the event of war between Japan and China, a matter that had been brought up by "some [foreign representative] colleagues."[27]

Mutsu replied that consuls had no such authority,[28] but he had been tipped off and was ready when, on July 23, he was handed a note from R. S. Paget, of the British embassy at Tokyo, on behalf of Lord Kimberley, asking that Japan give Great Britain "an undertaking that in the event of hostilities breaking out between Japan and China they [Japan] will abstain from warlike operations against Shanghai and its approaches."[29] Mutsu replied immediately and affirmatively to the request.[30]

Taking together the signing of the new Anglo-Japanese treaty, the conditional nature of Great Britain's warning against war, and the subtle shift of British concern from war in general to Shanghai in particular, we conclude that the Japanese resort to war was tacitly approved by Great Britain, prior to the attack on the Chinese troopship *Kowshing*, an event that opened hostilities on July 25. The fact that a British naval court at Shanghai subsequently adjudicated that Japan's sinking of the *Kowshing* (a British merchantman sailing under Chinese government charter) was justified in the circumstances was a further go-ahead signal to Japan.[31]

Like Great Britain, Imperial Russia gave Japan a seemingly stern remonstrance against going to war with China, but in the end softened this so much as to nullify its effect. Under instructions from Foreign Minister Nicholas K. Giers the Russian minister at Tokyo, Hitrovo, called on Mutsu at the Japanese Foreign Office on June 25. He told Mutsu that China had sought Russian good offices in the situation, complained that the Russian government had not been kept fully informed of developments and intentions by Japan, and sought assurances that Japan would not resort to war. To this approach Mutsu gave wordy explanations and guarded assurances.[32]

That Mutsu's explanations did not satisfy Russia is indicated by the fact that on June 30 Hitrovo delivered a formal note to Mutsu, in French, advising him of Japan's "serious responsibility" to withdraw all troops from Korea.[33] However, thereafter Russia softened this stand perceptibly, indicating willingness to accept Japanese assurances of generally peaceful intent, concern for Korean independence, and the like, and emphasizing Russian noninvolvement.[34]

To Washington's credit, the American advisement to Japan against war, though later in coming than the British and Russian, was sustained, at least until after hostilities had begun. Edwin Dun, American minister at Tokyo, delivered a note from Secretary of State Gresham to Mutsu on July 9, saying that Japan's demands were "the more remarked in view of the fact that China favors the simultaneous withdrawal of both the Japanese and Chinese troops," and that "the President will be painfully disappointed should Japan visit upon her feeble and defenseless neighbor the horrors of an unjust war."[35]

Mutsu replied with many words and excuses, to which the American response to the Japanese minister, Tateno, in Washington was that the dispute might then best be arbitrated and suggesting that, if Japan requested it, the president might arrange this.[36] However, any worry the Japanese Foreign Office entertained that this criticism from Washington was deeply held was quickly dispelled after the outbreak of hostilities. In response to Japan's request that the United States legation in Peking assume charge of Japanese interests and properties in China, the American chargé d'affaires at Peking, Charles Denby, Jr., replied on August 1 that "acting under the orders of the Honorable Secretary of State, I *hasten* [emphasis by author] to accede to your request."[37]

While it is true that the United States legation in Tokyo did the same for China and the United States joined Great Britain, Russia, and France in a belated joint mediation effort in October after the Japanese had all but won the war, it is also true that Denby's enthusiasm for protecting Japanese nationals in China had to be dampened by a State Department admonition that this did not include giving them general asylum and extraterritorial rights.[38]

All told, the conclusion seems inescapable that British, Russian, and American foreign policy was so permissive of Japan's course toward war as to have amounted to tacit approval of it. Of course, it may be argued that the Western powers expected China to win or that they really thought Japan was liberating Korea from a Chinese yoke. The latter is true to a point. The Chinese "resident," Yuan Shih-K'ai, had been, in Harrington's phraseology, "the biggest man in town [Seoul]" from 1885 to 1893 and all the Western representatives there resented his high-handed wire pulling at the Korean court.[39] However, events moved very rapidly in 1894 and by the summer of that year, as recent studies have shown, the American minister at Seoul, John M. B. Sill, legation secretary H. N. Allen, as well as a wide body of American official and nonofficial opinion were aware that Japan was the military power to be feared.[40] Great Britain and Russia were certainly as well informed on Japanese military strength as the United States was.

Another case in point was the Triple Intervention, which occurred on April 23, 1895, when Russia, France, and Germany presented identical notes to the Japanese Ministry of Foreign Affairs demanding that Japan back off from her Manchurian conquests and retrocede the Liaotung penninsula to China. The story is well known, but two aspects are of importance here: (1) Japan heeded the advice very quickly; (2) Germany, rather than Russia, was the initiator of the intervention.

The first point indicates that the Japanese foreign-policy leadership, then as in 1894 under the direction of Itō Hirobumi as premier and Mutsu as foreign minister, was extremely susceptible and responsive to the winds of international diplomacy, and the conclusion that, had an equivalent amount of pressure been applied in June or July 1894, there would have been no Sino-Japanese war at all, seems appropriate.[41]

The second point, German initiative, was uncovered in German documents by Frank Iklé, who shows that the motive was simply the Kaiser's post-Bismarckian determination to get in on East Asian as well as other imperialistic ventures.[42] This information underscores our previous point that Russia, who, with Great Britain, should have been the prime deflector of Japanese imperialism in Manchuria, was extremely dilatory in coming to a definite position. Had Russia and Great Britain, with even minimal American support, applied real pressure on Japan in the summer of 1894, Japan's course toward imperialism in East Asia might well have been permanently deflected. Unfortunately the Triple Intervention was too late to discourage the by then well-developed Japanese appetite for territorial aggrandizement at the expense of China.

To sum up the argument to this point: Americans DeLong and LeGendre stimulated Japanese expansionism against China early in the game, and Minister Young failed to seize on the neutralization of Korea as a way to halt it. Then Great Britain, Russia, and the U.S. failed to exert sufficient diplomatic pressure to deter it in 1894, when diplomacy (short of force) probably had its last chance.

After the Sino-Japanese War, Japan, having acquired military confidence, was much less inclined to listen to Western advice, although there may have been a few more chances. For example, Ernest Satow, whose advice, because of his long residence in Japan, was much respected by the Japanese, was sounded out in Peking just before the Russo-Japanese War. In December 1903, General Yamane asked Satow for his "private" view, whether Japan ought to fight now or delay. Satow said "yes" (fight), "for if Russia is left undisturbed in Manchuria out of which she will never retire willingly, she will end by taking Corea, and the position of Japan would then be imperiled."[43]

The Washington Conference provided another chance, and perhaps there were a couple more in the 1930s, such as the effort of Shidehara to contain the Manchurian militants in 1931 and Konoe's peace feelers to China in the late 1930s; also a final one in Nomura's diplomacy, which led to the ditching of Matsuoka in July 1941. It should be observed, however, that in these instances everything depended on the outcome of political infighting *inside* Japan, wherein the civilian-international-Shidehara–type orientation had to win if the course of Japanese aggression against China were to be deflected. That situation is quite different from the early Meiji occasions cited, when the civilian-international–type leadership (then represented by the Ōkubo-Itō-Mutsu line) was really in control and could make its decisions stick.

Thus in the post-Meiji-Manchu era the shoe was quite literally on the other foot. The Japanese military was so strong that it could not be deflected by the suasions of Western-style diplomacy, and it was China that needed to be warned of this. But unfortunately, from the presidency of Yuan Shih-k'ai onward, beginning with the ill-starred efforts of Paul Reinsch and Frank J. Goodnow to turn Yuan into an American-backed constitutional monarch, Westerners encouraged China to stand up to Japan, with words but not substance.[44]

And though China was always disappointed in the results, from the betrayal on Shantung at the Paris (Versailles) peace conference through the League of Nations' unhelpfulness on the Manchurian question in the 1930s, China's diplomacy under such leaders as Wellington Koo became more and more enmeshed in and dependent on Western diplomacy.[45] As a result, Japan-educated or -oriented Chinese, from Ts'ao Ju-Lin to Wang Ching-wei, who could at least communicate with Japanese leaders, were castigated as unpatriotic or traitorous.[46]

Of course, the unfortunate Western influences discussed above do not exonerate Japan from blame in the long, tragic course of Japanese relations with China. Li Hung-chang had given Itō Hirobumi some excellent advice while recovering from an assassin's wounds at Shimonoseki, where he had come to sue for peace in 1895. He said: "It matters little to Japan, in this time of her abounding prosperity and greatness and in the abundance of able men, whether she today receives a larger or smaller indemnity, or whether she enlarges her boundaries by the annexation of a greater or smaller portion of the territory now within reach of her armies; but it is a matter of vast moment to her future happiness of her people, whether or not by the negotiation now in hand, her Plenipotentiaries make of the Chinese nation firm friends and allies or inveterate foes."[47]

Unfortunately Itō and several subsequent generations of Japanese leaders did not heed his advice.

Notes

1. See Frances V. Moulder, "Comparing Japan and China—Some Theoretical and Methodological Issues," in Alvin D. Coox and Hilery Conroy, eds., *China and Japan: The Search for Balance since World War I* (Santa Barbara, Calif.: ABC–Clio Press, 1978), chapter 5.

2. See William D. Hoover, "Crisis Resolution in Early Meiji Diplomatic Relations: The Role of Godai Tomoatsu," *Journal of Asian History* 60, no. 1 (1975): 57–81.

3. Ōkubo Toshikazu, *Ōkubo Toshimichi Bunsho* (Ōkubo Toshimichi Documents) (Tokyo: Nihon Shiseki Kyōkai, 1927–31), 5, no. 708:53–63. See deBary, William T., ed. *Sources of the Japanese Tradition* (New York: Columbia University Press, 1958), pp. 658–62.

4. Hilary Conroy, *The Japanese Seizure of Korea, 1868–1910* (Philadelphia: University of Pennsylvania Press, 1960), pp. 286–97; Hagihara Nobutoshi, *Mutsu Munemitsu* (Tokyo: Chūō Kōronsha, 1973), pp. 233–60. Cf. Gordon Berger, trans., *Kenkenroku* (Tokyo: University of Tokyo, 1982)

5. Payson J. Treat's term; see his *Diplomatic Relations between the United States and Japan* (Stanford, Calif.: Stanford University Press, 1932), 1:353–88.

6. Ibid., pp. 411–12.

7. Treat observes that DeLong did not wait for instructions on these matters and that DeLong's and Soejima's ideas are difficult to distinguish. Treat, 1:474–75. DeLong and Soejima became great friends after initial differences over the *Maria Luz* Chinese coolie case, in which Soejima freed the coolies from the Peruvian ship and DeLong, representing Peru, ended up presiding at the auctioning off of the ship. Wayne McWilliams discussed this in his paper on "The National Rights Diplomacy of Soejima Taneomi" delivered at the Association for Asian Studies meeting of March 1973 at a session chaired by the author. See also McWilliams's article on "East Meets West: The Soejima Mission to China, 1873," *Monumenta Nipponica* 30 (Autumn 1975): 237–75.

8. Treat, 1:475–83; see DeLong to Secretary of State, November 6, 1872, no. 302, *Papers Relating to the Foreign Relations of the United States* (hereafter *FRUS*), 1873, pp. 553–56.
9. Fish to DeLong, December 18, 1872, no. 177, *FRUS*, 1873, p. 564; same to same, December 30, 1872, no. 164, *FRUS*, 1873, pp. 567–68; see also Treat, 1:482–83.
10. Treat, *Diplomatic Relations*, 1:543–50.
11. This was on the grounds that China and Japan were not at war and hence there was no legal obstacle to his being employed by a foreign nation. The previous cases of Frederick Townsend Ward and Henry A. Burgevine, who were once employed by China, were cited. Secretary of State Fish to Consul General Seward, August 26, 1874, no. 409, *FRUS*, 1874, pp. 332–34; Cadwalader to Seward, October 9, 1874, no. 416, *FRUS*, 1874, p. 346.
12. See Leonard Gordon, "Japan's Abortive Expedition to Taiwan, 1874," *Journal of Modern History* 37, no. 2 (June 1965): 171–85; Leonard Gordon, "Charles LeGendre: A Heroic Civil War Colonel Turned Adventurer in Taiwan," *Smithsonian Journal of History* 3, no. 4 (Winter, 1968–69): 63–76, especially pp. 72–76.
13. Richard T. Chang, "General Grant's 1879 Visit to Japan," *Monumenta Nipponica* 24, no. 4 (1969): 373–91, especially p. 381.
14. Ibid., p. 391; see also Treat, 2:100–104, 141–44, 179–81. The State Department refused to take notice when the final annexation occurred. Secretary of State to Minister Young, Peking, March 16, 1883, no. 95, National Archives, Diplomatic Instructions, Department of State, NA 713, micro. 77, roll 40, pp. 409–12.
15. Young to Secretary of State Freylinghuysen, December 28, 1882, no. 87; same to same, December 27, 1882, no. 86, National Archives, Diplomatic Despatches, China, 1882.
16. Secretary of State to Young, March 16, 1883, no. 94, National Archives, Diplomatic Instructions, Department of State, NA 713, micro. 77, roll 40, p. 409.
17. Secretary of State to Young, February 28, 1883, no. 90, National Archives, Diplomatic Instructions, pp. 402–3 and pp. 419–32. The quotation is from George M. McCune and John A. Harrison, eds., *Korean-American Relations: The Initial Period, 1883–1886* (Berkeley, Calif.: University of California Press, 1951), p. 5.
18. Phrase used by Foreign Minister Mutsu Munemitsu in Mutsu to Itō, August 16, 1894, Archives of the Japanese Ministry of Foreign Affairs on Library of Congress Microfilm (hereafter JFMA), MT (section) 1.6.1.5, pp. 539–40.
19. For treaty-revision correspondence of this period, see Gaimushō, *Nihon gaikō bunsho* (Japanese Foreign Office documents; hereafter NGB), 27:1 (1894), pp. 1–87; regarding "signing in English," see Mutsu to Aoki (London), July 13, 1894, no. 46, NGB, 27:1, p. 87.
20. Aoki (London) to Mutsu, July 15, 1894, no. 49, NGB, 27:1 (1894), pp. 88–89.
21. Treaty, etc., signed by Aoki and Lord Kimberley, dated July 16, 1894, enclosure in Aoki in Mutsu, July 17, 1894, no. 55, NGB, 27:1 (1894), pp. 90–105.
22. Enclosure in Kurino (Washington) to Mutsu, November 27, 1894, no. 143, NGB, 27:1, pp. 198–211.
23. Further details of treaty-revision negotiations with the U.S. in NGB, 21:1, pp. 155–216.
24. NGB, 21:1, pp. 218–36.
25. Aoki (London) to Mutsu, June 24, 1894, no. 619, NGB, 27:2, pp. 272–73.
26. Aoki to Mutsu, June 29, 1894, no. 627, NGB, 27:2, p. 281.
27. Okoshi to Mutsu, June 27, 1894, secret, item 1 of no. 733, NGB, 27:2, pp. 399–400.
28. Mutsu to Okoshi, June 29, 1894, item 2 of no. 733, NGB, 27:2, p. 800.
29. Paget to Mutsu, July 23, 1894, no. 734, NGB, 27:2, pp. 400–401.
30. Mutsu to Paget, July 23, 1894, no. 735, NGB, 27:2, pp. 401–2.
31. Henningsen (Shanghai) to Stone (Tokyo), August 29, 1894, attached document in Ōmori to Mutsu, no. 725, NGB, 27:2, p. 371. It is to be noted that Mutsu was prepared to "give satisfaction" to Great Britain if needed. Mutsu to Aoki (London), July 29, 1894, no. 711, NGB, 27:2, p. 333; same to same, July 31, no. 712, NGB, 27:2, pp. 334–35.
32. Resumé of conversation on Korean problem, June 25, 1894, no. 620, NGB, 27:2, pp. 274–77.
33. Hitrovo to Mutsu, June 30, 1894, no. 633, NGB, 27:2, p. 284.
34. See Krazny Archiv, "Russian Documents Relating to the Sino-Japanese War," *Chinese Social and Political Science Review* 17 (1933–34): 638–57; see also JFMA, section SP5, pp. 250–53.

35. Dun to Mutsu, July 9, 1894, no. 652, NGB, 27:2, p. 296.
36. Mutsu to Dun, July 9, 1894, no. 653, NGB, 27:2, pp. 297–98.
37. Denby to Jutaro Komura (Peking), August 1, 1894, attached doc. to no. 755, p. 431.
38. Secretary of State Gresham to S. Kurino, August 29, 1894, attached doc. to no. 791, NGB, 27:2, pp. 443–44.
39. Fred Harvey Harrington, *God, Mammon and the Japanese: Dr. Horace N. Allen and Korean-American Relations, 1884–1905* (Madison, Wisc.: University of Wisconsin Press, 1944), pp. 205–46; see also Conroy, *The Japanese Seizure of Korea*, pp. 184–85.
40. See Jeffrey M. Dorwatt, "The Independent Minister: John M. B. Sill and the Struggle Against Japanese Expansion in Korea, 1894–1897," *Pacific Historical Review* 44, no. 4 (November 1975): 485–502; Jack Hammersmith, "The Sino-Japanese War, 1894–1895: American Predictions Reassessed," *Asian Forum* 4, no. 1 (January–March 1972): 48–58.
41. Japan decided to capitulate on April 24, the day after receiving the demands, though some face was saved by delaying the formal reply until May 5. Documents telling the story are in JFMA, section SP5, pp. 446–504 and NGB, 28:2, pp. 1–223.
42. Frank W. Iklé, "The Triple Intervention: Japan's Lesson in the Diplomacy of Imperialism," *Monumenta Nipponica* 22, nos. 1–2 (1967): 122–30. In my study, *The Japanese Seizure of Korea* (1960), I reported the "change in German attitude" (pp. 290–91), but I did not realize the full implication of this until seeing Iklé's study. See also George A. Lensen, *Balance of Intrigue* (Tallahassee: University of Florida Press, 1982), I, pp. 259–324.
43. George Alexander Lensen, *Korea and Manchuria Between Russia and Japan, 1895–1904: The Observations of Sir Ernest Satow* (Tallahassee, Fla.: The Diplomatic Press, 1966), pp. 35–36.
44. On Reinsch and Goodnow, see *FRUS: Lansing Papers, 1914–1920*, 2:427–29; National Archives microfilm 329, roll 14, pp. 964–66, 978–83, 1046–47, 1115–41; Reinsch to Lansing, January 15, 1916, no. 892, *FRUS* (1916), pp. 54–55; Paul S. Reinsch, *An American Diplomat in China* (Garden City, N.Y.: Doubleday, Page and Co., 1922), pp. 172–73, 176. Western journalists also played a large roll in stimulating China's defiance of Japan. See Mordechai Rozanski, "The Role of American Journalists in Chinese-American Relations, 1900–1925" (Ph.D. diss., University of Pennsylvania, 1974).
45. See the revealing articles of Pao-chin Chu: "V. K. Wellington Koo: The Diplomacy of Nationalism," in Richard D. Burns and Edward M. Bennett, *Diplomats in Crisis* (Santa Barbara, Calif.: ABC–Clio Press, 1974), pp. 125–51, and "From Paris Peace Conference to Manchurian Incident," in Alvin D. Coox and Hilary Conroy, *China and Japan: The Search for Balance* (Santa Barbara, Calif.: ABC–Clio Press, 1978), pp. 61–82.
46. See Madeleine Chi, "Ts'ao Ju-lin (1876–1966): His Japanese Connections" in Akira Iriye, ed. *The Chinese and the Japanese* (Princeton, N.J., 1980), pp. 140–60, and Hang-sheng Lin's articles on Chou Fo-hai and Wang Ching-wei in Burns and Bennett, *Diplomats in Crisis*, pp. 171–93, and Coox and Conroy, *China and Japan*, respectively; see also in *Peace and Change* 1, no. 1 (Fall 1972), pp. 18–35; and John Hunter Boyle, *China and Japan at-War, 1937–1945: The Politics of Collaboration* (Stanford, Calif.: Stanford University Press, 1972).
47. Memorandum of the Ambassador of His Imperial Majesty The Emperor of China in Reply to the Draft of Treaty Proposed by the Plenipotontiaries of His Imperial Majesty The Emperor of Japan, April 5, 1895, NGB, 28:2, no. 1081, pp. 347–48.

Part 4
Problems and Solutions in Thought and Action

Jinrikisha: traditional transport in the Meiji era. *(Photo permission by Anna Brinton Collection. Reproduction by Masako Imai.)*

Introduction

In this section the reader will meet some of the best minds of Meiji Japan seeking solutions in thought to guide them in action. He has already met Fukuzawa, briefly in the general introduction and again on the women's-rights issue in the article by Mikiso Hane. Tokutomi Sohō and Uchimura Kanzō have been referred to in Professor Yamashita's article on Herbert Spencer and the general introduction respectively. But in the following essay on "Varieties of *Bunmei Ron*" these three are given the in-depth treatment they deserve as three of the most active minds of Meiji Japan. Their soul-searching efforts to find a way to "civilize" Japan *(bunmei ni suru)* without accepting subservience to the Western world in either thought or action are probed with the sort of analytical intensity that is almost peculiar to Japanese scholars of what is called "thought" *(Shisō)*.

The author, Matsuzawa Hiroaki, is the sort of scholar who weighs every word and worries about every nuance, not only in the writings of his subjects of inquiry but also in his own writing and the translation thereof. Such concern may seem excessive when a topic such as "civilization" has come to be viewed as an airy subject suited to witty parlor talk today, but as Professor Matsuzawa's essay shows, it was a subject of serious, indeed urgent, importance to the Meiji mind. That this was true may also be an important lesson for us, caught as we are in the vortex of change. Utilizing a Matsuzawa style of analysis, could we discover clues to the meaning of "civilization" today?

Peter Ch'en's study of Inoue Kowashi is the distillation of many years of research, and though the notes are somewhat incomplete because of the author's untimely death, it seems well worth presenting for several reasons. It shows precisely how Japan's Meiji constitutional leaning toward Germany occurred. It also suggests that Inoue was a much more important element in the construction of the Meiji system than previous emphasis on the role of Itō Hirobumi and other, more highly placed oligarchs has indicated. Here is revisionist history in the making, though, sadly, because of Dr. Ch'en's untimely death, it will have to be completed by others.

The third essay, on Mutsu, shows the remaking of a radical into first a liberal, then a cautious conservative determined to practice the art of the "possible" in government service. It will be recalled that Herbert Spencer preached "gradualism" to other Meiji leaders. But Hagihara Nobutoshi literally trailed Mutsu on his journey after political wisdom and found his point of conversion at the old house of Lorenz von Stein in Vienna. The article here is a condensation and translation by Hagihara of his book-length study of Mutsu in Japanese. Mr. Hagihara, a graduate of Tokyo University, is one of Japan's foremost critics. In addition to his study of Mutsu, he is the author of biographical studies of Baba Tatsui, Sir Ernest Satow, and Togo Shigenori. He has avoided what he calls "being institutionalized" with university or other affiliations.

9 Varieties of *Bunmei Ron* (Theories of Civilization)

Matsuzawa Hiroaki, with assistance in translating from the Japanese original by *Nagata Yoichi and Hilary Conroy*

In the midst of the confusion of the Meiji Restoration, the Japanese began energetically to coin new words and revive obsolete words in order to convey new ideas from the West. Some of these terms became very fashionable. *Kaika, bunmei,* and *bunmei-kaika* were among them. The Japanese believed that these were Japanese equivalents of the English word *civilization,* which was popular in Victorian Great Britain.

These fashionable words, *bunmei* or *kaika,* represented everything Western then in vogue, for example, beef, bowler hats, gas lamps, the telegraph, railways, and steam ships. These were favorite subjects of *nishikie* (wood-block prints) and *kaika-bon* (*kaika* literature), and of caricatures by people such as Bigot and Wirgman. They showed the robust and often flamboyant spirit of the age. There was, however, a reverse side to this coin, which has often been overlooked by historians. That is to say, the majority of people were drowning in the flood of products of Western civilization. They had left the old world forever. Yet they had no idea of where they were going. In 1876, in the midst of this situation, Fukuzawa Yukichi wrote that "according to doctors' reports incidents of nervous illness or insanity are on the rise in recent times."[1]

This combination of a vigorous and gay atmosphere on the surface and an undercurrent of anxiety and loss of direction was to some extent almost a natural result of the governmental policy of *bunmei-kaika*. The victors in the civil war gained power without any clear program. Thus, they were forced to begin modernization by imitating what they thought was Western civilization before homemade programs and theories of modernization were ready. Furthermore, the attitude of the government toward Western civilization was opportunistic. It avidly yet indiscriminately introduced the material products of Western civilization, regardless of their usefulness to and their effects upon the life of the populace.

As a result, the words and material objects of civilization flooded Japanese society very quickly. People however, had little idea of what civilization was and where they were moving in this deluge of *bunmei-kaika*. Facing these facts, nationalistic and liberal-minded intellectuals took upon themselves the task of establishing *theories* of civilization in Japan. On the one hand, they criticized the governmental policy of *bunmei-kaika*, particularly its opportunism and superficiality. On the other hand, they tried to show the bewildered people what civilization truly was and how they could attain it in Japan.

However, the work of constructing *theories* about civilization contained a dilemma. The intellectuals had no recourse but to refer to such theories in the Western nations, just as the government imported products of civilization from them. Materials for their theories were available at the time in Europe: Montesquieu's *De l'Esprit des Lois*, 1748; Guizot's *Histoire de la Civilization en Europe*, 1828–30; Buckle's *History of Civilization in England*, 1857 and 1861; Spencer's *Principles of Sociology*, 1873–96. Above all, the works of the "system makers"[2] Buckle and Spencer were read eagerly by intellectuals and students at the beginning of the Meiji era. Their translations too, became best-sellers. Why were they so appealing? First of all, they seemed to be the first theories that explained the development and nature of the mid-nineteenth-century European, particularly English, civilization. Furthermore, this explanation was based on what these theorists claimed were the scientific laws of civilization, which were universally valid not only for Europe but for the whole world, and which were as certain as natural laws. This "grand theory" and the "synthetic system" seemed to provide a clear perspective for Japan, which was at the mercy of the waves of Western civilization.

However, comprehensive theories such as Buckle's and Spencer's played a paradoxical role in explaining Japan's civilization. This paradox stemmed from complicated problems contained in the theories. While these theories assumed that laws of civilization were universal all over the world, they had a negative perspective on the non-Western world, that is, there was a dichotomy between the West and the non-West. These comprehensive theories originated in a rather hasty generalization made from the experience of English society during the very rapid industrialization of the eighteenth and nineteenth centuries. As is often the case in general theories, they could not always be applicable to individual cases. This was the case in the non-West, including Japan.

These theories only indicated a contemporary confidence that Europe, headed by England, was leading the world. They depicted the world in terms of a dichotomy between the developed and ever-progressing West and the underdeveloped, stagnant non-West. Furthermore, they tended to regard this gap as permanent. These theories furthered prejudice toward and ignorance of the non-West, because they often regarded Asia as one

Varieties of Bunmei Ron (Theories of Civilization)

undifferentiated whole and failed to recognize varieties of character within it. It took a long time before Japan was noticed as a nation with its own character.

Readers in Japan who had contact with these civilization theories were placed in a delicate situation. They had already been shocked by the enormous gap between the West and Japan in their civilization. Then on top of that, these theories arrived to explain and confirm this gap. The power of argument of these theories was overwhelming. The more persuasive they were, the more unbridgeable seemed the gap.

In this article the author will take three outstanding and influential intellectuals who were socially and culturally interrelated and who built up civilization theories between the 1870s and 1920s. They were Fukuzawa Yukichi, Tokutomi Sohō, and Uchimura Kanzō.

Fukuzawa Yukichi—*Bunmei-ron no Gairyaku (An Outline of Theory of Civilization)*

Bunmei-ron no Gairyaku came first and was most influential in the formation of civilization theory in Japan. Fukuzawa's uniqueness stemmed partly from his famous thesis, "one person, two lives" (一身二生) stated in the preface.[3] He argued that contemporary intellectuals had experienced both old Japanese traditions and new Western civilization through the upheaval of rapid Westernization that the Meiji Restoration brought about. In this sense they could compare traditional Japan based on their own direct experience with the new Western civilization. He concluded that Japanese intellectuals familiar with Western civilization were in a superior position to Western theorists. According to Fukuzawa, the Western theorists guessed at the non-West from a distance and from within an "already established civilization," whereas the Japanese were in the midst of a chaotic process of creating a new civilization and therefore had a clearer view of this process. It could be said that this was a kind of declaration of intellectual independence against the universalistic theories that had been produced in Europe.

Next, Fukuzawa implicitly criticized those intellectuals (some of whom were perhaps his colleagues in Meirokusha) who despaired of catching up with Western nations and so lost their confidence in Japan as they learned more of Western theories of civilization. On the other hand, he boldly assumed a critical attitude toward Buckle's *History of Civilization in England*. Although Fukuzawa did not always mention his debt to Buckle in *Bunmei-ron no Gairyaku*, his book followed closely the lines of Buckle's theory of the history of civilization. One of the basic motifs that ran through Buckle's argument was the dichtomy between civilization in Europe and what he called "civilization exterior to Europe." In this context Buckle believed that

Asia was the most important "civilization exterior to Europe" and that India could be taken to represent civilizations in Asia as a whole.[4] Thus, he described conditions in India at great length. The main points of the argument were two. First, in India "the heat of the climate has . . . caused an abundance of food and the abundance of food caused an unequal distribution, first of wealth, and then of political and social power."[5] Thus despotism and the eternal slavery of the populace was "the state to which they were doomed by physical laws utterly impossible to resist."[6] Second, people there were "oppressed by the pomp and majesty of nature."[7] Therefore, they were "intimidated" and lost control of "imagination," to use Buckle's own terms.[8] This can be said to epitomize the view that regarded Asia as one eternally doomed, stagnant society. On this point Fukuzawa criticized Buckle's argument decisively, but presumably deliberately without mentioning him by name. To quote Fukuzawa's argument in a rather free translation:

> Is this theory effective in analyzing conditions in Japan? If this is the case, then as the causes belong to the realm of natural laws, we can do nothing about it. What I intend is to discover the historical and social conditions which led to despotism. If I am successful, then hopefully we can find the way to break through despotism.[9]

This was one of the basic motifs of *Bunmei-ron no Gairyaku*.

In fact, his very definition of civilization was polemic. First he separated the "external elements of civilization" from "the spirit of civilization." The latter was crucial to the creation of civilization in Japan.[10] He attached most importance to strong intellectual independence as a core of "the spirit of civilization." In other words, it was "the spirit" that managed to produce and use "the external elements" by recognizing the laws of nature and society. Fukuzawa argued that the development of the spirit of civilization was promoted by the revolution in traffic and communication, changes brought about by the industrial revolution, and the ever-increasing diversity and frequency of human relations accompanying it.[11] It is perhaps obvious that this definition of civilization itself implied a radical criticism of the "civilization" policy of the Meiji government.

Fukuzawa built up a program for civilization in Japan through his definition of civilization. He, too, thought that for the immediate promotion of Japanese civilization it was necessary in Japan to accept models of Western civilization. However, he insisted that as "the spirit of civilization" was hard to accept, while "the external elements" were easy to accept, the acceptance of "the spirit of civilization" should have priority over what he called "the external elements".[12] This signified a proposal for radical Westernization that was diametrically opposed to the government's opportunistic policy of Westernization. Moreover, he understood "spirit"

Varieties of Bunmei Ron (Theories of Civilization)

as not just an idea, but as connected with a real social condition that would help the growth and functioning of the spirit. Therefore, he wanted the promotion of diversity and frequency in human relations along with the introduction of the spirit. Thus, he insisted that social relations should be completely liberated even at the level of the individual.[13] In his opinion the acceptance of Western civilization should be accompanied by the liberation of society in Japan.

As is commonly known, belief in the general progress of human beings lay at the root of Fukuzawa's theory of civilization. In addition, he did not worry about the gap between the civilization of the West and that of Japan, which made some intellectuals feel pessimistic. In a book written four years after *Bunmei-ron no Gairyaku*, he estimated that Japan was only twenty or thirty years, at the most fifty years, behind Europe in the introduction of modern technology.[14] Although he tentatively set Western civilization as Japan's objective, he never stated his approval of what Western civilization actually was. Because of his belief in incessant human progress, he expected that a day would come in the future when current Western civilization would be regarded as barbarous.[15]

Fukuzawa, however, never took a rose-colored view of the possibility of Japan's civilization. He did not believe in the simple rule that the more civilization advanced, the more evil decreased and good increased. Instead, he understood that progress of civilization would continually produce new problems, especially with regard to social differentiation and conflicts.[16] Above all in his inquiry into the future of civilization in Japan, Fukuzawa was much concerned with the problems that would be caused by contact between countries at different stages of civilization. In this context, Fukuzawa paid particular attention to the function of superior civilization. For example, he discussed the relations between an industrial nation and a raw-material-producing nation. Free trade, investment, and colonization along with the flow of the progress of civilization between the two nations would strike a blow at the raw-material-producing nation, and in the end eliminate the independence that was an essential condition for civilization.[17] This implied a decisive rejection of the gospel of free trade and the international division of labor that were based on Britain's supremacy in industry and lay at the root of the theories of Buckle and others. Fukuzawa, influenced by Buckle's theory, declared that the main aim in civilization theory was to discover "the laws" governing the progress of civilization.[18] On this point, it should be noted that, when he discussed the future of civilization in Japan, he never referred to anything like so-called objective or necessary laws of progress for civilization. According to Fukuzawa, Japan was on the verge of losing her independence as the result of the pressure of Western civilization. Internally she was in a state of great confusion, which had been caused by the Restoration. Therefore, the Japanese had to *create* civilization out of chaos. It was bound to be a life and death adventure. It was not belief in technology, productivity, objective and necessary "laws" of progress, or dependence on "the general trend in the world" that provided him with hope for Japan's civilization. It was, in the last analysis, just a belief in "the spirit" of civilization that would be strong enough to face and overcome this critical situation.

It is commonly said that Fukuzawa wrote *Bunmei-ron no Gairyaku* from a sense of crisis that he felt about Japan's civilization, but that subsequently in his later years, after the Sino-Japanese War, he became rather optimistic. Today he is sometimes criticized for a lack of understanding of the misery of the Japanese common people and the relations between "civilized" Japan and "barbarous" China and Korea. In retrospect, especially in view of the later fate of the Japanese Empire, it can be said that he was under an illusion about the progress of civilization in Japan. His failure showed how difficult it was for the people at a higher level of civilization to understand the impact that the progress of civilization had on people at a lower level of civilization, both in international relations and their own domestic societies. It is clear that Fukuzawa did have an understanding of this problem in his *theory*.[19] The reason that he could not pass this barrier seems, at least to some extent, to be attributable to the limitations of his notion of "the spirit of civilization." As in the case of Buckle's notion of "the mental laws of civilization," there was a partiality for intellect and a kind of dryness in Fukuzawa's ideas. In fact, it was this suggestion of dryness in his theory which lessened its appeal to younger generations in the later half of the 1880s.

Tokutomi Sohō—*Shin Nihon no Seinen (Youth of the New Japan)* and *Shōrai no Nihon (Japan in the Future)*

It was Tokutomi Sohō who, after a brilliant debut, took the place of Fukuzawa. His *Dai Jyūkyūseiki Nihon no Seinen oyobi sono kyōiku (Japan's Youth and Its Education in the Nineteenth Century)* of 1885 (the title of which was changed to *Shin Nihon no Seinen (Youth of the New Japan)* in 1887) and *Shōrai no Nihon (Japan in the Future)* of 1886 immediately brought him into prominence. These works inaugurated a new theory of civilization to replace Fukuzawa's. In both, Tokutomi tried to explore the course on which the new civilization would make progress in the midst of the great confusion engendered by the Meiji Restoration.

Tokutomi, like Fukuzawa, held forebodings over the future of civilization in Japan, because the old power structure remained strong and the new enlightened people establishing civilization were still immature. However, turning his eyes to the outside world, Tokutomi noted that a good support for Japan's civilization was gaining strength. In fact, more than one third of his *Shōrai no Nihon* was devoted to an analysis of what he called the "environment of the outside world" and "natural trends of society" in it. There, too, Tokutomi was not so naïvely optimistic. Competition over armaments, war, and proliferation of what he called "military organization" were rampant throughout the world. Above all, the Western powers were putting dangerous pressure on the parts of Asia around Japan.[20] However, what did make this competition over armament at all possible? It was nothing other than the development of what he called "industrial organization," which constituted the basis of and supported the military organization as a kind of substructure. This industrial organization, Tokutomi argued, was, by its nature, necessarily overcoming the military organization with an irresistible energy.[21] Accordingly, the character of the whole society was changing from "aristocratic" to "democratic," and free trade was making closer relations between nations and thus bringing about world peace.[22] This was the undercurrent of world history underlying power politics and gradually altering them. Tokutomi understood this undercurrent as the irresistible *sekai no taisei* (general trend of the world). Because Tokutomi pinned his hope on the incessant pressure of this irresistible "general trend of the world" on Japan, and on the suitability of Japan's geographical conditions for responding to this pressure,[23] he expected that the civilization of "new Japan" would break into open resistance against the old.

Tokutomi's perspective on "the world trend" in his *Shōrai no Nihon* was based on a dichotomy. He regarded all societies of the world, including Japan, in terms of a diametrical contrast of the "military type" versus the "industrial type." He argued that every society would progress from the former to the latter along a unilinear course. Although Tokutomi gave little credit to Herbert Spencer, these ideas were modeled on Spencer's *Political Institutions* (1883), the fifth part of his *Principles of Sociology*.[24] It was the dichotomy of "the military types of society versus the industrial type of society" that the provincial Radicals in England at the beginning of the nineteenth century had possessed in common, when the industrial revolution had brought about a striking change in the whole nation.[25] Spencer combined this dichotomy with the philosophy of organic revolution, and reformulated an idea of development into a theory of unilinear evolution, valid throughout world history. Scholars such as Buckle can be said to have looked down at the foothills of the world from the summit of world civilization, i.e., England, when he unfolded his grand theory of world civilization. Against this background, the counterposition of the old society vis-à-vis the new society in Spencer's dichotomy of "military type" versus "industrial type" implied the relative position of the non-West, including Japan, vis-à-vis Europe. Whereas Buckle's civilization theory had not dealt with Japan,[26] but with Asia, Spencer brought Japan into his "synthetic" system, discussing its feudal state as a typical case of an old "military type" society. Spencer's civilization theory implied that the progress of various nations would follow the course of England and converge with it. However, as was shown in his advice to Japanese politicians such as Mori Arinori, Itō Hirobumi, and Kaneko Kentarō, Spencer was apparently sceptical of the possibility of Japan's rapid modernization.[27] In contrast to Fukuzawa's critical attitude toward Buckle, Tokutomi naïvely followed certain arguments of Spencer that appealed to him and contended that Japan's civilization was actually approaching England's.

Tokutomi's program for Japan's civilization was rather simple. All that the program prescribed was to follow "the general trend of the world," and to introduce it into Japan appropriately. He did not go beyond the assumption that Japan would inevitably be "an industrial society," and as "an inevitable result," a "democratic society." In his *Shin Nihon no Seinen* he discussed an education program for youth a little more concretely. This program advocated acceptance of the Western "spiritual civilization" and "moral society" rather than "eclecticism" and "partiality for intellect," which were then prevailing. His insistence on fundamental Westernization undoubtedly had something in common with Fukuzawa's *Bunmei-ron no Gairyaku*. However, he referred little to the builders of "industrial society" and their future course. This suggests that the more difficult the predicament of Japan was, the more Tokutomi's optimism over the progress of civilization in Japan was supported merely by his trust in "the general trend of the world" emanating from the Western nations.

It took even less than ten years for Tokutomi's optimistic view of civilization in Japan to collapse. The shock of the Triple Intervention disillusioned him and made him realize that real international politics was heading away from international cooperation. His image of the general trend of the world broke down because of its great discrepancy with reality. The shock to him was all the greater because of the sincerity of his belief in the general trend. Why did this happen?

Tokutomi seems to have taken pride in the fact that his knowledge of current developments in the West, particularly in England, was richer than Fukuzawa's had been. Incidents that he quoted as signs of the progress of democracy and world peace were numerous, the speeches of Cobden, Bright, and John Morley, the establishment of the Anti-Agression League in 1882, in which Spencer had taken the initiative, the activities of the International Arbitration and Peace Society, and so on.

The problem lay in the frame of reference that selected and digested this information. Tokutomi agreed with Spencer's unilinear-progress theory that the old world would struggle against the new, and that in the end the old world would be defeated. Moreover, he believed this general trend to be irresistible. Nakae Chōmin was critical of this point and stated in an essay on Tokutomi's journal, *Kokumin no Tomo*, that Tokutomi was a looker-on dependent on the "God of Progress" (進化神).[28] Yet another problem lay in Spencer's theory itself. Spencer's first and most popular book, *Social Statics*, begins with the sentence, " 'Give us a guide,' cry men to the philosopher."[29] This cry epitomized a situation in which people were bewildered by the cataclysm of industrialization and symbolized Spencer's intention to provide them with a clear perspective. His means was to establish a certain and comprehensive world view. In this sense his theory, which he claimed to be a new science of society, is correctly described now as a kind of "theodicy."[30] If so, it is natural and valid that his theory would be synthetic, rigid, and dogmatic. However, all the more because what Tokutomi calls Spencer's "grand system" was rigid and dogmatic, it tended to fail to keep pace with the reality even from rather early days. When Tokutomi read *Principles of Sociology*, he found that Spencer himself had already been conscious of and worried about the rigidity in his theory.[31]

How and in what circumstances did Tokutomi read Spencer? The first chapter of his *Shin Nihon no Seinen* was entitled, "After This Deluge Another Deluge Will Come." Tokutomi, too, was seriously concerned about the bewilderment of Japanese youth in the 1880s. It was natural that he should have jumped at and believed in Spencer's "theodicy." Perhaps the appeal of Spencer to Tokutomi was no less strong than Spencer's appeal to contemporary English readers. Tokutomi's optimism over the future of the civilization in "new Japan" was supported by his belief in the "God of Progress" of "the general trend of the world," independently of the reality already existing in Japan. This "belief in the God of Progress" was related to Tokutomi's belief in Spencer's theory of progress, which he possibly considered the latest theory to emerge from the West. Thus Tokutomi's clear-cut picture of the progress of civilization tended to be separated from the reality of the world in a double sense.[32] The more literal Tokutomi's belief in the theory was, the stronger the shock of the disillusion that eventually came. "The Sino-Japanese War forced me, who had so far studied with books, to study with real facts for the first time. . . . The influence of the experiences of this war effaced that of Spencer, Cobden, and Bright. It was, of course, the Triple Intervention. . . . Thus I converted into 'Gospel of Power.' "[33]

Uchimura Kanzō—From *Chijin Ron (The Earth and Man)* to *A New Civilization*

The converted Tokutomi turned to approach the Meiji oligarchs, an action that caused him to lose credit with liberal-minded youth at the end of the 1890s. As this was happening, Uchimura Kanzō appeared and replaced Tokutomi as a prophet to dissatisfied youth. Uchimura belonged to the same generation as Tokutomi. In fact, Tokutomi opened the door of journalism for Uchimura by providing him with space to publish in his own magazine. Uchimura at first adopted the same position as Tokutomi on the subject of Japan's civilization. However, subtle differences of perception finally caused a split between them. While Tokutomi was shocked at the gap between the reality and the theory of the history of civilization, Uchimura was establishing his theory. As we have seen, Tokutomi abruptly abandoned the theory to which he had been committed for a decade. By contrast, Uchimura radically transformed his theory only through twenty years of agonized pondering over the gap between the reality and the theory. To understand Uchimura's thinking, therefore, it is necessary to see the whole course of the development of his theory of civilization.

As a foreign student and social work volunteer from 1884 to 1888, Uchimura was fortunate to have an opportunity to experience the reality of America and to compare it with the missionary ideology then prevailing in the United States and influential in Japan. Some people, he considered, "seem to imagine that the cause of the mission can be upheld only by picturing the darkness of heathens in contrast with the light of Christians."[34] So they made a "diagram showing heathens by jet black squares, and Protestant Christianity by white squares."[35] Therefore, this ideology prescribed that for the purpose of progress heathen nations should be converted to Christianity as the "religion of Civilization" and model themselves on the Christian nations that gave concrete form to it. Thus, the ideology could be regarded as a Christian version of a theory of unilinear progress civilization. Through his own observations, however, Uchimura could maintain a distance from such Christianity and "Christian civilization," and critically distinguish between what he considered their negative and positive aspects. On the other hand, he continuously searched for a "mission" that Japan could perform in the progress of worldwide civilization. He sincerely believed that "lagging," "heathen" Japan would surpass "advanced" Christian nations.[36]

Nevertheless, Uchimura did not have an optimistic view of the possibility of civilization in Japan. As Tokutomi did, Uchimura included in his program for Japan's civilization the introduction not only of the "material" results of Western civilization but also the "spiritual" foundation. This idea of fundamental Westernization led to the criticism that the contemporary policy of opportunistic and eclectic introduction of Western things resulted in confusion and bewilderment.[37]

This point was common to both Tokutomi and Uchimura. The difference was that Uchimura continued to promote this Westernization at a deeper level, even after Tokutomi gave it up altogether. Ultimately, Uchimura regarded the "spiritual civilization" at the base of Western civilization as nothing but pure Christianity. The problem in Japan's civilization was how to achieve a fundamental revolution of value and way of thinking by nationwide acceptance of Christianity.

Varieties of Bunmei Ron (Theories of Civilization)

Uchimura's earlier program for Japan's civilization was based on the historical theory of civilization unfolded in his writings, *Chijin-ron (The Earth and Man)*, revised edition of 1897 of the first edition with a title of *Chirigaku Ko (Geographical Studies)*, and *Kōkoku Shidan (A History of the Rising Nations)* in 1900. Both of them were influenced by a broad range of Western historical writings. In the case of the former, it was particularly influenced by Arnold Henry Guyot's (1807–84) *The Earth and Man—Lectures on Comparative Physical Geography in Its Relation to the History of Mankind* of 1849 and Anson Daniel Morse's (1846–1916) history lectures at Amherst College. While the theories of Fukuzawa, Tokutomi, Buckle, and Spencer were related to scientific and technological development after the industrial revolution, Uchimura's was remarkably idealistic. He understood that history made progress and that its progress was the gradual unfolding of the capabilities of humanity, especially its moral aspect. In other words, history was an educational process under the tutelege of God and in accordance with His plan,[38] supporting the righteous (義) and punishing the unrighteous (不義).[39] Thus it is clear that his historical theory of civilization was basically theological and teleological. In the historical process, the center of human civilization had started in the ancient Orient, had moved westward, and was about to come to Japan. Uchimura believed that this interpretation of events indicated the future of Japan's civilization. In this sense, his optimism concerning the progress of civilization through the world to Japan was, in the last analysis, supported by his belief in the world dominion of God.

However, Uchimura was frequently disappointed at the lack of progress of civilization both in the world and in Japan. What had supported his interpretation of events in Japan had been various movements for "social reform." But he eventually realized these reform movements, too, were not free from their own fatal defects. He seems to have concluded that, after all, he could not expect too much of the situation within Japan. He had to turn his eyes to the progress of "the general trend of the world" that was approaching Japan,[40] as Tokutomi had done. While the young Tokutomi (who had a longing for Western civilization yet had not had an opportunity to travel to the West), had gathered information from books and had constructed an idealized image of Western civilization, Uchimura was neither so prone to idealize the West nor to despair of Western civilization. Originally he believed that England and the United States, representing Protestantism, were the prime movers of the contemporary progress in the world. When he became generally disillusioned with these countries because of their imperialistic policy as in the Spanish American War and the Boer War, he anchored his hopes on the "remnants" in these countries, especially movements such as "Progressivism" and such men as W. J. Bryan or "The Peace Societies" in America.[41] However, in spite of the efforts of these "remnants," conditions in the world ran contrary to his hopes. The gap between the reality and the belief in the progress of world civilization under the dominion of God was becoming increasingly wider.

This ideological difficulty culminated at the outbreak of World War I in what Uchimura called his "second conversion." Following European "Christian nations," America joined the war and leaders of churches as well as peace and reform movements became, paradoxically as Uchimura saw it, fanatical advocates of war. Reality in the world and in Japan was far from progress. It was rather retrogressing from civilization to barbarism. In Uchimura, abandonment of belief in progress was equal to denying belief in God, who created human beings and was leading them to perfection. Through more than a decade of bitter spiritual struggle, he finally came to break the deadlock by a leap to belief in the Second Coming of Christ.[42] This new eschatology no longer assumed that reforms by human efforts would advance toward the achievement of the perfection of mankind. It meant, rather, that God would come at the end of human history and make human beings perfect once and for all. From 1918 to 1919, Uchimura strongly propounded this Second Coming of Christ, about 1924, in the twilight of Uchimura's life, when the antagonism between Japan and the United States over the prohibition of Japanese immigrants was becoming more severe, his eschatology underwent a fresh development. At this time he introduced a new idea of the correspondence of "the last day" with another concept that he referred to as "the type of the last days." According to this idea, sometime before the " last day" of human history, what Uchimura called "the type," i.e., a foreshadowing of this last day would occur.[43] This new idea in his eschatology showed Uchimura's serious concern over the fate of his nation and the world. In fact, in writings such as his "Nippon no Tenshoku" ("Japanese Mission") of 1924 and "A New Civilization" (originally written in English in 1926), he referred to what he saw as Japan's downfall and subsequent revival. According to Uchimura, American exclusion of Japanese immigrants symbolized a situation in which "the whole world is closed against Japan."[44] This "stalemate in all directions" (八方塞がり) took place, because, to quote his original English, "under its [sic] young, inexperienced politicians of the Meiji Era, she [Japan] adopted this Western civilization which is no civilization. . . . True, Japan by her adoption of the Western methods of warfare, has won her place among the Great Powers of the world within less than a century; . . . but she lost the love of the whole world. . . . Japan Westernized herself and the West has disowned her.[45] Therefore, Uchimura foresaw in Japan's future that she would "at least throw away her position as a first-class nation, if not her existence itself."[46] However, in the midst of despair he also looked forward to "Japan's genuine rising" beyond this national calamity. The expectation was as follows. Japan would revive as a nation, which would be small in its material aspects, but which would be great in its

Varieties of Bunmei Ron *(Theories of Civilization)*   221

contribution to the world in creating a new civilization. "She is to start a new civilization, . . . a warless civilization. . . . What a day will be when my own Japan, by its [sic] solemn decree, will decree the disarmament of the nation, and so bring in the new civilization to the whole world."[47] The spiritual basis of this "new civilization" was what he called "re-reformation"—a fundamental reconstruction of modern Christianity which he thought had degenerated into a "Religion of Civilization."[48]

It took just a half century from *Bunmei-ron no Gairyaku* to *A New Civilization*. During this period, the theories of civilization born in Japan came full cycle, from belief in progress to eschatology, from a sense of adventure in Japan's creation of a new civilization to expectation of a "new civilization" after the death of the old. It anticipated that modernization that was initiated by the *bunmei-kaika* policy of the Meiji government was coming full cycle.

Perhaps it could even be argued that in a certain sense it anticipated the cycle of the postwar history of Japan also.

Notes

1. *Gakumon no Susume (Encouragement of Learning)*, *Fukuzawa Yukichi Zenshū (Complete Works of Fukuzawa Yukichi*, henceforth referred to as *FZ*) (Tōkyō, 1959), 3:129.
2. W. E. Houghton, *The Victorian Frame of Mind* (New Haven, Conn., 1957), p. 165, n. 16. The writer is greatly indebted to this work, especially chapters 6 and 7, for his understanding of "dogmatism" and intellectual "rigidity" of these "system makers."
3. *Bunmei-ron no Gairyaku*, *FZ*, 4:5. For an incisive analysis of this thesis, see Maruyama Masao, "Kindai-Nihon ni okeru Shisōshiteki Hōhō no Keisei" ("Formation of Methods of Intellectual History in Modern Japan") in Fukuda Kan'ichi, ed., *Seijishisō ni okeru Sei-Ō to Nihon (The West and Japan in Political Thought)* (Tōkyō, 1961), vol. 2.
4. See *History of Civilization in England* (London, 1871), 1:22, and John M. Robertson's annotated edition of Buckle's work, *Introduction to the History of Civilization in England* (London, 1904), notes on pp. 40, 47, 74, 81. Fukuzawa read the 1872 New York edition (2 vols.), which is based on the second edition London (2 vols.) of 1858 and 1864. The writer has examined the personal copy that bears Fukuzawa's own annotations, but here quotes from the 1871 London edition.
5. *History of Civilization in England*, 1:81.
6. Ibid., p. 80.
7. Ibid., p. 146.
8. Ibid., p. 140.
9. *FZ*, 4:148ff.
10. Ibid., p. 19.
11. *Minjō Isshin (The People's Life Renewed)*, 1879, *FZ*, 5:5ff.
12. *FZ*, 4:19ff.
13. Ibid., p. 23.
14. *Minjō Isshin*, *FZ*, 5:8. See also his *Jiji Shōgen (Comments on Current Issues)*, 1881, *FZ*, 5:115.
15. *FZ*, 4:18ff.
16. *FZ*, 5:8ff, 31ff.
17. *FZ*, 4:193–97, 209–10.
18. *FZ*, 4:54ff. Fukuzawa refers here to Buckle's *History*, 1:22–28. See also ibid., pp. 3ff.
19. *FZ*, 4:198–200.
20. Chapters 3 and 4 of *Shōrai no Nihon*.

21. Ibid., chapters 5 and 6.
22. Ibid., chapters 7–9.
23. Ibid., chapter 11.
24. K. Pyle writes, "Several passages of *Shōrai no Nihon* appear to be almost direct translations of *Principles of Sociology,*" Pyle, *The New Generation of Meiji Japan* (Stanford, Calif., 1969), p. 211, n. 38.
25. J. D. Y. Peel, *Herbert Spencer—The Evolution of a Sociologist* (London, 1970), pp. 76, 194.
26. In *Common Place Book,* which is Buckle's own detailed and comprehensive record of what he read and which was included in vol. 3 of Helen Taylor's *Miscellaneous and Posthumous Works of Henry Thomas Buckle,* there are extracts from two books on Japan, Thunberg, *Voyage to Japan,* 1795, and Golownin, *Memoir of Captivity in Japan,* 2nd. ed., 1824. He did not however, even mention the name of Japan in his *History.*
27. D. Duncan, *Life and Letters of Herbert Spencer* (London, 1908), pp. 161, 215, 292ff., 319–23. For a painstaking account of Spencer's contact with and influence upon Japanese politicians, including Mori Arinori, see I. P. Hall's biography, *Mori Arinori* (Cambridge, Mass., 1973).
28. "Kokumin no Tomo Dai 15-gō," *Shinonome Shinbun,* February 8, 1888.
29. *Social Statics* (New York, 1884), p. 1.
30. Peel, *Herbert Spencer,* p. 245, and his introduction to *Herbert Spencer on Social Evolution* (Chicago, 1972), p. xxiv. For the Calvinist background of this "theodicy," see *Herbert Spencer,* pp. 29–31, 82–84, 102–11, 131–33.
31. *Herbert Spencer,* pp. 19ff., 29–32, 194, 232ff.
32. For example, in his argument concerning the general trend of the world toward democracy and peace, Tokutomi introduced the oranization of the Anti-Aggression League in 1882, in which Spencer took the initiative, as a sign of hope that the general trend was steadily overcoming power politics and expansionism (*Shōrai no Nihon,* [*Meiji Bungaku Zenshū,* vol. 34], pp. 86–87). In fact, however, what Spencer wanted to do by this league was to make a rather belated attempt to stem the gathering force of imperialism in England. Despite Spencer's dedication, the league came to nothing, and when Tokutomi celebrated the organization of the league in 1886, Spencer's disillusionment in the future had intensified.
33. Tokutomi, *Jimu Ikkagen (Personal Comments on Current Issues)* (Tōkyō, 1913) (*Meiji Bungaku Zenshū,* vol. 34), p. 277.
34. Uchimura, *How I Became a Christian* (Tōkyō, 1895), *Uchimura Kanzō Zenshū (Complete Works of Uchimura Kanzō,* henceforth referred to as *UZ*), 15:119.
35. Ibid.
36. Ibid., pp. 148ff. Also see Uchimura, *Japan and the Japanese* (Tōkyō, 1894), *UZ,* 15:271.
37. See, for example, "Uchi to Soto to" ("Outside and Inside"), *Tōkyō Dokuritsu Zasshi,* no. 7 (September 10, 1898), *UZ,* 2:508–13; "Nihon-koku no Dai-Konnan" ("A Great Difficulty of Japan"), *Seisho no Kenkyū,* no. 35 (March 10, 1903), *UZ,* 14:250–59; "Japan's Case," *The Yorodzu Choho,* April 6, 1897, *UZ,* 16:106; "Thoughts and Reflexions," *The Yorodzu Choho,* August 15, 1897, *UZ,* 16:232ff.; "Note and Comment," *The Yorodzu Choho,* February 4, 1898, *UZ,* 16:379.
38. *Kōzuiizen-ki (A History of the Antediluvian Period)* (Tōkyō, 1911), *UZ,* 3:55.
39. See, for example, "Yogensha Habakuku no Koe" ("The Voice of the Prophet Habakkuk"), *Seisho no Kenkyū,* nos. 46–48 (1903), *UZ,* 4:743ff., and "Nichiro-Sensō yori yo ga uketaru Rieki" ("Some Benefit I Derived from the Russo-Japanese War"), *Shin-Kobō,* no. 69 (November 10, 1905), *UZ,* 14:pp. 385ff.
40. *The Yorodzy Choho,* December 29, 1897; *UZ,* 16:349ff.; "Shun-Gyō-Mu" ("A Dream in a Spring Dawn"), *Tōkyō Dokuritsu Zasshi,* no. 27 (April 5, 1899), *UZ,* 2:611; "Hito no Shitsumon ni kotaete" ("In Reply to Someone's Question"), *Tōkyō Dokuritsu Zasshi,* no. 38 (July 25, 1899), *UZ,* 2:664.
41. "Beikoku no Daraku to sono Kyūsai" ("America's Fall and Her Salvation"), *Seisho no Kenkyū,* no. 56 (September 22, 1904), *UZ,* 14:360–63.
42. For the development of Uchimura's thought from this deadlock to his leap to belief in the Second Coming of Christ, the following two autobiographical accounts are particularly informative: "Sheisho Kenkyū-shayno Tachiba yori mitaru Kirisuto no Sairai" ("The Second Coming of Christ Seen from the Viewpoint of a Biblical Scholar"), *Seisho no Kenkyū,* no. 211 (February 10, 1918), *UZ,* 9:637–43; "Kirisuto Sairin o shinzuru yori kitarishi Yo no Shisō-jō no

Varieties of Bunmei Ron (Theories of Civilization)

Henka" ("Some Changes in My Thought as a Result of My Belief in the Second Coming of Christ"), *Seisho no Kenkyū*, no. 221 (December 10, 1918), UZ, 9:855–63.

43. "Matsujitsu no Mokei" ("The Type of the Last Day"), *Seisho no Kenkyū*, no. 279 (October 10, 1923), UZ, 14:538–43.

44. "New Civilization", *The Japan Christian Intelligencer* 1, no. 2 (April 5, 1926), UZ, 15:573.

45. Ibid., pp. 572ff.

46. "Nippon no Tenshoku," *Seisho no Kenkyū*, no. 292 (November 1924), UZ, 14:599.

47. "New Civilization," UZ, 15:573.

48. "Need of Re-reformation", *Seisho no Kenkyū*, no. 333 (April 10, 1928), UZ, 15:534.

For Further Reading
(Excluding books and articles cited in the notes.)

J. W. Burrow. *Evolution and Society—A Study in Victorian Social Theory*. Cambridge, 1966.

R. A. Nisbet. *Social Change and History—Aspects of the Western Theory of Development*. New York, 1969.

R. T. Handy. *A Christian America—Protestant Hopes and Historical Realities*. New York, 1971.

C. Blacker. *The Japanese Enlightenment—A Study of the Writings of Fukuzawa Yukichi*. Cambridge, 1964.

H. Matsuzawa. "Kindai-Nihon to Uchimura Kanzō" ("Modern Japan and Uchimura Kanzō"), in Matsuzawa, ed., *Uchimura Kanzō*. Tōkyō, 1971.

10 Inoue Kowashi: The Principles of Reform

H. Peter Ch'en

Inoue Kowashi's contributions to and influence on the government of Japan remain largely unknown. Yet, the Meiji statesman was deeply involved in the government of Japan during his twenty-two-year bureaucratic career, which lasted from 1872 to 1894, and was a key figure in the transformation of the Japanese state into a constitutional monarchy in the 1880s.[1]

Inoue Kowashi was born in 1843 in the Kumamoto domain in Kyūshū. He was well educated in Japanese and Confucian studies and was highly respected for his literary ability. He was also known by his pen name of Goin. In 1870, he went to Tokyo and began his official career in October with an appointment to the post of assistant dean *(shōshachō)* of the new government South Campus for Western Studies of the University (Daigaku Nankō), the predecessor of Tokyo University. He was promoted to associate dean *(chūshachō)* in January 1871, but resigned from the position within two months. A year later, at the age of twenty-eight, he was appointed as a tenth-grade official *(jittō shusshi)* in the Ministry of Justice (Shihoshō). This marked the beginning of a bureaucratic career that would continue until he resigned for reasons of health from the position of minister of education in August 1894 at the age of fifty, seven months before his death on March 15, 1895, from chronic tuberculosis.[2]

Inoue played an important part in the formation of state policies on the highest level, especially in foreign policy toward Korea, Taiwan, and China, in policy relating to treaty revision, and by advising and influencing the key policy makers of each phase of the early Meiji period: first Ōkubo Toshimichi and Iwakura Tomomi, next, Iwakura Tomomi and Itō Hirobumi, and finally Itō Hirobumi. Inoue came to the attention of Ōkubo in August 1874.[3] When Ōkubo, as the minister resident plenipotentiary of the emperor of Japan, was in Peking to negotiate a settlement of the Formosan Incident, Inoue assisted Ōkubo from September 12 to the end of October 1874 and drafted much of the official correspondence from the

Japanese mission to the Ch'ing government. He also prepared a draft treaty and other documents and continually offered his views and opinions.[4] Thereafter, Inoue continued to render assistance and advice to Ōkubo until sometime before the latter's death on May 14, 1878.

Inoue was the right-hand man to Iwakura from September 1876, possibly even earlier, until the latter's death on July 20, 1883, and influenced him greatly on numerous occasions. During June–July 1881, Inoue worked to guide Iwakura toward the solution of the key problem facing the ruling group—the problem of having to decide what kind of constitutional government should be established in Japan—by presenting information concerning constitutional government in Great Britain, Germany, and other Western countries, as well as his views and advice on various matters.

Inoue began to assist Itō Hirobumi when Itō "discovered" him in early 1875.[5] After Itō inherited the mantle of the deceased Ōkubo, he came to adhere to Inoue's advice and turned more frequently to Inoue for assistance. In late June and early July 1881, Inoue exerted great influence on Itō's attitude concerning the problem of the type of constitutional government the ruling group should establish in Japan. He convinced Itō, among other things, that in establishing constitutional government in Japan, the consequences would be grievous if the ruling group were to use the parliamentary government of Great Britain as the model for Japan, as Ōkuma Shigenobu, the senior councillor, had proposed in his memorial of March 1881. He also persuaded It that the ruling group should adhere to the principle of gradual progress and thus initate certain practices used in the constitutional government of Germany. Itō depended heavily on Inoue's assistance after his return from Europe in August 1883, especially in the task of establishing the constitution and ancillary laws. After the promulgation of the constitution, Itō continued to obtain Inoue's assistance until Inoue resigned from the government on August 8, 1894, because his health had deteriorated markedly. Even then, Inoue did not cease to offer his advice to Itō. In the winter of 1894, he sent from his sick bed in his home in Hayama a statement written in classical Chinese to Prime Minister Itō, who then was in Hiroshima directing the war against China.[6]

Inoue pointed out strategic and other advantages a country would enjoy by the possession of Taiwan and the disadvantages that Japan would suffer should the island fall into the hands of another country. He stated that, if Japan acquired Taiwan as spoils and, thus, concluded the war, future generations most probably would not regard Japan's undertaking as unrighteous and shameful. He warned that, should Japan miss this opportunity, after two or three years, Taiwan most probably would become a possession of another power, and if not, most probably would become a neutral land that could not be contested. Subsequently, Itō adhered to Inoue's advice.

In addition to his activities in the field of foreign policy, Inoue composed for Iwakura, Sanjō Sanetomi, Itō, and other members of the ruling group the memorials on constitutional government that they presented to the emperor. One such memorial was presented by Itō in December 1880. This was in compliance with the imperial order of February 1880, stating that each councillor submit his written opinion concerning the proper time and suitable method for establishing a constitution and a national assembly. Inoue wrote Itō's memorial upon the latter's request; and in a letter dated November 22, 1880, Itō commented:

> I have received your draft and will discuss with you further my ideas after reading it carefully. Although it is a hasty idea, I should like to attach a general discussion [sōron] to the two proposals of the Senate [Genrō-in] and the auditors [kensakan] and to add in this discussion something to the effect that I should like to have [the government] announce publicly by an imperial rescript that the decision on the time and method of drafting a constitution and establishing a popularly elected assembly is entirely up to the Emperor, and, thus, give direction to the people. Please give this your further consideration. I am leaving the details until I see you. I should be extremely happy if you would be kind enough to come at your convenience tomorrow evening to my Azabu residence.[7]

Inoue similarly drafted the memorial that Terashima Munenori and six other councillors presented on the night of October 11, 1881.[8]

Inoue drafted many laws, regulations, and ordinances for the government. In this field, his monumental work was the Constitution of the Empire of Japan, promulgated on February 11, 1889.[9] Nearly all imperial rescripts of the time were the work of Inoue Kowashi. One of the most famous is the Imperial Rescript (Mikotonori) of April 14, 1875, in which the emperor proclaimed that it was his desire to establish a constitution gradually.[10] Another is the Imperial Rescript (Chokuyu) of October 12, 1881, in which the emperor declared that he intended to convene a national assembly in the twenty-third year of Meiji, that is, 1890.[11] Yet another is the Imperial Rescript on Education (Kyōiku chokugo) of October 30, 1890, which emphasized the role of Confucian morality, loyalty to the state, and filial piety in education.[12]

Inoue participated in the work leading to the establishment of several major governmental institutions by drafting the regulations that defined the organization of these bodies and the duties and powers of their officials. His most important contribution in this area was his work that led to the organization of the first cabinet (naikaku), which was established on December 22, 1995.[13] Finally, while he was the minister of education (from March 7, 1893, until August 29, 1894), Inoue was the key figure in deciding upon educational policies. He planned and ordered the implementation of many reforms concerning primary education, secondary education, technical, industrial, and agricultural education, and higher education.[14]

The opinion that Inoue contributed greatly to the governance of Japan from 1872 to 1894 and in making preparations in the 1880s for Japan's transformation into a constitutional monarchy can be substantiated in part by the comments that Itō made on July 17, 1890, regarding Inoue's work and contribution in his letter to Tokudaiji Sanenori, the grand chamberlain *(Jijyūchō)*, and Motoda Nagazane, a privy councillor *(Sūmitsu komonkan)*. Itō wrote this letter to propose that Inoue be appointed a privy councillor or an imperial household councillor. Itō wrote as follows:

> As you know very well, he is a person second to none in trustworthiness and is especially versed in practical knowledge. Since 1875, he has not only had the confidence of the two elders, Iwakura and Ōkubo, but also has taken part in all the work of the top level government. For more than ten years, he has drafted seven or eight of every ten of the confidential documents concerning major policies for the military and the state. Since the death of the two elders, I have inherited their unfulfilled aims and have barely managed to continue their work; but I realize that the help he has given me in this is beyond reckoning. Particularly in the grave task of planning a constitutional system and formulating the constitution, it would be no exaggeration to say that he devoted his life's blood to each word and phrase.[15]

Insight into Inoue's thought and actions gives a clearer understanding of many aspects of Japan in the period from 1874 to 1895, including the following: the ability and views of the members of the ruling group, the respective roles of the high officials who instituted the changes and reforms, and the nature of the changes and reforms. The information that exists on these matters is meager, but Inoue's career offers new knowledge on the subject.

In this paper, I will show the concerns, thoughts, and beliefs—or let us say, the principles—that were components of Inoue's ideology and that guided Inoue's actions at a specific point in his career. The time was June 1881. The action was his contemplation of the nature of the constitutional government that the ruling group should establish, that is, the nature of the cabinet, of the popularly elected national assembly, and of the constitution. Inoue's thoughts on these topics can be seen in the opinions he expressed, on more than one occasion, in June 1881, to Iwakura, who was then the minister of the right *(Udaijin)* and probably the most influential member of the ruling group as well as in the measures he advised, and the reasons he presented for adopting these measures.

I

In *Iken dai ichi* (Opinion Number One),[16] which (Inoue) presented to Iwakura sometime between June 16 and June 19, 1881, he wrote:

In order to have constitutional rule and establish a people's assembly, it is, I believe, essential first to study what time is suitable for doing this and which system within the constitutional forms of government would be especially suited to our national character [*kokutai*] and popular customs [*minzoku*]. Now, if we suppose that the time is already ripe, we have come to the point of next inquiring into the suitability of the systems.

He continued:

[As to] the constitutional forms of government which are practiced in the countries of Europe, although their goals are generally the same, their methods and procedures vary to some extent in accordance with each country's degree of advancement, national character and popular customs. The case in point is that there are differences in the extent of the rights [*ken*] of the national assemblies. In the instance in which the rights of a national assembly are small, it merely participates in legislative deliberations; in the instance in which the rights are large, it holds actual administrative rights.

Inoue then pointed out that the power of the legislative body varies from country to country and described the situation in England:

The power [*seiryoku*] of the deliberative chamber [*giin*] varies as to country. That with the greatest power is none other than the English Parliament (except for republics). The deliberative chamber of England not only possesses legislative rights but also actual executive rights. A proverb of England has it that there is nothing which the English Parliament cannot do except that it cannot change a man into a woman and a woman into a man.

Why do we say that the deliberative chamber of England also possesses actual executive rights? According to the customary law of England, the English King does not himself rule but entrusts [government] entirely to cabinet ministers; and cabinet ministers are then appointed or dismissed by the parliamentary majority. The Cabinet is organized by the head of the majority party. Every time there is a change in the party holding the majority in the deliberative chamber, there occurs a change of Cabinet Ministers; the one turns and the other follows, just as in the case where one wheel moves and the second wheel responds to it. Hence, the King simply is controlled by the parliamentary majority and lets parties win or lose; he merely proclaims the result in accordance with formality; and he shifts about just like a flag in the wind.

Therefore, although in name the executive rights belong exclusively to the King, in fact, as the chief executive official is none other than the head of the party in control of the deliberative chamber, the actual executive rights are indeed in the hands of the party in [control of] the deliberative chamber; although in name the King and the deliberative chamber share sovereignty, in fact, sovereignty resides exclusively with the deliberative chamber; and the King merely holds an empty vessel.

Inoue contrasts the situation in Prussia with that in England:

> Contrary to this, [in a country] like Prussia the King not only reigns over [his] people but also manages the affairs of state, and, although he shares the legislative rights with the deliberative chamber the executive rights reside exclusively in his hands and are most certainly not ceded to others. The King selects his ministers and administrators regardless of the numerical strength of the circumstances, he often selects persons who have the confidence of the deliberative chamber, so far as the scope of his rights is concerned, he never permits interference by parties in the deliberative chamber.
>
> If we are to create a constitutional government in our country and establish a national assembly, this will indeed be a new undertaking for us. The question whether we should go the whole way [*isshin shite*] in imitating the party government of England, leaving the appointments and dismissals of administrators entirely to the majority in the deliberative chamber, or adhere to the principle of gradual progress, giving to the deliberative chamber only legislative rights and leaving the appointment and dismissal of the chief executive officials exclusively up to the Emperor's choice, and thus model our government on the present situation in Prussia—the choice between these two, being a matter which will establish the lasting foundations of [our government] and determine our fortune for a century is a problem of the greatest importance.

Inoue also explained why the choice between the two systems was so important:

> Students of politics are not in agreement on the similarities and differences between these two systems, but they do agree that in general, depending on the national character and popular feelings [*ninjō*] of countries, [their political systems] cannot be identical. If England were made to imitate the system of Prussia suddenly it would be inevitable that civil strife would immediately arise, just as if Prussia were made to imitate the practice of England, it would also be inevitable that its peace would be disturbed.

Which system did Inoue advise Iwakura to choose? He wrote:

> The great undertaking of establishing constitutional rule is just starting and has not undergone an actual test. Rather than rush ahead precipitately and end up with regrets, or be forced to take away later

what was previously given, it would be better, I believe, to learn from Prussia and move forward gradually step by step thus leaving room [for maneuver] in the future.

Why did Inoue believe that it would be a grave mistake to choose the English system? He believed that the duties of government would be neglected and the affairs of state unattended and, worse yet, the peace and unity of the country would be destroyed. These destructive consequences would ensue because, according to Inoue, Japan lacked two conditions that were prerequisite for successful functioning of a government based on the English system: the existence of two major parties and an ample supply of men capable of governing the nation. Inoue wrote:

> An English convention is that the formation of political parties generally results in two parties. Therefore when one party wins a majority the other party wins a minority. Now, in a country like ours no political parties have been formed, and even if they were, certainly several small parties would set themselves up independently and would not be able to develop into a grand union. Supposing that then the existing cabinet received a minority and [the Emperor] would dismiss it, would the party which would take its place be after all the one in which the esteem of the people [shūbō] resided and to which a majority went? The several small parties certainly would ride abreast, would compete with one another, and would be unable to combine. In attacking the existing government, they would temporarily join forces and, thus, fulfill their respective objectives, but when one of the parties would take the place of the existing government and form a cabinet, the other parties would certainly go into opposition; the position of the rights of the executive would be nothing more than a sort of battleground; the parties would attack each other one after the other; A would stumble and B would fall; there would be no stability; they would have no time to find out what the duties of government were or what was the state of national affairs; and in the end, they would unavoidably resort to arms. This is the first of the differences in conditions between us and them.
>
> In England, except for the fact that such officials as bureau and section chiefs and judicial officers are permanent officials, the various ministers, vice-ministers and secretaries-general are all made up of a single political party; and it is the convention that the important officials resign all together at the same time whenever the majority in the deliberative chamber changes and there is a change of the cabinet. Now, supposing that the cabinet of our country were to change and such officials as the councilors [sangi], the chief and vice-chief officials of each ministry, and the important secretaries were all at once to look for persons who could serve as their successors, except for two or three prominent men, would those men of talent and courage [shunketsu] out of office be the persons in whom the esteem and confidence of the people would be found? Or would we let youngsters

and clever men scramble [for these posts]? This is the second of the differences between them and us.

Since the Restoration, imperial influence has not yet permeated the people's minds; when the step of abolishing the *han* was taken, the feeling of resentment was directed no where but against the government. Now, if we were suddenly to imitate England's system of party government and follow in its footsteps of changing the government through the majority opinion of the people, it is perfectly obvious that we would be setting up a national assembly today only to have the cabinet changed tomorrow.[17]

In *Iken dai ni* (Opinion Number Two), which he presented to Iwakura in the latter part of June, perhaps on June 25, 1881, Inoue advised that the following measures should be adopted and explained why:

> If we want to have the cabinet administrators selected and appointed by the Emperor and not controlled by the national assembly, we should adhere to the following three points:
> First, we should put in the constitution the clear statement that "the Emperor selects and appoints, and also promotes and dismisses the ministers and other officials of the *chokunin* [imperial appointee] rank." If put in this clear statement, even though in reality it would be necessary for the Emperor, as far as possible, to select as administrative ministers men who have the popular confidence and to dismiss those who are against public opinion, the right of appointment and dismissal would reside entirely with the Emperor; and therefore, those who are ministers would rely on the favor of the Emperor, and the confidence of the nation would not be swayed by differing opinions and divergent utterances; but the ministers would decide their views firmly and would adhere to an unwavering course. Even if on one or two matters, they had [only] minority support in the deliberative chamber, still they would be able throughout to fulfill the functions of a cabinet and would not end up changing policies constantly (This is based on the constitution of Prussia.)
> Secondly, we should in the constitution fix the responsibilities of the ministers and divide these into those which they undertake jointly and those they undertake individually. . . . If, in imitation of England, all the ministers were supposed to assume joint responsibility unconditionally every time a minister made a mistake and was reprimanded by the deliberative chamber, the other ministers would, thus, have to resign together. In such a case, the cabinet would easily invite attacks from the deliberative chamber, would change frequently, and would become inevitably a battle ground. Moreover, logically speaking, if the mistake of an administrator must be made the responsibility of all the administrators, all executive business, in spite of the fact that there are shared duties and exclusive tasks in each department, must undergo first common deliberation by all the administrators. Actually, this would lighten the responsibility which each individual shoulders

separately. The reason why there is the system of joint responsibility in England is that it regards cabinet administrators as the corporate body of a political party and considers them as the same as a single person. The process of having different ministers and of establishing their functions in order to handle the business of the executive branch should differ in principle from having several members of a deliberative chamber band together to form a single corporate body.

Thirdly, in the constitution, we must imitate Prussia in having the following article. It is stated in Article 109 of the Constitution of Prussia: "Existing taxes shall remain in effect." The explanation of this is that, if the government and the national assembly do not agree on the annual budget, the budget of the previous year will continue in effect.

This article is the vital means by which Prussia, in her constitution, maintains executive rights. Without this article, if the deliberative chamber were to attack the cabinet and give only minority support to important cabinet bills, while the cabinet, relying on the Emperor's protection, were not to resign, the one recourse of the deliberative chamber in persisting in its position, would be to refuse to levy taxes and to deny funds and materials which the national treasury needs. Since the deliberative chambers have the power to refuse the taxes on which the state lives, countries like England, Belgium, and Italy must, on account of their deliberative chambers, organize party cabinets and win the popular esteem of their deliberative chambers. Now if we really want to imitate Prussia in keeping the cabinet free of the deliberative chamber, we must also depend on Prussia's budgetary article. Otherwise, even though there is an article to the effect that the Emperor appoints and dismisses Ministers, this would amount to little more than a mere fiction.

I believe that the above three points are necessary in order to maintain the principle of gradual progress and to preserve forever the welfare of the country.[18]

Now we know the real reason that in June, 1881, Inoue was strongly opposed to the proposal to establish a constitutional government modeled after British parliamentary government, and why he urged that Japan follow certain Prussian practices in establishing constitutional government. The ultimate conclusion was that, in contemplating a change in the political system, Inoue adhered to certain principles. Therefore, we also know that the view that Inoue favored the German model because he desired to maintain the political status quo was erroneous.

II

One of the principles that guided Inoue in June 1881 in his thoughts on the nature of the constitutional government that Japan should establish was that the peace and unity of the country must be preserved. Another principle was that the new political system must be suited to the national character *(kokutai)* and popular customs *(minzoku)* of Japan; for if it were not, the peace and unity of the country inevitably would be destroyed. Yet another one was that the cabinet under the new political system must be so stable and secure that it would be able to devote itself to its duties, to adhere to an unwavering course, and to realize its policies, some of which might be unpopular.

Were Inoue's political attitude and ideology conservative? Did he seek to rivet the status quo upon Japan at any point in his bureaucratic career? Concerning the real motives of the drafters of the Constitution of the Empire of Japan, Robert A. Scalapino has expressed the following opinion: "The climax of these developments was the Meiji Constitution of 1889, a fundamental law superbly timed and written to fit the oligarchic cause. . . . It was a document written largely for the oligarchs, highlighting their own political concepts. By it, they succeeded in riveting upon the nation a status quo which was more strongly oligarchic than representative and one which perpetuated and strengthened the myth of Imperial absolutism."[19] On the same subject, John W. Hall has stated: "The constitution was carefully devised to maintain the political status quo."[20] Was Inoue a devoted steward of the oligarchy who endeavored tirelessly to strengthen and prolong its power? Did Inoue's work and influences serve Japan well? Our knowledge of the principles to which Inoue adhered in June 1881, in his consideration of the nature of the constitutional government that Japan should establish sheds light on these questions.

Notes

1. This article is based upon a paper of the same title presented at a panel entitled "Young Intellectuals and the 'Establishment' in Meiji Japan" presented at the annual meeting of the Association for Asian Studies in 1971. Because of the untimely death of the author, it has been edited by Sandra T. W. Davis.

2. Inoue's appointments, orders, ranks and honors, rewards, and annual salaries are listed in his curriculum vitae, which is kept in the Inoue Kowashi Archives (Goin Bunko). The archives are owned by Inoue Kowashi's heir but have been on loan to and maintained by the Kokugakuin Daigaku Toshokan in Tokyo since 1957.

3. For the way in which Inoue came to be known to Ōkubo, see Kimura Tadashi, *Inoue Kowashi kun Kyōiku jigyō shōshi* (Tōkyō, 1894), p. 135; Kobayakawa Hideo, "Inoue Goin sensei" in Hirata Nobuharu, ed., *Motoda Inoue ryōsensei jiseki kōen roku* (Kumamoto, 1913), pp. 8–9; Morimoto Yonekazu, "Inoue Kowashi sensei" in Morimoto Yonekazu, ed., *Saichōen no homare* (Kumamoto, 1932), pp. 6–7.

4. See Morimoto "Inoue Kowaski," pp. 7–9; Katsuda Magoya, ed., *Ōkubo Toshimichi nikki*, 2 vols. (Tōkyō, 1927), 1:310–37; Kiyosawa Kiyoshi, *Gaiseika toshite no Ōkubo Toshimichi* (Tōkyō, 1942), chapters 5, 7. See also Sophia Su-fei Yen, *Taiwan in China's Foreign Relations* (Hamden, Conn. 1965), chapter 9. The drafts of the correspondence to the Ch'ing government, memoranda pertaining to the negotiations, other documents that Inoue wrote, and also the drafts of the statements of opinion that Inoue presented to Ōkubo are in the Goin Bunko.

5. In his speech at the assembly hall of the Kumamoto Prefectural Assembly in April 1900, Itō told his audience the time and circumstances in which he "discovered" Inoue. The speech is quoted in Morimoto, "Inoue Kowashi," pp. 36–40.

6. The statement is quoted in Kobayakawa, "Inoue Goin," pp. 19–20.
7. The letter is found in the Inoue Monjo (Inoue Kowashi Documents), which are in the possession of Inoue Kowashi's heir.
8. A draft of the memorial, written in Inoue's handwriting, on six sheets of the Council of State (Dajōkan) paper, is found in the Inoue Monjo. It is contained in the envelope on which are written seven Chinese characters by Inoue, *jū yo nen ki mitsu mon jo* (1881 Secret Documents).
9. For Inoue's work in drafting the constitution, see Inada Masatsuga, *Mei ji kempō seiritsu shi*, 2 vols. (Tokyo, 1960, 1962), vol. 2.
10. See Inada, *Meiji kempō*, 1:245.
11. Ibid., pp. 521–24, and 527.
12. Umetani Noboru, "Kyōiku chokugo seiritsu no rekishiteki haikei," in Sakata Yoshio, ed., *Meiji zenhanki no nashonarizumu* (Tōkyō, 1958), pp. 85–128; Umetani Noboru, *Meiji zenki seijishi no kenkyū* (Tokyo, 1963), pp. 266–305, 368–99; Kaigo Tokiomi, *Kyōiku chokugo seiritsushi no kenkyū* (Tōkyō, 1965).
13. Inada, *Meiji kempō*, 1:732–58.
14. For Inoue's work in education, see Kimura Tadashi, ed., *Inoue Kowashi kun kyōiku jigyo shōshi* (Tōkyō, 1894); Nihon Kindai Kyōikushi Kenkyūkai, ed., *Inoue Kowashi no kyōiku seisaku* (Tōkyō, 1963); Uchida Tadashi, "Meiji nijūnen dai ni okeru gakusei kaikaku mondai no kenkyū—Inoue Kowashi no chūgakkō seido no kaikaku o chūshin toshite," *Ippan Kyōiku Kenkyū*, no. 7 (January 1964), pp. 27–47; Kaigo Tokiomi, ed., *Inoue Kowashi no kyōiku seisaku* (Tōkyō, 1968).
15. Itō's letter is quoted in Morimoto, "Inoue Kowashi," pp. 35–36. According to Morimoto, the letter was written in 1888; but it actually was written in 1890.
16. A document entitled "Iken daiichi" is found in *Itō Hirobumi hisho ruisan* (Itō Hirobumi's Classified Collection of Secret Documents). The printed text based on this document is contained in Itō Hirobumi, *Kempō shiryō*, 3 vols. (Tōkyō, 1934), 1:49–52. A document with only inconsequential differences but with the same title is found in the Makino Nobuaki Monjo in the Kokuritsu Kokkai Toshokan Kensei Shiryō Shitsu. The handwriting of this document is not that of Inoue Kowashi, but he appears to have added several corrections and notations to it. It is bound together with four other documents by Inoue under the date June 1881. Details are contained in the author's unpublished manuscript which he was working on at Harvard University when he became terminally ill (Editors' note); part 2, chapter 2.
17. H. Peter Ch'en, unpublished Harvard MS, part 5, chapter 2.
18. Ibid., part 2, chapter 4.
19. Robert A. Scalapino, *Democracy and the Party Movement in Prewar Japan: The Failure of the First Attempt* (Berkeley and Los Angeles: University of California Press, 1953), p. 42.
20. John Whitney Hall, "A Monarch for Modern Japan," in Robert E. Ward, ed., *Political Development in Modern Japan* (Princeton, N.J.: Princeton University Press, 1968), p. 57.

11 Mutsu Munemitsu in Europe, 1884–85: The Intellectual in Search of an Ideology

Hagihara Nobutoshi

Mutsu Munemitsu (1844–97), who served as Japan's foreign minister from 1892 to 1896 during the Sino-Japanese War, negotiated the revision of the unequal treaties with the West. The son of an influential bureaucrat in Kishū (Wakayama Prefecture), Mutsu joined the loyalist movement in Kyoto during 1863–64 and developed close ties with the Tosa samurai and *ronin* who later were to help lead the Restoration and the new regime. Mutsu held important positions in Kishu after the Restoration and was sent by the clan to Europe in 1870–71 to hire German military instructors to train the clan army. He served in various posts in the Meiji government, but gradually became alienated with the Satchō monopoly of power and especially with the Satsuma leadership. In 1878, Mutsu assisted a group of former Tosa clansmen in a plot designed to assassinate government officials and was arrested and imprisoned. Since he was a student of the Chinese classics and of English, he devoted his time in prison to studying and translating the ideas of the British utilitarian philosopher, Jeremy Bentham.[1]

In 1885, Mutsu Munemitsu, then forty-two, went to Vienna to study privately with the famous German social scientist, Lorenz von Stein. According to letters sent to his wife, Ryōko, Mutsu stayed in Vienna from June 20 to August 15, 1885, a period during which he appeared to have had lessons with Stein several hours each day.[2]

From late 1870s until the autumn of 1890, when Stein died, it was fashionable for Japanese travelers to Vienna and nearby areas to pay what may be called the "Stein visit." This is indicated by the numerous calling cards left by well-known and unknown Japanese at Stein's home. Nearly everyone, except the students, held an official title: important members of the government, officials from every ministry, diplomats, military officers, judges, professors, and local officials.

Needless to say, this practice was initiated by Itō Hirobumi. Itō visited Europe from 1882 to 1883 as part of his investigation of European constitutions; and during this time, he took private lessons from Stein. It is well known that he was so fascinated with Stein's personality and intellect that he invited him to Japan as the principal adviser to the Meiji government. In a message sent from Vienna to Inoue Kaoru on October 22, 1882, Itō stated:

> I will ask by telegram for Stein's appointment in the near future. I regard it as beneficial for the future of the nation. I would like you to support it. There are not many great scholars who advocate *Monarchische Prinzip* as does Stein. Most of them, following the fashion of the day, favor democracy, which would be useless for us to adopt. If Stein is invited, he will be an adviser to the government and also, at the same time, will work primarily to reform the school system. In reforming the mental outlook of the people, the first task is to improve the textbooks.[3]

Itō's request was approved by the leaders of the Meiji government and by the throne, but the appointment never materialized. Because of infirmity and old age, Stein declined the invitation. Stein was sixty-six years old at the time. Instead, he offered to be available at any time to answer questions on European law and politics from the Meiji government. Although he would not be able to go to Japan, he would assist the Japanese who came to Europe, especially Vienna, to study. On November 15, 1882, Stein wrote Itō:

> I will help young students staying here from your country, not only by placing them in a university but also by recommending that they study with me as my students. In so doing, I would like to be the center for Japanese students studying about Europe and the transmitter [of ideas] to establish a university in the future in your country.[4]

This is the background to the "Stein visit" undertaken by so many Japanese. The initiative taken by Itō led Mutsu to follow the same path. Even though Stein's appointment to a position with the Meiji government was not realized, with Itō's request as the precedent, Stein's eldest son, Ernest von Stein, who was a lawyer, was invited to visit Japan. Ernest remained in Japan for about six months in 1887–88. During his visit, he was received with great warmth and was often invited to the imperial palace for chrysanthemum-viewing parties and duck hunting and to dinners and dances held by the government at the Rokumeikan.

Among the correspondence the author found in the Stein house were letters from many Japanese: seven from Itō Hirobumi, two from Itō Miyoji, three from Matsukata Masayoshi, six from Kuroda Kiyotaka, five and a diagram from Kaieda Nobuyoshi, three from Tani Kanjō, eleven from Toda Ujitomo, seven from Miyoshi Taizō, two from Matsuoka Yasutake, eight from Watanabe Renkichi, two from Kawashima Atsushi, nine from Fujinami Kototada, and eight from Mutsu Munemitsu. There are also letters to Ernest, Stein's eldest son; but they are mainly letters of introduction, calling cards, and brief personal notes whose content is not very worth noting. However, it was Kaieda Nobuyoshi's letter of condolence that had the most genuine expression of feeling on the death of Stein in September 1890.

Only Mutsu's letters are truly worth noting. To be precise, seven letters Mutsu wrote to Stein while he was in Europe are the most important for historical research. The eighth, dated October 5, 1887, is a letter of introduction he wrote after his return to Japan, for Toda Ujitomo, who was appointed to succeed Saionji Kimmochi as minister to Vienna. Mutsu's letters are written characteristically without ostentation and are filled with frank and clear statements. Moreover, there is no touch of hesitation toward the renowned scholar Stein.

What makes Mutsu's letters so simple and so solid? During his study abroad, Mutsu felt he had to decide where he stood politically; and before he could make that decision, he had to be sure of his own ideological viewpoint. Indeed, among the Japanese who studied under Stein, Mutsu was, except for the younger students, the only man who had no official status at the time.

After the Satsuma Rebellion was suppressed, Mutsu was arrested for participating in the antigovernment movements of the Tosa Risshisha (Rights Society of Tosa). He was sentenced to five years' imprisonment and was imprisoned in Yamagata and Sendai from September 1878 to December 1882. His sentence was shortened because of the amnesty granted at the end of 1882 under "the policy of generosity and oppression" of the Meiji government. When Itō Hirobumi was consulted on this matter during his stay in Vienna, he wrote to Iwakura Tomomi, "As the government has no objection as far as Mutsu and Ōhe [Taku] are concerned, I would like you to deal with them as generously as possible."[5]

It was January 1883 when Mutsu was released from prison. In August, Itō returned from Europe after almost a year-long investigation of European constitutions. Mutsu had difficulty reaching decisions on his attitude toward politics after he was released from prison; and the political situation in Europe as well as Stein's theories which Itō, his longtime friend, related to him seemed very attractive. Itō also invited Mutsu to visit Europe. In fact, Mutsu's letter to his wife, Ryōko, suggests that he was urged to undertake the visit by Itō with financial support from Inoue Kaoru and Shibusawa Eiichi.

Mutsu left for Europe via America in April 1884, fifteen months after he was released from prison. However, one should not be led to the conclusion that he had made up his mind to cooperate with the *hanbatsu*, a clan-dominated government against which he had committed acts of treason. Though we cannot deny that Mutsu was inclined to cooperate with his former opponents, he had a "problem of conscience" to resolve before committing himself to a political ideology. There was no better place to try to solve the problem than England, just as Itō's positive desire to oppose British and French democratic theory had led him directly to Germany as the first place to visit on his trip to Europe to investigate Western constitutions. We note that Mutsu, however, left for England, although his trip was at the urging of and supported by Itō.

Mutsu arrived in London on July 8, 1884, after a month and a half of travel in America. According to a letter written to his wife on July 10, 1884, Mutsu at first appears to have planned to stay in London for about six months, until the end of the year; but his departure was delayed for another three months until the end of March 1885, and he remained in England for a period of nine months. The reason that he postponed his trip to Vienna for several months was that Stein, whom Mutsu was going to visit toward the end of the year in order to receive private lessons, was not in good health. Mutsu appears to have sent a letter of introduction written by Itō to Stein soon after he arrived in London. This letter is no longer among Stein's correspondence, but Stein's answer was written on September 14. Stein seems to have written that he was ill at the time and asked if Mutsu was in London in order to study English. Mutsu replied, "My stay in England is not as you appear to think wholly on account of my desire to acquire a knowledge of the language, but is also due to other important business."[6] Furthermore, in the same letter, Mutsu asked Stein about the possibility of having private lessons, namely, lectures for several hours a day for a few weeks, with him. Stein replied without delay on October 8. This letter appears to have caused Mutsu to postpone his visit to Vienna until the following spring because of Stein's illness. However, Stein, in the same letter, before replying to Mutsu's request for private lessons, appears to have asked the reason for his request. It seems that Stein, despite Itō's introduction, must have wondered about Mutsu, who had no official title, as he was used to meeting government officials from Japan. Who was this "unknown" who wanted to study political science with him?

> As my honourable friend, Count Itō, will have told you in his letter of introduction, the object of my visit to Europe is to study the constitutions and administrations of European states. His Majesty, our Emperor, as you may have heard, issued an edict a few years ago to the effect that a Constitution shall be established and a National Assembly summoned in the year 1890; and his government is actively engaged in preparations for the national event. But these preparations ought not to be wholly entrusted to the government, and a private individual outside of it, like myself, should contribute, if he can, to ensure the success of the coming reform. That is the object of my visit to Europe; but I cannot put the details on a sheet of note paper. I shall therefore reserve them for our future interview.[7]

Stein must have understood Mutsu from his frank and clear answer, which ended his doubts and resulted in his acceptance of Mutsu as a private student.

On the other hand, Stein's questions may have reminded Mutsu of his four years and four months in prison and also of his position as a man out of office at the time. Yet, there was England before his eyes, the motherland of Bentham and the birthplace of parliamentary politics.

While in prison, Mutsu translated Bentham's major work, *An Introduction to the Principles of Morals and Legislation*, and after he was released, published it under the title of *Rigaku seishū (Principle of Utility)* (2 volumes, 1883). It is obvious from the works he wrote in prison, such as *Menpeki dokugo (A Monologue Facing the Wall)*, *Fukudo dokugo (Fukudo's Monologue;* Fukudo was Mutsu's pen name) and *Shiji seiridan (Philosophical Discussions)*, how deeply he became impressed with the utilitarian liberalism of Bentham after translating Bentham's work.

What Mutsu explained to Stein as his "important business," and what may be called "the problem of conscience," was Mutsu's need to reexamine the theory of English liberalism and the practice of parliamentary politics in England on the spot, which he had known previously only through books.

According to Mutsu's letters from London to his wife, however, it is difficult to envision how hard he studied. In regard to this experience, he wrote on January 9, 1885, that he took private lessons for three weeks during the winter vacation at Cambridge, noting that "I have been in this town of Cambridge since December 26. Since I take two lessons a day, I am very busy; but I am going to return to London in several days." There is only one description, dated October 24, 1884, about a visit to Parliament and to a politician, a letter in which Mutsu states: "I visited a session of Parliament. It was so active [*nakunoka seidai*] that I found it of great use. Prime Minister Gladstone made a speech in that session, and I found some ladies among the spectators, too. I now am going to see Mr. [Henry] Fawcett. His wife is very famous, for she writes books and helps her blind husband greatly. Therefore, I intend to meet Mrs. Fawcett, too. I will write [to you] what she tells me about etiquette for ladies."

Mutsu was in London during the latter days of the second Gladstone cabinet and saw the passage of the revised election law and universal male suffrage. Henry Fawcett, whom Mutsu mentioned in his letter, was an active member of the Liberal party, who lectured on economics at Cambridge and was postmaster general in the second Gladstone cabinet. However, since Fawcett passed away twelve days after Mutsu wrote this letter, on November 6, they could not have had time to become friends.

Mutsu's letters to Ryōko, showing his concern for her health and even for what she read, reveal him to be a devoted husband. During his travels, he wrote to her on June 18, 1884: "As a couple, we are traveling companions; as a couple, we share joys and sorrows even if we are not together."

Furthermore, he promised her from London on December 19 that "if you should become ill, which I hope will not happen, please let me know as soon as possible by telegram. I will return at any time to you." In a long letter, written from London on March 6, 1885, he wrote:

> I hope you read many books. If you have time, read the editorials in the newspaper as it is very important for you to understand today's world. Generally, the women in this county read the newspaper. Therefore, although their knowledge is rather superficial, they still can speak in an entertaining fashion with gentlemen.
>
> I will tell you a few reasons why Japanese women do not have much knowledge of the world. First, due to old customs, they do not try to associate with people. Second, even if they have friends, they do not have sufficient topics to discuss. Therefore, they cannot help but live in a small world.
>
> These are many topics of conversation. The best way to have things to discuss is to read newspapers and then novels such as *Hakken den* [*Legends of Eight Dogs*], *Yumiharizuki* [*The Waning Moon*], and the like. After reading these books, you can talk about the past and the present while enjoying yourself greatly. Moreover, you will become very knowledgeable. Therefore, start out with a solid work such as the *Nihon gaishi* [*Unofficial History of Japan*] and the *Ju hasshi ryaku* [*Eighteen Outline Histories*], translated Western books, and so forth. In addition, read the newspapers every day. The best is *Tokyo nichi nichi shimbun*. Papers with small circulation are not as good. Read *Hakken-den*, too. It is better to ask Usami about it. Get Saya [their oldest daughter, then age thirteen] to read a little every night.
>
> In addition to reading, you need to exercise once a day. The women here go out at least once daily. I know you are a stay-at-home, so at best go out into the garden or somewhere for about half an hour a day. Furthermore, it is good for you to walk in Ueno Park occasionally. Even if you do not like to exercise at first, I am sure you finally will come to enjoy it after you begin.
>
> You are right to urge me to return to Japan in every letter. I am sure it is reasonable for you to write thus. Actually, it is very inconvenient for me to live in a country where I cannot understand the language well. Moreover, I have to do everything myself. For example, I have to handle trivial matters and even mail letters by myself. I cannot have my own way here as in Japan. Therefore, I also want to come back to Japan as soon as possible, but I cannot return now. It would injure my reputation to return to Japan without achieving anything. . . . However, I am going to leave here in June or July. Please be patient. We can expect to live together for another twenty years. Please endure the present inconvenience with the expectation of a happier life in the future.

Ryōko had begun to ask Mutsu to return as soon as possible. Although he had planned at first to stay abroad for a year, Mutsu's schedule of foreign travel gradually was postponed because of Stein's illness. He wrote he would be back in June or July, but he actually left Europe for Japan at the end of 1885. While Mutsu was in London, his seventy-six-year-old mother, Date Masako, died; and his young wife, who longed even more for his return, had to face the mourning period alone. Ryōko was his second wife and was twelve years younger than Mutsu; she was twenty-nine or thirty when he left to study abroad. In addition to her youth, she was a famous beauty of whom Mutsu was very proud. Ernest Satow, the British diplomat who served in Japan for a total of twenty-five years during the late Edo and Meiji periods and who rarely praised the beauty of Japanese women, referred to Ryōko's beauty.

It was July 1886, six months after Mutsu returned to Japan, when Satow, then British consul general in Bangkok, came to Japan on his summer vacation. Traveling from Nikko to Ashio, he happened to meet Gōtō Shōjirō, Shibusawa Elichi, and Mutsu Munemitsu, who were staying at Ashio with their families. Mutsu's second son, Junkichi, his son by his late wife, Renko, had been adopted into the Furukawa family; and as a result, Mutsu was related to Furukawa Ichibei, the manager of the Ashio copper mine. At Ashio, Satow met Ryōko for the first time; and he described her in his diary: "Mutsu's second wife, a very pretty young woman with fine eyes and splendid eyebrows."[8]

On July 16, 1884, Mutsu also asked his wife to send him her photograph, preferably in Western dress. In November, he wrote Ryōko:

> I am as happy to receive your pictures as though I were seeing you again. Since every picture was taken so well, I gave one to the old couple who are my landlords. The old woman asked whether or not you were my sister and said you resembled me closely. In the eyes of foreigners, all Japanese resemble one another because of our build. Nonetheless, I appreciate your beautiful photograph very much.

On October 16, Mutsu asked Ryōko, "Please take care of yourself and wait for me, knowing we will see each other again. Like you, I, too, found the summer nights long; but we can recall these days with found memories in the future." On a more comical note, he wrote, "I have had some trouble with my teeth, so I had a false tooth inserted. I am too old to be of any use. Laugh at me!"

However devoted Mutsu was to Ryōko, it is impossible to imagine that he would spend the entire nine months of his stay in London just writing to her or looking at her photograph. Now we must examine that part of Mutsu's life which is not revealed very clearly in his letters to Ryōko, namely, his life as he undertook what he calls his "important business." That aspect of his life is reflected in seven notebooks, now in the custody of the Kanazawa Bunko (Library) in Kanagawa Perfecture. The thick notebooks, written in English, prove how eagerly he studied and his ambition to profit from his study abroad. The titles on four of the works that appear to have been written in London were *International Law; Constitutional Law and History*, volume I, *The English Constitution, Historical Sketch to the Accession of Charles I; The English Constitution, Historical; Responsible Ministers.*

The first work dealt with international law; the second and third contained notes on constitutional history, sovereignty, Parliament, political parties, the cabinet, judicial powers, democracy, class differences, and so forth. In short, he dealt rather fully with and carefully coordinated the important elements of English politics. From the writing style, it appears he did not transcribe these notes from books but rather took notes of lectures and then recopied them in the notebooks. The fourth book is different in that it consists of questions he asked primarily about the relationship between Parliament and the cabinet and the answers of his teacher. These notes appear to be a result of the private lessons he took at Cambridge, and the volume of work appears to indicate a longer period of study than three weeks. From a notation in the second notebook, "From Dr. Waraker of Cambridge, November 1884," it appears that Mutsu studied privately with a Dr. Waraker in London before going to Cambridge. Thomas Waraker was a lawyer and member of Lincoln's Inn who served as law coach and lecturer at Cambridge and apparently came to London often.[9] He was the author of a work entitled *Naval Warfare of the Future, A Consideration of the Declaration of Paris, 1856* (London, 1892). He may have been introduced to Mutsu by Suematsu Kenchō, who had just graduated from St. John's College at Cambridge. Mutsu's questions, as documented in the fourth notebook, were based on what he had learned from Waraker's advice and lectures, his three weeks of private lessons at Cambridge, his reading, his experiences in London and prior knowledge of English politics and law that he had gained from reading translations of the major works of Jeremy Bentham. These questions represent the climax of his foreign study as he sought to resolve the problem of the English method of thought, which he studied with an intensity second only to the Japanese and Chinese classics. The questions, which were written down and often repeated, especially those on the relationship between Parliament and the cabinet and on the status of the emperor *(tennō)* went to the core of the subject of Japanese polity, which was reborn in his mind. The questions he asked dealt with the following topics: responsible cabinets, the two houses of Parliament, the election of representatives, standing committees, on the reform of the constitution, on the interpretation of law, impeachment, party discipline and the action of members, the suspension of members from a parliamentary borough who had been reelected, single-member constituencies, the democratic tendency in England, political parties, on financing Parliament, and on the payment of members of Parliament.

Mutsu began the questions by stating:

> The real essence of a constitutional government seems to be in the fact that the cabinet hold their power only so long as they are supported by a majority in the representative house, and resign it over to their successors as soon as it becomes apparent that they have lost the necessary confidence of that majority.

He thought constitutional government and the system of responsible cabinets were inseparably related. Mutsu, of course, recognized that it was only in England among the European nations where the principle of responsible cabinets was realized and functioned effectively. He said in his notebook that "this was not so much owing to any act of commission on her [England's] part as to the gradual and almost unconscious growth and amalgamation of customs as usages of generation after generation." Yet, we know that Mutsu had in mind the fact that less than twenty years had passed since Japan had abolished the feudal system that divided the country into more than 200 fiefs, had established a unified country, and now was trying to abandon absolute monarchy in order to establish constitutional government.

Mutsu realized that the cohesion of the former clansmen remained and the interests of various groups clashed. Therefore, Mutsu asked the lecturer: "Could a genuine form of government by responsible ministers be effectively adopted in such a country as Japan? If the question is answered in the negative, then what is the good of adopting a constitutional form of government without its real essence?" Waraker answered negatively: "It is doubtful whether in such a country as Japan, government by responsible ministers could be adopted at once. In England it has been the growth of two centuries." Moreover, "Its adoption has everywhere led to the diminution of royal authority, and the gradual assumption of supreme power by the representative branch of the legislature. If the English system be adopted, the Mikado must be prepared to surrender a very considerable part of his power into the hands of his ministers and the representatives of the people."

Since Mutsu was sure that constitutional government and responsible cabinets were inseparably related, he repeated his question, saying:

> I quite agree with you and am not without some doubt as to whether the system could be adopted at once in Japan. But the point of my question in this respect in my former letter was whether without adopting this system sooner or later a constitutional form of government would be of no good to the people, or even wanting this one

element, still the government which is constitutional and takes into consideration the voice of the people to a greater or less extent would not be of vast benefits to them as compared with a despotic monarchy.

Waraker's answer again was negative. Moreover, he emphasized the need to distinguish constitutional polity from responsible cabinets, saying, "I think that a constitutional government might usefully be introduced without proceeding so far as, at once, to constitute responsible ministers with all the incidents of the English system."

According to Waraker, the establishment of responsible cabinets would result in a decline in the power of the imperial family and the highest authority would move increasingly to members of the House of Representatives. Mutsu again asked about the status of the emperor relating to these opinions, adding his own specific viewpoint, which is very interesting:

> This is quite true, and I think, were it not for that, a constitutional government will do no good to the people who may adopt it. At the same time I further think that the diminution of royal authority in this way is really the most effective means of securing and perpetuating the safety of Royalty, and therefore those who have loyalty to a Crown at heart cannot do better than reform the government and making it a constitutional one.

Mutsu's opinion on the emperor system in Japan was opposed to the status of the emperor in the Constitution of the Empire of Japan, which was prepared by Itō Hirobumi and his *hanbatsu* followers and promulgated four years later, in 1889.

How did Mutsu reach such an opinion on the emperor? Did he arrive at his conclusions through the study of the history of the British royal family? Was he very familiar with the history of Japan in regard to the emperor system? Or was it based on his knowledge of the secret of the Japanese emperor system, which had survived through long periods of war and peace by remaining in the position of the symbol of authority while delegating power to the shogunate? Or was he, as a man out of office, so free as to propose a bold opinion on the emperor system? While the reasons for his views are difficult to analyze, his discussion of the English system shows that Mutsu adhered to the system of responsible cabinets. He maintained his honor as a man different from those who joined groups that were organized by the strong feudal clans because he had spent more than four years in jail as a political prisoner.

Waraker answered:

> My remarks were offered by way of caution. The government of the state, I have no doubt, would be improved by popular control. But

is the Mikado prepared to surrender his power and prerogratives to a representative assembly? He ought at all events to be advised regarding the probability and not as a remote consequence of the adoption of the English system.

Mutsu then narrowed his question and asked what was the most important fact in regard to the English example. Waraker replied that the Mikado needed to transfer his power to the cabinet and representatives. Waraker said:

> In England, ministers are responsible at once to the Queen and to parliament, but in effect they are obliged to shape their policy so as to secure the support of the House of Commons. If they cannot secure the continued confidence of that House, they no longer serve the Crown. Hence their responsibility to the Queen has become little more than nominal, while their responsibility to the House of Commons is direct and absolute. In this way, without any transfer of the power of the Crown to ministers, that power has practically passed into the hands of the leaders of political parties who happen to command a majority in the House of Commons.

However, Waraker only repeated what Mutsu already knew; and Mutsu had finished his questions on constitutional government and responsible cabinets.

They then discussed the bicameral system. Mutsu said he supported this system, and gave his views on the formation of the House of Lords—the House of Peers in Japan. Mutsu's opinion becomes the more interesting when we remember that the peerage system went into effect in July 1884, just after he began his foreign travels, and that the new titles and court ranks had gone primarily to the former *daimyō* and leaders of the *hanbatsu*. Mutsu told Waraker that peers in Japan had little influence politically and socially compared to England. Then he suggested that the upper house should consist of imperial nominees for one generation, excluding representatives from the hereditary nobility. He gave two reasons for this. First, imperial nominees to the House of Peers who served for one generation should be, as quoted from Mutsu's notebook, "comparatively free from the pressure of public opinion." Second, "they would not be able to practice unnecessary and reckless obstruction of popular will."

It is hard to judge whether Mutsu considered only the former *kuge* (court nobility) as the new peerage and hereditary nobility or whether he included the leaders of the strong feudal clans who received titles and ranks in the new peerage system. In the former case, Mutsu would refer to his experiences in the pre-Restoration era; in the latter case, he would relate to events after the Restoration. As he wrote that imperial nominees to the House of Peers were to serve for one generation, so Mutsu insisted on ability as a more important criteria than birth and former status in the feudal clans. After Waraker stated that he was not sufficiently familiar with the situation in Japan to reach a conclusion in these discussions, he said it would be best to adopt a system that consisted of both representatives from the hereditary nobility and imperial nominees to the House of Peers for one generation.

While insisting on responsible cabinets, what views did Mutsu have on suffrage for the lower house?

> I think that in these days when the opinion of equality and freedom is gaining strength day by day among mankind and the intellectual powers of man are being developed almost hour by hour the cry for the reduction of the franchise will become louder and louder and never cease to be heard until universal suffrage is granted. This seems to me to be an inevitable thing sooner or later.

As Mutsu used the expression "sooner or later" at this point, he did not insist on adopting universal suffrage "at once." However, as he regarded the process of political democratization and the realization of universal suffrage as an "inevitable thing," he had a different perspective from that of the *hanbatsu* forces. In fact, the election law for the House of Representatives that was proclaimed in 1889 gave the right to vote to about 1.24 percent of the population, thereby adopting a restrictive qualification for suffrage.

In response to Mutsu's statement of his views, Waraker said: "The policy of creating the lowest franchise at once and before it is asked for, may well be doubted."

As we read through the major points in the dialogue between Mutsu and Waraker in the fourth notebook, the fundamental structure of Mutsu's political viewpoint becomes obvious. Mutsu began his discourse with the statement that the essence of constitutional government was responsible cabinets. He regarded it as inevitable that imperial sovereignty be decreased drastically; and unless this was done, there was no reason to adopt the system of constitutional government.

If we compare Mutsu's views to those of Itō Hirobumi, the central figure of the *hanbatsu* government, his position becomes more distinctive. Itō's words are from a letter written to Iwakura Tomomi while he was investigating European constitutions:

> Though I cannot describe all that I have investigated since I came to Europe on a piece of paper, I will write to you later on as to how I comprehend the outline of the national organization as advocated by the well-known scholars [Rudolf von] Gneist and [Lorenz von] Stein in Germany. I can understand their views sufficiently so as to lay the basis for the imperial house without lessening imperial authority. The

current situation in our country is that the writings of radical liberals in England, America, and France are believed as though they were the golden rule to the extent that the country is almost brought to ruin. However, I have obtained the reasons and means to correct this situation. Now is the time to realize my real feelings for the nation, and I regard it as essential to practice my beliefs. I feel as if I had discovered a place to die with respect, both in office and out of office. We are full of hope for the future.[10]

Itō's letter to Iwakura expressed his pleasure at finding sufficient "reason and means" in Germany with which to confront and defeat the liberal faction. On the other hand, Mutsu still maintained in his mind the spirit of liberalism, which he had absorbed from Bentham even though he had come to Europe at the request of and with the support of Itō.

Mutsu, however, while in England, had to face a situation in which he was to part from the liberal radical faction in a way different from that of Itō. To be exact, Mutsu had reaffirmed in England what he felt before he came to England. His answer to Waraker's last question was: "Now in Japan it would be very difficult to adopt at once the system of responsible ministry in its essential and effective form." These words may be said to express Mutsu's farewell to "the first half of his life."

The problem that Mutsu recognized even before Waraker pointed it out was the historical time lag between England and Japan, the undeniable fact that it took 200 years for responsible cabinets to take root in England. This is why Mutsu always qualified his answers by saying "sooner or later" instead of "at once." However, what Japan then needed was the theory of immediacy, not gradualism. In this situation, how was he to act?

It would seem that Mutsu, after considering the long span of British history, finally decided to seek office with the clan government rather then join the movement for popular rights. The *hanbatsu* government and the popular-rights movement did not differ from each other regarding the theory of "immediacy." The difference was that the objective of the former was a system of transcendental cabinets and the goal of the latter was a system of responsible cabinets. Between these two, Mutsu advocated the theory of "gradualism," that is, he regarded responsible cabinets as inevitable, although he was on the side of those favoring transcendental cabinets; and this distinguished Mutsu's position as one unique from that of both the *hanbatsu* power and the popular-rights faction.

In the political world, the order of priorities is all-important. To meet the needs of Japan, therefore, Mutsu gave precedence to the *theory* of "immediacy" tentatively and kept that of "gradualism" to himself. The combination of personal experience and study in England, in short, his sense of history, finally forced Mutsu to make this choice. The "important business" that Mutsu mentioned to Stein indicates his effort to reach this conclusion. Mutsu, to be sure, had to solve this personal conflict while in England before he could visit Stein.

It can be assumed that Mutsu resolved his "important business" at the end of January 1885, after he had taken private lessons from Waraker for about three weeks. Toward the end of February, he received a letter from Stein, the first since October 1884. Stein explained that he had been ill but would now accept Mutsu as a private student. Stein's infirmity had caused Mutsu to postpone his return home and to change his plans several times, all of which increased Ryōko's anxiety. Three days before he left England, on March 27, Mutsu wrote Ryōko, "You will have to wait and endure loneliness while I am absent."

On March 30, Mutsu left England; he stayed in Paris for several days and arrived in Berlin on April 18. Soon after his arrival, Mutsu wrote to Stein for information and received an answer on April 28. He replied to Stein: "I wish to see you as soon as possible, but according to your direction I will stay here till the end of June, when I shall leave Berlin for Vienna."[11] Stein probably had set July as the time to give private lessons to Mutsu. Because of this, Mutsu had to stay in Berlin for two months; but in any case, at last he could make plans for his return home. While in Berlin, he took private lessons and studied the constitutions and administrations of Germany and Prussia as indicated in the fifth notebook, kept in the Kanazawa Bunko and entitled "German and Prussian Constitutions, Etc."

Mutsu's serious attitude toward his studies is reflected in a letter to Ryōko written on May 11 from Berlin:

> Although you ask me in every letter to tell you interesting things about this place [Berlin], I am not able to do so in a letter. Furthermore, I am spending almost ten hours daily studying, so I have no time for amusements which could be described to you. Moreover, unlike England, I cannot communicate in this place, and I have to request an interpreter for everything, which troubles me greatly. I am afraid there is nothing interesting to write. However, when I return home before long, we will be able to talk to one another and rejoice together.

While Mutsu had put a "seal" upon the liberal, British way of thinking with which he had been familiar in England, this does not mean he turned his back on it permanently. He merely pushed it to a corner of his mind for a while. On the other hand, as far as political ideology was concerned, the main purpose of his study abroad had been attained in England. The sense of relief Mutsu felt after reaching this conclusion made it easier for him to learn the German thought pattern quickly, which was a political necessity and was unknown to him. This led to his strenuous study of "about ten hours a day." Now free of the "difficult problem" of ideological orientation, he could concentrate his great reserve of intellectual energy on absorbing new knowledge. In fact, of the seven notebooks Mutsu wrote while abroad, the fifth is the richest in content. The 300-page large-sized notebook is filled with notes in English, while he listed under four headings: "A General Sketch of the German Constitution"; "A General Sketch of the Prussian Constitution"; "Prussian Administration"; "Prussian Administration, continued. The Kompetenz of the Government Officials and the Courts of Administration."

While in Berlin, Mutsu started to prepare for his return home in earnest. The reason for using the words "in earnest" is that Mutsu, in his situation, had to do more than plan the trip to Japan. On April 29, 1885, Mutsu wrote to Ryōko from Berlin, "Though my return home was reported in the newspaper there [in Japan], it is mistaken. As I have asked Imamura before, I would like you to send me a copy of it no matter what the article may have reported in the newspaper concerning my homecoming." After completing his private lessons with Stein in July in Vienna, Mutsu toured the Continent before going back to England in late August or early September. Yet, in regard to his plans for his return to Japan, Mutsu told his wife on May 11, 1885, "I would like you earnestly to keep this to yourself."

Mutsu's "secrecy," as we will see later, gradually came to have a tinge of intrigue that almost seemed unreasonable to Ryōko as his return drew near. What made him do this? Mutsu, in the letter of May 11, continued: "I can imagine that you must be feeling more nervous over my absence than the last time. I feel the same. I would like you to understand the situation." This can be taken as an apology to Ryōko, but it is questionable if she was convinced of anything concrete. (By the "last time," Mutsu meant the years spent in prison in Yamagata and Sendai.) Before dealing with this problem, let us follow Mutsu to Vienna, where he would study under Stein after a stay of two months in Berlin.

The first letter Mutsu wrote to Ryōko from Vienna, on June 25 said, "I left Berlin on the nineteenth of this month and arrived in Vienna (capital of Austria) the next morning. As I wrote to you before, I will stay here for a while and attend lectures by a famous scholar named Stein." Mutsu worked as hard in Vienna as in Berlin and informed his wife on July 2, "I am studying every day as much as possible in this place so far from home." Saionji Kimmochi, then minister to Vienna, confirmed this in a letter to Itō Hirobumi on July 3:

> Mutsu Munemitsu is staying here and studying under Stein. Although in the past Mutsu was inclined toward the English way of thinking, he seems to have invented some other method since he came to the Continent. He is studying intensely.[12]

If Saionji's observation was correct, Mutsu, who was reputed to be a follower of English liberalism, had changed his outlook to the German way of thinking as if he had "invented" something. As a matter of fact, Saionji may have understood Mutsu's ideas in this way. Nonetheless, it is questionable whether Saionji, who had studied in France for about ten years from 1870 to 1880 and had edited the *Eastern Liberty Newspaper (Tōyō jiyū shimbun)* with Nakae Chomin, was writing to Itō frankly. Saionji and Mutsu did not deal directly with each other as one was a Japanese minister and the other "a private person out of office." But both of them had put a lid on the faith in liberalism in their minds, the one having left *Tōyō jiyū shimbun* and the other imprisonment as personal history behind them.

It follows that what Saionji meant by "invented" some other method was not Mutsu's conversion to the German way of thinking, but the "political necessity" that compelled him to put aside his liberal ideas. We do not know what Saionji and Mutsu actually discussed about the *hanbatsu* forces during their stay in Vienna. It is certain, however, that the friendship in Vienna of Mutsu and Saionji, who was Mutsu's junior by five years, resulted in a close relationship in political affairs, a relationship that continued until Mutsu's death in 1897. Mutsu's studies of political science, his serious efforts to absorb what he learned, and his daily lectures with Stein must surely have surprised Saionji.

From the end of his stay in London and certainly after he came to Berlin, Mutsu had been suffering from a flareup of his chronic ailment, tuberculosis. Nevertheless, he answered Ryōko's inquiries about his health in July 9, saying, "You must have heard of my illness. The nature of the disease is chronic. If anyone visits and asks about it, tell him that I am suffering from an ache in my chest." Although he did not make it sound very serious, Mutsu must have been suffering from both serious discomfort and anxiety.

When Stein welcomed Mutsu, he was sixty-nine years old and had just retired from the University of Vienna, where he had taught for thirty-one years, since 1854, as a professor of state science (political science). The last two of Mutsu's seven notebooks written during his study abroad tell about the private lessons taken from Stein. Volumes 6 and 7 are entitled "The Plan of State Science, by Prof. von Stein" and "Supplementary Notes on State Science," respectively. The sixth notebook is in Stein's own handwriting, and it seems that he gave it to Mutsu as reference material for a lecture. In this comparatively thin booklet are enumerated the themes of "state science" according to Stein. In the larger seventh volume, Mutsu copied and summarized Stein's lecture, which, at the request of Mutsu, Stein supplemented and corrected in his own handwriting.

Stein began his lectures with the following words: "There are two ways in which we may think of a State, namely philosophically and practically. . . . The combination of these two produces a proper intellectual conception. And this is what we want here." Stein went on to point out the drawbacks of communism and socialism and ended his lectures by discussing the possibility of social reform through the intervention of the government. There is not sufficient room here to introduce Stein's lectures in detail nor is there any reason for doing so as research on this has already been done in Japan. In addition, the main purpose of Mutsu's study abroad had been attained in England. The purpose of his trip was not for his "inner" (ideological) development but to further his own political career. For this reason, his objective had shifted to acquiring new knowledge. His "inner" trip had been replaced by a voyage into politics.

The evidence indicates that Mutsu had difficulty when he shifted his thought pattern from that of England to that of Germany. He seems to have had difficulty in understanding Stein's ideas and terms, which were influenced by Hegelian philosophy. For example, in the seventh notebook, Mutsu wrote, "A government in itself is a dead organization," only to be corrected by Stein to read: "The idea of government in itself is an abstract structure." When Mutsu sent the seventh notebook to Stein and asked him to go over it, Stein complimented him on his serious study and comprehension of his theories:

> I received your letter and the notebook on the lectures which you sent a few days ago. I not only read through the notebook closely, but I appreciated it very much. To tell the truth, I was impressed with your hard work in compiling the notebook of over a hundred pages in the short time since we last met.
> . . . I will write a summary on each chapter before I return it to you. . . . As a matter of fact, the notebook is based on and summarizes the discussions we had this summer, so I do not think there is any more to add in my comments.[13]

In the midst of a difficult battle with the "state science" of Stein, Mutsu sent the following message together with his photographs to his wife: "Once again I am sending two photographs of me. What do you think of them compared with the previous ones? You should look at them when you are alone."[14] Mutsu completed his private lessons with Stein at the end of July or the beginning of August. He left Vienna on August 15 for a two-week trip to Russia, traveling to Petersberg, Gorky (then Nizhnii Novgorod), and Moscow, and visiting the famous world's fair in Nizhnii Novgorod.[15] On September 14, he returned to London by way of Berlin.

Mutsu wrote to Ryōko that he had been planning to return since spring, as soon as he could find a ship going to Japan, but a new situation was keeping him in London for another three months. Although details are not clear, Furukawa Ichibei and Shibusawa Eiichi asked him to inquire about copper and copper miners. Mutsu wrote to Ryōko on September 25, "These days, I am engaged in work as if I were a copper broker." He could not decline the request as he had been supported by Furukawa and Shibusawa since the time he had been in prison.

While traveling in Russia and working in London, Mutsu went over his notes from Stein's lectures and wrote to Stein as questions arose.[16] In a letter dated December 1, Stein bade farewell to Mutsu, saying, "After you return home and are engaged in business in the real world, you may face problems other than those we discussed. In that case, I would like you to remember me and to ask any questions."[17] As soon as Mutsu received the letter along with the seventh notebook, which had been annotated and corrected, he wrote his farewell letter to Stein. This was the last letter Mutsu wrote to Stein while in Europe.

> I thank you heartily for your kind letter and revision of my manuscript. I should like to answer it specially, but as I am now busily engaged with the preparation of my journey, I take the liberty of postponing it till I reach home, when I shall examine the manuscript more closely and ask for your further advice. At present I send to you my hearty words of gratitude and farewell, with my best congratulation for your happy and prosperous seventieth birthday.[18]

Having completed his foreign study, Mutsu waited for a ship going to Japan; and his main concern was what his political activities would be after he returned home. On May 11, he wrote to Ryōko from Berlin to tell her the schedule for his return and admonished her to inform no one except Tsuda Izuru, a cavalry major and Mutsu's senior and fellow clansmen from Wakayama. Since these instructions made Ryōko anxious about him, he explained his desire for secrecy in a letter from Vienna on July 31:

> I do not have to conceal my homecoming schedule; but as you know, when I last returned from Miyagi prefecture, in other words, from jail in Sendai, people gave me too many welcoming dinners and receptions. Therefore, I think it would be fun to return and have no one notice. There is nothing wrong with me. Don't be upset about me.

Mutsu's real reasons for this secrecy remain in doubt. However, he used other methods to prevent the news of his return from leaking out. He informed Ryōko on July 31, "When I send the telegram, I will send only one word, 'Today.' Then you will know that I started out from England on that day. I will go via Indian Ocean. . . . If by any chance, I stop in the United States, I will send a telegram saying 'Today, America.'" Since the telegrams would be written in English, he advised her to have his eldest son, seventeen-year-old Hirokichi, read them. "If he cannot understand them, Tsuda will help you. Even if you have Hirokichi and Tsuda read them, please keep them quiet." As a result, there is no reference in his letters of the date of his return.

The key to Mutsu's secrecy lies in his character and in the political situation. He kept his return a secret from all his friends and acquaintances, including Furukawa Ichibei, his financial patron, Itō Hirobumi and Inoue Kaoru, his friends in the dominant *hanbatsu* group, Gotō Shōjirō, his old friend in the popular-rights movement, and informed only Isuda, his *sempai* from his home province whom he entrusted with his affairs while in jail and during his foreign travel.

Why did Mutsu act this way? The author would suggest that this reflects the change from ideological or "inner" travel to political travel. If politics is the art of the possible, the essential need of the politician is to allow room for this selection, for freedom of movement. Since Mutsu had left prison, his activities had been watched by both the government and the popular-rights group. While staying in London, Mutsu had decided which group he would join on his return to Japan. However, he thought that no one could predict what would happen next in the political world. His secrecy in regard to the date of his return was a precautionary measure to allow himself as much freedom of action as possible. Thus, while in Europe, he had begun to use what might be called "Mutsu diplomacy" on both the strong *hanbatsu* group and the popular-rights group. In a letter written to Ryōko on June 18, 1884, at the beginning of his travels, he said, "It seems to me that during these travels that there is some trouble in the midst of joy while there was some joy in the midst of trouble in Miyagi." On February 1, 1886, Mutsu reached Kobe; and his foreign travel had come to an end.

Soon after Mutsu returned, Itō Hirobumi received a letter of recommendation in regard to Mutsu from Saionji Kimmochi in Vienna that read:

> I heard Mutsu Munemitsu left England for Japan last winter. I think he will have arrived in Japan by the time you get this letter.
>
> He studied very hard in Europe. I believe he will look different when you meet him. I am sure it is a heavy loss for him to be out of office. Moreover, I don't think it is good for the government to keep him out of office.
>
> Why don't you employ him as soon as possible? This employment is necessary not only for him but also for the government.[19]

This letter was timed to correspond exactly with Mutsu's return. If we remember that Saionji and Mutsu met and spoke with one another at Vienna, we can understand that Saionji was very serious in recommending Mutsu to the strong *hanbatsu* government.

On October 28, 1886, Mutsu was asked to accept an official position with the government. He was appointed resident minister of the Ministry of Foreign Affairs. As he explained later, his feelings at this time were:

> I had spent almost three years traveling in foreign countries since I was released from prison, although I received various advice from

my friends, both inside and outside the government, about my future. Then, after I came home, my friends again gave me a variety of advice; and I had to decide which course I should take for my life, whether to enter government service or to remain outside the government. At the time, unlike most government officials, I did not regard the political parties that were outside the government as anything more than groups of vagrants, utterly harmful and useless. On the contrary, I believed that if we cultivated and encouraged these groups they would become an influential force that would have a positive effect in the political world of our country in the future. However, when I look back upon my past, I have to realize that I was a person who had committed major crimes and had been imprisoned for a long time. And I did not feel immediately at ease to position myself, with such a past record, in the place of opposition to the government. If I could make any choice, I thought I should first enter government service.

At this juncture, Count Itō and Count Inouye were most anxious to advise me to accept a government post, and thus, I got this post. But, my old friends, especially those who came from the same prefecture as I, namely, Wakayama, were very disappointed with my decision though they did not explicitly object to it. This was because they placed too great an expectation upon my political future.[20]

Notes

1. Editor's note: An earlier version of this work was published as "Mutsu saikai," in Japanese. See Hagihara Nobutoshi, *Mutsu Munemitsu*, vol. 35 of *Nihon No meicho* (Tōkyō: Chūō Koronsha, 1973), pp. 7–45. Translated by Shiju Nobuko, Yoko Yuki and Sandra T. W. Davis. Adapted and edited by Sandra T. W. Davis.
2. In the article, Hagihara notes that he traveled from London to Weidlingau village, near Vienna, in December 1969 to visit the home to Lorenz von Stein. In July 1970, Stein's grandson, Dr. Manfred von Stein, permitted him to visit the Stein house and to study letters and other materials sent to Stein. Mutsu's letters were among those remaining in Stein's files. Editor's note.
3. Shumpo-ko Tsuishō Kai, *Itō Hirobumi den*, 3 vols. (Tōkyō: Shumpō-Ko Tsuikō-Kai, 1940), 2:320–21.
4. Ibid., pp. 322–23.
5. Ibid., pp. 286–94, 294–99.
6. Letter from Mutsu to Stein dated September 29, 1884, in Lorenz von Stein documents.
7. Letter from Mutsu to Stein dated October 15, 1884, in Lorenz von Stein documents.
8. Manuscript dated July 31, 1886, in Ernest Satow Papers, Public Record Office. London.
9. Hagihara notes that Thomas Waraker's name and profession were listed in the *Alumni Cantabrigienses*, part 2, 1752–1900, vol. 6. Editor's note.
10. *Itō Hirobumi den*, 2:294–99, from Vienna, August 11, 1882.
11. Letter from Mutsu to Stein dated April 28, 1885, in the Stein documents.
12. Watanabe Ikujiro, *Mutsu Munemitsu den* (Tōkyō: Kaizosha, 1941), p. 162.
13. Ibid., p. 159–62, Letter from Stein to Mutsu dated December 1, 1885.
14. Letter from Mutsu to his wife, Ryōko, dated July 31, 1885, Mutsu's letters to his wife are in the Kensei Shiryo shitsu, National Diet Library, Tokyo. They are reprinted in Hagihara, *Mutsu Munemitsu*.
15. Letter from Mutsu in Berlin to Stein, dated September 8, 1885, in the Stein documents. The Stein house at Weidlingau has been taken down and Stein's books and papers

have been moved into the Lorenz von Stein Institute für Vewaltungswissenschaften, Kiel, Federal Republic of Germany.

16. Letters from Mutsu to Stein dated September 8, 1885, from Berlin and October 1, 1885, from London, ibid.

17. Watanabe, *Mutsu Munemitsu den*, p. 159–62.

18. Letter from Mutsu to Stein dated December 7, 1885, Stein documents.

19. Letter from Saionji Kimmochi to Itō Hirobumi dated January 15, 1886, and quoted in Watanabe Ikūjiro, *Mutsu Munemitsu den*, pp. 162–63.

20. Mutsu Hirokichi, comp., *Hakushaku Mutsu Munemitsu Iko (The Posthumous Works of Count Mutsu Munemitsu)* (Tōkyō: Iwanami Shoten, 1929), p. 764.

Part 5
The Darker Side

Early telegraph system in Yokohama. *(Photo permission of Anna Brinton Collection. Reproduction by Masako Imai.)*

Introduction

The preceding four sections of this volume have pictured the Meiji mind as innovative and adaptive, progressive and conservative, idealistic and realistic. In the interplay of these opposing tendencies, a balance was struck that permitted Japan to survive and prosper with an internal political structure that had recently left behind its feudal Tokugawa antecedents, and within an international system that was dominated by Western imperialism.

It is tempting to declare the Meiji period a time of success in both internal and external affairs and to look to the 1930s for excesses in repression internally and imperialism abroad. Yet Meiji Japan had its victims too, and their stories must be told not only to provide a necessary corrective to an overly rosy view of the period, but also to link later tragic developments to their Meiji precedents.

This fifth and last section considers the plight of some of the victims of the Meiji success story: workers, women, peasant farmers, peace movements, and Korea. The three articles that follow attempt to describe why and how the above came to be victims of a darker side of the Meiji mind.

In the first article, the late John Lin, whose article was completed by Dr. Reginald Rajapakse, demonstrates how Meiji definitions of stability, unity, and progress worked to promote policies detrimental to the welfare of workers, peasants, and women. Labor unions, peasant associations, and women's groups, which arose during the Taishō era (1912–26), were subject to repression in favor of big business, landlords, and male supremacy. Professor Lin concluded that the stifling of these voices contributed to the stifling of democratic and egalitarian impulses in prewar Japanese society.

Sharlie C. Ushioda's essay on the life and times of Fukuda Hideko serves to highlight in a case study the problems faced by a liberated woman in a male-dominated society. When Fukuda's unconventional wisdom becomes entangled with pacifism, an unpopular position at a time of expansion abroad, the result is an increase in the repressive actions of the Meiji government. How Fukuda fares against forces both societal and governmental provides an especially instructive chapter in the study of women in Meiji Japan.

The final essay, by Wayne Patterson, looks at the nation of Korea as yet another victim of the imperial expansionism that characterized the later years of Meiji Japan. Indeed, Korea was Japan's first step in the long road to the Pacific War. Like the peace movement that threatened the goals of Meiji leaders as described in the preceding essay, the unrestricted flow of Koreans across the Pacific had to be prevented if the Japanese takeover of Korea was to be successful. Professor Patterson's research into the means and reasons for the Japanese action against Korean immigration shows in this case study how Japanese imperialism operated to consolidate its hold over Korea, which, it should be noted, received a higher priority from the Meiji government than improving the lives of the common people in Japan.

To be sure, the history discussed in these last three essays should serve to temper any excessive adulation of the achievements of Meiji. At the same time, it should not blind us to the achievements that Japanese society attained during this period. Like any period under historical scrutiny, Meiji Japan had its share of visionaries and ideologues as well as hardheaded realists. This mixture of varying ideas and personalities served to produce a dynamism never before experienced by Japanese society. The essays in this volume have attempted to capture the essence of the dynamism of the Meiji mind in thought and action.

12 Workers, Peasants, and Women in Taishō Japan: Legacy of the Meiji Mind

*John Lin with Reginald Rajapakse**

The reputation of the Taishō era, 1922–26, as a time of liberalism and democracy in Japan tends to obscure the reality of the situation for workers, peasants, and women. This was undoubtedly a period of great advances in Japan's overall political and economic development. It witnessed the transformation of the narrowly limited constitutional government erected by the Meiji oligarchs into an almost full-fledged parliamentary system based on universal male suffrage, freedom of the press, two-party rivalry, and party-controlled cabinets.[1] It saw a tremendous expansion of the Japanese economy, particularly in the industrial sector, which was rapidly modernized by technological innovation and heavy capital investment.[2] The benefits of these developments were inequitably distributed, with the major share accruing to owners of property (landlords, industrialists, bankers, merchants, moneylenders), high government officials, and professionals. The dichotomy between democratic institutions and social reality in this period was epitomized in the increasing distress and repression of both the agrarian and urban poor and the increasing concentration of economic power and political influence in the hands of the *zaibatsu*.

The sharp contrast between the rising affluence of the well-to-do and the worsening plight of the masses generated social tensions and class antagonisms unprecedented in Japanese history. Labor strife, evidenced by an increasing number of industrial strikes, tenancy disputes that erupted with disconcerting frequency and, above all, the rice riots of August 1918 reflected the growing desperation and anger of the poorer classes.

During the rice riots, some 700,000 persons in 36 cities, 129 towns, and

---

*Professor Lin's illness and death while this volume was in preparation made it impossible for Dr. Rajapakse and the general editors of the volume to arrange with him the documentation of many Japanese primary source materials he used in this article. The interested reader is referred to his doctoral dissertation (see note 9).

145 villages smashed the shops of rice merchants, ransacked the homes of the well-to-do, and rampaged in the streets for more than two weeks. The government's response to this massive and largely spontaneous popular outburst against the inflation of rice prices was a policy of ineffective price controls and import subsidies intermixed with pious admonition and swift repression of rioting mobs. Many areas were placed under martial law, and troops and police dispatched to maintain order and protect property. Several thousand were arrested; and, by the end of 1918, over 6,000 persons had been tried and sentenced, some to pay fines and others to jail terms, ranging from six months to life.[3]

The government's tendency to rely more on force than on remedial measures to solve pressing social and economic problems was a blatant feature of public policy throughout the Taishō era. It involved far more than governmental indifference to economic hardships inflicted on the poor, which in itself was morally reprehensible. Indeed, there was a fundamental, antidemocratic aspect to this policy, namely, a systematic, calculated effort to deny basic rights, such as equality before the law, freedom of association, speech, and press, to the underprivileged groups in society: workers, peasants, women, and others.

The background and setting for the political developments and social problems of this era was provided by far-reaching economic changes. The Taishō period witnessed both rapid growth and transformation of the economy, owing largely to the impact of World War I and its aftermath. During the war and the resulting temporary withdrawal of Western competition from the markets in South and East Asia, Japan found itself in the position of the sole supplier of a multitude of goods and services. Aided by wartime demand and monopolistic market conditions, Japan's foreign trade and domestic industrial production expanded rapidly.[4] There was a tremendous increase in the number of business enterprises, in the capacity of the industrial plant, and in the amount of capital investment, much of it generated by the accumulation of large surpluses of specie through export trade. Rapid growth marked the development of both old and new industries. There was considerable growth in the textile industry; but the most significant expansion came in heavy industry, which produced the industrial supplies and equipment that supported the wartime boom: shipbuilding, chemicals, metal refining, and machine tools. "The World War I boom was tremendous", a scholar recently observed. "It engendered the most rapid industrial and overall growth Japan ever had."[5]

Accelerated industrial growth, especially in the area of heavy industry, and increased capital investment strengthened the trend toward business consolidation and the concentration of economic power in the hands of the *zaibatsu*. During the war many small and medium businesses, owned by individual proprietors and partnerships, were merged into larger ones. There was a marked increase in the number of joint stock companies, which became the predominant form of corporate organization. This process of consolidation was furthered by the postwar deflation, which stimulated a "rationalization" movement in Japanese industry. Essentially, this meant attempts to increase productivity and to save labor costs by maintaining a higher level of investment and adopting improved technology.[6] Rationalization led to the elimination of thousands of small and medium businesses that lacked the capital necessary to carry out cost-cutting improvements.

A similar process of consolidation was under way in the banking business. The decade of the 1920s witnessed a sharp reduction in the number of small banks. While aggregate bank deposits increased by one-quarter from 1920 to 1929, the number of banks declined in the same period from 2,041 to 1,008. Financial power came to be centered increasingly in a handful of big private banks and trust companies, largely owned or controlled by the *zaibatsu*. Since there was no capital market for public issues, the commercial banks in Japan were the chief external source of private capital for business firms. Thus, through their banks and trust companies, the *zaibatsu* could wield controlling influence over their smaller industrial and trading competitors.

The net effect of these developments in the war and postwar years was to concentrate economic power in the hands of the great financial combines or *zaibatsu*. Already dominant in large-scale industry, foreign trade, and banking, the *zaibatsu* now extended their control over an increasing share of small-scale commerce and manufacturing. The larger groups, notably Mitsui and Mitsubishi, developed into towering conglomerations of heterogeneous enterprises spread over such fields as trading, shipping, banking, insurance, manufacturing, mining, and real estate.[7] "In economic development [during this period]," notes George O. Totten, "the sprawling *zaibatsu* battened, while the overwhelmingly large number of so-called middle and small enterprises starved for want of capital, markets and raw materials, and remained stunted in the shadow on the sufferance of the giants."[8]

While, on the one hand, the impact of World War I and its aftermath tended to concentrate economic power in the hands of a few, on the other, it tended to impoverish the masses. The prosperity of the wartime boom produced the *narikin*, the new rich, whose fortunes were made, if not overnight, at least within a short space of years. At the same time, however—and this is more important for our consideration—it enormously increased the ranks of the urban industrial proletariat and the landless peasantry. The immediate problem for these two groups was the rising cost of living, the result of a wartime inflation, which was exacerbated by the accumulation of Japan's specie reserves, the increase in the circulation of currency, and the relative scarcity (or stagnation in the production) of consumer goods.

The rate of inflation was unprecedented. Prices rose from a base index of 100 in 1914 to 122 in 1916, to 202 in 1918, and 248 by 1919. On the other hand, wages climbed much more slowly. The wage index rose from a base of 100 in 1914 to 102 in 1916, to 153 in 1918, and to 218 by 1919. But even this lag between nominal wage and price increases does not fully convey the magnitude of the problem created by the rising cost of living for the poorer classes. It is essential further to take into account the fact that the price of rice, which occupied an important part of working-class budgets, increased about fivefold during the period 1909–19.[9] It became the cause of mounting social discontent that culminated in the rice riots of August 1918.

The government's confused and unsympathetic response to this massive and largely spontaneous expression of economic grievances by the poor can be seen in the situation of workers, peasants, and women, and in government policies toward their aspirations.

A social change of great long-run significance that resulted from the wartime boom was the rapid expansion of the urban industrial proletariat. The total number of factory workers increased dramatically during these years, from 948,200 in 1914 to 1,520,400 in 1919, an increase of about 60 percent. Not only the size of the labor force but also its composition and character underwent profound change. First, there was a marked increase in the number of male workers because of the rapid growth of heavy industry. Second, the male labor force in the heavy industries tended to be different both in social background and in outlook from the largely female labor force in the textile industry. It was older, probably better educated, and more urban than rural in origin. It was also relatively better paid and less subject to the paternalistic supervision and discipline that was common in the textile industry. These differences made for a less submissive, more independent attitude on the part of the male labor force in heavy industry. Not surprisingly, it was among this section of the working class that the labor movement of the Taishō era gained initial strength and, in the long run, achieved its greatest success.[10]

There is little to be said about the earlier history of the labor movement in Japan. A few craft unions were organized by printers, ironworkers, and others in the late 1890s; but this activity was strangled in its infancy by the Meiji government with the help of the Public Peace Police Ordinance enacted in March 1900. The ordinance restricted the rights of assembly, demonstration, speech, and press. Article 17 in particular circumscribed the activity of labor. It required all public meetings to be reported to the authorities in advance, empowered the police to supervise and control such meetings, and declared strikes illegal, making them an offense subject to criminal conspiracy.[11] Carried over into the Taishō era and applied broadly, this ordinance was to plague popular movements of the period.

Although workers often resorted to strikes—despite the ordinance—in the years preceding World War I, the only significant labor organization that came into being was the Yūaikai or Friendly Society, founded by Suzuki Bunji and a few other moderate middle-class intellectuals in 1912. The aims of the Yūaikai reflected the beliefs of its founders. Its central purpose was to reconcile the interests of labor and capital, and to promote labor's well-being by education, mutual aid, self-help, and cooperation with employers.[12] (The underlying assumption was that, for both practical and theoretical reasons, the interests of labor and capital were not fundamentally opposed, but mutually dependent. Antagonism between the two would be to the economic advantage of neither.)[13]

Economic developments during World War I gave a powerful impetus to the growth of the labor movement in Japan. Not only did the number of strikes and labor disputes, and the number of workers involved in them, increase enormously, but there was also a significant increase in the number of trade unions. The Yūaikai, for instance, grew from its modest beginnings in 1912 to a sizable labor organization with a membership of 30,000 and 120 branches by 1918.[14] Behind this growth in unionization and mounting labor strife were two basic causes: (1) the rapid expansion of the industrial labor force, especially in heavy industry, and (2) the hardships inflicted on workers by the rising cost of living and the conditions of work in the incessantly operating wartime factories. Furthermore, mass production and industrial expansion meant an influx of unskilled labor. As a result, trade unionism expanded to include both skilled as well as unskilled workers.[15] The first Japanese factory law did not go into effect until 1916, and even then it had limited application. Labor demands in these years centered on purely economic demands: wage increases and improvement of working conditions, especially reduction in the hours of work.

Based on these foundations and influenced by ideological concepts from abroad, "a small but highly self-conscious and politically oriented labor movement"[16] developed in the postwar years. It was distinguished not only by a proliferation of trade unions and the growth of labor federations, but also, more important, by a pronounced class consciousness that had hardly existed during the war years. The emergence of this phenomenon was the result of the interaction of ideological influence from abroad, notably the impact of the Russian Revolution, with Japanese labor's disappointing experience with management during the course of the war. It had become increasingly clear to labor leaders as well as to middle-class intellectuals that employers were interested in "the cooperation of capital and labor" only in order to assure industrial peace and continued profits.[17] By the war's end, a disproportionately large share of the increased income produced by the boom had "accrued to the well-to-do classes in the forms of rent, dividend, interest, and corporate savings,"[18] leaving the workers feeling unrewarded. Real grievances, made the harder to bear by envy, as those who reaped profits from the wartime prosperity indulged in extravagance and display, awakened the class consciousness of Japanese labor.[19] It was given form and direction by proletarian concepts imported from abroad after the war.[20]

Symbolic of this growing class consciousness among labor was the transformation of the Yūaikai into the Nihon Rōdō Sōdōmei (General Federation of Labor in Japan) in 1919. It was no longer a "friendly society," seeking to reconcile the interests of capital and labor, but a purely working-class organization devoted to securing the rights of labor. The new program of the organization, inspired partly by the labor provisions in the Versailles Peace Treaty (1919), called for the legal recognition of basic working-class rights—for example, the right to organize, the right to strike, and the right to vote—all of which required the action of government, rather than the action of individual employers.

While economic issues such as higher wages and better working conditions continued to provide the driving force for trade-union organization and activity directed against management, the emergence of class consciousness and the assertion of basic rights tended to integrate as well as politicize the labor movement. By 1920 there were over 200 unions, most of them newly formed, and they had begun to organize in larger groups. The years from 1919 to 1921 witnessed a wave of industrial strikes generated by the postwar deflation,[21] concerted attempts by union leaders to secure recognition of collective bargaining rights from management,[22] and, above all, a nationwide campaign by organized labor for universal suffrage.[23] All these efforts, however, ended in failure in the face of combined opposition from government and corporate management.

The Seiyūkai party cabinet of Premier Hara Kei (October 1918 to November 1921), which was in power during these years, showed little enthusiasm for either democratic reform or social legislation. Rather than attack labor unrest at its source by devising remedial measures, Hara's government turned increasingly to the tactics of control and repression to deal with the labor problems. From the end of 1919, it made every effort to combat the growing number of strikes by rigorously enforcing Article 17 of the Public Peace Police Ordinance, by encouraging employers to fire or refuse to employ striking workers, and by arresting labor organizers and agitators. The government resorted to direct police action in case of strikes in critical industries. In January 1920, for instance, it dispatched regular police as well as secret police *(kempeitai)* units to break up a strike at the Yawata Steel Works. In February, it called up the *kempeitai* to subdue striking streetcar workers in Tokyo. More ominous for the future, the government began to create special agencies within the law-enforcement authorities (Police and Justice Departments) to carry on surveillance and to stamp out left-wing movements and radical or "subversive" ideologies.[24] However, the most staggering blow dealt by the Hara government to labor aspirations was the defeat of the universal-suffrage bill in 1920.[25]

The inevitable consequence of this increasingly repressive policy pursued by the government and the setback to democratic rights, namely, universal suffrage and collective bargaining, sought by labor was the temporary eclipse of the moderate element in the labor movement, and the ascendancy of those who advocated radical solutions. Hence, after 1920, Socialist- and Communist-inspired efforts to form proletarian parties on the one hand, and on the other, a growing receptivity to "anarcho-syndicalism, expressed in ideological terms a simple, down-to-earth alienation from both workplace and politics and a consequent resort to 'direct action.' "[26] The largest and strongest working-class organization, the Sōdōmei and its affiliated trade unions, was now hnadicapped by bitter feuds among competing factions, anarcho-syndicalists, social democrats, and Communists. An attempt, begun in April 1922, by the Sōdōmei and its rival, Rōdō Kumiai Dōmeikai (Federation of Labor Unions), to organize a national general federation of labor broke down owing largely to the irreconcilable ideological differences among the competing factions, even before the government finally suppressed the attempt in September 1922.[27]

The syndicalist surge in the labor movement waned after 1922, leaving Communists and social democrats still to resolve their differences. The process was aided indirectly but quickly by the government, which stepped up its attacks on the radicals, while, at the same time, it began to make consessions to the moderate Left. Repression reached its climax in September 1923, when, following the great Kanto earthquake, police raids and mass arrests crushed both Communists and anarchists.[28] The moderates or social democrats, who now regained ascendancy in the labor movement, turned away from the revolutionary course. It had brought on repression by government, constant defeat of strikes by management, and a consequent decline in trade-union membership. With moderates in control, the Sōdōmei, at its general meeting in February 1924, announced its shift to what it called a more "realistic direction." This meant, in essence, a resumption of efforts to secure working-class rights through the parliamentary process. The Sōdōmei's lead was promptly followed by other labor organizations.[29]

In order to encourage this moderate course, the government, in turn, revised its policy toward labor in 1924 by allowing the larger trade unions to elect the workers' delegates to the International Labor Conference, instead of appointing them as it had done before. This modest change had the effect of promoting "union organization almost as much as if a trade union law had been enacted guaranteeing the right to organize."[30] Union membership more than doubled from 1923 to 1926 (see table). These years also witnessed a great many strikes and a resurgence of radicalism in the labor movement. While the moderates gained the upper hand in the Sōdōmei, its affiliated Communist-inspired unions broke away in May 1925 to form an organization of their own: the Nihon Rōdō Kumiai Hyōgikai (Council of Japanese Labor Unions). Its radical platform and

Table

Year	Number of Trade Unions	Membership	Number of Strikes
1923	432	125,551	
1924	469	228,278	333
1925	457	254,262	293
1926	488	284,739	495

Source: Kyōchō Kai, *Saikin no shakai undō*, p. 221.

militant leadership attracted many followers as well as government intervention. Within a year of its founding, the Hyōgikai had gathered fifty-nine affiliated unions and a membership of 30,000, and it led far more labor disputes than the Sōdōmei. At the same time, over 5,000 of its members were detained by police for questioning and 196 imprisoned for instigating strikes. The Hyōgikai's turbulent career came to an end shortly with its suppression by massive police arrests and brutality in March 1928.[31]

From 1924, the government's new policy toward labor was largely one of concessions to moderates and suppression of radicals. Suppression and concession were symbolized best by the almost simultaneous passage by the Diet of the Peace Preservation Law and the Universal Manhood Suffrage Act in May 1925.[32] The latter extended the vote to males over twenty-five years of age; the former provided penalties of up to ten years' imprisonment for participation in any society that was designed to overthrow the Japanese form of government or abolish private ownership of property. Directed ostensibly against Communists and anarchists, the Peace Preservation Law added enormously to the already extensive powers conferred on the police, as seen by regulations dating as far back as 1900, for carrying out censorship, arrest, and even violence against men and women of left-wing sympathies. The law lacked precision in its wording, and thus it opened the way for many kinds of interference with personal liberties, and did not by any means confine their application to extremists.[33] Under this law, the government banned the first proletarian party, Nōmin Rōdōto (Farmer-Labor party), just thirty minutes after it came formally into existence on December 1, 1925. The involvement of suspected Communist elements in the party's formation was sufficient cause for official intervention.[34] The same law, as already mentioned, led to the suppression of the Hyōgikai and massive police arrests of Communists and Communist sympathizers in March 1928.

Nor did the moderates in the labor movement fare any better at the hands of the government. While they escaped the ruthless suppression meted out to the radicals, they were not rewarded for their moderation by any significant concessions. There were only two concessions made by the government, and both were of relatively minor importance. First, there was the limited respectability conferred on trade unionism by government recognition of trade unions for voting purposes for the ILO in 1924, and second, there was the abrogation in 1926 of the infamous Article 17 of the Public Peace Police Ordinance, which removed certain handicaps to trade unions when on strike. Taking advantage of these concessions, moderate labor oganizations, like the Sōdōmei, Nihon Rōdō Kumiai Dōmei (Federation of Japanese Labor Unions), and Nihon Rōdō Kumiai Sōrengo (General Alliance of Japanese Labor Unions), successfully negotiated collective bargaining agreements with various managements. However, these agreements remained purely voluntary because the government refused to enact a trade-union law giving legal recognition to collective bargaining rights.[35]

Instead, the government, responding to big business and conservative interests, sought to promote harmony in industrial relations by providing conciliation machinery for the ad hoc settlement of labor disputes. In 1927, it enacted the Labor Disputes Conciliation Law (Rōdō Sogi Chōtei Hō), which provided for the establishment of conciliation committees whenever demanded by both sides to a dispute. The law, however, remained largely ineffective. A more successfully operated device to promote harmony was the works council, an idea borrowed from Great Britain and the United States. Favored largely by management and conservative pressure groups, such as the Kyōchō Kai (Harmonization Society), these works councils or factory consultative committees were established in many enterprises as a substitute for collectively bargained enforceable contracts.[36] In this way, the government avoided making a clear legal specification of labor's rights and duties.

Similar policies were followed in dealing with the rights of peasants and women. While the urban industrial proletariat had to contend with hardships caused by conditions of work, rising wartime inflation, and then postwar deflation, the hardships afflicting the peasantry sprang from more deep-rooted causes, stemming largely from the adjustment of agriculture to the needs of a commercial, industrial economy.

To begin with, Japan's villages had little arable land, much labor, and produced rice as their staple crop, and, since the 1860s, raw silk as their main secondary product. The small farm, operated with family labor, remained the fundamental pattern of organization in agricultural production. Despite industrial growth, agriculture continued to be the predominant form of economic activity, employing half the working population, over 14 million people, as late as 1930.[37] Land fragmentation and the small size of holdings, inevitable in such a situation, were a basic cause of peasant discontent. In the 1920s, for instance, almost 50 percent of Japanese farmers held less than half a *cho* (1 *cho* = 2.45 acre) of land. About 24 percent held between half a *cho* and a *cho,* and 18 percent between one *cho* and three *cho.* More important, two-thirds of the farmers were wholly or partly tenants of the land they cultivated.[38]

The growth of tenancy and the concentration of ownership in the hands of landlords, many of them absentee or, to use the Marxist term, "parasitic," had proceeded steadily with the commercialization of agriculture and the Meiji reforms in land tenure and land tax in the 1870s.[39] The reforms abolished feudalism, gave the cultivator formal title to the land, and imposed a land tax to be paid in money. The poor farmer lost out, either in the initial redistribution, or subsequently through his inability to pay taxes and cope with the vagaries of a money economy. By 1880, it was estimated that more than 30 percent of the cultivated area had already passed into tenancy.[40] The process continued to operate, thinning the ranks of the middle farmer who produced for the market. His level of expenditure rose as he had to buy fertilizer, tools, new strains of seeds, and a variety of household goods, as well as pay taxes, while the prices he received for his products tended to fluctuate. Many owner-cultivators were unable to solve the problems this situation posed, and they invariably contracted debts and eventually sank to the status of tenants. The proportion of tenanted land gradually increased to 46 percent, and the proportion of wholly and partly tenant families to 69 percent by 1919. Others, the more successful, became landowners on a larger scale, marking the continued separation of the village into rich and poor.

The farmer's income, whether owner-cultivator or tenant, depended largely on the price he received for his products. This determined for many the difference between solvency and bankruptcy. The wartime inflation that caused so much hardship to the city worker did not adversely affect the farmer to the same extent. Although his cost of living and operating expenses tended to rise, he was sufficiently compensated by sharp increases in the price of farm products. The price for rice, for example, soared from 16 yen a *koku* in 1917 to 39 yen in 1918, and to 55 yen by 1920. Then the postwar trade recession and ensuing deflation broke and reversed the upward trend in farm product prices. The price of rice dropped precipitously. The cost of a *koku* of rice fell from 55 yen in 1920 to 25.5 yen in 1921, while the wholesale-price index dropped from 343 to 265 in the same two years. This meant real poverty for farmers, especially as their most important subsidiary crop, raw silk, suffered a similar decline in value.

Price support programs sponsored by the government and a recovery in silk prices induced by boom conditions in the United States did something to improve the situation in the next few years. Improvement was, however, only temporary. A prolonged and much steeper decline occurred after 1925, owing largely to the import of cheap rice from Taiwan and Korea and to the gradual collapse of the American market for raw silk. Prices farmers received for their products dropped by 53 percent between 1925 and 1931.[41] The index of raw-silk prices (1914 = 100) slumped from 222 in 1925 to 151 in 1929, and to 67 by 1931. Over the same period, the index for rice fell from 257 to 114.[42]

The agrarian price declines in the 1920s caused widespread poverty in rural areas. The burden of agricultural debt increased enormously, from 14 million yen in 1917 to 4.5 billion yen by 1929. Most of this debt, 56.5 percent, was owed to moneylenders and other individuals who were not directly engaged in agriculture.[43] Villages suffered, too, from the fact that they acted as a shock absorber for urban unemployment. Although population increase forced many to the towns to find jobs in shops and factories, each setback to the industrial economy drove them back to seek refuge in their native villages. Conditions became so desperate that farmers even resorted to "human traffic" in their own daughters.[44]

The worst affected were the poorest farmers, especially the tenant farmers, who were at the mercy of their landlords. By the 1920s, this meant something like half the agricultural population, for 49 percent held plots of under one and a quarter acres, and over two-thirds were tenants for all or part of their land. Tenancy agreements invariably favored the owner because of population pressure and scarcity of land. Thus, rents were payable in kind, which deprived the tenant of most of the benefits of inflation. They were also high, amounting to as much as half the crop on ricepaddy, a third for dry fields.[45] In the absence of a law protecting tenant rights, there was no security of tenure. Landlords sought to minimize their losses by raising rents and taking back the lands of indigent tenants.[46]

The severity of such conditions had been mitigated before the war by the rapid expansion of agrarian production; but as this slowed down, so the agreements became the focus of rising tension. Tenancy disputes, which had usually been occasioned in the past by floods, typhoons, and similar catastrophes, became more frequent, more extensive, and more highly organized, especially around the periphery of urban areas. Tenant unions, patterned after labor unions, multiplied rapidly, increasing in number from 88 in 1918 to 625 by 1926. All of them campaigned actively for changes in the existing system of land tenure, in addition to acting as representatives of their members in specific local disputes.

Like the labor federations that developed in the trade-union movement, tenant unions came to be organized in larger groups. The most prominent of these farmer federations was the Nihon Nōmin Kumiai (Japan Farmers' Union), founded in April 1922. Initially organized with fifteen tenant unions, it expanded rapidly, bringing within its fold 300 unions and over 10,000 tenant farmers by 1924. It developed under left-wing leadership, and played a significant role in the formation of the first proletarian party, the ill-fated Nōmin Rōdōto (Farmer-Labor party) in 1925 and later the Rōdō Nōminto (Labor-Farmer party) in 1926.[47]

Tenant unrest accompanied the increased activity and organization of tenant farmers. The number of tenancy disputes grew at an alarming rate after 1920. Faced with the threat posed by this development, landlords responded by organizing themselves for self-defense. local landlord unions were formed to resist tenant demands, and in 1926 a national organization emerged.[48] In this conflict between tenant and landlord, the government once more took the side of privilege, as it had done in the conflict between labor and management.

Just as in the case of urban unrest, the government relied more on repression than on remedial measures to deal with the problem of agrarian unrest. The Public Peace Police Ordinance of 1900 was again the main instrument of repressive action. Applying this ordinance with no moral restraint, the government directed the police to break up tenant meetings, arrest the leaders of tenant unions, and protect the fields of landlords. In addition, local authorities, taking their cues from government policy and responding to landlord pressure, passed special bylaws to punish tenant conspiracy. By 1926, at least seventeen prefectures had bylaws that provided for twenty to thirty days' imprisonment for such offenses as forcing others to enter tenant unions or demanding interviews with landlords after sundown.[49] Although acts of physical violence at the height of tenancy disputes were not uncommon, the general level of violence was not so high as to justify wholesale suppression of basic rights and indiscriminate police action.

On the positive side, the government did little to alleviate agrarian discontent. The measures it adopted in the 1920s, such as the price-support programs and the establishment of the Hypothec Bank for agricultural credit, were palliatives at best. The obvious social inequities of the agrarian system were barely touched. The government did nothing to check the growth of tenancy by providing tax relief and cheap credit for the small owner-cultivator. The tax burden remained heavy and usury flourished through the countryside.[50] Worse still, the government, acting under landlord influence, quashed all attempts in the 1920s to use legislation to protect tenant rights. Instead, it sought to preserve the traditional unity and harmony of rural life by providing conciliation machinery for the ad hoc settlement of tenancy disputes. In 1924, it enacted the Tenancy Disputes Conciliation Law, which provided for the appointment of mediators by the district courts to arbitrate the disputes between tenants and landlords. Although tenants were allowed to have their own representatives at the arbitration, the act specifically debarred tenant unions from participation. Thus, as in the case of trade unions and labor rights, the government refused to give legal recognition to tenant unions and tenant rights. The policy was much the same in the area of women's rights.

Japanese women in the Taishō period had to contend with social and political disabilities imposed on them by feudal traditions as well as by laws dating back to the Meiji era. The Civil Code of 1900 denied them legal equality with men, while electoral laws accompanying the constitution of 1889 barred them from participating in the political process. Not only were women denied the right to vote and the right to seek election to the Diet, but they were also forbidden to join political parties, or even attend meetings of a political nature, the latter restriction being reaffirmed by Article 5 of the Public Peace Police Ordinance of 1900. Organized efforts by women to overcome these disabilities did not begin until after World War I. By then the ranks of working women in Japan had greatly increased, women in some Western countries had achieved political rights, and the movement for democracy had begun to gather momentum.

Women workers in industry were among the first to seek improvement in their status. Although labor unions such as the Yūaikai had enrolled women in their ranks, they were not treated as equals with men. The Yūaikai, for instance, maintained this invidious distinction by assigning regular membership only to men and relegating women to associate membership. By 1917, however, pressure from an increasing number of women workers within the organization forced the Yūaikai to amend its charter and admit women to regular membership. When the Yūaikai was converted into the Sōdōmei (General Federation of Labor) in 1919, women were elected to directorships in the executive council. The organizing of women workers in trade unions ran into far greater opposition from management, which distrusted the labor movement as a whole. In 1920, for instance, a strike by some 500 women workers of the Sōdōmei against the Fuji Spinning Company ended in not only a defeat of the strike but in a forcible disbandment of the union. Management refused to rehire the strikers unless they withdrew from membership in the Sōdōmei. Facing increasingly strong opposition from management, women soon became disillusioned with trade unionism.[51]

Women's efforts to secure political rights met with similar resistance. The Shin Fujin Kyōkai (New Women's Association), founded in Tokyo in 1920, launched a campaign for the repeal of Article 5 of the Public Peace Police Ordinance, which forbade women to join political parties or even attend political meetings. The association established many branches in various parts of the country, issued a periodical to publicize its views, and petitioned the Diet to repeal the obnoxious article. The campaign was carried on despite the opposition of conservative groups and harassment by police. Both major political parties, Seiyūkai and Kenseikai, were willing to grant women the right to attend political meetings but opposed their joining political parties. A bill to this effect passed the forty-fourth session of the Diet, but it was rejected by the House of Peers. Finally, in May 1922, both houses voted an amendment to Article 5, giving women the right to attend political meetings. However, the New Women's Association did not last much longer after this partial success. Its activity was disrupted by police intervention as well as by internal feuds among rival ideological factions, and the association went into voluntary dissolution in December 1922.[52]

The campaign for women's political rights was then taken up by the Fujin Sansei Dōmei (Women's Suffrage League), which was organized toward the end of 1923. With the legislation of universal suffrage becoming a distinct possibility, a number of women's organizations, including the Women's Suffrage League, Women's Christian Temperance Society, and Federation of Women (Fujin Renmei), came together to form the Association for the Attainment of Women's Suffrage (Fujin Sanseiken Kakutoku Kisei Dōmeikai) in December 1924. The association canvassed party politicians, circulated petitions, and carried on a great deal of propaganda activity.[53] Despite these efforts, however, the campaign for women's political rights ended in failure. The Universal Manhood Suffrage Act passed by the Diet in May 1925 did not extend the vote to women. The women of Japan had to wait until the constitution of 1947 to realize full legal and political equality with men.

Notes

1. For a perceptive study of the political developments in this period, see Peter Duus, *Party Rivalry and Political Change in Taisho Japan* (Cambridge, Mass.: Harvard University Press, 1968).
2. For an authoritative study of the economic developments in this period, see William W. Lockwood, *The Economic Development of Japan: Growth and Structural Change, 1868–1938* (Princeton, N.J.: Princeton University Press, 1954).
3. Kyōchō Kai, ed. *Saikin no shakai undō (Recent Social Movements)* (Tōkyō: Kyōchō Kai, 1930), p. 690.
4. Lockwood, *Economic Development*, pp. 38–42.
5. Hugh T. Patrick, "The Economic Muddle of the 1920s," in James W. Morley, ed. *Dilemmas of Growth in Prewar Japan* Princeton, N.J.: Princeton University Press, 1971), p. 224.
6. Kazushi Ohkawa and Henry Rosovsky, "A Century of Japanese Economic Growth," in William W. Lockwood, ed. *The State and Economic Enterprise in Japan* (Princeton, N.J.: Princeton University Press, 1965), p. 79.
7. Lockwood, *Economic Development*, pp. 59–60, 210–12, and 215–32.
8. George O. Totten, "Collective Bargaining and Work Councils as Innovations in Industrial Relations in Japan during the 1920s," in R. P. Dore, ed. *Aspects of Social Change in Modern Japan* (Princeton, N.J.: Princeton University Press, 1967), p. 204.
9. For details, see Jung-shun Lin, "Popular Movements in Japan during the Taishō Era (1912–1926)" (Ph.D. Diss., University of Pennsylvania, 1960), pp. 308–9. Between January 1917 and August 1918, the price of rice rose from 16 yen per koku (4.96 bushels) to 39 yen per koku.
10. Duus, *Party Rivalry*, pp. 122–24.
11. See Lin, "Popular Movements," pp. 415–21, for details of this earlier phase of labor activity.
12. Katsumaro Akamatsu, *Nihon shakai unoō shi (The History of Social Movements in Japan)* (Tōkyō: Iwanami Shoten, 1952, p. 155; see also Kyōchō Kai, ed., *Saikin no shakai undō*, p. 202.
13. Duus, *Party Rivalry*, p. 126.
14. Lin, "Popular Movements," pp. 326–28, 330.
15. Totten, "Collective Bargaining," p. 208.
16. Ibid., p. 239.
17. Duus, *Party Rivalry*, p. 126.
18. Lockwood, *Economic Development*, p. 41.
19. Kentarō Hayashi, "Japan and Germany in the Intewar Period," in James W. Morley, ed. *Dilemmas of Growth in Prewar Japan* (Princeton, N.J.: Princeton University Press, 1971), p. 466.
20. Totten, "Collective Bargaining," pp. 205, 240.
21. See Duus, *Party Rivalry*, pp. 126–27; see also Shigetada Murayama, *Nippon rōdō sōgishi*

gaikan (An Outline of the History of Labor Disputes in Japan) (Tōkyō: Bunmei Kyokai, 1930), p. 27; also Shakai Keizai Rōdō Kenkyūjo, ed. *Kindai Nihon rōdōsha undō shi (Recent History of the Labor Movement in Japan)* Niigata: Hakurinsha, 1947), p. 20, Table 6; also Bureau of Police Affairs, Ministry of the Interior, *Rōdō sōgi no gaikyō (Outline of Labor Disputes)* (surveyed in December 1919), January 1920, classified as a secret document, p. 2.

22. Totten, "Collective Bargaining," pp. 205, 209.
23. Duus, *Party Rivalry*, pp. 128–32.
24. Lin, "Popular Movements," pp. 425–28.
25. Duus, *Party Rivalry*, pp. 152–57.
26. Totten, "Collective Bargaining," pp. 209–10.
27. Lin, "Popular Movements," pp. 436–41.
28. George M. Beckmann, "The Radical Left and the Failure of Communism," in Morley, ed. *Dilemmas of Growth in Prewar Japan*, pp. 143, 150.
29. Kyōchō Kai, *Saikin no shakai undō*, p. 221.
30. Totten, "Collective Bargaining," p. 210.
31. Shakai Keizai Rōdō Kenkyūjo, *Kindai Nihon*, p. 62.
32. Duus, *Party Rivalry*, pp. 203–6.
33. W. G. Beasley, *The Modern History of Japan* (New York: Praeger, 1963), p. 234.
34. Lin, "Popular Movements," pp. 462–65.
35. Totten, "Collective Bargaining," pp. 210–11.
36. Ibid., pp. 216–20.
37. Lockwood, *Economic Development*, p. 44.
38. Beasley, *Modern History of Japan*, p. 218.
39. Takao Tsuchiya and Saburō Okazaki, *Nihon shihonshugi hattatsushi gaisetsu (An Outline History of the Development of Capitalism in Japan)* (Tōkyō: Yūhikaku, 1948, 2nd ed.), pp. 472–81.
40. Lockwood, *Economic Development*, p. 552.
41. Patrick, "Economic Muddle of the 1920s," pp. 216–17.
42. Lockwood, *Economic Development*, pp. 56–57.
43. Patrick, "Economic Muddle of the 1920s," p. 218.
44. Kentarō Hayashi, "Japan and Germany," p. 481.
45. Beasley, *Modern History of Japan*, p. 230.
46. Kyōchō Kai, *Saikin no shakai undō*, p. 390.
47. Seizaburō Shinobu, *Taishō Seijishi (A Political History of the Taishō Era)* (Tōkyō: Kawade Shobō, 1953), 3:765, 770.
48. R. P. Dore and Tsutomo Ōuchi, "Rural Origins of Japanese Fascism," in Morley, ed., *Dilemmas of Growth in Prewar Japan*, pp. 187–89.
49. Ibid., p. 186.
50. Lockwood, *Economic Development*, pp. 54–55, 100, 555.
51. Lin, "Popular Movements," pp. 345, 347–48.
52. Shinobu, *Taishō Seijishi*, p. 811.
53. Lin, "Popular Movements," pp. 358–61.

13   Fukuda Hideko and the Woman's World of Meiji Japan*

Sharlie C. Ushioda

A search through the pages of English-language sources on modern Japanese history and culture reveals little information on the role that Japanese women have played in the development of their country. Although significant advances have been made in the past few decades in many areas of Japanese studies, the field of Japanese women's history was, until recently as one scholar noted, "somewhere back in the neolithic age in concepts and in the importance attached to it."[1] While it is generally known that the status of women in traditional Japanese society was quite low[2] and that a number of important changes in Japanese society took place in the decades following the Meiji Restoration that presumably affected women as well as men, there are as yet few adequate studies in English on the status of women, women's movements, or individual women leaders of the period.

Despite the fact that Western historians of modern Japan have seldom ventured into the field of Japanese women's history, a number of Japanese scholars have done some important work in the area. Most of the results of Japanese scholarship on women can be found in a special category of historical writing called *joseishi* (women's history). General perusal of several of these *joseishi*-type books indicates that the history of women in modern Japan is a fascinating and complex subject that deserves the attention of serious scholars for the new insights it can provide into many facets of the development of modern Japan.

One method of beginning to gain some understanding of the role of women in prewar Japan is to study the lives and thoughts of women leaders of the period. Since very few women are mentioned in standard

---

*Ms. Ushioda read a brief paper on Fukuda Hideko at the Annual Meeting of the American Historical Association in Washington, D.C., December 1976, an essay that was subsequently published in *Peace and Change* 4:3 (Fall 1977), pp. 9–12, entitled "Women and War in Meiji Japan: The Case of Fukuda Hideko, 1865–1927."

historical texts, however, the task of locating women leaders on whom to focus is no simple problem. After searching through a number of sources for "important women," one finds that a few candidates appear to stand out as having been particularly noteworthy for their involvement in and effect on the events of their time. These include Tsuda Umeko (1864–1933), a Christian educator and founder of Tsuda College; Fukuda Hideko (1865–1927), a political activist and writer; and Yosano Akiko (1878–1942), a poet and social critic.

The following paper is an attempt to begin to piece together the life of one of these women, Fukuda Hideko. The paper will begin with a brief description of the position of women in Meiji society, and then continue with a biographical sketch of Hideko and a preliminary discussion of some of the most important activities in her life. Because much more research needs to be done before any real understanding of her life and its meaning can be reached, this paper does not pretend to be a thorough analysis of her, but rather has the very limited objective of simply clarifying the kinds of concerns she had and the people with whom she associated. A bibliographical essay on sources for further research is appended.

Women in Meiji Society

Before focusing our attention on Fukuda Hideko, it is necessary first to say a few words about the period in which she lived, and particularly the position of women in Meiji society.

The Meiji-Taisho era (1868–1926) was one of the most exciting periods in all of Japanese history. It was a time when, after two and one-half centuries of self-imposed isolation from the outside world, Japanese leaders threw open Japan's doors to the world in order to learn how best to make their country into a strong, modern nation, and in the space of a few decades Japan changed from an isolated feudal nation to a modern world power. Two important aspects of modernization had an especially large influence on Japanese women: (1) so-called enlightenment thought and (2) the development of capitalistic production.[3]

Enlightenment thought, that is, the study of Western political and social philosophies, science, and history, inevitably brought with it some feminist ideas. By the middle of the Meiji period both "bourgeois feminism" as represented by John Stuart Mill and Henrik Ibsen, and "proletarian feminism" as advocated by Karl Marx, Frederick Engels, and August Bebel were known in Japan.[4] Important Japanese men leaders who showed some interest in the status of women were Fukuzawa Yukichi and Mori Arinori. Steps were taken as early as 1871 to establish public schools for girls in order to "awaken" the female sex to the "sense of responsibility"[5] that each individual must cultivate in order for Japan to become strong, and a number of private schools for girls were established as well, especially by Christian missionaries. Also in 1871 the Meiji government sent five young girls abroad to observe Western life and become models for Japanese women.[6] Thus, some attention was paid to the enlightenment of women during this era.

The development of capitalistic production also affected women's status and role, since the need for workers in the new industries of the period (especially silk production) opened the doors to a female labor force. Many young women left their villages to become wage-earning factory workers in the cities, thus stepping out of their traditional role in the home.

However, although the coming of both enlightenment thought and capitalistic production held the possibility of a change in women's status in Japan, this same period also saw the formulation of a number of laws designed to keep women in their traditional place despite modernizing changes in other sectors of society. The most important of these laws were (1) the Meiji Constitution of 1889 and the Law of Election in which no females were given voting rights (even in 1925, when "universal suffrage" was enacted, women were not included); (2) the Law on Assembly and Political Association of 1889, later incorporated into Article 5 of the Peace Police Law *(Chian Keisatsu Hō)* of 1900, which explicitly excluded Japanese women from the right to join political parties and attend political gatherings even in the form of lecture meetings;[7] and (3) the Meiji Civil Code of 1898, which spelled out women's legal inferiority in numerous ways, including classifying married women as "incapacitated persons" (along with minors, the mentally ill, the deaf, dumb, and blind) and bypassing them in favor of males in almost all questions of inheritance and succession.[8] Furthermore, although public schools were indeed begun for women, the aim was not to produce independent, self-sufficient women, but rather, as in traditional times, to train good wives and mothers who would be obedient and submissive and manage the home skillfully.[9] While the development of capitalistic production did present the opportunity for some women to become wage earners, they did not become *independent* wage earners, for most of the women workers were young, unmarried, and lived in dormitories, and their extremely low wages were used simply to supplement their parent's income as they worked "for filial piety."[10] In addition, as Japanese society modernized, individual households became less and less self-sufficient and money was needed for almost all basic necessities. Wives who did not earn a money salary thus became completely dependent on their husband's earnings and women's status sank lower and lower. It is against such a background that Fukuda Hideko's life must be seen.

Biographical Sketch[11]

Fukuda Hideko was born Kageyama Hideko on October 5, 1865, in the city of Okayama in the province of Bizen, the daughter of Kageyama Katashi, a samurai, and his wife Umeko. At the time of Hideko's birth her father was thirty-four years old and her mother forty; and the family consisted of an older sister Sawako, age nine, and an older brother Hiroshi, age six. In 1869 when Hideko was five years old her younger brother, Atsuhirō, was born.

Information on the Kageyama family ancestry is somewhat obscure, and Kageyama Katashi's role in the disturbing *bakumatsu* years between Admiral Perry's second visit and the Meiji Restoration is also unclear. It is known, however, that Hideko's father was in the lowest rank of samurai and, like others of his class, was in a rather poor financial situation.[12] Since his stipend was not sufficient to support his family, he was forced to have a side job. Thus, from 1849 until 1871 he operated a temple school *(terakoya)* and, sometime after the 1872 conscription law abolishing the samurai class was announced, he obtained employment as a policeman in Kojima-gun, a county about twelve miles from his home. He was not a very enterprising man, however, made only a very small salary, and does not seem to have been very suited to the occupation of policeman. His lack of success as the wage-earning head of his family probably had an important influence on Hideko's later insistence on independence and self-support for women.[13]

Hideko's mother, Umeko, had an even stronger influence on the development of Hideko's personality. A strong-willed woman, she was once married to another man, but is said to have left him when she was insulted by his brother's wife. After her marriage into the Kageyama family, because of her husband's insufficient salary, she had to work first as a teacher in the school run by her husband, and later as a teacher in the newly established prefectural girls' school. Hideko remembered being ashamed, as a child, of her mother's short haircut and unfashionable clothes since people snickered at her as she walked to school to teach; but later, after realizing how difficult her mother's life was in trying to take care of four children as well as help support the family, she was extremely proud of Umeko's independence and determination.[14] Hideko came to be greatly influenced by her mother's strong-mindedness, and mother and daughter grew to be very close.[15]

From Hideko's earliest childhood days, Umeko was particularly concerned with educating her, and while she left her oldest daughter at home when she taught, Umeko took Hideko to school with her. Thus, unlike her sister, who received no formal education, Hideko learned to read and write at a young age. When she was ten she entered primary school, where she was exposed to the new Western learning as well as to traditional Japanese and Chinese studies. She appears to have been an excellent student, since immediately after graduation in 1879 she became an assistant teacher in the same school. In addition to her teaching duties she also did private tutoring after school and, at her mother's suggestion, studied tea ceremony, flower arrangement, and other feminine proprieties. At the age of fifteen Hideko was well on her way to becoming an educated and indepedent woman.

At the time Hideko was graduated from primary school and becoming a teacher, Japan was going through the very turbulent and exciting period of the Popular Rights Movement (*Jiyūminken undō*) as so-called enlightenment thought was spreading throughout the country. Although Okayama was somewhat removed from the center of things, by 1882 the movement had become known to Hideko through her acquaintance with several of its Okayama members. These included her older sister's husband, Sawada Masayasu, who was a member of the prefectural assembly and a leader of the movement to petition for the establishment of a parliament; and her older brother's friend, Kobayashi Kuzuo, a young activist. Her real "awakening" to the movement, however, came in 1882, when one of the few female members of the group, Kishida Toshiko, came to Okayama to speak on the subject of women's rights.[16] A brilliant young woman and talented public speaker who had once served as lecturer to the Empress, Kishida in her speeches attacked the "evil practice"[17] of subjugation of women and expressed the belief that, in order for society to progress, men and women must have equal rights. Her ideas had a strong influence on some of Okayama's women, and after she left, they formed a group called the Women's Lecture Society (*Joshi enzetsukai*) at which they gave speeches and discussed problems relating to women. Hideko is said to have given a speech entitled "The Theory of the Equality of Human Beings" at one of these meetings. Also at about this time Hideko, her mother, and a few others established a private girls' school in order to help women get an education, and Hideko turned down her first marriage proposal.

Thus, by the time Hideko was nineteen years old, she had already become an active member of Okayama society. However, she had much wider interests, and in 1884, at the age of twenty, she decided to broaden her horizons by leaving Okayama for Tōkyō. Upon arriving in Tōkyō, she first entered a missionary girls' school, but before long, she became involved in larger national and international movements, and it is from this point that her career as one of Meiji Japan's most remarkable women begins.

Fukuda Hideko's activities for the next thirty years centered around three major concerns: (1) her opposition to Meiji government policies, (2) her dissatisfaction with the role and status of Japanese women, and (3) her search for personal happiness in her relationships with close friends and family. During different periods of her adult life one or another of these concerns assumed priority, although she was often simultaneously concerned with all of them.

Between the years of 1885 and 1889 opposition to the foreign policy of the Meiji government dominated Hideko's existence. She became associated with a remnant of the Popular Rights Movement that became involved in a plot known as the Osaka Incident. In 1885 she joined with Liberal party leaders Ōi Kentarō, Kobayashi Kuzuo, and several others in a plan to aid a Korean revolutionary movement, was arrested, and received a prison sentence of one and a half years.

Family matters took priority in Hideko's life from 1889 to 1900. From 1889 until 1891 she was involved in an unofficial common-law relationship with Ōi Kentarō, which resulted in the birth of a son in 1890. This relationship turned out to be very unhappy for Hideko, however, since Ōi became involved with another woman.[18] She left him and in 1892 married another liberal intellectual, Fukuda Yūsaku, who had been a student at the University of Michigan and was interested in the American labor movement. Between 1893 and 1899 Hideko gave birth to three sons. She and Yūsaku were leading a satisfactory married life when suddenly in 1899 he became very ill. He died in 1900 and Hideko found herself a widow with four children to support.

In order to earn money for herself and her family, Hideko turned to her earlier profession of teaching. Having from girlhood days been very sensitive to the problem of women's economic independence, she decided to establish a women's technological school for the purpose of teaching other women to be self-supporting. Her interest in education and jobs for women soon brought her in contact with another group that opposed Meiji government policies, and in 1901 she joined the Japanese socialist movement.

Association with Japanese socialists dominated Hideko's life during the years 1901–7. During this period she was connected with such organizations as the Heiminsha (Commoner's Society) and the Shin Kigensha (New Era Society), and supported various political and social causes such as the petition movement for revision of the Peace Police Law[19] and the Yanakamura Problem.[20] She also began her writing career at this time, in 1904 publishing her autobiography entitled *Half of My Life* (Warawa no han shōgai), and in 1905 publishing a novel entitled *My Reminiscences (Warawa no omoide)*.

In 1907 Hideko's attention again became focused on the status of Japanese women, and she began perhaps her most ambitious project, the publication of a journal called *Sekai Fujin (Women of the World)*. The purpose of this journal was to advocate reforms to improve the status of women in Japanese society. It began as a semimonthly magazine, but by 1908 it had become a monthly, and it ran for thirty-eight issues before it was supressed because of antigovernment articles and publication was suspended. In addition to articles by Hideko herself, this magazine also included a number of articles by such prominent Japanese socialists as Abe Isoo, Kōtoku Shūsui Sakai Toshihiko, and Ishikawa Sanshirō. Important topics discussed in it were the Japanese marriage system, revision of the Peace Police Law, social problems such as those surrounding the above-mentioned Yanakamura and the *eta* class, women's movements in foreign countries, socialist theory, economic independence for women, women's suffrage, and women's education.

The time of publication of *Sekai Fujin* appears to have been Hideko's most active period, and after its suspension, she seems to have written very little. She continued, however, to concern herself with social and political problems, and occasionally submitted articles to journals such as the newly established feminist journal *Seitō (Blue Stockings)*, begun by Hiratsuka Raichō in 1911. From 1918 on she lived with one or another of her sons, and for a time seems to have been rather poverty-stricken, supporting herself by peddling clothes.[21] In early 1927 she wrote her last article on the topic of women's suffrage. She died of a sudden illness in May of 1927 at the age of sixty-three.

It is evident from this biographical sketch that Fukuda Hideko was not the traditional obedient and submissive type of Japanese woman, submerged in the wife-mother role. Rather, she was a strong-willed woman who, breaking out of the traditional stereotype, was determined to make her voice heard on the critical issues of her day. Despite the fact that as a woman she had no right to vote and was legally barred from joining political groups and listening to political speeches, she was very concerned with questions of national and international importance and devoted much of her life to trying to enlighten other women to their significance. Let us now focus on two of the most important groups with which Hideko was associated in order to get a better understanding of the causes in which she was involved and her role in them.

Fukuda Hideko and the Osaka Incident

The first turning point in Hideko's career came as a result of her involvement in the so-called Osaka Incident of 1885 when she was but twenty years old. This incident happened as a consequence of Sino-Japanese rivalry over Korea and the Japanese government's failure to support Korean progressives in their struggle to overthrow their conservative rivals. The originators of the plot were Kobayashi Kuzuo, Hideko's old friend from Okayama days who was now secretary of the Liberal party, and Ōi Kentarō, who has been described as "perhaps the most dynamic exponent of liberty and equality in the entire Japanese liberal movement."[22] In the background of the incident was the Korean uprising of 1884. This uprising was a coup staged by Korean progressives (the Independence party), many of whom had studied in Japan and whose leader, Kim Ok-kiun, had been a student of Fukuzawa Yukichi and wanted Korea to modernize as Meiji Japan was doing. However, the government of Korea was in the hands of a conservative faction that, supported by influential representatives of China's Manchu Dynasty, was attempting to keep Korea from modernizing and trying to force the country back into a Confucian tributary relationship with China. In this power struggle the Korean progressives hoped that the Meiji government would support them. Although they did manage to convince the Japanese minister in Korea to assist them briefly, the Japanese government was not very favorably inclined toward Korean progressives because of their ties with Japanese liberals and other government critics, and it was not willing to risk war with China over their cause. Thus, at the critical moment the Japanese government withdrew support from the rebels and the attempted revolution failed.

Ōi and Kobayashi along with some other Japanese liberals became very angry at their government's refusal to help Korean progressives and, after an appeal from Korean leader Kim Ok-kiun, they decided to organize an expedition to Korea to put the Independence party back into power. Early in 1885 they drew up a proclamation of Korean independence and, espousing liberal principles and regarding themselves as "latter-day Lafayettes helping Korea toward independence and progress as Lafayette had helped America," they determined to kill themselves "for righteousness."[23]

Hideko had been studying in Tokyo at the time of the Korean uprising, and she became aware of the plight of the Korean Independence party through conversations with her friend, Kobayashi. The situation seems to have captured her youthful imagination and she became very indignant about the Japanese government's failure to support the progressives. Although Kobayashi at first did not want to tell her of his and Ōi's plans, she urged him to include her and finally he agreed. She quit school and began an active fund-raising campaign for the Korean revolutionary movement. As the scheme progressed, Hideko was also chosen to carry explosives collected for the mission, and these she moved from the Tōkyō area to Osaka. When she reached Osaka, she was asked by Isoyama Seihei, the leader of the band that was actually to go to Korea, to accompany the expedition, and she left for Nagasaki for embarkation. Meanwhile, however, the police were hot on the trail of the group. While waiting for a ship in Nagasaki, they were all caught and rounded up. Over sixty people were arrested and sent back to Osaka, where they spent the next year in detention. The trial was held in May of 1887 and Hideko and her friends were charged with crimes against the state, possessing bombs, and inciting riots. Ōi and Kobayashi received six-year sentences, while Hideko received an eighteen-month sentence.[24] As the only female member of the group, Hideko received wide publicity and she seems to have caused quite a sensation for being the first woman jailed for a political crime. Therefore, although the attempt of the Osaka Incident conspirators to promote the establishment of a progressive regime in Korea was abortive, as a result of her participation in the plot Hideko became a public figure.[25]

Hideko was released from prison along with several other political prisoners (including Ōi) under the terms of amnesty granted when the Meiji Constitution was promulgated in February of 1889.[26] Although in later writings she indicated that much unhappiness accompanied her association with the Osaka Incident,[27] and her motives for joining the group have been questioned,[28] there can be no doubt that her experiences in the incident and her prison term played an important part in determining the course of her future career. The next ten years were difficult ones for her as she became involved in various personal misfortunes, but she did not completely submerge herself in her sorrows and continued to be interested in the critical issues of the day. Soon after the death of her husband in 1900, she decided to pull herself together again, and with "great determination"[29] she set out on a "new departure."[30] The center of her attention this time was the newly formed Heiminsha.

Fukuda Hideko and the Heiminsha

The Heiminsha was an organization founded by two Japanese socialist leaders, Kōtoku Shūsui and Sakai Toshihiko, for the purpose of promoting "commonerism" (*heiminshugi*), "socialism" (*shakaishugi*), and "pacifism" (*heiwashugi*).[31] The primary organ for the spread of their ideals was a newspaper, the *Heimin Shimbun*, and in the English column in the first issue of the paper published in November 1903 they elaborated (in somewhat ungrammatical but well-meaning English) on their purposes for the benefit of interested socialists "all over the world":

> The growing complicacies [sic] of our industry and the gradual absorption of wealth of capitalists are increased more and more dissatisfaction with the existing institutions of our society among our laboring classes. The corrupted state of our political societies is, also, separating gradually those ruling classes from the rest of the people whose dissatisfaction with the actual order of things is growing rapidly. These are the causes which give birth to the socialist movements in our country now spreading all over the country. There was, however, no paper which represents our socialistic ideas . . . [so] to propagate our socialistic ideas among our community we resolved on issuing this journal. . . .
>
> It is said that liberty, equality, and fraternity are three cardinal principles of human life.
>
> In order to secure liberty amongst men, we support the principle

of democracy, and desire to destroy all class distinctions and oppressions. . . .

In order to bless men with equality we insist upon socialism and we desire to make all the means of production, distribution, and exchange the common property of men. . . .

In order to favour men with fraternity, we adhere to peace policy and we endeavor to actualize disarmaments. . . . It is our ideal that perfect liberty, equality, and fraternity for the greater mass of men should be secured, and we shall make every attempt, in realizing this idea, to rouse public opinion.[32]

In order to achieve these ideals of rousing public opinion to fight for liberty, equality, and fraternity, the Heiminsha published articles and sponsored public meetings on a variety of different relevant topics of the day. These included reporting on labor problems such as unemployment, strikes, low wages, and factory and mine accidents; discussing important socialist movements and leaders in other countries; criticizing corruption and dishonesty in Japanese government and industrial circles; and discussing socialist philosophy and the progress of socialism in Japan. However, although all of these topics were important, the Heiminsha is most famous for its stand in international affairs—that is, the pacifism of its members—and in particular their unwavering opposition to the Russo-Japanese War. Virtually every issue of the newspaper from the time of its conception in 1903 until its suspension in 1905 because of government harrassment and the arrest of its editors contained antiwar articles. An editorial discussing a resolution presented by Japanese socialists to the International Congress held in Amsterdam in 1904 summed up the attitude of the Heiminsha members toward the Russo-Japanese War:

> Whereas the Russo-Japanese war is carried on by the Capitalist governments of both nations and in consequence brings a great deal of suffering upon the working classes in Russia and Japan, therefore be it Resolved that the Japanese Socialist Association ask the members of the International Socialist Congress . . . to pass a resolution to the effect that they will do their best to urge their respective governments to take proper steps to put an end to the Russo-Japanese War as soon as possible.
> By passing this resolution we do not mean to ask our comrades in Europe and America to use some direct means to urge their respective governments to interfere with the war, but we believe our comrades can use their pens and tongues so as to make their influence felt directly.[33]

The Heiminsha is considered the first organized antiwar group in modern Japanese history.[34]

Although it seems probable that Hideko had some knowledge of the developing Japanese socialist movement through her late husband's labor interests and her earlier connection with the liberal movement, Hideko's involvement with the Heiminsha seems to have begun as a result of a chance meeting in 1901 with one of the group's leaders, Sakai Toshihiko, who happened to be living next door to Hideko.[35] At this time Hideko had just emerged from her period of personal troubles and was busy trying to support herself and her children by establishing her girls' technological school. Sakai turned out to be very sensitive to women's economic problems (he often wrote articles on the subject), and, being introduced by him to his socialist friends, Hideko became very interested in the group's activities. Before long, she was a regular visitor to the Yūrakuchō offices of the Heiminsha.

In scanning the pages of the *Heimin Shimbun*, one looks in vain for a by-lined article by Hideko. However, despite the fact that she seems not to have written anything for publication in the newspaper, there is evidence that she had some important input into the group. For one thing, she seems to have been instrumental in getting support funds for the paper, a vital part of any operation, since, according to scholar Itoya Toshio, she introduced editor Sakai to Katō Tokijirō, a wealthy doctor who became a "counselor" of the paper.[36] Second, it was evidently through Hideko's introduction that the young Ishikawa Sanshirō, who soon became one of the most active members of the socialist group, was brought into the Heiminsha.[37] Furthermore, Hideko's name is prominently listed in the section "Brief Biographies of Important Participants in the Heimin Shimbun" included in the published collection of the newspapers.[38] Thus, it is likely that she wrote or at least had some hand in writing some of the many unsigned articles.

Although one can find no evidence of Hideko's writing activity in the *Heimin Shimbun* itself, her association with the group was very important in her development as an author and a public figure, for in the years 1904–5 she wrote two full-length books that were published by the Heiminsha. The first, an autobiography up to the establishment of her techological school for girls in 1901 entitled *Half of My Life*, was a very frank account of the difficulties she encountered during her younger years. It centered around her emotional reactions to her involvement in the Osaka Incident, her years in jail, and her unhappy relationship with Ōi Kentarō. The book was written in fluent literary Japanese and was evidently widely read, since it was reprinted once in the year of its publication and five times in the following year.[39] Today it stands as Hideko's major claim to fame and it continues to be reprinted and read by a new generation of Japanese as a fascinating account of a Meiji woman's fight for liberation from the restrictions imposed on her as a result of her sex. Translation of the last paragraph of her prologue to the autobiography illustrates clearly the influence of socialist thought on her mind at the time. It also alludes to her associa-

Fukuda Hideko and the Woman's World of Meiji Japan 287

tion with the Popular Rights Movement and offers a glimpse into the complexities of her motivations:

> Previously I was angry at the monoply of political power and went along enthusiastically with the cry for people's freedom. Now I am resisting monopoly of power by the capitalists and I am involved in the salvation of the unfortunate poor. The reason why I dare to describe half of my life so frankly without hiding anything is not only to express my regrets at my past sins, but more to declare what I call a new war against society and myself.[40]

A partial recounting of Hideko's prison experience follows, translated from *Warawa no hanshōgai (Half of My Life)*:

Chapter 7   Serving My Sentence

1. The Prison Chief's Admonition

More than ten of us were sent to Ise and we were all sentenced to a one-and-a-half-year term. If this had been an ordinary trip, I could have enjoyed the scenery, which was a fine as one could make into poems, during our travels through the fifty-three stations of the Tokaido. I, however, was guarded by a policeman and wearing a persimmon-colored [prisoner's] uniform with even a rope attached to my hip, and that made me uninterested in writing even a poor poem. Besides, all the policemen who came along from Osaka were changed to other ones at Kusatsu and I missed familiar faces and spent a lonely time until we arrived at the prison at Tsu City, Mie Prefecture. Although we arrived at dusk, the prison chief must have received the news and specially arranged to come to his office. He gathered us in a waiting room and, with such a loud voice that I still now cannot forget it, he gave us the following orders: "I, Gito Hiramatsu, am the chief of this prison. You are prisoners who have been transferred here from the Osaka prison. You are now under my supervision. Needless to say, you should strictly follow the rules of this prison and try to be granted amnesty as soon as possible. Now tell me your names, occupation, and possessions." When my turn came he admonished me with a tear of sympathy saying, "I know your name without being told. You must be Kageyama Hide[ko]. Your parents must not know that you are here in front of me as a result of planning such a big scheme in spite of the fact that you are a young woman. They must be worried about where you are and what you are doing, every time it is hot or cold. You must not have been thinking about your parents. It was your unlucky mistake that you thought your deeds were for the sake of the country. You must think of your parents. One who is patriotic to his country should also be dutiful to his parents." Listening to that, I suddenly felt bitter grief, and tears of homesickness that I had tried not to show my comrades started to fall endlessly so I could not raise my face for a while. The chief was silent for a few moments and then he told me that he could understand my feeling, that now I should follow the prison rules and try to lead other delinquent women prisoners and make them repent, and that I should teach the feeble-minded citizens and should fulfill my long-time desire for loyalty and patriotism. He told me that even if my term was one and a half years, I might be given the special privilege of a reduced term, hence I should try to be released as soon as possible and go home to fulfill my duty to my parents. On later days he still encouraged me every time he came to look around the prison. I at last forgot the fact that I had a light sentence and worked hard to lead other women prisoners.

2. Women Prisoner's Assignment

I used to wake up at five o'clock in the morning and get dressed. When the chief warden came to unlock the ward I sat with the other prisoners and paid respect to her. Then we went to the well to wash our faces and had our breakfast at the working place. After that we started to work on the day's assignment; some of us sewed red kimonos, some of us wove and spun thread. I will tell you first about our sewing assignments. If we were making red kimonos without linings, we were supposed to finish three of them a day. If we were making lined kimonos, we were supposed to finish two of them a day, and if we were making quilted kimonos, we were supposed to finish one and a half of them a day. Second, our assignment of making undergarments was to finish four pairs of them a day; and for repairing old garments a regular amount of them was also assigned, depending on how large the repair job was. Thus the chief warden assigned those jobs to each of us. I originally was not assigned any of those jobs and no one would blame me even if I spent the whole day reading. I, however, wanted to correct people's mistaken impression of me by fulfilling a woman's duty so I joined voluntarily with the ordinary women prisoners to finish my assignment every day until two hours before the end of the working time, when I went back to my own ward for reading. Therefore, when I was released I was paid a suitable amount of wages and it came to more than ten yen even after the allowance was subtracted. That is to say, persons who received heavy sentences had to pay seven-tenths of their wages to the government and owned three-tenths of them. On the contrary, I was to pay three-tenths of them to the government and owned seven-tenths of them. Thus if I were to stay in prison a long time, I could save quite a large amount of money, which would be useful when I was released.

Hideko's second published work during her period of association with the Heiminsha was a novel entitled *My Reminiscences*. Although as a literary work it was not nearly so successful as her autobiography, the novel is important for the further light it sheds on Hideko's major concerns of the period. According to Hideko's biographer, Murata Shizuko, the novel centers around three major themes: (1) belief in Christian socialism,[41] (2) the need for vocational training and economic independence for women, and (3) criticism of war.[42] The antiwar theme seems to be particularly well-developed, for Hideko has her characters make such statements as:

> War is really a crime.
>
> The army is a place where no one's personality is recognized. Why should the army be allowed to exist?
>
> Why do I have to stop my studies and be drafted?[43]

Thus, Heiminsha ideals had a definite influence on Hideko's writings at this time.

Hideko's association with the Heiminsha can therefore be seen as a second turning point in her career. In the company of such dedicated socialist thinkers as Abe Isoo, Kōtoku Shūsui, Sakai Toshihiko, and Ishikawa Sanshirō, Hideko's own talents were encouraged and she developed into a social activist and writer more determined than ever to play a noticeable part in the making of modern Japan.

Conclusion

After the forced disbanding of the Heiminsha in 1905, Japanese socialists began to go through a period of ideological dispute that resulted in the division of the movement into two groups: the "Christian" wing, led by Ishikawa Sanshirō, Abe Isoo, and Kinoshita Naoe, which began a newspaper entitled *Shin Kigen* (New Era), and the "materialist" wing, led by Nishikawa Kōjirō and Yamaguchi Kōkan, which began another journal, entitled *Hikari* (Light).[44] Hideko for a time joined the staff of the more Christian-oriented *Shin Kigen*, but her eyes were focused on more important things for the future. By then, Hideko had twice been involved in the activities of radical groups that stood in defiant opposition to the prevailing policies of the Meiji government, and her association with both of them had contributed greatly to the development of her thought. From her involvement with the Osaka Incident she had learned of the excitement of being concerned with foreign policy and experienced the hardships and glories of being convicted of a crime against the state. From her involvement with the Heiminsha she had become aware of the ideals of socialism and their application to national and international affairs, and had developed her talents as a writer. However, in neither of these groups was Hideko a leader or a policymaker. She was only a loyal follower and supporter of others' ideals. Now she was finally ready to begin her own group. In 1907, at the age of forty-three, with the support of many of her

Heiminsha friends, Hideko turned to the activity that represents the pinnacle of her career, the publication of the journal *Sekai Fujin*. Having been the only woman involved in the Osaka Incident and one of few women in the early socialist movement, she became convinced of the importance of enlightening more Japanese women to the realities of politics and society, and *Sekai Fujin* became her vehicle to inspire women to participate in activities of national and international importance.

Analysis of the contents of this journal is beyond the scope of this paper. The importance of its publication can be seen, however, in the fact that it marks the beginning of the rise of a conscious, organized feminist movement in Japan.[45] The purpose of the journal, stated Hideko in the first issue, was to:

> study the nature and mission of women without regard to the laws, customs, and moral circumstances which [presently] surround them, and to encourage and develop reform movements on the basis of the true, inborn characteristics of women.[46]

As the first feminist journal in a country where the subjugation of women had been institutionalized for centuries, the publication of *Sekai Fujin* was an important landmark in modern Japanese history.

Thus, as a result of her experiences in the Osaka Incident and the Heiminsha, Fukuda Hideko became the "pioneer of the women's liberation movement" in Japan.[47] Although surrounded by laws and customs that not only discouraged but often forbade her participation in the critical issues of her day, she refused to succumb to conservative pressures and forged ahead in the long struggle to enlighten her fellow countrywomen to the responsibilities of being a citizen of modern Japan. While she died long before her efforts and the efforts of the brave women who followed her example came to any fruition (women were not given legal equality in Japan until after World War II), her name stands as an inspiration for later women activists in modern Japan.

Notes

1. Marlene J. Mayo, "Some Reflections on New Texts in Japanese History and the Current State of American Scholarship on Japan," *Journal of Asian Studies*, 31, no. 1 (November 1971): 164. See also Thomas R. H. Havens, "Women and War in Japan, 1937–45," *American Historical Review* 80, no. 4 (October 1975): 913–34, and Joyce Lebra, Joy Paulson, Elizabeth Powers, eds. *Women in Changing Japan* (Boulder, Colo.: Westview Press, 1976).

2. For a typical statement on the position of women in traditional Japanese society, see Edwin O. Reischauer and John K. Fairbank, *East Asia: The Great Tradition* (Boston, 1960), p. 556. Regarding women in feudal Japan it states, "Women were eventually excluded from inheritance and relegated to the socially and legally inferior status that they were to retain until the twentieth century."

3. See Sampei Kōko, *Nihon no Josei* (Tōkyō, 1957), p. 63.

4. These terms were used by Shidzue Ishimoto in her autobiography, *Facing Two Ways, The Story of My Life* (New York, 1935), chapters 30 and 32.
5. Ibid., p. 361.
6. Ibid., p. 362. See also Sampei, *Nihon no Josei*, p. 64. The five girls were Yamakawa Tsutematsu (age twelve); Ueda Yoshiko (age fifteen); Tsuda Umeko (age eight); Yoshimasu Ryōko (age fifteen); and Nagai Shigeko (age ten).
7. Ishimoto, *Facing Two Ways*, p. 364; also see George Oakley Totten, III, *The Social Democratic Movement in Prewar Japan* (New Haven, Conn., 1966), p. 360.
8. Sampei, *Facing Two Ways*, p. 71; also, unpublished paper by Christine Bransfield, "The Legal Status of Women Under the Meiji Civil Code of 1898" (UCLA, 1971).
9. Sampei, *Facing Two Ways*, p. 74.
10. Ibid., pp. 76, 85.
11. For biographical information on Fukuda Hideko I have relied on Murata Shizuko, *Fukuda Hideko* (Tōkyō, 1959); Itoya Toshio's commentary in Fukuda Hideko, *Warawa no hanshōgai* (Tōkyō, 1968), pp. 97–118; and Nagoya Joseishi Kenkyūkai, ed., *Fukuda Hideko Kenkyū* (Tōkyō, 1962). In this article we shall use the first name Hideko to refer to Fukuda (Kageyama) Hideko.
12. Murata, *Fukuda Hideko*, p. 4.
13. Ibid., p. 6.
14. Ibid., p. 7.
15. Ibid., p. 7. This point is also brought out in Murakami Nobuhiko, *Meiji Joseishi*, series volume "Jōkan yo Ie" (Tōkyō, 1972), p. 103; and is given further proof by the fact that at the time of her mother's death Hideko devoted a whole issue of the magazine *Sekai Fujin* to Kageyama Umeko. See Rōdōundōshi Kenkyūkai, ed., *Sekai Fujin* (Tōkyō, 1961), p. 305.
16. On Kishida Toshiko, see Murakami, *Meiji Joseishi*, pp. 74–101; and Furuya Tsunatake, "Meiji Women," *Japan Quarterly*, July–September 1962, pp. 323–24. A more recent article on Kishida is Sharon L. Sievers, "Feminist Criticism in Japanese Politics in the 1880's: The Experience of Kishida Toshika," scheduled for publication in *Signs*.
17. Murata, *Fukuda Hideko*, p. 21.
18. Ibid., p. 63. The "other woman" was a fellow activist and friend of Hideko's, Shimizu Toyoko. On Shimizu, see Murakami, *Meiji Joseishi*, pp. 127–66.
19. As noted above on Article 5 of the Peace Police Law prohibited women from engaging in political activities. Other articles of this same law forbade workers from organizing and striking, and restricted rights of suffrage and party membership in certain categories of adult males (e.g., students). See Robert A. Scalapino. *Democracy and the Party Movement in Prewar Japan* (Berkeley, Calif., 1962), p. 299.
20. The Yanakamura Problem was a case that involved farmers in the village of Yanakamura fighting against the takeover of their land by wealthy, government-supported landowners for the purposes of consolidation of land holdings. The leader of the opposition group that Hideko joined was Tanaka Shōzō. See Ōshika Takashi, *Yanakamura Jiken* (Tōkyō, 1958).
21. Itoya in Fukuda Hideko, *Warawa no hanshogai*, p. 117.
22. Hilary Conroy, *The Japanese Seizure of Korea* (Philadelphia, 1960), p. 162. On Ōi, see also Marius B. Jansen, "Ōi Kēntarō: Radicalism and Chauvanism," in *Far Eastern Quarterly*, May 1952, pp. 305–16.
23. Conroy, *Japanese Seizure*, p. 164.
24. Murata, *Fukuda Hideko*, p. 60.
25. Murakami, *Meiji Joseishi*, p. 117.
26. Jansen, "Ōi Kēnterō," p. 312; also Murata, *Fukuda Hideko*, p. 54.
27. This fact is brought out in Fukuchi Shigetaka, *Kindai Nihon Joseishi* (Tōkyō, 1963), p. 41 and is one of the underlying themes of Fukuda Hideko's memoir, *Warawa no hanshōgai*.
28. See Murakami, *Meiji Joseishi*, pp. 109–16.
29. Fukuda, *Warawa no hanshōgai*, p. 93.
30. Murata, *Fukuda Hideko*, p. 87.
31. F. G. Notehelfer, *Kōtoku Shūsui: Portrait of a Japanese Radical* (Cambridge, England, 1971), p. 94.
32. Hattori Shisō and Konishi Shirō, eds., *Shūkan Heimin Shimbun* (Tōkyō, 1953–58), 1 (English Section): 3.

33. Ibid., 2 (English Section): 18.
34. For more details on the antiwar aspects of the Heiminsha, see Matsushita Yoshio, *Meiji Taishō hansen undōshi* (Tōkyō, 1949), chapter 3.
35. Murata, *Fukuda Hideko*, p. 92.
36. Itoya in Fukuda, *Warawa no hanshōgai*, p. 114; and *Shūkan Heimin Shimbun*, 3 (English Section): 12.
37. Itoya, ibid., p. 114.
38. *Shūkan Heimin Shimbun*, 1:21.
39. Murata, *Fukuda Hideko*, p. 99.
40. Fukuda, *Warawa no hanshōgai*, p. 12.
41. I have as yet been unable to find any evidence that Hideko ever became a Christian. She was, however, in close contact with Christians such as Abe Isoo, and was presumably affected by their thinking.
42. Murata, *Fukuda Hideko*, pp. 110–17.
43. Ibid., p. 112.
44. Notehelfer, *Kōtoku Shūshi*, p. 118.
45. The Seitōsha (Blue-Stocking Society), organized by Hiratsuka Raichō in 1911, is usually considered to be the first important feminist organization in Japan, but it seems clear that Hideko's *Sekai Fujin* preceded it. See Mizuno Shikiko, "Fukuda Hideko to Hiratsuka Raichō," in Nagoya Joseishi Kenkyūkai, ed., *Fukuda Hideko Kenkyū*.
46. *Sekai Fujin*, I, 1(1907), p. 1.
47. Murata, *Fukuda Hideko*, subtitle of book.

Bibliographical Note

The above discussion of the highlights of the career of Fukuda Hideko indicates clearly that much further research on her experiences and the experiences of other important Meiji women needs to be done before any real understanding of the role of women in modern Japan can be reached. The following books and articles, should prove useful for further investigation.

In the general area of women in Meiji society there are few satisfactory English language works. Two books, Alice M. Bacon, *Japanese Girls and Women* (Boston, 1891), and Mary R. Beard, *The Force of Women in Japanese History* (Washington, D.C., 1953) give a few clues as to the situation, but neither provides any sort of structural scholarly analysis. Three shorter pieces by Japanese scholars, however, prove to be quite useful for the insights they give into the impact of Enlightenment thought on Japanese women: Jinzō Naruse, "The Education of Japanese Women," in Count Shigenōbu Ōkuma, ed., *Fifty Years of New Japan*, volume II (New York, 1909); "The Life of Women," in Yanagida Kunio, ed., and Charles S. Terry, trans., *Japanese Manners and Customs in the Meiji Era* (Tōkyō, 1957); and Furuya Tsunatake, "Meiji Women," in *Japan Quarterly*, July–September 1962. Sharon L. Sievers, *Flowers and Salt: A History of Women in Meiji Japan* (scheduled for publication by Stanford University Press), which the author has read in manuscript, is a welcome addition to English language sources on Meiji women.

As far as Japanese-language sources are concerned, the following "women's history" type books provide good introductions to the subject: Sampei Kōko, *Nihon no Josei (Women of Japan)* (Tōkyō, 1951); Inoue Kiyoshi, *Nihon Joseishi (History of Japanese Women)* (Tōkyō, 1967); Fukuchi Shigetaka, *Kindai Nihon Joseishi (History of Women in Modern Japan)* (Tokyo, 1963); and Mitsui Reiko, *Kindai Nihon no Josei (Women of Modern Japan)* (Tokyo, 1953). As the titles indicate, the former two books trace the history of Japanese women from earliest times to the present, while the latter two concentrate on the modern period. All of them survey the various political, economic, and social changes of the Meiji period and examine their impact on women. They also give brief biographical sketches of some of the more prominent women of the time. For a much more detailed treatment of women in Meiji society, Murakami Nobuhiko's recent four-volume series entitled *Meiji Joseishi (History of Meiji Women)* (Tōkyō, 1972) provides a highly interpretative analysis.

On Fukuda Hideko herself, a number of sources is available. Primary source materials consist of the writings of Fukuda herself and the memoirs of people with whom she was associated. Works by Fukuda available in local libraries are her autobiography, *Warawa no Hanshōgai (Half of My Life)* (Tokyo, 1904, reprinted 1959), and the collected issues of the journal she edited, *Sekai Fujin (World of Women)* (Rōdōundōshi Kenkyūkai, ed., Tōkyō, 1961). Friends who have written about her include Ishikawa Sanshirō in his *Jijoden (autobiography)* (Tōkyō, 1956) (see especially chapter 20, "Fukuda Hideko"); and Sakai Toshihiko in *Sakai Toshihiko Zenshū (Collected Works)* (Tōkyō, 1934). (See, for example, volume 3, pages 157–58, "Warawa no hanshōgai o yomu") ("Reading *Half of My Life*").

The most comprehensive secondary source on Fukuda is Murata Shizuko's biography, *Fukuda Hideko* (Tōkyō, 1959). It contains an excellent bibliography of Hideko's published writings. A number of interpretive articles that examine particular aspects of Fukuda's life are collected in a volume entitled *Fukuda Hideko Kenkyū (Study)*, edited by the Nagoya Joseishi Kenkyūkai (Tōkyō, 1962). Some of the articles included in this collection are "Fukuda Hideko to Yanakamura Jiken" ("Fukuda and the Yanakamura Incident"), "Fukuda Hideko to Ishikawa Sanshirō" ("Fukuda and Ishikawa"), and Fukuda Hideko no genzaiteki igi" ("The Modernity of Fukuda"). A more recent article on Fukuda is Ōki Motoko, "Fukuda Hideko ni okeru fujinkan no kiseki" ("The Locus of Feminist Views in Fukuda Hideko") in *Rekishigaku Kenkyū*, July 1967. Other secondary sources that mention Fukuda in some detail are Ōshika Takashi, *Yanakamura Jiken (Yanakamura Incident)* (Tōkyō, 1958); and Hirano Yoshitaro's biography of *Ōi Kentarō* (Tōkyō, 1966).

14 Japanese Imperialism in Korea: A Study of Immigration and Foreign Policy

Wayne Patterson

For nearly three decades after the Meiji Restoration of 1868, the Japanese government rejected the counsel of those who advocated expansion abroad. Japan followed a cautious foreign policy because of the need to direct energy inward to modernize and the need to avoid antagonizing the Western powers. By the 1890s, it was clear that the policy had been a success. Japan had modernized and had freed itself from the unequal treaties imposed by the West.

As a result of Japan's newly gained independence and big-power status, a new and bolder foreign policy could be pursued. Just as the Western powers were expanding their influence into Asia, Africa, and Latin America, Japan moved toward a leadership role in East Asia. In this process, it was Korea, Japan's nearest neighbor, that attracted the most attention. Whether the end was the modernization and enlightenment of Korea, the safeguarding of Japan's national security by assuring stability in Korea, or the expansion of the Japanese empire onto the mainland of Asia, all agreed that intervention in Korea was the proper means to serve these ends.[1] When China threatened to disrupt the attainment of these ends, the result was the Sino-Japanese War of 1894–95. When China's defeat allowed Russia to compete for influence in Korea, Japan made ready to wage its second war in a decade, the Russo-Japanese War of 1904–5. By the turn of the century, Japan's dealings with Korea were based upon the premise that conditions in Korea were of great import to Japan and that Japan was prepared to intervene in the internal affairs of Korea. It was within this pattern of dominance that Japan dealt with the problem of immigration to the United States.

In January of 1903, after seven years of trying, the Hawaiian Sugar Planters' Association brought the first of sixty-five shiploads of Korean laborers to the sugar-cane fields of Hawaii. The planters desired Koreans to offset the preponderance of Japanese laborers in Hawaii and in so doing to reduce the number of strikes by the Japanese, who held a virtual monopoly

Japanese Imperialism in Korea

of plantation labor. Moreover, Chinese labor was not available because Hawaii had recently been annexed by the United States and had to comply with the Chinese Exclusion Act of 1882. It was this movement of about 7,000 Koreans to Hawaii between 1903 and 1905 which was opposed by the Japanese government. It will be instructive to examine not only the reasons for this opposition but also the methods employed to halt it. In the end, Japanese efforts to halt Korean immigration to Hawaii form a significant, and heretofore unknown, part of the overall Japanese takeover of Korea in the first decade of the twentieth century.

At first, the arguments put forward in opposition to the immigration were based upon the quite natural desire of Japanese diplomats to protect Japanese immigrants in Hawaii and assure their economic well-being. Once the flow of Korean laborers to Hawaii was assured, the planters were no longer under any pressure to increase wages and, in fact, even entertained the notion of cutting wages now that the Japanese were in the process of losing their labor monopoly.[2] These economic considerations were not lost upon one Japanese diplomat in Seoul; and two months after the beginning of Korean immigration, one of the planters in Honolulu noted: "My letters from Korea by today's mail is [sic] not very satisfactory as there is evidence of Japanese meddling with Korean emigration, the Japanese Minister at Seoul [Hayashi Gonsuke] having informally notified the Korean Government that their emigration to Hawaii is interfering with Japanese emigrants and he therefore looks upon it as unfriendly."[3] To the great relief of the planters, it turned out that Hayashi had been acting on his own, without instructions from Tōkyō. Nothing came of the incident and Koreans continued to arrive in Hawaii.

The initial attempt to oppose the movement of Koreans to Hawaii failed because the Japanese lacked not only a strong will but also the strength to carry out any threats. Simply put, they realized that what the planters were doing was perfectly legitimate just as the action of the Korean government in allowing emigration was perfectly within its sovereign rights as an independent nation. While the Koreans were being used as strikebreakers, in effect, against the Japanese in Hawaii, and while this definitely worked an economic hardship upon the Japanese there, it certainly did not warrant extreme exertions on the part of the Japanese government. Moreover, although Japan was undoubtedly the strongest power in Korea by the early months of 1903, it was not in such a position that it could simply demand a halt to emigration. Yet the Japanese Foreign Office continued to monitor the emigration, receiving factual despatches from time to time from Japanese diplomats in Korea.[4] In addition, a more ominous note had been sounded as this minor incident left Korean emigration policy with a powerful enemy in Hayashi Gonsuke, the highest-ranking Japanese diplomat in Korea.

The second set of arguments opposing the movement of Koreans to

Hawaii came more than a year later, in the summer of 1904. The source this time was private Japanese emigration agents in Tōkyō, who were concerned that Korean immigration to Hawaii would lessen the demand for Japanese laborers and thus reduce their profits. Because the Hawaiian Sugar Planters' Association "could very well afford to reduce the number of [Japanese] men, particularly as the Korean question was turning out so satisfactorily," the number of Japanese immigrants was, in fact, reduced from 1,500 per month to 1,000 per month.[5] Although undoubtedly motivated by their own narrow economic interests, the argument of the Japanese emigration agents added a new element to the issue, the national interest of Japan. The protest came in a letter to the Japanese foreign minister, Baron Komura Jutarō:

> Everyone is sure that the nation profits from emigration enterprises. Specifically, emigration to Hawaii brings more profit to our imperial nation. Emigration enterprises for Hawaii were begun in 1885 by the government and were then transferred to private enterprises in 1894. Until now, the number of emigrants to Hawaii numbered about 160,000 and those still remaining now in Hawaii number about 70,000. The number of those emigrants is approximately more than half of the total population of Hawaii. Therefore, many kinds of facilities—fifty or sixty elementary schools, charity hospitals—were built and the Japanese colony resembles a self-governing body. Accordingly, trade between Japan and Hawaii has been making great strides every year and the total amount of remittances from the emigrants exceeds one hundred million yen a year. Recently, the total amount of donations for the Artillery Ministry made by the emigrants in Hawaii has totalled about ninety thousand yen since the opening of the Russo-Japanese War, and for the first national loan they desired to buy three million yen worth of bonds. Since the emigrants have succeeded in Hawaii they can afford to contribute to the public profit as mentioned above; however, they could not save even one yen in Japan before emigrating. I believe that the success of the emigrants in the future is also promising. However, since last year an American has been running the Oriental Development Company [sic] and recruiting Koreans who desire to emigrate to Hawaii in competition with Japanese emigrants. The number of emigrants is increasing and as a result the success of the Japanese emigrants in the future will be adversely affected. I think that we should not stand by and watch the Korean emigrants suddenly encroach upon the Japanese emigration which has been established for about twenty years and seems to be prospering. If the Koreans are actually encroaching, those facilities such as schools and hospitals for which the agents for the emigrants have been raising funds for several years might become useless. I believe that we should take some measures to meet this situation. I recommend the following plan: some Japanese should ask permission from the Korean government to handle the emigration business for the whole country. On

receiving permission, you should appoint an influential person to organize the company, or the government itself run the business for Korean emigrants to Hawaii as long as the Koreans would not encroach upon the rights of the Japanese emigrants. As I would like to ask the Korean government to permit the emigration business in the near future, I hope that you will support us so far as you think proper. I tell you this in advance.[6]

When more than six months elapsed without a reply from Komura, who had ignored the appeal, a second letter went out, in February of 1905, covering many of the same points and concluding:

> We deplore deeply the fact that the public profits from the emigration to Honolulu, formerly great, have been decreasing as a result of the Korean emigration as mentioned above. We want you to discuss ways of preventing Koreans from emigrating to Honolulu in order to protect the Japanese emigrants, since the Korean government is now supervised by the Japanese government. Since we believe that the problem is seriously disrupting the national profit at a time when we are expanding the national dignity in the world, we dare harm your dignity by making these comments.[7]

Even though the agents appealed to the national interest, Komura and the Japanese Foreign Office remained unmoved even after the receipt of this second letter. They remained unconvinced that lessened demand and continued low wages for Japanese in Hawaii and falling trade and remittances justified official intervention to halt Korean emigration. As a result, this second effort to stop Koreans from going to Hawaii ended in failure. However, there was a portion of that second letter from the emigration agents in Tokyo that would take on extraordinary import quite soon when a third reason arose to prevent Korean immigration to Hawaii, a reason so powerful that the effort to halt the immigration would be sponsored by Foreign Minister Komura himself.

This third and most powerful reason surfaced less than a month later, in March of 1905, and was contained in a cable from the Japanese Consul in San Francisco to Komura. The cable read: "State Senate of California passed March 1st a resolution to call attention of the President and State Department to menace of Japanese immigration and to request that immediate action will be taken by treaty or otherwise to limit and diminish the further immigration of Japanese labourers in the United States. The resolution will probably pass the Assembly today."[8]

This was a matter of serious concern to Foreign Minister Komura. In 1882 the United States had passed the Chinese Exclusion Act because of the pressure of public opinion, mainly from California, against the large number of Chinese immigrants. Now, a generation later, similar pressure was being exerted on the American government from California to pass a

Japanese exclusion act. While it was one thing to bar Chinese—after all, China was still backward in Japan's eyes—it would be quite another to bar immigrants from the modern nation of Japan. It was more than a question of racism pure and simple. Japan prided itself on having become a member of the advanced nations of the world. If America were to treat Japan in the same way as China, all the gains of the Meiji period would be for nought. To put Japan in the same league as hapless China would be a devastating psychological blow to Japan's dignity.

It was clearly in the interest of Japan to prevent the United States from passing a Japanese exclusion act. One solution was offered by the Japanese minister to the United States in Washington in a lengthy cable to Komura:

> You are now doubly fully informed by our Consul-General at Honolulu of the impossibility of preventing Japanese immigrants to Hawaii from coming to the United States and also by our Consul at San Francisco, of passage through State Senate and Assembly of California of resolution to take necessary measures to restrict Japanese immigration. In my opinion, it is important that our position regarding the matter should be clearly defined, informally communicated to the United States Government, and if needs be, American public by means of press. In fact, Japanese immigrants to the United States proper coming directly from Japan are not of a large number on account of restrictions placed on them in Japan and, if those coming via Honolulu are excepted, they are only a few thousand of better class people but this fact is not universally known, and because larger number of them mostly composed of those from Honolulu are of lower class, it is considered that Japanese emigration is unrestricted and injurious to American interests, not speaking of uneasiness caused to people of Pacific Coast in consequence of superior strength by Japan in the War as reported by our Consul at San Francisco. I would submit for your consideration question as to whether Imperial Government take measures to prohibit Japanese or any other immigrants of the labouring class to Hawaii or other insular possessions to come to the United States proper. I am not certain whether or not the United States Government can take such measure, but if approved, I may propose to the United States Government to take the matter into consideration to appease people of Pacific Coast.[9]

Takahira was clearly choosing the lesser of two evils. That is, it would be better to have the American government enact a law preventing the Japanese in Hawaii from moving to the mainland than to have it enact a Japanese exclusion act. Ironically, it may have been this suggestion from the Japanese minister in Washington which caused President Roosevelt two years later to issue an executive order preventing the movement of Japanese and Korean laborers from Hawaii to the mainland United States.

In any event, it was clear that the situation was serious and that drastic measures such as Takahira's proposal had to be considered. Japan had for some time been aware of the problem of the migration of Japanese immigrants from Hawaii to California and had tried to devise ways to prevent it. Since it was legally impossible to prevent immigrants from going to California after reaching Hawaii, other methods were tried. Upon leaving Japan, for instance, emigrants were told that they were prohibited from moving on to California without the permission of the Japanese consul in Honolulu, Saito Miki. In addition, the words "To Hawaii Only" were written in English in passports issued to Japanese emigrants to Hawaii.[10] Neither of these ruses was effective as the Japanese in Hawaii soon learned that there was no legal barrier preventing them from going to California, where the fruit orchards paid up to twice the wages of the sugar plantations of Hawaii.

Thus, Foreign Minister Komura was faced with a difficult problem. Japan migration from Hawaii to California had to be stopped or else the United States would very probably enact a Japanese exclusion act. Yet attempts to bluff and intimidate Japanese emigrants had proved ineffective, and Takahira's proposal, while representing the lesser of two evils, still smacked of official action against Japanese immigrants by the United States government. It was Komura's job to find a way to prevent Japanese from moving from Hawaii to California that was not only effective but also avoided official American action against Japan.

A third alternative to ruses or official American action suggested itself to Komura in a passage that he had read in the second letter from the Tokyo emigration agents. The agents, while not aware of the political consequences, were quite astute in ascertaining the basic reasons for Japanese migration from Hawaii to California:

> Since the balance between the demand for and the supply of labor has been lost, the wages of the laborers are falling because of competition, and the attitude of the employers toward the laborers is changing. We suppose that the Japanese immigrants cannot compete with the Koreans when wages are decreasing, since the Korean immigrants do not need money for sanitation and education, and are satisfied only with sufficient money for food and clothes. As a result, there is a tendency for the number of Japanese immigrants trying to move to the American continent by boat to increase, despite the prohibition law, while the Korean immigrants to Honolulu are increasing. We are afraid that this situation will destroy the standard of living of the Japanese immigrants.[11]

Since Komura had received the agents' letter in February, it was still fresh in his mind when, a couple of weeks later, he received the cable from San Francisco telling of the possible political consequences of continued large-scale migration of Japanese from Hawaii to California. On the same day that he received the cable from San Francisco, Komura sent a letter to Saito Miki, the Japanese consult in Honolulu, part of which read: "I regret for the sake of our Japanese emigration businesses that Korean emigration has shown these successes in such a short time—less than two years. Looking at the future from the situation of today, I think that we cannot waste one day and it is necessary to consider measures to prevent Koreans from emigrating to Hawaii." The remainder of the letter sought information about Korean immigration.[12] On the same day, Komura also drafted identical letters to Japanese consuls in the four Korean cities of Inch'ŏn, Mokpo, Kunsan, and Pusan to solicit additional information on the subject.[13]

The issue of Korean immigration to Hawaii had thus become joined with Japanese immigration to the United States. The cable from San Francisco and the drafting of the letters to Hawaii and Korea that occurred on the same day make it evident that Komura, despite his professed concern for the welfare of the emigration businesses of Tokyo, was reacting to adverse public opinion in California. Komura now agreed with the emigration agents that Korean emigration should be stopped, but for different reasons. If Korean immigration to Hawaii were halted, then the Japanese laborers there would retain their labor monopoly. Consequently, when striking for higher wages and better working conditions on the plantations, the Japanese would succeed because their strikes could no longer be broken by Koreans. As a result, the economic conditions for Japanese workers in Hawaii would improve, making California less attractive economically. Fewer Japanese would be induced to migrate to the mainland, reducing the anti-Japanese sentiment on the coast and therefore reducing pressure on Washington to exclude Japanese.

If imperialism consists of both ends as well as means, then Japan had settled upon the ends to be pursued in this problem. Here finally was an issue important enough to cause Komura to abandon his noncommittal attitude toward Korean immigration and to pressure the Japanese government to intervene actively. Simply put, Korean immigration to Hawaii would have to be sacrificed to prevent Japan from losing face internationally.

Yet Japan still lacked the means to enforce its will upon the Korean government. While Japan certainly had a preponderance of power in Korea in the spring of 1905, it nevertheless needed an opportunity to press for the end of Korean emigration. Japanese imperialism at this point was still incomplete because it lacked means, not ends. So, aside from writing to Hawaii and Korea for information, Komura could only await developments in Korea for an opportunity. His wait was not to be a long one.

Only one month later Komura read in the local newspaper that the Korean government itself had temporarily suspended the emigration of Koreans to Hawaii and Mexico.[14] The good fortune of this move was not lost on Komura, who cabled the Japanese minister in Korea, Hayashi Gonsuke, the following day: "It is very convenient that the Korean government has recently prohibited the emigration of Korean workers because the Koreans abroad compete with our Japanese emigrants and are in confrontation with them. . . . In light of this situation, please consider maintaining the prohibition for some time."[15]

This was just the opportunity Komura needed to press his aim to halt the emigration of Koreans. What Komura did not know was that Hayashi Gonsuke, who had been opposed to the emigration almost from the beginning, had taken action in the matter without waiting for orders from Tōkyō. Hayashi's role in these early stages was crucial. The Korean government had learned about the difficulties surrounding the emigration of some Koreans to Mexico and the Korean foreign minister "originally intended to prohibit the emigration of Koreans to Mexico, but that upon consultation with His Excellency the Japanese Minister to Korea, the Japanese Minister [Hayashi Gonsuke] pointed out that it would be unfair to discriminate in favor of any emigration Company or country and that if one were stopped all must stop."[16] So, unlike the first time, when he had acted on his own, this time Hayashi had correctly anticipated Komura's thinking on Korean emigration and had effected the extension of the prohibition to include Hawaii. Thus, the first step had been taken in the process of enforcing Japan's will upon Korea in the emigration issue. Now Hayashi and Komura could turn their attention to preventing the renewal of emigration, as Komura's cable to Hayashi revealed.

The second step in this case of Japanese imperialism in Korea presented the Japanese government with the necessity of solving short-term, immediate concerns before turning to longer-range and more crucial concerns. By the middle of April 1905, the letters soliciting information that Komura had sent out the previous month began to bear fruit. Detailed information on emigration was now being accumulated by the Japanese Foreign Ministry in Tokyo.[17] It was the kind of information that Foreign Minister Komura needed to deal effectively with the issue. Disquieting to Komura, however, were indications contained in letters written after the Korean government had prohibited emigration that Koreans still continued to leave for Hawaii.

Worried that the Korean Foreign Office was lax in enforcing the ban, Komura cabled Hayashi in Seoul instructing him to inform Japanese consuls in the port cities of Korea to keep their areas under surveillance and to exert pressure to ensure enforcement of the prohibition.[18] The disturbing reports continued,[19] causing Komura to cable consuls in Inch'ŏn and Chinnamp'o,[20] and, a week later, to the Japanese chargé d'affaires in Korea, Hagihara Morikazu, who was the highest-ranking Japanese diplomat in Korea as Hayashi Gonsuke, the Japanese minister to Korea, had returned to Tōkyō briefly. Komura told Hagihara that he had "received a cable telling of the Korean government's having repealed the law against the emigration of Korean laborers. Please check if it is true and answer by cable."[21] Two days later, Hagihara answered:

> There is no evidence of the government's having repealed the law against the emigration of Korean laborers which you mentioned in cable number 95. But in the instructions dispatched to each controlling center at the ports, the government permitted those Korean laborers who had contracted before the prohibition law to emigrate regardless of the law. I suppose that the misunderstanding might have come out of this instruction.[22]

Even as Hagihara was reassuring Komura that the prohibition was still in effect, Japanese pressure on the Korean government to tighten enforcement increased. A week later, a Korean newspaper reported that "the Japanese Chargé d'Affaires [Hagihara] wrote to the [Korean] Foreign Office stating that the ninety Korean emigrants who had recently left Chinnamp'o for Hawaii had been collected after the prohibition had been declared and that therefore the *kamni* [port official] of both Chinnamp'o and Chemulp'o [Inch'ŏn] should be punished."[23] Three weeks later, after Hayashi had returned to his post in Seoul, the Japanese minister continued to apply pressure on the Korean government by lodging a formal request with the Korean foreign minister to order the *kamni* of every port city to stop all emigrants."[24]

While Hagihara and Hayashi were busy twisting arms in Seoul, the Japanese Foreign Ministry in Tokyo decided to investigate the Japanese link to Korean emigration, as the Koreans changed ships and underwent quarantine checks in Kobe. Accordingly, the following letter was sent to the prefectural governor:

> The emigration of Koreans for the purpose of earning money abroad has already been prohibited by the Korean government. But we have been informed of the following: since the prohibition law, agents for the emigrants have been skillfully evading the law and have been bringing some ten or twenty laborers to Kobe Bay by every ship on the pretense that they are coming to Japan. The emigrants are guided to one building in the port for lodging and when they total approximately one or two hundred, they start for Honolulu as emigrants for Hawaii. Please confirm the credibility of this information and if it is true please inform us of the names of the agents and the details after the inquiry as soon as possible.[25]

After the governor replied two weeks later that the reports were untrue,[26] Komura was finally satisfied that by mid-June the prohibition was finally being enforced by the Korean government with less than gentle prodding by Japanese diplomatic officials in Korea. It had taken nearly three months to accomplish this second step. Now that the immediate problem of proper enforcement of the prohibition had been solved, the Japanese government could now turn to the longer-range aspects of preventing the renewal of Korean emigration.

Japan was able to take the third step in its policy of imperialism because of political factionalism and mismanagement in the Korean government. When emigration had begun in early 1903, the Korean government had created the Department of Emigration within the Imperial Household Department to manage the process and issue passports. The order creating this new department also included rules and regulations governing the operation of the department and the safeguarding of the emigrant. The head of the Imperial Household Department, Yi Yong-ik, however, did not approve of emigration and soon afterward canceled the order creating the department. Emigration still continued, of course, as passporting functions were assumed by the Foreign Office. However, when the order creating the Department of Emigration was canceled, the accompanying rules and regulations were also abolished along with the department. From that point on, emigration proceeded on a dubious legal basis, with no rules to protect emigrants.

Hayashi Gonsuke, who had followed the situation closely from his vantage point in Seoul since the beginning of emigration, was well aware of the vulnerability of the Korean government regarding appropriate regulations. The Japanese minister had first approached the Korean government in June 1904 to request a copy of the regulations. When nine months passed without his request's being honored, Hayashi's discovery of a weak link in the emigration process was confirmed.[27] This weakness was to be exploited as an integral part of Japan's imperial strategy to prevent the renewal of Korean emigration to Hawaii. Japan's strategy was revealed when the recruiter of the emigrants talked with Yi Ha-yŏng, the Korean foreign minister, shortly after Yi had talked with Hayashi. The recruiter wrote that Foreign Minister Yi had "asked the writer to stop the work until such a time as the rules and regulations contemplated could be put into effect. . . . The writer pointed out to Mr. Yi that he would personally be very glad to work under such rules and regulations as the Korean Government saw fit to enact to protect their countrymen and that the enforcement of the same would have his fullest sympathy and support."[28]

The full extent of Japanese strategy became clear two weeks later, when the Korean Foreign Office drew up what it deemed to be appropriate regulations governing emigration only to have the new rules rejected.[29] While no explanation was given for the rejection, it became increasingly evident that Minister Hayashi had argued successfully that the new rules were inadequate. Japan's position was that the regulations had to be based upon a complete and thorough investigation of emigration and that until the Korean Foreign Office was willing to invest its resources in such a manner, Japan would continue to veto any emigration rules that might be drawn up. By erecting stiff requirements for new regulations, Japan could be fairly confident that Korean government compliance would probably fall short. An expedient method to prevent the renewal of emigration to Hawaii had been found nestled snugly within the folds of "humanitarian concern" for the welfare of Korean emigrants.

The lack of suitable emigration regulations was not the only weakness that the Japanese government exploited. There was a second, corollary issue that, like the first, can be traced to mismanagement within the Korean government. Despite the urgings and advice of Americans, Russians, Japanese and Koreans in Korea and Hawaii, the Korean government consistently refused to send a consul to Honolulu. By 1905, there was still no Korean consul in Honolulu. Moreover, the Korean government permitted emigration to Mexico early that year despite the fact that there were no Korean diplomats in that country. The Korean government had failed miserably in providing diplomatic protection for its emigrants abroad—these actions were so basic to normal diplomatic intercourse that Japan could argue with some justification that emigration could not proceed until this matter also was solved.

It would be difficult at such a late date, the spring of 1905, for Korea to appoint diplomats to Honolulu and Mexico. Since the beginning of hostilities with Russia, Japan had been pressing the Korean government to recall all its missions abroad and to replace them with Japanese officials.[30] By the fall of 1904, in a specific reference to Hawaii, Minister Hayashi told the Korean government that, if it was not prepared to establish a consulate there, it should put the matter into the hands of the Japanese consulate.[31] Soon afterward, Hayashi began spreading rumors around Seoul that the Korean emperor had in fact appointed the Japanese consul in Honolulu, Saito Miki, as honorary Korean consul there.[32] As Japanese strength grew in Korea, so too did the pressure to replace Korean diplomats abroad with Japanese.[33] By May of 1905, the Korean government acceded to Japan's demands and appointed Saito Miki the honorary consul for Korea at Honolulu.[34]

These moves by Japan, preempting Korean initiatives, made independent action by the Korean government much more difficult. It was also convenient for Japan to have one of its own diplomats oversee the Korean emigrants in Hawaii, where anti-Japanese agitation was becoming more forceful. The Japanese Foreign Office was able to coerce the Korean government in the issue of diplomatic representation abroad because of the increasing diplomatic support that Japan was able to muster over all aspects of Korean-Japanese relations. It was within this context of ever-increasing strength vis-à-vis Korea that Japan managed the immigration issue.

When the Russo-Japanese War broke out in early 1904, Japan forced upon Korea a treaty of alliance, embodied in the protocol of February 23, 1904, which made Korea a virtual protectorate of Japan. Great Britain, Japan's ally since 1902, did not object, nor did the United States under President Theodore Roosevelt. Russian influence, affected adversely as the war progressed, became nil. With a free hand in Korea, Japan could announce that "the Korean government in regard to the making of any treaty, conducting any diplomatic intercourse, or conceding any franchises or contracts to a foreigner, must consult the Japanese government beforehand." The second protocol, signed on August 22, 1904, also stipulated that a Japanese (Megata Shutarō) be appointed adviser to the Finance Department and that a foreigner, recommended by Japan, be appointed adviser to the Foreign Office. The latter was an American, Durham White Stevens.[35]

Under these conditions it would be difficult for the Korean government to act independently on any issue, much less on emigration. However, in the summer of 1905, the issue of emigration came to symbolize for Korea the loss of its own sovereignty as an independent nation. Within the Korean Foreign Office the decision was made to reassert Korean independence by obtaining the renewal of Korean emigration to Hawaii. Japan was equally determined that any such attempt to assert independence from Japan would not succeed.

The Korean government had determined that in order to effect the renewal of emigration it would have to draw up rules and regulations that would be acceptable to Japan. By June of 1905 it became obvious that prerequisite to the drafting of these rules, there would have to be a fact-finding tour of Hawaii and Mexico by a high-ranking Korean diplomat. Upon the completion of the investigation, suitable regulations would be drawn up that could not fail to meet Japan's strictest criteria. That done, it would be difficult for Japan to justify continued opposition to Korean emigration. More important for Korea, it would lend symbolic support for its reassertion of independence in the conduct of foreign relations. The stakes had been raised far higher than the movement of several thousand laborers and had now become a crucial bone of contention between imperial Japan and faltering Korea.

The Korean vice-minister of foreign affairs, Yun Ch'i-ho, was selected to make the trip. His dairy provides valuable details about the emigration issue:

> Mr. Stevens in his audience with the Emperor on the 15th inst. suggested to His Majesty that I be sent to Japan and also to Hawaii to investigate the condition of the Korean emigrants to the Sandwich Islands. His Majesty promised he would. Mr. Stevens had a talk with Yi Ha-yong, Hayashi and Megata on the subject. They all agreed that it was an excellent idea, but none of them seems particularly anxious to put the proposal into effect.[36]

Yun prepared to depart, even though Stevens had not mentioned the need to visit Mexico. In mid-July, Yun arrived in Tōkyō on the first leg of his investigation. While in Tōkyō, Yun visited the Japanese Foreign Ministry to discuss his mission:

> Concerning the controlling regulations, the Trade and Commerce Director of the Foreign Ministry [Ishii Kikujirō] had several talks with the Vice-Minister of the Korean Foreign Ministry, Mr. Yun Ch'i-ho, when Yun came to Tokyo last year. At that time the director gave him a full explanation of our protecting laws for emigrants and Vice-Minister Yun agreed with most of our points. They concluded that after going back to Korea, Yun would have a talk with Mr. Stevens, who is adviser to the Korean Foreign Office, and would try to get the Korean government to draw up the proper regulations.[37]

While the preceding Japanese account shows Yun in apparent agreement with the Gaimushō officials, his diary reveals that he was aware of Japanese duplicity in the matter:

> While in Tokyo, I learned that the Japanese Govern't intends to keep Koreans out of Hawaii, the Eldorado for the Japanese laborers. Now just think of it. Japan whose surplus coolies, titled and otherwise, pour into Korea in tens and hundreds of thousands to grab everything in sight, to kick and cuff and cuss the Koreans as ingrates and savages for not being grateful for being kicked, cuffed and cussed. This generous and altruistic Japan grudges the few miserable dollars which the Korean laborers may pick up in the dust and mud of the Hawaiian cane-fields![38]

The Japanese Foreign Ministry was aware that Yun

> seems to be afraid that the Japanese government is completely against the emigration of Koreans to Hawaii and intends to stop it. I told him of our view that the Japanese government is not completely against the emigration and is willing to allow emigration with certain limitations when the Korean government enacts a law similar to the protection law for Japanese emigrants. . . . I also told him that we have no objection to the voyage of Mr. Yun.[39]

Despite his misgivings, Yun was determined to carry out his mission, and by the end of August he was ready to depart for Hawaii. Yun's diary notes that, while the Japanese government did not mind his visit to Hawaii, it did not seem enthusiastic about the proposed visit to Mexico:

> Last night, returning from the famous teahouse of Akasaka Park where we had been invited by the Nisshū Insurance Company, I got a telegram from the Seoul F. O. about 12. It ran: "Proceed to Hawaii and

Mexico. Transmitted 1000 yen to the Japanese Bank, Seoul." Busy all day going about to get ready for my trip. Stevens said, "Oh never mind Mexico. Besides, 1000 yen—only 500 dollars U.S. gold hardly enough for the Hawaiian trip."[40]

Nonetheless, Yun left Tōkyō for Yokohama and on August 30

went on board of the S. S. Manchuria at 11 A.M. Weighed anchor at 4 P.M. Well, good-bye to Japan for a month. . . . Oba, the agent of the Taeryuk Sikmin Hoesa [Continental Colonization Company], came on board to see me off. I don't like him very much—too much cunning. He told me that the Taeryuk Hoesa men are opposed to the Korean immigration to the Hawaiian island as that would interfere with the Japan's immigration and that they would like to see the Korean immigration directed to countries—like Mexico for instance—where Japanese are not found. I see from this little talk why the Japanese Legation in Seoul was so anxious to stop the Korean emigration.[41]

Upon his arrival in Honolulu, Yun "stated yesterday that there were no stories of ill-treatment of Koreans in Hawaii. He said he heard of ill-treatment of Koreans in Mexico and he was going there to investigate."[42] The problems in Mexico, in which Korean emigrants were rumored to have been sold into slavery on sisal plantations there, had been the cause for the Korean government to prohibit emigration in April. While Yun's investigation would have to be complete and included visiting both Hawaii and Mexico, it was the Mexican situation that was the main stumbling block. If the Mexican situation were fully investigated by Yun, then much of Japan's objections to emigration could be overcome.

By the fall of 1905 then, it became increasingly evident that Korean emigration to Hawaii depended upon a complete investigation by Yun, if rules satisfactory to Japan were to be drafted. However, a complete investigation by Yun required that he visit not only Hawaii but also Mexico, where the real problem was. The reluctance of Stevens to allow Yun to travel to Mexico thus takes on added significance. For Japan, a situation had developed in which the path of least resistance would be simply to prevent Yun from going to Mexico. The result would be an incomplete report, inadequate to serve as a basis for the drawing up of new emigration rules. It was in the interest of the Japanese government to prevent Yun's trip to Mexico not only because it might lead to the renewal of emigration but also because it might serve as a prelude for the establishment of a Korean legation in Mexico. Such a move on the part of the Korean government would conflict with Japan's desire to replace Korean missions abroad with Japanese diplomatic missions already stationed in those places. Moreover, it would signal a degree of independence in foreign policy that Japan at this time would regard as intolerable. The following report, which circulated in Seoul at this time, lends credence to this interpretation:

Mr. Hayashi has proposed to the Korean government that the interests of Korean emigrants in Mexico be cared for by the Japanese Consul in that country. It is thought no direct answer will be given until after Yun Ch'i-ho has made his report of conditions as he finds them on his tour of inspection.[43]

But how could Japan prevent Yun from going to Mexico now that he was already halfway there in Hawaii? The answer lay in his financial situation. Yun had arrived in Hawaii on September 8 and immediately began to visit all plantations that employed Koreans. Yun had been given one thousand yen, about 500 dollars, for his traveling expenses; but after nearly two weeks in Hawaii, Yun had spent most of the sum. His diary records:

By the way, this morning Mr. Saito came and showed me a telegram from F. O. Seoul which ran thus: "Get 490 Yen from Specie Bank. Yun Ch'i-ho travelling expenses Mexico. Foreign Office, Seoul." Mr. Saito went with me to the Bank and cashed the money 490 Yen—$242. Mr. Swanzy found out from a man who had been to Mexico that the trip to and from Yucatan would take four weeks and cost $360 in travelling expenses alone.[44]

Consequently, on the following day, Yun sent the following cable to Seoul: "490 Yen received. 300 American dollars more for Mexico. Yun."[45]

Upon receiving Yun's cable, the Korean Foreign Office asked the Finance Department to forward the necessary funds.[46] It now became a simple matter for Japan to prevent Yun from traveling to Mexico: Megata Shutarō, the Japanese adviser to the Korean Finance Department, simply vetoed the expenditure.[47] Although he was in Hawaii, Yun had no alternative but to return to Korea with his mission only partly accomplished. Japan had apparently prevailed in the emigration issue.

Yun knew that the cause was all but lost. Nonetheless, what he had learned in Hawaii was enough to convince him that emigration to Hawaii, at least, should be restored. Yun revealed his state of mind on the matter on the day of departure when he met with the planters:

The President stated that Mr. Yun had visited all of the Islands and Plantations and is returning to Korea by the steamer leaving today; that he had requested another meeting with the Trustees before departing to finally discuss the matter of Korean immigration. Mr Yun stated that he had visited all the Plantations where there are Koreans and that he found that the Koreans were well treated by the managers. . . . Mr. Yun stated that his business was to find out how the Koreans are doing here and to report what he has seen and heard to his Government; that a renewal or suspension of the immigration to these Islands rests with the Government, but that he would strongly recommend a renewal of the immigration.[48]

Arriving back in Japan in mid-October, Yun came face to face with a set of circumstances that seemed to shift the balance in Korea's favor in the emigration issue. These more favorable circumstances arrived in the form of a cable from the Korean Foreign Office in Seoul with 600 yen for Yun to make the trip to Mexico after all. Of course, the equivalent of 300 dollars was insufficient for Yun to travel from Tōkyō to Mexico, but, more important, where had the money been obtained? Perhaps there was more to be had? The Japanese had certainly not relented, allowing Megata to disburse funds from the Korean Finance Department. The money, in fact, had come from none other than the Korean emperor himself.[49]

Having circumvented Japanese efforts to deny Yun the necessary funds, it now seemed very likely that the trip to Mexico might be made after all. The prospect made the Japanese very nervous and Yun reported three days later that stronger and more direct Japanese action was in the offing to prevent the trip: "Lunch at the Tokio Club with Stevens. Mr. Hayashi was of the party.... At the suggestion of Hayashi, Stevens sent a telegram to Seoul advising the Foreign Office not to send me to Mexico."[50] Six days later, Yun commented on this startling turn of events:

> The Tokio weather, since I have been here, has been miserable. Rainy, gloomy, and chilly—like the Japanese in their attitude to Korea.... Stevens phoned me this morning that Pak Jai Soon [the new Korean foreign minister] had answered his telegram insisting that I should go to Mexico. I sent another long message insisting that I should be in Seoul. So far as I am concerned I am willing enough to go, if I had money enough.... In Pak Jai Soon's telegram to Stevens, the Yen 600 was said to have been given by His Majesty. Stevens thinks that the Palace is anxious to send me to Mexico not out of any solicitude for the Koreans in Yucatan but of some political motive—to show the foreign nations that the Korean government is managing its own foreign affairs—In either case I do not think the Palace is wrong for this once.[51]

Even though Yun still lacked sufficient funds, the Japanese Foreign Ministry was taking no chances that additional money might be forthcoming to enable Yun to go to Mexico. So on the same day, Komura cabled Hagihara Morikazu in Seoul:

> The Korean Emperor has demanded that Yun Ch'i-ho take an official tour to Mexico to inspect the situation of the Korean emigrants there, but Yun requested the Emperor to stop plans for his official tour to Mexico since Stevens expected Yun to return to Korea soon. In spite of his desire, the Emperor insisted on the necessity of Yun's tour and had the Foreign Minister order his tour. Since Stevens has been in Mexico once before, he can tell the Emperor sufficiently about the situation in Mexico if he is requested to. Consequently, it is not neces-

sary now to insist on Yun taking the tour. We hope that you will acquaint the Emperor with this information and try to persuade him to cancel this order.[52]

On the following day, Hagihara answered:

> This letter concerns Cable Number 252. I was informed that the Korean Foreign Minister had despatched a cable to Yun through [Korean] Minister [to Japan] Cho saying, "Inform Yun Ch'i-ho to return." Since that is a sufficient order for Yun, he can leave for Korea soon. If someone objects in the Korean imperial court, I, as Minister, will speak on Yun's behalf. I hope that you will tell this to Yun Ch'i-ho and persuade him to come back to Korea soon.[53]

Hagihara, acting in Hayashi's absence, had coerced the new foreign minister of Korea into disobeying the wishes of his sovereign and ordering Yun to return to Seoul. Yun, still in Tōkyō and unaware of this correspondence, cabled: "Traveling expenses for Mexico not come. Shall I return? Answer." Later that evening he received the message to return to Seoul.[54] Thus ended Yun's last hope of going to Mexico and, with it, Korea's last hope to renew emigration to Hawaii. Symbolically, it also represented the end of an independent foreign policy for Korea.

The editor of the influential *Korea Review*, Homer Hulbert, after visiting Hawaii, took an indirect slap at Japanese policy:

> Hon. T. H. Yun who was sent from Korea to look after the interests of the Koreans here has just finished his investigation and has returned to Korea. . . . I do not see how he can do otherwise than advise that the coming of Koreans to Hawaii be not discouraged. Everything that I heard and saw made me believe that no one who has Korea's welfare at heart can continue to oppose their coming here.[55]

Hulbert's editorial and Yun's return to Seoul on November 6 made no difference to Japan. Within two weeks Marquis Itō Hirobumi had arrived in Korea and forced Korea into a protectorate of Japan. Korea had formally lost its independence and now all matters pertaining to emigration resided in the hands of the Japanese resident-general's office, which announced that "from now on all passports, demanded . . . by Koreans who wish to leave their country . . . will be issued at the office of the Resident-General instead of at the Korean Foreign Office as heretofore."[56]

In January of 1906, the American recruiter of Korean laborers for Hawaii approached the American Legation in Tōkyō for aid:

> A period of nine months now having elapsed, it would seem that ample time had been had to have investigated emigration conditions and to have enacted suitable laws and regulations by which emigra-

tion could be carried on. The delay and interruption that this work has had has been of great financial loss to me, and I have the honor to request that you will be kind enough to make such representations to the authorities at Tokyo as may seem best likely to tend to any early revival of this work.... It is the writers [sic] firm belief that there is no objection on the part of the Imperial Japanese Government to the emigration of Koreans, properly regulated and the writer will be very glad to comply with any reasonable regulations which the Imperial Japanese Government may see fit to impose. Begging for the above your kind consideration, I am, Sir, respectfully yours, D. W. Deshler.[57]

One week later an American Legation official personally handed to the new Japanese foreign minister, Katō Takaaki, Deshler's written request and his own comments:

> Mr. Deshler seems simply to want the embargo on Korean emigration removed, and apparently the date when this shall be done awaits only the promulgation of appropriate regulations. He therefore asks me to try to enlist the cooperation of Your Excellency's Government to hasten the drawing up of the emigration regulations and the removal of the embargo. What Mr. Deshler asks seems to me entirely unobjectionable, and so I think Your Excellency's Government may be quite willing to exert its influence in favor of the desired end. I shall be very glad if this matter receives favorable attention.[58]

Japan was not about to change its policy to accommodate either a private American citizen or even the American Legation in Japan, and so no reply was forthcoming from the Japanese Foreign Ministry. Nevertheless, the topic of emigation was still alive within the Japanese Foreign Ministry as part of a standard foreign-policy review on the occasion of the appointment of a new foreign minister. In February 1906, four unsigned position papers circulated within the Japanese Foreign Ministry. Their general conclusion was that the policy on emigration had been correct and that "since the emigration of Koreans for Hawaii and Mexico has been completely stopped because of his prohibition, our Japanese emigrants in Hawaii have no competitors there and they again hold a monopoly on the labor in Hawaii." A notation in the margin indicated that Itō, the resident-general in Korea, agreed completely with the findings.[59]

Because of the success of the policy, the resident-general, who then was placed in charge of Korean affairs, proposed a slight modification to allow Korean emigration under the strict control of Japan for its positive public-relations value.[60] The Gaimushō agreed,[61] and by late March, a new protection law for Korean emigrants was drafted "after considering the situation of the Korean people and the experience of our own protection law." The action was taken because "we think that to continue this policy of depriving freedom of emigration is not a proper policy." In mid-April, the resident-general "advised" the Korean government to enact the new rules; and, on July 12, 1906, the new emigrant-protection law was passed.[62] Publicly, Japan was to claim:

> As there was no representative of the Korean Government to take any measures in their behalf the Korean Government temporarily prohibited in April, 1905, any Korean labourers from proceeding abroad. Soon afterwards, the Residency-General of the Japanese Government being established, it was charged with the duty of protecting Koreans abroad also, and it caused the Korean Government to promulgate a law in July, 1906, protecting emigrants. By this law, Korean emigrants could not proceed abroad without permission of the Minister of Agriculture, Commerce and Industry.[63]

The new law, known officially as "The Mining and Emigration Regulations,"[64] rather than creating opportunities for Koreans once again to emigrate to Hawaii, in fact did just the opposite. The change had been in name only and Koreans still remained unable to emigrate to Hawaii. Once again, Homer Hulbert was to comment on the issue:

> There is something pathetic in the way Japan is providing "protection" for Koreans where no protection is required. . . . No one would deny that the government should exercise a certain oversight over emigration but these laws seem to be simply putting obstacles in the way of emigration rather than helping the Koreans to gain an honest livelihood in the labor market abroad. The Korean has as much right to go abroad and work as has the Japanese but these laws practically prohibit this. . . . As for the emigration laws one is almost forced to believe that successful Korean competition with Japanese labor in Hawaii has much to do with these stringent regulations. We do not affirm this but the fact of such competition combined with the further fact that all so-called reforms in Korea, so far, have looked to the sole benefit of the Japanese themselves make it look very much as if more than mere protection of the Korean were involved.[65]

Two months later, in September, Hulbert again commented: "This is only one more encroachment upon the rights of Korea. If Japan is sincere in her professed desire to see Korea advance the more Koreans go abroad the better, but this change is manifestly for the purpose of restricting emigration rather than for encouraging it."[66]

Finally, in November of 1906, a missionary who had been influential in encouraging Koreans to go to Hawaii wrote: "If a thousand selected Koreans a year could be permitted to emigrate to Hawaii in a few years they would return and develop the natural resources of Korea, adding many fold to the value and financial resources."[67]

All of these protests were, of course, futile. Japan was committed to its policy. Technically, the Japanese policy of prohibiting Korean emigration to Hawaii had been a success. After all, the United States had not, in fact, passed a Japanese exclusion act, sparing Japan the same fate as befell the Chinese in 1882. On the other hand, events outran Komura's economic solution to the problem. The more distasteful solution suggested two years earlier by the Japanese minister in Washington became reality in March of 1907, when, by executive order of President Theodore Roosevelt, Japanese and Korean laborers were forbidden to enter the mainland of the United States from Hawaii. Furthermore, soon afterwards, the gentlemen's agreement effectively ended all Japanese labor emigration to Hawaii or the mainland United States, even though it was, in reality, a thinly disguised exclusion act for face-saving purposes. The reasons for prohibiting Korean emigration to Hawaii by Japan had become moot; but, by that time, it was too late for Korea and Korean emigration to Hawaii. Soon afterward, in October of 1910, the final act was played out when Korea was annexed and was to remain a colony of Japan for the next thirty-five years.

Notes

1. See Hilary Conroy, *The Japanese Seizure of Korea, 1868–1910: A Study of Realism and Idealism in International Relations* (Philadelphia: University of Pennsylvania Press, 1960); see also C. I. Eugene Kim and Han-kyo Kim, *Korea and the Politics of Imperialism, 1876–1910* (Berkeley, Calif.: University of California Press, 1967).
2. Walter M. Giffard to William G. Irwin, February 13, 1903, Walter M. Giffard Papers, University of Hawaii Archives, Honolulu, Hawaii.
3. E. Faxon Bishop to Charles M. Cooke, March 19, 1903, Bus Files B, Charles M. Cooke Papers, Hawaiian Mission Children's Society Library, Honolulu, Hawaii.
4. The Japanese Foreign Ministry received three reports on Korean emigration during the first six months of 1903, after which time there was a period of two years without any reports from Japanese officials in Korea.
5. Giffard to Irwin, December 12, 1902, Giffard Papers.
6. Makoto Morioka to Baron Komura Jutarō, July 5, 1904. *Kankoku seifu Hawai oyobi Mokushika yuki Kankoku imin kinshi ikken—tsuki hogo itaku kankoku no ken (The Issue of the Prohibition of Korean Emigration to Hawaii and Mexico by the Korean Government—Recommendation and Protection)*, 3-9-2-18. Meiji Sanjū Hachi (1905). Gaimushō Gaikō Shiryō Kan (Diplomatic Records Office), Tōkyō, Japan (hereafter *Kankoku Imin*).
7. Makoto Morioka, Hinata Terutake, and Tomiochi Chūtaro to Komura, February 5 (?), 1905, *Kankoku Imin*. Hinata was the director of the Dairiku Shokumin Kaisha (Continental Colonization Company).
8. Uyeno, Japanese Consul in San Francisco, to Komura, March 3, 1905, Cable No. 1025, No. 8 in *Zai Bei ryōji rai* (Consuls, January–June, 1905), in English. Later that day Uyeno cabled again to report: "The resolution reported in my telegram eight was passed by the Assembly this morning" (Cable No. 1029), No. 9 in *Zai Bei ryōji rai* (Consuls, January–June, 1905), in English. Gaimushō Gaikō Shiryō Kan (Diplomatic Records Office), Tōkyō, Japan.
9. Takahira, Japanese minister to the United States, to Komura, March 18, 1905, Cable No. 1299 (Received in Tokyo March 20, 1905), No. 54 in *Bei Rai*, pp. 3091–93, in English. Gaimushō Gaikō Shiryō Kan (Diplomatic Records Office), Tōkyō, Japan.
10. Ishii Kikujirō, supervisor of the Office of Trade and Commerce, to Saito Miki, Japanese consul in Honolulu, August 28, 1905 (Secret), *Kankoku Imin*.
11. Makoto Morioka, Hinata Terutake and Tomiochi Chūtaro to Komura, February 5 (?), 1905, *Kankoku Imin*.

12. Komura to Saito, March 9, 1905 (Drafted March 3, 1905), Secret Transmission No. 3, *Kankoku Imin*.

13. Komura to Katō Motoshirō, Consul in Inch'ŏn, March 7, 1905 (Drafted March 3, 1905 and approved March 6, 1905), Secret Document No. 9; Komura to Wakamatsu Usaburō, Consul in Mokpo, March 7, 1905 (Drafted March 3, 1905 and approved March 6, 1905); Secret Document No. 9; Komura to Ariyoshi Akira, Consul in Pusan, March 7, 1905 (Drafted March 3, 1905 and approved March 6, 1905), Secret Document No. 7; Komura to Yokota Saburō, Branch Chief in Kunsan, March 7, 1905 (Drafted March 3, 1905 and approved March 6, 1905), Secret Document No. 7, *Kankoku Imin*.

14. Komura to Hayashi Gonsuke, Japanese Minister to Korea, April 5, 1905, 2:10 P.M. (Cable No. 253), No. 64, *Kankoku Imin*. The newspaper was the *Hōchi Shimbun*.

15. Komura to Hayashi, April 6, 1905, 8:00 P.M. (Cable No. 260), No. 65, *Kankoku Imin*.

16. David W. Deshler to Huntington Wilson, Chargé d'Affaires, United States Legation, Tokyo, January, 1906 (n. d.), Enclosure No. 2 in Wilson to Elihu Root, Secretary of State, January 27, 1906, U.S. Department of State, U.S. Embassy, Japan. Despatches from U.S. Minister to Japan, 1855–1906. Washington: National Archives and Records Service, 1946. This document can also be found in Carter–U.S. Departments. State, October 1905–June 1907, Archives of Hawaii, Honolulu, Hawaii. Also in Wilson to Katō Takaaki, January 19, 1906, *Kankoku Imin*.

17. Yokota Saburō (Kunsan) to Komura, March 27, 1905, Secret Document No. 5; Katō Motoshirō (Inch'ŏn) to Komura, March 29, 1905, Secret Document No. 6; Katō to Komura, April 4, 1905, Official Report No. 67; Wakamatsu Usaburō (Mokpo) to Komura, March 16, 1905, Secret Document No. 19; Ariyoshi Akira (Pusan) to Komura, March 14, 1905, Secret Letter No. 13; Saito Miki (Honolulu) to Komura, April 24, 1905, Official Letter No. 58, *Kankoku Imin*.

18. Komura to Hayashi, April 13, 1905, 6:05 P.M. (Cable No. 276), No. 69, *Kamkoku Imin*.

19. Wakamatsu Usaburō to Komura, April 13, 1905, Secret Document No. 20 (Received April 19, 1905); also Hagihara to Komura, April 29, 1905, No. 62, (Received May 8, 1905, No. 6247); also Someya Nariaki (Chinnamp'o) to Hayashi, April 22, 1905, No. 6; also Someya to Komura, May 8, 1905, No. 9 (Received May 15, 1905), *Kankoku Imin*.

20. Komura to Someya Nariaki, Vice-Consul in Chinnamp'o, April 29, 1905, Secret Document No. 15. A message for Katō Motoshirō, consul in Inch'ŏn, was appended. *Kankoku Imin*.

21. Komura to Hagihara, May 6, 1905 (Cable No. 356), No. 95, *Kankoku Imin*.

22. Hagihara to Komura, May 8, 1905, 3:20 P.M., No. 174 (Received 9:10 P.M., No. 408), *Kankoku Imin*.

23. *Cheguk Sinmun*, May 16, 1905.

24. *Hwangsŏng Sinmun*, June 9, 1905.

25. Ishii Kikujirō to Hattori Ichizo, Governor of Hyōgo Prefecture, June 1, 1905 (Drafted May 31, 1905), No. 810, *Kankoku Imin*.

26. Hattori to Ishii, June 14, 1905, No. 8466 (Received June 16, 1905, No. 4490-2), *Kankoku Imin*.

27. *Korea Review*, March 1905, p. 116.

28. Deshler to Wilson, January, 1906 (n.d.). See note 16.

29. *Hwangsŏng Sinmun*, April 17, 1905.

30. Horace N. Allen, U.S. Minister to Korea, to Gallaudet, August 25, 1904, Allen MSS, New York Public Library, New York City; also, *Korea Review*, August, 1904, p. 366; also, Allen to John Hay, Secretary of State, September 10, 1904, Despatches from U.S. Ministers to Korea, 1883–1905, Washington, National Archives and Records Service, 1949.

31. *Korea Review*, September 1904, p. 415.

32. *Hwangsŏng Sinmun*, September 6, 1904.

33. *Korea Review*, April 1905, p. 157.

34. *Hansŏng Sinbo*, May 5, 1905.

35. *Kwanbo (Official Gazette)*, September 9, 1904.

36. Yun Ch'i-ho *Ilgi (Diary)*, June 20, 1905 (Seoul: Kuksa P'yŏnch'an Wiwŏnhoe [National History Compilation Committee], 1977), in English.

37. Chinda Hiromi, Vice-Minister of Foreign Affairs, to Tsuruhara Jyōkichi, Director-General in the Resident-General's Office (Seoul), March 20, 1906 (Drafted February 28, 1906), No. 69, *Kankoku Imin*.

38. Yun Ch'i-ho *Ilgi*, November 29, 1905.
39. Ishii to Saito, August 28, 1905 (Secret), *Kankoku Imin*.
40. Yun Ch'i-ho *Ilgi*, August 28, 1905.
41. Ibid., August 29, 30, 1905.
42. "Jap Laborers Will Continue to Come," *Pacific Commercial Advertiser*, September 9, 1905.
43. *Korea Review*, September 1905, p. 359.
44. Yun Ch'i-ho *Ilgi*, September 18, 1905.
45. Ibid., September 19, 1905.
46. *Korea Review*, September 1905, p. 354.
47. *Ibid.*, October 1905, pp. 393, 397.
48. Hawaiian Sugar Planters' Association Trustees, Minutes, October 3, 1905, Aiea, Hawaii.
49. Yun Ch'i-ho *Ilgi*, October 16, 25, 1905.
50. Ibid., October 19, 1905.
51. Ibid., October 25, 1905.
52. Komura to Hagihara, October 25, 1905, 3:50 P.M. (Cable No. 873), No. 252, *Kankoku Imin*.
53. Hagihara to Komura, October 26, 1905, 10:50 P.M. No. 407 (Received 12:10 A.M., October 27, 1905, No. 1120), *Kankoku Imin*.
54. Yun Ch'i-ho *Ilgi*, October 28, 1905.
55. Homer Hulbert, "The Koreans in Hawaii," *Korea Review*, November, 1905, pp. 411-13.
56. *Korea Review*, February 1906, p. 79.
57. Deshler to Wilson, January 1906 (n.d.). See Note 16.
58. Wilson to Katō Takaaki, January 19, 1906 (Handwritten), *Kankoku Imin*.
59. The document is dated February 6, 1906, and bears the seal of the minister and vice-minister of foreign affairs, *Kamkoku Imin*.
60. Tsuruhara Jyōkichi to Chinda Hiromi, February 19, 1906, No. 447 (Receiving No. 2834), *Kankoku Imin*.
61. Hiromi to Tsuruhara, March 20, 1906 (Drafted February 28, 1906), No. 69, *Kankoku Imin*.
62. Tsuruhara to Chinda, July 16, 1906, No. 813 (Received July 20, 1906, No. 3607), *Kankoku Imin*.
63. Government-General of Chosen, *Annual Report on Reforms and Progress in Chosen (Korea), 1910-1911*, Keijō (Seoul), December 1911, pp. 36-37.
64. *Japan Weekly Mail*, July 14, 1906.
65. Homer Hulbert, "The Korean Emigrant Protection Law, *Korea Review*, July 1906, pp. 256-58.
66. Homer Hulbert, *Korea Review*, September 1906, p. 356.
67. Reverend George Heber Jones, "The Koreans in Hawaii," *Korea Review*, November 1906, pp. 401-6.

Notes on the Contributors

JAMES B. LEAVELL received a B.A. and M.A. from Baylor University and received his Ph.D. from Duke University in 1975 in East Asian History. He has held NDEA Title IV and Fulbright-Hays grants. Mr. Leavell has taught in Hong Kong and Japan, as well as at Hardin Simmons University and the University of Maryland. He has been with the History Department at Furman University since 1974, spending a sabbatical year, 1982–83, in Japan.

JAMES L. HUFFMAN, associate professor of history at Wittenberg University, combined professional training in both history and journalism. A graduate of Marion College and Northwestern University, he spent two years as a reporter for the *Minneapolis Tribune* before taking an M.A. and Ph.D. at the University of Michigan. He has taught at Marion College (Indiana) and at the University of Nebraska, and has served as senior translator for the *Japan Interpreter*. In addition to several articles his publications on Japanese history include *Press and Politics in Meiji Japan: The Life of Fukuchi Gen'ichirō* (Honolulu: University Press of Hawaii, 1980).

YAMASHITA SHIGEKAZU is a graduate of Tokyo University and has been a professor of political science at Kokugakuin University, Tōkyō since 1971. His works include *Igirisu seiji shisō shi* (Tōkyō: Komine Shoten, 1968), *J. S. Mill no shisō keisei* (Tōkyō: Komine Shoten, 1971), and *J. S. Mill no seiji shisō* (Tōkyō: Bokutakusha, 1976). He has translated into Japanese Jeremy Bentham's *An Introduction to the Principles of Morals and Legislation* and J. S. Mill's *Consideration on Representative Government* and is the author of many articles on Japanese and English political thought.

MIKISO HANE was born in California and lived in Japan from 1933 to 1940. He received B.M., M.A. and Ph.D. degrees from Yale University, where he taught Japanese between 1943 and 1957. From 1959 to 1961 he taught at Toledo University and, since 1961, has been at Knox College, where he is professor of history. His publications include *Japan, A Historical Survey* (New York: Scribners, 1972); a translation of Masao Maruyama's *Studies in the Intellectual History of Tokugawa Japan* (Tōkyō and Princeton, N.J., 1974); *Peasants, Rebels and Outcastes* (Pantheon, 1982); *Emperor Hirohito and His Chief Aide De Camp, the Honjō Diary, 1933–1936* (Tokyo, 1982). He has received research grants from the Fulbright program, Japan Foundation, and the National Endowment for the Humanities.

ELLEN P. CONANT received her education at Bryn Mawr College and New York University. She concentrated on Japanese art history, which she studied under the direction of Alexander Soper. She is a resident of New York City; and has served as chair of the Columbia University seminar on modern Japan.

Notes on Contributors

SANDRA T. W. DAVIS is a specialist in Meiji politics and thought and in U.S.–Japan trade. She is the author of *Intellectual Change and Political Development in Early Modern Japan: Ono Azusa, A Case Study* and numerous articles on Japanese history, politics, and trade. She received her Ph.D. in 1968 from the University of Pennsylvania, and subsequently taught at Hunter College, N.Y., and North Carolina State University at Charlotte, N.C., as well as at Sophia University in Japan. She now is Manager, International Research, Corporate Marketing Research and Development Department, of the American International Group, Inc., in New York.

RICHARD T. CHANG was born in Korea and received his doctorate from the University of Michigan in 1964. He is the author of *From Prejudice to Tolerance: A Study of the Japanese Image of the West, 1826–1864* (Tōkyō, 1970), *Historians and Meiji Statesmen* (Gainesville, Fla., 1971), *Historians and Taishō Statesmen* (1977) and numerous articles on Meiji Japan. Professor Chang has taught at Kent State University, the University of Kansas, the University of Pittsburgh and, since 1966, has taught at the University of Florida, where he is professor of history. He is coordinator of the Florida Japan Seminar for 1979–82. His new book entitled "The Justice of the Western Consular Courts in 19th Century Japan" is scheduled for publication by the Greenwood Press.

HILARY CONROY is a professor of Far Eastern history at the University of Pennsylvania, where he has taught since 1951. He received his doctorate at the University of California, Berkeley, and he has from time to time taught there, as well as at Swarthmore College, the University of Colorado, the University of Hawaii, International Christian University (Tōkyō). He was a Fulbright scholar at Tōkyō University in 1954 and a senior specialist at the Institute for Advanced Projects, East-West Center, Honolulu, in 1965–66. He has written, edited, and coauthored many books and articles on Asian history, including *China and Japan: Search for Balance Since World War I* (with Alvin D. Coox; Santa Barbara, Calif.: ABC–Clio Press, 1978) and *Japan Examined* (with H. Wray; Honolulu: University Press of Hawaii, 1983). He was chairman of the Graduate Group in East Asian Studies at the University of Pennsylvania in 1979–80, of the American Historial Association Committee on the J. K. Fairbank prize for the best book on East Asian history 1981–82, and currently is Chairman of the Interchange for Pacific Scholarship.

MATSUZAWA HIROAKI is a graduate of the Faculty of Law at the University of Tokyo where he studied modern Japanese history under Masao Maruyama. He is currently professor of the history of Japanese political thought at Hokkaido University in Sapporo, Japan.

NAGATA YOICHI did graduate work in International Relations at the University of Pennsylvania.

H. PETER CH'EN studied Japanese history under Edwin Reischauer and Albert Craig at Harvard University, where he received his Ph.D. and where he was a research fellow at the East Asian Institute. He taught at Keene State University in New Hampshire, where he was social-science chairman and also taught at the University of Pennsylvania, where he was a visiting professor. His untimely death in 1977 cut short a promising academic career.

HAGIHARA NOBUTOSHI was born in Tōkyō in 1926 and studied under Oka Yoshitake of the Tōkyō University Law Faculty. He has been a visiting scholar in residence at the University of Pennsylvania and at St. Antony's College in Oxford, England. Among his many publications in Japanese are a book on Baba Tatsui, a Meiji radical, a commentary on the diaries of Sir Ernest Satow and a biography of Togo Shigenori. A free-lance critic, he is a frequent contributor to *Chuō Kōron* and *Mainichi Shimbun*.

JOHN LIN received his Ph.D. in political science from the University of Pennyslvania in 1960. He was professor of political science at SUNY–New Paltz and a longtime member of the Columbia University Seminar on Modern Japan, where he frequently contributed to discussion sessions of that organization. He died in 1979.

REGINALD RAJAPAKSE received his Ph.D. from the University of Pennsylvania in South Asian history with a study of Ceylon–U.S. relations in the nineteenth century. He taught in the history department at SUNY–Albany. Dr. Rajapakse's contribution was made possible in part by a project of the Interchange for Pacific Scholarship, which assists scholars of Asian descent in publishing the results of their research in English.

SHARLIE C. USHIODA received her undergraduate training at the University of Pennsylvania and earned an M.A. in East Asian studies at Harvard University. She has taught Japanese language, history, and culture at the University of California at Irvine and at Saddleback College, Mission Viejo, California. As a Ph.D. candidate at UCLA, she is studying the status of women in Japan and has published several articles on this subject.

WAYNE PATTERSON received his undergraduate training at Swarthmore College and earned his Ph.D. from the University of Pennsylvania. He is the coauthor of two books on Koreans in America and has published several articles on East Asian history and international relations. He is currently working on a book on Korean immigration to Hawaii at the turn of the century. After holding teaching positions with the University of Pennsylvania and the University of Maryland, he is currently associate professor in the History Department of Saint Norbert College in Wisconsin from which he was on leave with research fellowships at the University of California, Berkeley and Harvard University (1983–84).